GILBERT HOBBS BARNES

THE ANTISLAVERY
IMPULSE

1830-1844

with a new Introduction by

WILLIAM G. McLOUGHLIN
Brown University

GLOUCESTER, MASS.

PETER SMITH

1973

To
ULRICH BONNELL PHILLIPS

INTRODUCTION TO THE HARBINGER EDITION

by William G. McLoughlin

Gilbert Hobbs Barnes was for twenty-five years a professor of economics at Ohio Wesleyan University. He died in 1945 at the age of fifty-six. During his lifetime he wrote only one book, and this was in the field of history, not economics. Yet by this book, first published in 1933, Barnes established for himself a distinguished and permanent position among the significant interpreters of the American Civil War.

In one sense this might be considered an accident—if it is an accident when a scholar in the course of his research discovers a long-forgotten trunk of important historical papers. In another respect it may also have been accidental that Gilbert Barnes undertook this book and found these papers at a particularly important turning point in the course of American historiography and in his own attitude toward the writing of history.

But, of course, in the long run, no great historical work is ever an accident. It is the combined result of hard work, intrinsic talent, and competent knowledge which the scholar applies to the task he has undertaken. *The Antislavery Impulse* is rightly considered a classic in its field, and Gilbert Barnes has a rightful claim to distinction.

While this book was immediately recognized by reviewers in 1934 as "significant," "important," and even "revolutionary," it was also considered highly provocative, controversial, and contentious. For in establishing what was a major reinterpretation of the causes of the Civil War, Barnes directly refuted or seriously qualified most of the prevailing interpretations of his day. And historians do not easily give up the interpretations which they have established or learned with much care and effort. The measure of Barnes's achievement is that his book has stood the test of time and of the most searching historical criticism to which his professional colleagues could subject it. Although some of his minor claims have been successfully challenged and some of his major points qualified by subsequent research and by the utilization of new sources and methods, nevertheless his interpretation of the antislavery impulse still stands today essentially as he presented it. Consciously or unconsciously a whole generation of students have assimilated it as their fathers assimilated the interpretations he challenged.

On the surface the most exciting thing about Barnes's book when it first appeared was his discovery of the long-forgotten letters and papers of Theodore Dwight Weld and Angelina Grimké Weld. These opened up a rich, untapped area of source material for the study of the abolition movement. Prior to 1933 Weld had been an almost unknown figure in American history, and even the most scholarly monographs on the antislavery movement passed him by with scarcely a reference. But more important than raising Weld himself to his rightful place in American history was the fact that through his letters and papers Barnes became aware of a whole new aspect of the antislavery movement. Previously, as Barnes says in his Preface, discussions of the antislavery movement had centered primarily around the work of William Lloyd Garrison and his coterie of New England supporters—men whose religious outlooks ranged from the "come-outer" anticlericalism of Garrison himself to the Quakerism of John Greenleaf Whittier and the transcendentalism of Theodore Parker. But through his study of Weld Barnes discovered that the records told "a different and incomparably more significant tale." A tale which began with the Great Revival in the "burned-over" region of New York inspired by Charles Grandison Finney (a man as neglected as Weld by historians) and which led through the conversion of Weld and his conversion of other westerners to the formation of a mighty wave of evangelical antislavery sentiment west of the Appalachians; this sentiment brought about the formation of countless abolition societies and the arousing of a religious crusade against slavery which was more significant and important in the election of Lincoln and the outbreak of the Civil War than the work of Garrison in the East.

But this tale, which Barnes made so simple and told with such dramatic gusto, was not received with universal acclaim by American historians. It was accepted as interesting and important, but it was also considered very controversial. Many critics said that he rode his thesis too hard. That he was unfair in his attempt to debunk Garrison. That he exaggerated the roles of Weld and Finney. That he ignored important political and economic aspects of the antislavery movement. That he made his story so simple and smooth as to neglect some conflicting and contradictory aspects of his heroes and villains. In fact, it appeared to some that he had really thrown the whole controversy over the causes of the Civil War back seventy-five years and was returning to the view of contemporaries of the event who saw the war in terms of praise and blame—the devil theory of history —instead of recognizing that certain inexorable forces were at work which were beyond the power of anyone to control.

By writing this book Barnes placed himself in the middle of a battle about the war which has been going on among historians ever since 1861 concerning precisely what its causes were and how they are to be ranked in importance. And this battle was raging with particular vigor in 1933 because American historiography was then going through one of its periodic crises of reassessment. The consensus which had prevailed for a generation was undergoing sharp attack, and a new consensus was slowly being worked out. And for a time it was not altogether clear which side Barnes was on in this reorientation. Some critics are still unsure.

At the time Barnes wrote, five major lines of argument concerning the Civil War and its origins were being thrashed out. First and foremost there was what Thomas J. Pressly has called "the nationalist tradition," which had evolved in the years between 1890 and 1920 and which still had many followers. Not the least of these was Arthur C. Cole, whose *Irrepressible Conflict* (1934) stated the standard argument in terms of the inevitable organic evolution of the United States as a modern nation-state: the North and South were, by 1860, essentially different cultures; and the South, being anachronistic in its social, political, and economic institutions, simply had to give way before the manifest destiny of the industrialized, centralized America which the North represented: "Then emerged at length the glories of a modern America."

Second, though less important, there was the Marxist interpretation of the Civil War, which saw it as the beginning of the American proletarian revolution—a war waged by Northern bourgeois capitalism against a decadent Southern agrarian feudalism; the proletariat benefited little from this stage of the dialectic of history, but their oppression by postwar Robber Barons was the beginning of the end for American capitalism whose doom was sealed by the stockmarket crash of 1929.

Third, there was a new Southern view of the war, developed principally by Ulrich B. Phillips, which claimed that slavery would probably have died out soon after 1860 had the South been left to itself; but unfortunately Northern economic exploitation of the South and the hysteria whipped up by the abolitionists forced a war which was probably as unnecessary as it was bitter.

Fourth, and probably the most influential and popular view at the time Barnes wrote, was that expressed in the work of Charles and Mary Beard: this was essentially an economic interpretation of the war supplemented by the Progressive reform views of "the new history"; it minimized the social and political issues preceding the war, ignored the moral issue entirely, and asserted that while the war was inevitable, because of the sharp economic cleavage between the agrarian South and the industrial North, its consequences were by no means as glorious or beneficial as the previous generation of historians who created "the nationalist tradition" had claimed.

And finally, there was the argument put forward by those who are now known as the Southern revisionists, led principally by Frank L. Owsley, Charles W. Ramsdell, and Albert J. Beveridge (and soon joined by James G. Randall, Avery O. Craven, and Merle E. Coulter). These historians argued that the war was not only repressible but that it was a terrible blunder, precipitated if not perpetrated by Northern fanatical abolitionists and those fire-eating Southern hotheads who responded to them in kind. Without defending slavery as such, these historians declared that the moral issue was not a real or valid one, that the South was perfectly justified in fighting to preserve its conservative, agrarian, organic, democratic, high-minded culture against the materialistic, commercial, exploitative, plutocratic, selfish, atomistic system to which the North, by sheer weight of numbers and political tyranny, was forcing the South to pay colonial tribute.

Inasmuch as Barnes dedicated his book to his former teacher, Ulrich B. Phillips, and acknowledged him as the man under whose direction he had undertaken this study of the antislavery movement, it is not surprising that many reviewers in 1934 and many critics since have claimed that *The Antislavery Impulse* clearly belonged in the same interpretative vein as did Phillips's books. Phillips was a distinguished historian whose volumes on the slave system in the pre-Civil War South are still important in their area. Like Barnes, he broke new ground in historical research by discovering and interpreting original source materials which previous historians had neglected—notably the managerial and financial records of the large Southern plantations. Although he began his work in 1903, he was never really in harmony with the nationalist tradition of his day.

Southern by birth and a student of William A. Dunning, Phillips maintained that his own research proved that the slavery system was bound to die out in the latter half of the nineteenth century because of the exhaustion of the soil, the unavailability of new land for cotton culture, and the increasing unprofitability of maintaining slaves. Taking the more "objective view" of his generation concerning the moral issue of slavery, he found that it had certain benefits to the slave and the master because of its civilizing and stabilizing control over the millions of uneducated and backward Negroes still only a generation from savagery. While he did not dwell at length upon the matter, it is clear from his books and articles that Phillips held the Northern abolitionists, with their fanatical moralism, more to blame than any other factor for the precipitation of the war itself—though he was sufficiently sophisticated to insist, like his contemporaries, that no single cause could be named and that there were inexorable causes at work beyond the sphere of human effort.

Richard Hofstadter has summed up Phillips's work and viewpoint in words which should be kept in mind by those who would compare him with Barnes:

> He was a native of Georgia, to whom the Southern past always appeared in a haze of romance. His conception of the Negro was characteristically Southern, and his version of slavery has been described by a relatively impartial historian as "friendly." His books can best be placed in the course of our intellectual history when it is realized that they represent a latter-day phase of the pro-slavery argument.

It does not seem to me that a close and careful reading of Barnes's book will admit of its being characterized in a similar way. Barnes was born in Nebraska. His view of the Old South was scarcely romantic. His attitude toward the Negro showed no signs of racism. And there was no indication that he was for any reason even vaguely friendly toward the slave system.

The only point upon which Barnes and Phillips were in apparent agreement was in their view of the abolitionists. In fact, Barnes was so severe in his denunciation of Garrison that a number of historians have argued that *The Antislavery Impulse* really belongs in the category of Southern revisionism. Thomas J. Pressly, for example, in his book *Americans Interpret Their Civil War* (1954) took this view:

> The most significant feature of Barnes' volume from the stand point of changing opinions on the Civil War was its unsympathetic attitude

toward the antislavery movement. Previous accounts of organized opposition to slavery had been written by historians Albert Bushnell
Hart (the son and grandson of abolitionists), Theodore Clarke Smith
(long-time resident of Massachusetts and a graduate student of
Hart's at Harvard in the 1890's), and Jesse Macy (a veteran of the
Union Army whose family had actively supported the underground
railroad in the 1840's and 1850's). As was to be expected, Hart, Smith,
and Macy were all sympathetic to the antislavery cause; . . . By
contrast, the tone implicit throughout Barnes' book was hostile to the
antislavery cause and to its leaders. The antislavery leaders were
pictured as emotional, and at times irresponsible, propagandists who
should rightly bear a considerable part of the blame for sectional
conflict and civil war.

Pressly therefore concluded that Barnes's book "occupies a place in
the emergence of the 'revisionist' viewpoints." And to document this
he referred to the book reviews written in 1934 by Avery O. Craven
and James G. Randall.

There can be no doubt that the revisionists did seize upon the book
as clearcut evidence to sustain their claims. Avery Craven's review
in the New York *Herald Tribune* was headlined, "Fanatic Source
of the Anti-Slavery Crusade," and Craven said of Barnes in the
review: "Two generations of scholars have repeated the errors of
America's most successful venture in propaganda. . . . His findings
are revolutionary." For Craven, Barnes had at last succeeded in giving
the admirers of abolitionism their come-uppance and exposed the
abolitionists for the zealous bigots and deluded fanatics they were—
men who heedlessly and vindictively pushed the nation into a fratricidal holocaust simply to justify their own moralistic convictions
that the Southerners deserved to be punished for sinning against God.
With obvious relish Craven summed up what Barnes's book meant
to the revisionists:

> The antislavery crusade is one of the least understood episodes in
> American history. As usually described, it is a simple story of de-
> voted men under the leadership of the even more devoted William
> Lloyd Garrison painfully winning the "right-minded" to a great cause
> and, in the end, leading a nation to destroy human slavery. The truth
> is quite different. The abolition movement was a failure and Garrison
> was generally a hindering factor in it. The reason for such a mis-
> understanding is quite simple. When war broke out between the
> sections in 1861 Northern men were called out to shoot Southerners.
> They could do this only for the glory of God and the well-being of
> mankind. The abolition contention that slavery was a crime and

slaveholders criminals supplied the moral force needed. The despised or ignored fanatic suddenly became "respectable" and his distorted attitudes the justification for a holy war. His reward was a place in history so mythical as to justify the charge of "lies agreed to."

A similar point of view was expressed in James G. Randall's review of the book in the first volume of the *Journal of Southern History* (a magazine which owed its existence to the growing cleavages between Northern and Southern historians after 1930). Randall bluntly said, "The function of this book may be described as the revisionist interpretation of the antislavery crusade." Even reviewers who did not adhere to the revisionist school were struck by Barnes's characterization of the abolitionists. Louis Filler summarized the book as "a studied attack on Garrison." And of course it was.

Barnes clearly disliked Garrison and enjoyed debunking "the legend" about him. Barnes was also just as clearly antagonistic toward religious zealots. He attacked the abolitionists for denouncing the sins of others in precisely the same vein in which H. L. Mencken was then attacking the Prohibitionists, censors, and Sabbatarians. He portrayed the Puritans and their Calvinistic doctrines as narrow-minded and repressive, just as James Truslow Adams and V. L. Parrington were doing at this time. Anyone who reads *The Antislavery Impulse* with an eye which is receptive to the revisionist argument will have no difficulty in finding ample evidence to support Randall's claim: Garrison is denounced on page after page as "a figurehead of fanaticism," an "egregious fanatic," a deluded, obsessed schemer with "no qualifications for leadership," a man "always ready to think well of himself," who played a "lofty role," appearing "like Moses from Sinai" to worshipping followers who took his "convictions of grandeur" at face value. This "evil genius of the antislavery movement," unaware of "the sinister quality of his fame," indulged in "his rancorous denunciations and his brawling, ferocious abuse" of everyone so bold as to question his views.

The abolitionists who followed Garrison are characterized as being equally self-righteous fanatics: "visionaries and reckless agitators, ultras of the time" who "joined the society because of its very ill repute"; "doctrinaire" zealots, "persons with whom all temperate reason . . . is thrown away"; "propagandists" and "agitators" who courted martyrdom; "casuists of immediatism" whose insane plan was to turn millions of slaves loose at once without any restrictions; "radicals" so deluded with the righteousness of their cause that they resolved "that indifference to this movement indicates a state of mind more culpable than was manifested by the Jewish nation in rejecting Jesus as the Messiah. . . ." Barnes seemed to give his true estimate of the movement when he stated,

> The American Anti-Slavery Society was to achieve its end by per- suading citizens in the non-slaveholding North to denounce slavery in the slaveholding South. Its first concern was not the abolition of slavery, it was the "duty of rebuke which every inhabitant of the Free States owes to every slaveholder." Denunciation of the evil came first; reform of the evil was incidental to that primary obliga- tion.

The revisionists found further proof that the book was on their side in the fact that Barnes traced the root of the antislavery impulse to frontier revivalism with all its connotations of emotionalism, hysteria, hell-fire-and-damnation sermons, fundamentalist literalism, and irrational, fanatical zeal. Like those journalists in the 1920's who ridiculed the current revivals of Billy Sunday and echoed Mencken's jibes about "the Bible belt" and the imbecility of the Scopes Trial, Barnes vented considerable scorn upon those early-nineteenth-century revivalists and their converts who delighted in denouncing the sins of others—teetotallers who got "saved" and denounced drinkers, Sab- batarians who found religion and denounced non-observers. Religious revivalism, said Barnes, seemed to have "fulfilled its purpose when moral people were persuaded to denounce the immorality" of others.

One revisionist wrote his own interpretation of the antislavery impulse six years after Barnes did and based a large part of his con- clusions upon what Barnes had written in this vein. Arthur Y. Lloyd's *The Slavery Controversy, 1831-1860* (1939), written under the guid- ance of Frank L. Owsley, purported to "throw new light upon the slavery controversy as a part of the sectional struggle preceding the War Between the States." It divided the antislavery sentiment in the North into three groups: one led by moderate philosophers like William Ellery Channing, one led by politicians like Lincoln, "and finally the radical abolitionists, led by Garrison, Weld, Bourne, Foster and others, that demanded the immediate abolition of slavery without compensation or any plan of adjustment and denounced the South in harsh terms."

And yet the case is by no means so simple as Pressly and the revisionists made out. The truth of the matter is that Barnes was ambivalent toward the abolitionists. He was both repelled by them and attracted to them. There is evidence that he could not really make up his mind whether he wished to lay the blame for the Civil War upon them as moralistic fanatics or whether he wished to applaud them and to repudiate those interpretations which maintained that moral issues were not really involved.

One obvious sign of his ambivalence and his unwillingness to express his own historical judgment on the issue can be seen in his Preface, where he stated frankly his attempt to withdraw from the problem:

> The antislavery impulse unfolded into a narrative so unorthodox that I did not have the hardihood to interpret it in my own words. I have, therefore, let the documents tell the story.

And as if this abdication from judging were in itself a virtue which placed him on the side of scientific objectivity as a historian, he added, "The manner of its telling, I hope, makes for a reconstruction rather than a reinterpretation of the facts." If Barnes really believed this, he was expressing a naive view of historical writing. For obviously by the very selection and ordering of "facts," by choosing what is important or relevant and what is not, the historian is making judgments and building up an interpretation which it is idle to deny. And who can read the colorful, exciting prose which Barnes uses and the intensely dramatic scenes he reconstructs without recognizing the creative imagination of the critical historian at work? Barnes was deceiving only himself if he thought he was "letting the documents tell the story." I do not think that he really believed what he said here. It is true that throughout the book he often chose to express his views, or to express a view, by means of quotation from some contemporary source, particularly when he wished to be harsh toward the abolitionists. But the mere fact that he chose these critical quotations (and frequently contradicted them by value judgments of his own) was itself an act of interpretation.

There is no need to charge Barnes with conscious duplicity or cowardice about this, however. He was indeed entering a field which was not his own, one in which there were long-standing and fiercely held traditional views which the newcomer challenged at his peril. But Barnes demonstrated throughout his text, whatever he may have said in the Preface, that he was not afraid to speak bluntly in the face of the ancient and honorable Pooh-bahs of tradition where he believed them to be wrong. In fact, it was suggested by many reviewers that perhaps he had rushed in where angels feared to tread.

At the heart of the book's ambivalence lies the fact that Barnes himself was undergoing a serious ideological reorientation, along with the rest of American intellectuals, in the years 1925-1935. The shift was not of the same proportions as that crisis of identity which Eric Erikson constructs in his reinterpretation of the career of Martin Luther, but Erikson's argument applies here: "In some periods of his history, and in some phases of his life cycle, man needs (until we invent something better) a new ideological orientation as surely and as sorely as he must have air and food." By "ideology" Erikson means "an unconscious tendency underlying religious and scientific as well as political thought: the tendency at a given time to make facts amenable to ideas, and ideas to facts, in order to create a world image convincing enough to support the collective and the individual sense of identity." Surely this is what transpired during T. S. Eliot's great personal and intellectual struggle in the 1920's and 1930's. Surely this is what lay behind Joseph Wood Krutch's similar malaise in *The Modern Temper* (1929), Aldous Huxley's brilliant satire in *Brave New World* (1932), and Reinhold Niebuhr's burning indictments in *Moral Man and Immoral Society* (1933) and *Reflections on the End of an Era* (1934). And these symptomatic examples belong only to the Anglo-American phase of a reorientation in western intellectual life of which Karl Barth's neo-orthodoxy, Jean Paul Sartre's existentialism, Jacques Maritain's Thomism, and the new theologies of Jaspers, Heidegger, and Buber are the prominent European counterparts. This reorientation has been called the revolt against positivism, against naturalism, against scientism, behaviorism, and "social engineering." But by whatever name, it was a *crise de conscience* in western civilization which was just becoming manifest when Barnes wrote and which is with us yet. And Barnes himself shared in it.

Without resorting to a psychoanalytical study of Barnes himself, it is possible to demonstrate the shift taking place in his outlook by the simple expedient of contrasting the views which he expressed in a collaborative textbook published in 1926 with the views implicit in *The Antislavery Impulse*. The textbook was called *A Gateway to the Social Sciences,* and in writing it Barnes teamed up with three of his colleagues, Ben A. Arneson, a professor of political science, Charles W. Coulter, a professor of sociology, and Henry C. Hubbart, a professor of history. Barnes himself wrote as a professor of economics. The four authors stated in their preface that this book was designed as an undergraduate textbook for an introductory interdisciplinary course which would unite the social sciences.

Discarding "the historical-survey type" of elementary course, Barnes and his friends had attempted to create at Ohio Wesleyan in the early 1920's a course which was partly historical and "also structural, biological, and behavioristic." The authors stated that "this course has even more significance and value to the student of history than to students in other departments of the social sciences"—presumably because the student of history was, for reasons of intellectual and cultural lag, less familiar with the new trends in science and hence more old-fashioned in his reluctance to see behaviorism as the key to human development. "We feel that the student of history should see history as the unfolding institutional life of mankind. Too often detailed narrative history leaves little room for the constant elements, the laws and generalizations that the political scientist, the sociologist, and the economist are striving to arrive at." In short, what Barnes and his social scientist friends were trying to inculcate into their students in 1926 was almost precisely the opposite of the point of view which Barnes expressed in 1933.

The authors of *A Gateway to the Social Sciences* were strong advocates of John Dewey's Instrumentalism and James Harvey Robinson's "scientific history." Rejecting the block universe of social Darwinism, with its laissez-faire opposition to reform, they stated:

> From the scientific viewpoint we shall find that this social order of ours is infinitely plastic, that it is possible in the course of time for a fundamentally different social order to be brought about, and that not one ideal need be eliminated from consideration because it is unlike our present order.

This textbook was in effect a classic example of the paradoxical nature of the American temperament—the irreconcilable clash between the inherent idealism and pietistic moralism (which has been inbred in Americans from the days of the Puritans and Roger Williams) and the pragmatic faith in science and technological know-how (which it inherited from Jefferson and the Enlightenment). The dilemma is epitomized on page three of the textbook, where the student was told, "The Kingdom of heaven on earth is not an impractical dream but a sober possibility from the scientific point of view."

The book, however, stressed most emphatically that it was only possible "from the scientific point of view." It stated disapprovingly,

"We all deplore utopias," even while it held out the promise of achieving them. In other words, in 1926 Barnes was thoroughly committed (or seemed to be so far as this book was concerned) to the view that men whose utopian ideals flew in the face of behaviorist psychology and pragmatic sociology were doomed to failure. Only those who mastered the laws of social science and operated within the framework of existing mores (the authors inconsistently drew heavily upon William Graham Sumner's *Folkways* throughout) could ever hope to achieve reform.

Barnes's intellectual metamorphosis, or at least the critical conflict which his research into the antislavery movement posed, is succinctly demonstrated by the stance which the textbook of 1926 took on such crucial questions as slavery, abolition, religion, war, and utopian reform movements. The index of the textbook contained no entries under slavery, religion, Civil War, abolition, or Garrison: "We are following the lines of development that have led to the modern order; and the plantation system, based on negro slavery, is gone." Insofar as the book took any stand on the Civil War, it supported the prevailing "nationalist tradition" and certain aspects of Charles Beard's economic interpretation; i.e., the war was simply an incident in the rise of "the modern order," and its principal significance was that it showed how anachronistic the Old South had become. Like Beard, however, the authors maintained that laissez-faire capitalism in 1926 was itself out of date, and they frankly deplored the fact that in those days of Harding and Coolidge "we are still dominated by a philosophy a century outworn."

In a curious passage, reminiscent of John Dewey's tortured debate with Randolph Bourne in 1917, the textbook tried unsuccessfully to reconcile the problem of reform without war. With Sumnerian conservatism the authors noted that attempts to modify and change the mores in American society "must not transcend certain limits set by tradition." But within certain limits "variations are interesting and welcome"—if they are scientifically undertaken. Unfortunately, in our past, there have been times when there were so many radical reforms advocated that "the country seethes with them. Their invention and promulgation bring the reformer recognition if not notoriety." Then came this ambiguous passage:

> A cataclysm in the social order—an invention which revolutionizes industry, a plague, a scourge, an earthquake or other disaster, a catastrophe like the World War—now [while "the country seethes

with" reforms of all kinds, "many of them untried and extreme"]
shakes up the moral variations and permits selection to operate
directly, eliminating the unadaptable and useless variants and permitting the favorable ones to persist. There is a rearrangement of
institutional elements and relations in the social order. This cataclys-
mic change simply hurries the process of social evolution. We can
now see it working. The air is clearer, as after a thunderstorm, and
a consistency in the mores is again restored.

This mystical reliance upon the God of thunder to restore the benef-
icent laws of natural selection and bring resolutions *ex machina* to
the social order when seething reforms get out of hand, seems a
strange conception for the students of social science to assimilate
in this textbook. But it points out with startling clarity how confused
and basically unhappy most Americans have always been with an
ideology which rests solely upon the laws of science. Barnes seemed,
in 1926, to have adopted the prevailing ideology of behaviorism and
instrumentalism and to have accepted the scientific history as the true
historiography.

Yet within seven years Barnes had virtually reversed himself. The
assumptions, the style, the whole mood and spirit of *The Antislavery
Impulse* are entirely different. Not only is the later book completely
free from the dated jargon of behaviorism and sociology which burdened the textbook, but its implicit tone was one of impassioned
commitment to a point of view which repudiated the calm objectivity
and "healthy skepticism" that the earlier book sought to inculcate.
Instead of dwelling upon the inexorable forces of economic and
political science or the gradual laws of social evolution, the later book
held up the religious faith of individuals, the moral ideals of heroes,
the dedicated efforts of a handful of determined men, a Holy Band,
who pitted themselves against the political might, the economic power,
and the social folkways of a whole nation, in order to stand up for
what their hearts told them were eternal, universal, "higher" spiritual
laws.

The evidence for this reading of *The Antislavery Impulse*, it seems
to me, is far more convincing than the evidence for interpreting it as
a revisionist book. It is true that Barnes seldom had anything good
to say about Garrison, but when he did, it was important. In sum-
ming up Garrison, he took an almost existential ground in stating
that Garrison's friends "knew the man himself, the austerity of his
life and his singleness of purpose. They knew that the harshness of

his writings was derived from his righteous absolutes of faith, never from vindictiveness; and that his intolerance was for the principles that he hated, and not for the men who followed them. For all his 'I-ness'—his obsessive self-importance—Garrison was truly what his followers believed him to be, the embodiment of devotion to a cause." Barnes seems to have been trying hard to dissociate the man from his method, or perhaps, more accurately, to attack the falsity of the legend about Garrison rather than the cause for which Garrison fought. "To the public," Garrison seemed harsh and intolerant, said Barnes; "If the hateful self-portrait which Garrison's own words depicted in the *Liberator* had been true, its effect could not have been more ruinous to the antislavery cause. . . ." *If* it were true; but apparently it was not.

When Barnes attacked Garrison's methods he almost always did so because they were "ruinous to the cause." Garrison and his followers were lamentable because they were " 'dead weights to the abolition cause.' " Barnes never dissociated his judgment as a historian from the moral validity of the antislavery cause, and he seemed genuinely to regret that Garrison was such an impediment to its success: "To such a level had the greatest in 'the noble sisterhood of Christian charities' descended." And if he noted that it was Garrison who raised the South to "a level of hysteria," he also made it clear with thinly veiled sarcasm that the South itself was both super-sensitive and hypocritical:

> American opinion, in 1831, had much dignity and little humor, but that dignity had a quality of juvenile self-importance peculiarly intolerant of criticism and rebuke. Nowhere in the nation was this sensibility so tender as in the South, the home of Southern chivalry and the duelling code.

Revisionists overlooked this comment just as they overlooked the far more significant point that Barnes, throughout his book, took great pains to differentiate the abolitionism of Weld from that of Garrison. A. Y. Lloyd made a serious mistake in lumping the two together and treating their motivations, their arguments, and their methods as part of the same vindictive crusade against the South. "The Boston abolitionists made the Garrison legend history," Barnes wrote, and the revisionists were slow to unlearn the legend, preferring to add Barnes's castigation of it to their own and then to include the western abolitionists as part of the same legend.

The key figure in the book, of course, was Weld. After reading

Weld's papers and studying his career, Barnes could not help but admire him. And he expressed his admiration freely, not only by the heroic portrait he drew of Weld and those who followed him, but by contrasting his "modesty," "his magnetic presence," his leadership, his self-sacrificing selflessness with the total absence of all of these ennobling qualities in Garrison. If Barnes was harsh in his debunking of Garrison, this was largely the result of his ill-concealed sense of outrage that Garrison should for so long have received all of the credit which rightly belonged to Weld. If Garrison was "the evil genius" of the movement, Weld was its savior: "Weld was more than a lobbyist; he was an evangelist as well, the genius of the abolition revival; and the power which had wrought miracles of inspiration . . . in every group which his magnetic presence had invaded—that power was still his own." In contrast to Garrison's self-righteous, vituperative journalism, Barnes praised Weld's "thrilling eloquence" by a quotation from one who heard him: "He . . . uttered no malice; sharpened no phrase so that its venomed point might rankle in another's breast. . . . His great soul was full of compassion for the oppressor and the oppressed." Barnes's own estimation was just as strong: "Selfless and lovable—among all the abolitionists in later years only Weld and the gentle Whittier, his beloved friend, were unslandered by their co-workers. . . ."

The reader will find equally stirring words and portraits for the other members of that "roll of heroes" to whom Barnes was so anxious to render their long-overdue praise and fame: Charles Stuart, the Tappan brothers, the Lane Rebels, the Seventy, Joshua Leavitt, James G. Birney, Henry B. Stanton, the Grimké sisters, Joshua Giddings, Orange Scott. All of them were presented with their best sides forward. One of the highlights of the book was Barnes's magnificent re-creation of that great battle which crusty old John Quincy Adams waged singlehanded in the halls of Congress for the right of petition, not only in the teeth of raging Southerners but against the bitter anger of all the members of his own party.

Barnes's ambivalence toward the antislavery impulse was equally obvious in his treatment of Charles Grandison Finney and the Great Revival. While he had no use for Finney's hysteria-arousing sermons and his manipulatory "new measures," he could not help but admire the way the forthright western preacher demolished the cruel doctrines of Calvinism and defied the imprecations of Lyman Beecher. (But when Beecher's own congregation demanded to hear Finney, the Bostonian had to eat his own words of wrath.) "Finney was a portent, one of the notable figures in the moral history of the nineteenth century, and one of the greatest of modern evangelists." And what made him epochal was not those aspects of his revivalism which the Menckenites ridiculed, but the doctrine of "disinterested benevolence" which he preached—the doctrine which "released the mighty impulse toward social reform" and paved the way for the new antislavery impulse. If Weld and his followers were heroes, the fact that Finney was their spiritual father and greatest source of inspiration and strength surely reflected to Finney's credit. Furthermore, Barnes gave Finney credit for opposing the denunciatory aspects of some of Weld's abolitionist followers. Finney feared that "a censorious spirit" such as that of Garrison and some western radicals would "roll a wave of blood over the land." Barnes clearly regretted the fact that the Great Revival declined and "the antislavery impulse ceased to be a missionary movement to save the slaveholders." It was at this point, in 1839, that Barnes believed the war became irrepressible: "The decline of the Great Revival and the rise of Southern resentment made inevitable what he [Finney] feared."

There is one final but important point in Barnes's analysis of the antislavery impulse to which the Southern revisionists failed to pay due attention. This was his frontal attack upon the economic interpretation of the coming of the Civil War. The economic argument was central to the revisionist interpretation of the war because the revisionists held not only that it was economic differences which produced the different cultures and philosophies between the North and the South but also that these economic differences would never, by themselves, have brought a war. For prior to the furor aroused by the abolitionists, with their irrational fanaticism, the conflicts between Northern and Southern views had often been settled by compromises: in 1787, in 1815, in 1820, in 1828, in 1832.There was no reason to believe, said the revisionists, that rational men could not have continued amicably to compromise (as Henry Clay and Stephen A. Douglas tried to do) until slavery died out of its own accord or was gradually abolished by some mutually convenient arrangement. (The revisionists, incidentally, were by all odds the most disillusioned intellectuals following World War I and the most ready to denounce all wars as the result of irrational propaganda. Arthur Schlesinger, Jr., himself a product of the new ideology which Reinhold Niebuhr helped to expound for chastened liberals after 1930, ranked the revisionists in 1949 with those who failed adequately to cope with the great intellectual reorientation of their day: "The vogue of revisionism is connected with the modern tendency to seek in optimistic sentimentalism an escape from the severe demands of moral decision . . . in the name of a superficial objectivity. . . .")

The historian who did more than any other to "despiritualize" the causes of the Civil War (as Pieter Geyl put it), and the man whom Barnes was most clearly refuting in this book, was Charles A. Beard. Beard and his wife produced the most influential statement of the economic interpretation of American history in 1927 in *The Rise of American Civilization*. In chapters entitled "The Sweep of Economic Forces," "The Politics of Drift," and "The Approach of Irrepressible Conflict," the Beards, in dramatic and flowing terms, expanded upon the theme that "Under the drive of economic forces, it was the cotton interest that led the slave states into the appalling crisis." At the same time in the North, "By an inexorable process beyond the will of any man or group, the sovereignty of King Cotton and the authority of his politicians were rudely shaken" by the rise of industrial capitalism. "The supreme question to be debated, if contemporaries had only known it, was whether the political revolution foreshadowed by the economic flux was to proceed peacefully or by violence." It was to this point that the revisionists continually addressed themselves, and, like Beard, they first despiritualized the war's causes by making slavery irrelevant and next maintained that human reason plus intelligent awareness of the economic forces at work could have settled the conflict of interest peacefully if only the abolitionists and fire-eaters had not overheated the atmosphere.

The Beards, however, unlike the revisionists, gave short shrift to Garrison and the other abolitionists—"a tiny minority of agitators" —and they never mentioned Weld or Finney. Their comment on the origin of the antislavery impulse was, "The sources of this remarkable movement are difficult to discover." By and large, they concluded, "the smoke [of the movement] was larger than the fire." "If the realization of the abolition program had depended on the capture of a majority of the voters, if other factors than moral education had not intervened, the agitators might have waged a forlorn battle indefinitely." Barnes came down hard on this point, maintaining with great insistence that the religious impulse of antislavery was transferred directly into votes through the petition crusade and the efforts of the Conscience Whigs. But the Beards were convinced that

> In the economy of Providence, as the orators were fond of saying, abolition agitators were to be justified by history, not by the work of their own hands or by any of the political instruments they had forged. . . . Many an orator who might have forgiven the South for maintaining a servile labor system could not forgive it for its low tariff doctrines and its opposition to centralized finance. By forces more potent than abolition agitation, slavery was therefore swept along with vital economic issues into the national vortex at Washington.

By making the tariff "the outstanding issue" in "this clash of sectional interests," the Beards seemed at times to be transferring American irrational emotionalism from moral to economic issues, but they did not see this. In their eyes the Civil War (which they dubbed "The Second American Revolution") was merely an incident in the inexorable economic transformation of America from an agrarian to an industrial nation: "The roots of the controversy lay . . . in social groupings founded on differences in climate, soil, industries, and the labor systems, in divergent social forces, rather than in varying degrees of righteousness and wisdom, or what romantic historians called 'the magnetism of great personalities.' "

Barnes's refutation of this viewpoint was both explicit and implicit from cover to cover in *The Antislavery Impulse*, and today this refutation, rather than his destruction of the Garrison legend, appears as the central feature of the book. Barnes's concluding paragraphs make his view crystal clear:

> Indeed from first to last, throughout the antislavery host, the cause continued to be a moral issue and not an economic one. Neither in their propaganda nor in their sentiments was the economic issue dominant.

And lest anyone think that he was referring only to the leaders of the antislavery crusade and not to the American public at large, he added,

> Moreover, the areas of their antislavery strength coordinated with no simple Northern interest. They were to be found near to the South and far away; tributary to Southern trade and independent of it; close to the territories in dispute between North and South and at the farthest confines of the nation.

In thus refuting the despiritualizing aspects of the economic interpretation and reasserting the moral issue of human freedom, Barnes was

clearly pointing the way to that new interpretation of the Civil War
which has become the established consensus among historians since
his day. This viewpoint was given one of its most forceful, if extreme,
expositions in 1939 by Dwight L. Dumond in *The Antislavery Origins
of the Civil War*. Dumond drew heavily upon Barnes's work and
was of course roundly denounced by the Southern revisionists. It is
significant that when Barnes sought a co-editor for the Weld-Grimké
papers in 1933, he chose Dumond, and it is not surprising that since
1939 the revisionists have frequently lumped Dumond and Barnes
together among their opponents (a belated recognition of where
Barnes's real emphasis lay). It is significant too that Arthur Schlesinger, Jr., highly praised Dumond's book for reasserting this moral
issue which the "objective" sentimentalists had suppressed.

There is one final bit of fortuitous evidence which may be cited to
indicate that Barnes was not as ambivalent as he seemed or as objective as he claimed to be. In the copy of his book that is currently
in the library of Pembroke College in Brown University, there is
the following inscription written in Barnes's hand:

> To Larry and Christine Sears
>   from the author,
>   Gilbert H. Barnes.
>
> Designed as written, in part for the education of the first named,
> who once remarked in the author's hearing that no revival of religion
> had or could produce a social movement of intrinsic importance.

If Barnes did indeed design this book to prove that religion was not,
as most intellectuals in the 1920's maintained, a rather impotent if
not malicious force in American history, then *The Antislavery Impulse* fits squarely into the ideological reorientation which I have been
trying to outline. William Warren Sweet, then the dean of American
church history, in reviewing the book for *The Christian Century* in
1934, looked for and found this design in it. Sweet was happy to note
that by repudiating Garrison's anticlerical leadership of the movement,
Barnes had now demonstrated that the ministers and churches of
America were a part of the crusade from its outset to its conclusion.
One can almost sense the relief of church historians like Sweet at finding someone outside the churches who was ready to say a good word
for them. "Mr. Barnes has proved, I think," said Sweet, "that the
churches had a far more honorable part in the anti-slavery crusade
than has hitherto been accorded them." Is it stretching the point too

far to suggest that Barnes's book, or what it represents, had something to do with the reassertion by the clergy of its own self-respect
which was epitomized in 1935 by Harry Emerson Fosdick's famous
sermon declaring that the churches must go beyond sentimental
"modernism" and obsequious conciliations to science and take the high
road to a new orthodoxy? I think not.

And I think good evidence for this can be educed by contrasting
H. Richard Niebuhr's two classics of American religious history,
The Social Sources of Denominationalism, published in 1929, and
The Kingdom of God in America, published in 1937. In the first of
these books, Niebuhr, speaking in the accents of the religious historian *qua* sociologist, derogated most of the religious fervor of American life by explaining the proliferation of American Protestant
denominations in terms of Ernst Troeltsch's sociological theory of
the social and economic derivations of religious diversity. But eight
years later Niebuhr wrote that he was no longer satisfied with this
view of America's religious development because

> Though the sociological approach helped me to explain why the
> religious stream flowed in these particular channels, it did not account
> for the force of the stream itself. . . . While it could deal with the
> religion which was dependent on culture, it left unexplained the faith
> which is independent, which is aggressive rather than passive, and
> which molds culture instead of being molded by it.

Niebuhr always argued, at least in private conversations, that
these two books were complementary rather than contradictory.
Nevertheless, it is clear now that the first was written in the mood
and spirit of "modernism," while the second was written in the mood
and spirit of what we have since come to identify as "neo-orthodoxy."
In 1929 Niebuhr treated the antislavery movement precisely as the
Beards had done: "The difference in attitude toward slavery" on the
parts of the Northern and Southern churches, he wrote, was not "due
in the main to any excellence of disinterested moral insight on the
part of the North" but, on the contrary, it "was rooted in a difference
of economic interest and structures, of culture and tradition." And
he documented this interpretation by quotations from *The Rise of
American Civilization.* He did not mention William Lloyd Garrison,
Weld, or Finney in this book. But when he came to write *The Kingdom of God in America,* he devoted a whole section to the antislavery

movement because it spoke so clearly, he believed, for the millennial spirit which dominated the pre-Civil War American mind. In place of quotations from the Beards, his account of the antislavery movement in 1937 was drawn almost wholly from Barnes's work. (And, incidentally, swinging now to the opposite pole, he neglected again to mention William Lloyd Garrison because, apparently, Barnes had convinced him of his unimportance. Nevertheless, his was a more accurate application of Barnes's book than A. Y. Lloyd's book which appeared the same year.)

Having stated the major ambivalences and contributions of *The Antislavery Impulse,* I must conclude with a word about its shortcomings. The most obvious defect, of course, was that it did, as the reviewers said, ride its anti-Garrison thesis far too hard and concomitantly exalted Weld and Finney more than they deserved. John L. Thomas's brilliant (and neo-orthodox) re-evaluation of Garrison in his biography, *The Liberator* (1963), has now redressed the balance. While Thomas does not deny the importance of the western revival and the abolition leaders who grew out of it, he forcefully demonstrates that Garrison was much more than a "negligible" dead weight upon the cause. Moreover, he makes it clear that Barnes has misinterpreted Lyman Beecher by making him a whipping boy for the James Truslow Adams version of Calvinism. Beecher was himself an epochal figure, along with Nathaniel W. Taylor, the Yale theologian, overthrowing the more harsh and doctrinaire aspects of neo-Edwardsian theology which dominated New England between the First and Second Great Awakenings. In the broad view, Beecher and Finney were really fighting the same evangelical fight—only with a slightly different emphasis. And, as a number of scholarly works have since demonstrated, the reform impulse and "the Benevolent Empire," of which Beecher was a prominent leader, were well under way before Finney came on the scene.

Barnes erred also in attributing to Finney the doctrine of "disinterested benevolence." Had Barnes been a little more widely read in New England theology he would have discovered that this doctrine owed its origin to Jonathan Edwards and that it received its most eloquent statement at the hands of his pupil, Samuel Hopkins, himself one of the first of the antislavery host. Finney, of course, was vehement in denouncing Hopkins's neo-Edwardsian "triangular" version of Calvinism, but at the same time he was unconsciously developing,

or over-developing, Hopkins's neo-Edwardsian version of "applied
Christianity." Barnes made a serious mistake too in failing to consult
the Finney Papers at Oberlin. And he did not play entirely fair with
his readers in relegating to his notes in the back of the book the
evidence of Finney's vigorous opposition to Weld and the abolition
movement, though this is apparent in the Weld-Grimké letters.
Finney not only expressed his strong fears of a wave of blood result-
ing from Weld's denunciatory spirit, but he actively pitted all of his
prestige and eloquence against Weld in trying to dissuade the Lane
Rebels and various members of the Seventy from preaching abolition;
he wanted them to confine themselves to soul-winning. Robert S.
Fletcher in his excellent history of Oberlin College stated that the
reason why the college produced "so few abolitionist lecturers" between 1835 and 1860 was that Finney dominated the college and he
insisted that "the cause of Christ must come first" while the cause of
abolition could wait upon it. No wonder the Tappans considered
Finney a "coward," a traitor to the cause, who was "sinning against
conscience" by his refusal to pray for abolition in public. There was
in Finney's perfectionism (which Barnes slights) a strong element
of escapism, an over-optimistic reliance upon the Holy Spirit to
perform the difficult task of freeing the slaves. And if "the antislavery
belt" voted for Lincoln in 1860, it should be noted that later, when
Finney's perfectionism met the intransigence of the South, he decided
that even Lincoln was not sufficiently righteous in his policies and
supported Benjamin F. Butler for President in 1864.

Less important, perhaps, but nevertheless a shortcoming, was
Barnes's failure to define adequately what he called "the antislavery
belt." Whitney Cross's book, *The Burned-over District* (1950), has
supplied this defect, explaining precisely what the circumstances were
that made Finney's revivalism, abolitionism, and other reforms so
popular in western New York; Cross also corrected several minor
errors of fact in Barnes's book. Barnes also appears to have been
too hasty in explaining the Presbyterian schism of 1837 in terms of
the abolition issue; subsequent studies have placed more emphasis
upon theological, institutional, and disciplinary aspects of the schism.
Nor was it entirely satisfactory to neglect the pre-1830 phases of
antislavery and to have the book come to such an abrupt end in 1844,
a decision which seems to have been made primarily because Weld
dropped out of the picture at that time. Those who wished to dismiss

the abolition movement of the thirties as essentially a failure or a
forgotten incident by 1860 could find support for this in Barnes's
book. Those who wanted to know more about Weld had to wait for
Benjamin Thomas's biography in 1950.

And finally one must say something about the deficiencies in organization and presentation of the book. There is no question about
its brilliant and dramatic narrative; it has a driving momentum and
graphic vividness which grip the reader in a way that few monographs have ever done. But it achieved this at a heavy cost. Barnes
committed the grave sin of over-simplification and failure to qualify.
He made all of the parts of the story dovetail too neatly into a simple
one-to-one relationship. The development resembles the nursery
rhyme about the house that Jack built—only here it is the abolition
movement that Weld built, that Finney inspired, that the Tappans
financed, that the Seventy preached, that Adams took to Congress,
that Lincoln climaxed. Barnes was aware of this, but he sought to
make up for it by placing all of his qualifications and amplifications
in copious notes at the end of the book. It was a poor compromise.
An author whose notes constitute one-third of the total pages in his
book has obviously misjudged the purpose of notes and failed to
distinguish the relevant from the irrelevant. Barnes's notes are almost
as fascinating and at times more important than some aspects of his
text. They are far from being the documentation or citation of sources
which is ostensibly their purpose.

The Presbyterian schism, for example, appears only in a note at
the back though it was a crucial turning point in the religious and
humanitarian movements of the day. The failure of Weld's agents to
invade Indiana and Illinois is reduced to a note and dismissed as the
result of Weld's illness at the moment. Weld's many idiosyncracies—
his insistence on wearing shabby "John Baptist attire," his taking a
cold water bath every day, his conviction that he was an agent of
God—items which today's psychoanalytic historians would delight
in, Barnes buries in the notes. Some of the kinder and more laud-
able aspects of Garrison's character and behavior are placed in the
notes. And a serious qualification of the support of the New England
Baptists for abolitionism is dismissed in a note, though it gravely
undercuts a more general statement in the text concerning their
attitude.

But in the end it is a measure of the importance of this book that it transcends all of these shortcomings and that it has provided a stimulus and a source for some of the most significant scholarship on the pre-Civil War era which has appeared since.

It is appropriate to reissue this book now, one hundred years after the Civil War, when America is once again in the midst of a revolutionary effort to implement its moral ideals. Thanks to the victory in that war, this current revolution for human equality and freedom will find its ultimate solutions in Congress and the courts—though not without violence and bloodshed in the streets. Those who fail to sense the moral urgency of the present struggle would do well to read Barnes's book. If the book tells us anything, it is that moral commitment is not only an inherent ingredient of the American character but an essential element in any meaningful concept of history—a force as inexorable as any physiographic, economic, or geo-political force and one which cannot be separated from the nature and destiny of man without ultimately denying his humanity.

SUGGESTIONS FOR FURTHER READING

I. Primary Sources (published)

Beecher, Lyman, *Autobiography,* ed. Barbara M. Cross (Cambridge, Mass., 1961).

Birney, James G., *Letters,* ed. Dwight L. Dumond (New York, 1938).

Finney, Charles G., *Memoirs* (New York, 1876).

Stanton, Henry B., *Random Recollections* (Johnstown, N.Y., 1885).

Tappan, Lewis, *The Life of Arthur Tappan* (London, 1870).

Weld, Theodore Dwight, *Letters of Theodore Dwight Weld, Angelina Grimké Weld and Sarah Grimké, 1822-1844,* ed. Gilbert H. Barnes and Dwight L. Dumond (New York, 1934).

II. Secondary Sources

Beale, Howard K., "What Historians Have Said about the Causes of the Civil War" in *Theory and Practice in Historical Study: A Report of the Committee on Historiography* (Social Science Research Council, 1946), pp. 55-102.

Bodo, John R., *The Protestant Clergy and Public Issues, 1812-1848* (Princeton, 1954).

Cole, Charles C., *The Social Ideas of the Northern Evangelists, 1826-1860* (New York, 1954).

Craven, Avery O., *The Repressible Conflict* (Baton Rouge, 1939).

Cross, Whitney R., *The Burned-over District* (Ithaca, 1950).

Dumond, Dwight L., *Antislavery Origins of the Civil War in the United States* (New York, 1939).

Filler, Louis, *The Crusade Against Slavery, 1830-1860* (New York, 1960).

Fladeland, Betty, *James Gillespie Birney* (Ithaca, 1955).

Fletcher, Robert S., *A History of Oberlin College* (Oberlin, 1943).

Fosdick, Harry Emerson, "Beyond Modernism," *The Christian Century,* LII (1935), pp. 1549 ff.

Foster, Frank H., *A Genetic History of the New England Theology* (Chicago, 1907).

Garrison, W. P. and F. J., *William Lloyd Garrison* (New York, 1885-1889).

Geyl, Pieter, "The American Civil War and the Problem of Inevitability," *New England Quarterly,* XXIV (1951), pp. 147-68.

Griffin, Clifford S., *Their Brothers' Keepers: Moral Stewardship in the United States, 1800-1865* (New Brunswick, N.J., 1960).

Haroutunian, Joseph, *Piety Versus Moralism* (New York, 1932).

Hart, Albert B., *Slavery and Abolition* (New York, 1906).

Hofstadter, Richard, "Ulrich B. Phillips and the Plantation Legend," *Journal of Negro History,* XXIX (1944), pp. 109 ff.

Lloyd, Arthur Y., *The Slavery Controversy, 1831-1860* (Chapel Hill, 1939).

McLoughlin, William G., *Modern Revivalism* (New York, 1959).

Mead, Sidney E., *Nathaniel William Taylor, 1786-1858* (Chicago, 1942).

Pressly, Thomas J., *Americans Interpret Their Civil War* (Princeton, 1954).

Seldes, Gilbert V., *The Stammering Century* (New York, 1928).

Smith, Theodore C., *The Liberty and Free Soil Parties in the Northwest* (New York, 1897).

Smith, Timothy L., *Revivalism and Social Reform in Mid-nineteenth Century America* (New York, 1957).

Thomas, Benjamin P., *Theodore Weld* (New Brunswick, N.J., 1950).

Thomas, John L., *The Liberator: William Lloyd Garrison, A Biography* (Boston, 1963).

Tyler, Alice Felt, *Freedom's Ferment* (Minneapolis, 1944).

PREFACE

This is the centennial year of antislavery history. In August of 1833, Great Britain abolished slavery in the West Indies, and, in December of the same year, the American Anti-Slavery Society began its agitation for emancipation in this country. Like all organized propagandas, the American agitation had two concurrent histories. One was the course of public events which could be exploited for antislavery purposes. Some such events—the petition campaign in Congress, for instance—were developed by the organization itself; but usually they happened fortuitously. Well-placed mobs, striking martyrdoms, and the like could not be planned. They came as windfalls, and the history of them throws little light on the organization that exploited their occurrence. Coincident with the narrative of events was the other history, the chronicles of the organization itself; not the fair, consistent front turned to the public view, but the inspirations, the strategies, and the controversies that shaped the movement. It is the latter history which accounts for the nature and progress of the antislavery agitation.

Many of the antislavery leaders—and their descendants—have recorded their interpretation of this history with such minuteness and consistency that, except for a few special pleaders, a generation of historians have followed its outline, and even to-day it has the authority of an orthodox tradition. Of recent years, however, most historians have found this traditional story inadequate to explain the sectional struggle which culminated in the Civil War. The tendency has been to regard the movement of the 'thirties as inconsiderable and to refer the rising antislavery sentiment of the 'forties and the 'fifties to economic factors.

If the traditional story of antislavery beginnings is accepted, some such appraisal of its significance is inevitable. But contemporary records of the movement, especially outside New England, do not fit into the traditional story. They tell a different and incomparably more significant tale of a religious impulse which began in the West of 1830, was translated for a time into antislavery organization, and then broadened into a sectional crusade against the South. In this

aspect the movement of the 'thirties was not inconsiderable: it was
a major factor in the rise of sectionalism and a prime cause of the
final conflict. It is this history of the antislavery movement which I
propose to trace from its beginnings to its diffusion throughout the
North.

For an excess of quotations from the documents I beg the reader's
indulgence. The antislavery impulse unfolded into a narrative so un-
orthodox that I did not have the hardihood to interpret it in my own
words. I have, therefore, let the documents tell the story. The manner
of its telling, I hope, makes for a reconstruction rather than a reinterpretation of the facts.

For the plethora of references I make the same apology. The narrative developed in such unlooked-for ways that it demanded
reference almost point by point to the documents from which it came.
Since many of these documents are not accessible to scholars, I
have included in the notes enough of their contents to elucidate the
points on which they bear.

Amid a host of obligations too numerous to be listed, I acknowledge with especial gratitude my debt to Theodore Weld's grandson,
Dr. L. D. H. Weld, who made the Weld papers available. I am
under a similar obligation to Weld's granddaughter, Dr. Angelina
G. Hamilton; to Mr. Dion S. Birney, grandson of James G. Birney;
and to Dr. Philip G. Wright, grandson of both Elizur Wright, Jr.
and Beriah Green, for permitting me to use the manuscripts in their
possession. I am also indebted to Dr. Thomas Martin of the Library
of Congress for securing permission to use the Lewis Tappan papers and to Professor Andrews of Yale University for his careful
reading of this work in manuscript and for his many helpful suggestions.

My chief obligation is to Professor Ulrich B. Phillips, now of
Yale University, whose teaching first moved me to begin this study
and whose unwearied faith and help encouraged me to continue it
through the ensuing years.

GILBERT H. BARNES

Ohio Wesleyan University, 1933.

CONTENTS

THE ANTISLAVERY IMPULSE
1830–1844

CHAPTER I

The Great Revival

1830

At the beginning of the decade of the 'thirties, William Ellery Channing, the New England liberal, summed up the spirit of his age. It was, he observed, "an age of great movements" which had shown, as had no other age, a "tendency and power to exalt a people." Behind these great movements—the triumph of the Jacksonian democracy, the extension of popular knowledge, and the enlargement of economic opportunity—Channing discerned a common basis in a new perception of human brotherhood. "Every age teaches its own lesson," he declared. "The lesson of this age is that of sympathy with the suffering, and of devotion to the progress of the whole human race." [1]

In 1830, this new movement was working a transformation in religion no less significant than the changes in politics and education. As devotion to the common man increased, the dogmas of Calvinism lost authority. Though still the official creed of the Presbyterian and Congregational denominations, orthodox Calvinism had long been opposed in the East; and in the West—which, in 1830, was anywhere west of the Eastern highlands—thousands were ripe for apostasy. It was among these that the Great Revival began, and it grew wherever belief in Calvinism declined.

To the millions of Calvinists in New England and the West, the democratic faith in the common man which pervaded the Great Revival seemed unnatural and unsound. For the core of Calvinistic belief was a damnatory suspicion of mankind, expressed in its doctrine of original sin. Technically, the original sin was Adam's disobedience in the Garden of Eden, but Calvinists taught that it was our sin too: "When Adam sinned, we, being in Adam's loins as branches in the root, sinned in him." To use a biological figure, Adam's sin infected the human germ plasm with his guilt, and it was "conveyed from our first parents . . . by natural generation, so that all . . . are conceived and born in sin." To Calvinists there was nothing formal about our Adamic guilt; for by its vileness all of us are

3

born "wholly defiled in all the faculties and parts of soul and body. . . . wholly lost to all ability or will to any good." [2]

Left to the justice of a Calvinistic vengeance, how hopeless and helpless is man! Of himself he has no choice but to die in his sins and straightway go to hell to burn forever. Such, indeed, is to be the fate of all of us save a few sound Calvinists, God's elect, who do not merit salvation by any virtue of their own, but are saved by a decree which God uttered when eternity began, foreordaining salvation for a few and damnation for the remainder of mankind. Even these few do not know that they are predestined to be saved until God commands them by a "special calling" to repent of their sin. If they are truly elect, they do repent, and God performs on them a miracle. By the awful agency of the Holy Ghost He cleanses their guilty souls of original sin and they are thereby converted from damnation to salvation. They escape God's vengeance and the burning lake. They are saved!

Before the nineteenth century began, orthodox believers had observed that the Holy Spirit, that mysterious third person of the Trinity, chose to visit with peculiar power congregations gathered at revivals. There the elect heard most clearly the "special calling," while revivalists denounced sinners and summoned the heirs of salvation to repentance. The Great Awakening of 1800, as well as hundreds of local, sporadic "seasons of refreshing" throughout the land, had habituated orthodox Calvinists to expect the miracle of conversion primarily in revivals. But revivals themselves were unaccountably dangerous. During the process of conversion, the operation of the Holy Spirit filled the clergy with perplexity and dismay. Sinners would shriek and faint; they would be shaken with strange ecstasies, would babble with strange tongues. Repeatedly these "excitements" brought revivals into disrepute; but though whole congregations were "overthrown" by the power of the Holy Spirit, though whole communities went mad with terror and joy, the faith of the orthodox remained unshaken that salvation was a miracle wrought by the Holy Ghost through revivals. Long before 1830, revivals had become necessary properties in the Calvinistic drama of the escape from hell. By the clergy they were dreaded for their power to destroy decorum and feared as the abiding place of the Holy Spirit, but nevertheless they were valued for their effects in enlarging the congregation. Liberals here and there opposed them, but the nation as a whole believed and trembled. [3]

The Calvinistic creed was a terrible thing, especially to those who believed it. Even Timothy Dwight, famous theologian, president of Yale and pillar of orthodoxy, admitted that perhaps no doctrine was more reluctantly received by the human mind. "I confess," he said, "that if I saw any mode of avoiding the evidence by which it is established, I would certainly reject it also." But even in his day, liberal theologians were finding modes of avoiding the evidence, and attacks on the doctrine multiplied, especially in New England. By 1830, the Puritans had softened and grown merciful and kind; much of New England was apostate, and Calvinism pure and undefiled was to be found rather in the South and West. Here Old-School Presbyterians grimly defended the sacred doctrine from the softening influence of New England heresy and viewed with rancorous distrust the expanding benevolence of the times.

The most vulnerable point of Calvinism was its doctrine of infant damnation, which was a corollary of the doctrine of original sin. Since infants inherited the guilt of Adam's sin, they were born damned; and, if they died before they were old enough to heed the "special calling," they were damned eternally. This doctrine had never been popular, and it had become, by 1830, a reproach to Calvinism. But it was still preached even in New England as a terrible reality. "Hell is paved with the skulls of infants one span long," one conservative told his congregation, "and their parents look down upon them from Heaven, praising God for the justice of their damnation!" Of course such thoroughgoing conservatives were rare; but their doctrinal position was sound, and as long as they represented orthodox Calvinism, more liberal defenders of the faith were put to shame.[4]

The most stalwart and eloquent of the defenders of the faith was Lyman Beecher, "father of more brains than any man in America." He was a mighty orator, the foremost revivalist in the Congregational Church, and the most famous clergyman of his time. Early in his ministry Beecher had found that Calvinism was an indifferent creed for revivals. Its tendency, he discovered, was "to paralyze wonderfully the feelings of the soul"; and its doctrine that all men were predestined before their birth either to be saved or damned, made it hard "to treat converts as reasonable beings." But however irksome the old creed was, Beecher realized that its amendment would be dangerous. The damnation of infants he did venture to interpret as "consisting chiefly, if not entirely, in the loss of that holy enjoyment in heaven for which their depravity disqualified them; and if they suffered a positive evil at all, it was of the very mildest kind." But even this mitigation of Calvinistic orthodoxy he dared not unite to the doctrine of original sin, fearing "that the policy is unwise of making that doctrine the hinge of controversy between the orthodox . . . because, as it respects the character and destiny of infants, it gives the enemy the advantage of the popular side."[5]

Beecher was no philosopher. Like most famous orators, he made up his creed to secure popular approval; and while at all times he vigorously claimed a liberal attitude, he was timid toward ideas mistrusted by conservatives. In "the swamp of Calvinism" he remained until a safe way out was discovered by the New Haven theologians.[6]

From the beginning, attacks upon Calvinism beat most fiercely on the centers of learning. Princeton was immovable, and Andover was staunch; but Harvard went over to the Unitarian enemy, and Yale sought a middle ground. It was at Yale that Dr. Nathaniel W. Taylor, a gentle and scholarly professor of theology, began to write early in the century on the subject of original sin. Without formally abandoning the doctrine that our first parents' "corrupted nature . . . was conveyed to all their posterity," he denied that infants could inherit the actual guilt of Adam. Though they did inherit Adam's depraved nature, he declared that it was only in the form of "an unyielding determination to sin." They did not inherit the sin itself, and, therefore, they did not inherit Adam's title to everlasting punishment. Taylor concluded that infants were born sinless, that they could not sin until they were accountable for their acts, and that all sin, therefore, consisted in "voluntary exercises." With extraordinary ingenuity he argued that this was the true doctrine of original sin, true Calvinism and not heresy.

Orthodox Andover was deeply disturbed. A conference of its divines with those of Yale was arranged, and a spokesman put to Dr. Taylor the pregnant question: " 'Does the infant need regenerating grace in the first month of its existence?' Dr. Taylor replied, 'No.' 'Does he need this grace in the second month?' Again he answered, 'No.' " The inquiry was pursued to the sixth month. At that point Dr. Taylor, a prolific father, replied, "I don't know but that the child may then need renewing grace." The Andover professors departed more disturbed than before.[7]

To New Haven, Beecher brought his doctrinal perplexities; and when Nathaniel Taylor told him how he could preach to sinners a liberal gospel of responsibility and still subscribe to original sin for theological purposes, he was overjoyed. He proceeded to develop and preach his "famous technic," based on Taylor's ideas, "which will," he said, "carry us *all* out of the swamp together !" [8]

In this he succeeded. "While Dr. Taylor and others have written and reasoned and philosophized and mysticized," an indignant Calvinist wrote him, "you have rendered the same system palpable and practical in your preaching and ministrations, subserving their cause far more effectually than they have done themselves." In his Hanover Church in Boston, Beecher revived his people year by enlarging year, preaching the old Calvinism and the new liberalism at one and the same time, with never a sense of incongruity, conflict, or discord. "The time shall come," he said, "that the fundamentals unite us, and theories cannot divide: Then . . . Satan's power is broken, and the millennium is at the door !" [9]

Across the mountains, in 1825, came news to Boston of a mighty revival in western New York, such a "shower of refreshing" as had not been known since the Great Awakening. It began in 1824, but quickly spread in widening circles about Oneida, to Troy on the east and to Auburn on the west. Oneida County was completely "overthrown by the Holy Ghost," so that "in consequence of this display of divine power, the theatre has been deserted, the tavern sanctified." In the communities affected, it was reported that court business had fallen off and jails were standing empty. "The whole customs of society have been changed. Amusements and all practices . . . the object of which is simply pleasure, have been abandoned, and far higher and purer enjoyment has been found in exercises of devotion." Many thousands entered into salvation, while the orthodox rejoiced and infidels were confounded.[10]

In 1826, Boston began to hear a dissonance in the harmony of the western revival. Certain irregularities and extravagances were reported. It was charged that its moving spirit, the great revivalist Mr. Finney, was denunciatory and extreme. He preached from such texts as "Ye generation of vipers, how can ye escape the damnation of hell?" With violent posturings and groaning he prayed for sinners by name: "Oh God! Smite that wicked man, that hardened sinner. . . . Oh God! Send trouble, anguish and affliction into his bed chamber this night. . . . God Almighty, shake him over hell!" But more serious was his invention of "new measures." These consisted

in unduly protracting his meetings, usually for four days but sometimes for weeks; in using as helpers a "holy band" of new converts,
whose enthusiasm and assurance were a great trial to the local ministry; in instituting the "anxious seat" in front of the congregation,
to which those under conviction of sin could repair; and in permitting
women to pray in public meetings. In the language of the president
of Williams College, "the method of the revivals is complete radi-
calism!" [11]

Lyman Beecher, defender of revivals, was wroth. "Satan as usual,"
he declared, "is plotting to dishonor a work which he cannot withstand." Orthodox Calvinists, forgetting their suspicions of Beecher's
doctrines in the face of common danger, summoned him to defend
the repute of revivals; and Beecher, convinced that the church was
"on the confines of misrule and moral desolation," answered the
summons. He decided on a conference with Finney himself. "Ministers must come together and consult," he declared. "The mask must
be torn off from Satan coming among the sons of God and trans-
forming himself into an angel of light." [12]

In order that the ministers might tear off the mask from Satan
himself, Beecher arranged to meet Finney at New Lebanon, New
York, in 1827. Over the mountains with Beecher came a group of
notables, giants in the Eastern church. Among them were the president of Amherst; the veteran Justin Edwards of Andover; Joel
Hawes of Yale; and Nettleton, the famous orthodox evangelist.
Finney summoned to the conference his Western supporters, ministers whose churches he had revived by his labors. Pursuant to the
quaint fashion of the time, resolutions were put; after discussion, a
vote was taken, and by majority the resolution was judged true or
false. After innocuous preliminaries, the Eastern giants began: "Resolved That in social meetings of men and women for religious worship, females are not to pray." But this very part of western New
York was the land of Elizabeth Cady Stanton, Susan B. Anthony,
and the woman's rights movement. The Westerners rose to defend
the right of "the female brethren" to self-expression, and the resolution did not carry. Then: "Resolved That audible groaning in
prayer is . . . to be discouraged." This resolution received a grudg-
ing assent, though Finney was still convinced that there was such
a thing as "being in a state of mind in which there is but one way
to keep from groaning; and that is, by resisting the Holy Ghost."
Then the Westerners proposed a series of resolutions with a gen-

eral purport that it was not seemly for workers in one part of the Lord's vineyard to impose their judgments upon workers elsewhere. When asked to vote on these resolutions, Beecher, speaking for the Easterners, replied, "As the above does not appear to us to be, in the course of Divine Providence, called for, we therefore decline to act."

The tension broke; Beecher lost his temper and said: "Finney, I know your plan, and you know I do; you mean to come into Connecticut and carry a streak of fire to Boston. If you attempt it, as the Lord liveth, I'll meet you at the state line, and call out the artillerymen and fight you there." The brethren separated sorrowfully and the Easterners went back over the mountains. From this clash between Beecher and Finney there lingered an animosity which was to affect a second conflict big with consequences to the antislavery movement in years to come.[13]

Charles Grandison Finney was a portent, one of the notable figures in the moral history of the nineteenth century, and one of the greatest of modern evangelists. He was practising law in western New York when he came under the preaching of George W. Gale, the Presbyterian minister who later founded Oneida Institute and Knox College. Finney was soon converted. He immediately entered the church, was ordained, and began to preach with such intimacy of appeal and such fervor of conviction that his ministry quickly took on the emotional color of revivals. Calls for his services elsewhere made it impossible for him to remain with a single congregation, and he entered upon his extraordinary career as an itinerant revivalist.

Finney was a radical. A successful lawyer, he had a large contempt for the Calvin-burdened clergy, who tangled "election, predestination, free-agency, inability, and duty in one promiscuous jumble," and confounded the sinner "with you can and you can't, you shall and you shan't, you will and you won't; you'll be damned if you do, and you'll be damned if you don't." While he was preparing for ordination he flatly refused to attend Princeton, telling his ministerial advisers that he had no desire to subject himself to such influences as had made them what they were. He deplored the "mouthing . . . lofty style of preaching" popular in his day, and talked in the pulpit "as the lawyer does when he wants to make a jury understand him perfectly . . . the language of common life." To his colloquial, simple, downright style, he united a frank, open manner. But he had "great, staring eyes . . . never was a man whose soul looked out through his face as his did," and at the climax of his revivals, he would frighten his hearers into hysterics with his terrific, denunciatory eloquence. At such times, "surrounded by anxious sinners, in such distress as to make every nerve tremble, some overcome with emotion and lying on the floor . . . others shrieking out as if they were going to hell," Finney would seem by modern standards to have merited Beecher's condemnation. But standards alter with the years, and in western New York a century ago such a display of emotion was not considered excessive; it was regarded merely as "the natural expression of convictions . . . very pungent and deep." [14]

The time was one of emotional release. Contemporary revivals among Methodists and Baptists were orgies of religious hysteria, and in the West even Presbyterian revivals were sometimes marred by emotional excesses. "The best Presbyterian Revival preachers here preach nothing but the loose, disconnected rhapsodies of Methodists in the main," remarked a Western expert in revivals. "Their preaching is exhortation and appeal, dwelling upon the love of Christ &c, and all addressed to mere sympathy. They reason little and investigate less." In contrast, Finney "pressed the anxious sinners with the closely reasoned truth." Only after he had won their minds did he address himself to their "sympathy." Even then he exercised his gift of hypnotic eloquence with moderation, and never for a moment did he let the emotions of his converts get beyond his iron control. By contemporary revivalists he was accounted a conservative; and even his critics were forced to admit that in his revivals there was "less appearance of mere sympathy and excitement than usual." [15]

What made Finney an epochal figure was not his eloquence or his "new measures"; it was the new doctrine that he preached. He was far keener and bolder than Beecher, and the orthodox clergy of the West and South rightly saw in Finney the heresiarch of Calvinism, the first preacher "who adequately attempted to employ the theology of New Haven in its practical relations." Thanks to his freedom from theological training, Finney felt no restraining obligation to reconcile the new spirit moving in the churches with the old Calvinism. His attacks were not oblique but frontal. To him original sin was not "some constitutional depravity which lies back and is the cause

of actual transgressions": it was simply "a deep-seated but voluntary . . . self-interest. . . . All sin consists in selfishness; and all
holiness or virtue, in disinterested benevolence." [16]

Going far beyond any orthodox creed of his time, Finney tore
away the mystical terrors that veiled the workings of the Holy Ghost
in human hearts during conversion. "It is not a miracle or dependent
on a miracle in any sense," he declared. "It is purely a philosophical
result of the right use of constituted means." What is more, "a revival of religion is not a miracle . . . it consists entirely in the right
exercise of the powers of nature." These powers Finney admitted
to be merely those arising from emotional "excitement"; but they
were not to be deplored on that account. "Mankind will not act until
they are excited. . . . How many there are who know they ought
to be religious, but they . . . are procrastinating repentance until
they . . . have secured some favorite worldly interest. Such persons
never will . . . relinquish their ambitious schemes till they are so
excited that they cannot contain themselves any longer." Thus, Finney
concluded, it was the sinner himself who accomplished his conversion.
Indeed, "if the sinner ever has a new heart, he must . . . make it
himself," not through some obscure miracle of the Holy Ghost, but
by "changing the controlling preference of the mind." Instead of a
"preference for self-interest," he must exercise a "preference for
disinterested benevolence." [17]

This break with orthodoxy changed for Finney's converts the whole
emphasis of religious experience. Calvinism had made salvation the
end of all human desire and fear of hell the spur to belief; whereas
Finney made salvation the beginning of religious experience instead
of its end. The emotional impulse which Calvinism had concentrated
upon a painful quest for a safe escape from life, Finney thus turned
toward benevolent activity. Converts, he declared, did not escape life:
they began a new life "in the interests of God's Kingdom." In this
new life "they have no separate interests. . . . They should set out
with a determination to aim *at being useful in the highest degree
possible.*" [18]

Among Finney's converts this gospel released a mighty impulse
toward social reform. A contemporary remarked acutely that the new
doctrine had made over Calvinism into "a very practical affair, and
adapted it well to American tastes and habits. It encourages mankind
to *work* as well as to *believe.* Let loose from the chains of predestina-

tion, and in accordance with this new light, the scheme has been set on foot in America, of converting the world *at once* . . . a very natural excess of such emancipation of the mind, and of the overflowings of benevolence." [19]

As the number of the new-born in the Kingdom increased by the thousands, the ten thousands and, after the Great Revival year of 1830, by the hundred thousands, their enthusiasm overflowed into "all the great objects of Christian benevolence," such as temperance, education, and the ministry of the gospel.

Beecher had feared that Finney's "new measures" would appeal peculiarly to the youthful, and that into the ministry from these revivals "a host of ardent, inexperienced, impudent young men would be poured out, as from the hives of the North, to obliterate civilization and roll back the wheels of time to semi-barbarism." His fears were justified, for in each community that he invaded, Finney left groups of young men emancipated from sin and Calvinism and overflowing with benevolence for unsaved mankind. One of these was Theodore Dwight Weld, a student at Hamilton College near Utica when Finney found him. Weld was a prize to win. He was more mature than his fellow students; he had journeyed through the South during the three previous years, lecturing on the "science of Mnemonics"; and he had used his extraordinary personal gifts among his fellow students to talk down Finney's revivals. Weld was inveigled into a revival meeting, and for an hour Finney preached at him from the text, "One sinner destroyeth much good." He was "overthrown," and left college to labor in Finney's company as one of his Holy Band, being "instrumental . . . in the hopeful conversion of a great many souls." [20]

To his evangelistic labors Weld brought the constitution of a hero. His immense physical energy, always ready to "shake hands with Toil and call Peril by his middle name," was united to a vivid personal charm—"a finely expressive countenance, a smile . . . like a glorious vision of benevolence," and a "melodious voice . . . full and musical, and often peculiarly thrilling." During his first week in Finney's Holy Band he began his career of reform. Revolted by the current tradition that "the modesty of women's unperverted nature" enjoined their silence in public meetings, he urged the women of Utica "both to pray and speak if they felt deeply enough to do it, and not to be restrained from it by the fact that they were females." This

innovation made a great deal of talk and discussion throughout western New York, but with rare sagacity Weld refused to argue the
principle involved, and continued to encourage the practice. As it
spread, he observed that "wherever the *practice* commenced first, it
always held its own . . . but where it was first laid down as a doctrine . . . it generally prevented the practice and shut it out. . . .
Let intelligent women begin to pray and speak, and men begin to be
converted to the true doctrine; and when they get familiar with it they
like it and lose all their scruples." Weld continued to urge this innovation upon Finney's congregations: "The practice of female praying
in promiscuous meetings grew every day; and now all over that region
nothing is more common in revivals of religion." [21]

Thus did Weld plant the seed of the woman's rights movement in
the land of its origin. Beecher's resolve that "in social meetings of
men and women for religious worship females are not to pray" was,
had he only known it, directed not against Finney—who had nothing
to do with the practice—but against Weld, the first successful champion of the right of women to a public hearing. It was a conflict of
principle, strangely prophetic of a deeper conflict yet to arise between
Weld and Beecher.[22]

But it was among the young men that Weld chiefly labored in the
revivals, admonishing them at the anxious seat, helping them over
the black hours of conviction, and guiding their way to the great decision. Selfless and lovable—among all the abolitionists in later years
only Weld and the gentle Whittier, his beloved friend, were unslandered by their co-workers—he gained the lasting loyalty and affection
of his young converts. Among them developed "disinterested benevolence" in the form of a ministerial ambition. As years passed, their
numbers grew. They interchanged confidences and ambitions in a
loosely knit fraternity of friendship, and through Weld, their leader,
agreed to gather some day for theological training. This was the "host
of ardent, inexperienced, impudent young men" of Beecher's imagin-
ing, who were destined to "obliterate civilization and roll back the
wheels of time to semi-barbarism." [23]

Most of this ardent host, Weld among them, needed further school-
ing before studying theology; and, in 1827, Finney's early pastor,
George W. Gale, founded Oneida Institute at Whitesboro, New
York, to prepare them for the seminaries. Here Weld enrolled with
some scores of his brethren in the Kingdom to complete his academic
preparation. Funds for his maintenance were supplied by another of

Finney's converts, Captain Charles Stuart, whose love for Weld was to influence profoundly the antislavery cause.

Stuart was a Jamaica-born Englishman, a retired officer in the British army, and "a heavenly-minded follower of the Lord." He had resigned his commission after thirteen years of honorable service, and had migrated to America, where he taught in boys' schools during the winters and distributed Bibles and tracts at his own charges during his vacations. Stuart was a singular personality. "His looks, dress, manners, whole air and bearing are so peculiar," said a contemporary, "that strangers stare at him and some think him a lunatic." But his reputation for piety transcended all his peculiarities of manner, and he was everywhere regarded as "a man of God whom all must *love* who love the Savior." He was one of those who have no taste for marriage and who express their emotional life in religion and good works.[24]

When they first met, Stuart was principal of the Utica high school, a man of maturity and standing in the community, and Weld was hardly out of childhood. But despite the difference in their ages, the lonely bachelor forthwith conceived for the boy a regard which was "more than a father's affection for his first born." To Stuart the pattern of his attachment was the Biblical friendship of David for Jonathan; but his feeling for Weld was clearly more than a normal friendship. "He would die for me any time at a moment's warning," Weld wrote. "He would suffer in my stead the most refined and protracted torture and thank God for the privilege of doing it." With more than a friend's solicitude he watched over Weld's development, and at times his "almost passionate expressions of affection" perplexed his young disciple. Their association, however, never fell below the plane of a noble and uplifting comradeship; and to the end of his days Stuart regarded Weld simply as his "beloved brother and son and friend." [25]

Boy though he was, at their first meeting Weld found in Stuart a kindred soul. "I felt," he said, "that I had never met with one who drew me with such irresistible attraction." To Weld the bond of attraction was Stuart's piety. Even after his boyish enthusiasm had long been tempered by maturity, Weld still experienced "a sense of conscious, and sometimes almost overpowering unworthiness" at the thought of Stuart's heavenly character. "I have never known such a character!" he cried. "Like the eagle he flies alone!" With the en-

thusiasm appropriate to his youth and temperament, he straightway
became Stuart's ardent disciple.[26]

For Weld the fruit of this association was a life-long impulse
toward reform. With affectionate persuasiveness Stuart admonished
him "to help the helpless, be eyes to the blind, feet to the lame, a
tongue to the dumb, to raise the fallen, bind up the bruised and guide
the wandering." Their intimacy—so close that "it was an indivisible
existence"—kept Weld from the entangling trifles and limited ends
of youth. It turned his maturing ambition toward "a preference for
disinterested benevolence," and molded him for a reformer's career.[27]

When the Great Revival reached Utica, Stuart became, like Weld,
a member of Finney's Holy Band. In entire sympathy with the ministerial ambitions of his young disciple, he advanced funds for Weld's
education at Oneida Institute, demanding in return only a quarterly
report of his spiritual development. Stuart's aid enabled Weld to remain at the Institute for several terms. During vacations, though he
returned at intervals to Finney's Holy Band, he labored mostly
throughout the West for the American Temperance Society. In this
cause his eloquence and devotion were such that, more than once,
liquor dealers who heard him went home and emptied their barrels
into the gutter. By 1830, he was reputed to be the most powerful
advocate for temperance in the West.[28]

As his powers matured and his reputation grew, Weld was urged
with increasing frequency to leave the Institute and begin at once his
service for the Lord. In the midst of revivals, Finney commanded his
presence again and again without avail. Ministers besought him to
come and hold revival; and philanthropists in the East made application for his services. One of them was Lewis Tappan, a wealthy merchant of New York City, whose friendship for Weld was later to
mean much in the antislavery cause. He urged Weld to come and
evangelize his city. "A powerful inroad may be made here . . . into
the dominions of Satan," he wrote. "As to your not having studied
Theology . . . there is too much Theology in the church now, and
too little of the gospel." But to all of these applications Weld made
steadfast refusal. Each term he returned to Oneida Institute in order
to complete his preparation for the ministry.[29]

Meantime Finney had carried his "new measures" to increasingly
fervent listeners and to progressively larger cities. In 1828, he stormed

Philadelphia, which he found in a dreadful state. "Instead of being the 'radiating point,' the 'mainspring' . . . of the Christian enterprise of the Presbyterian Church," the city was "almost solid darkness. She reeks of corruption, and in her putrid embrace, she holds all the regions North and south locked up in loathsome horrid death." Finney longed for Weld's aid. "I should insist upon your coming and staying," he told him, "did I think I could prevail." But the revivalist conquered Philadelphia.[30] Then he turned north and converted Connecticut, and despite the protests of conservatives he carried a streak of fire to Boston. Lyman Beecher himself was forced by the members of his congregation to swallow his words and ask Finney to come to Hanover Church. He even labored with a specious willingness in Finney's Holy Band.

Finney moved on amid a growing excitement. Wherever he preached, the contagion spread to the countryside and to distant towns. At the turn of the decade, in 1830, the revival burst all bounds and spread over the whole nation, the greatest of all modern revivals. Tens of thousands turned from selfishness and chose "benevolence as a controlling preference of the mind." Praising God they resolved to "save the American church and nation from the judgments of heaven" by "a spirit of expansive benevolence." To the new-born converts and their rejoicing brethren fresh from the ardor of revival, social ills seemed easily curable and dreams of reform were future realities. On the crest of this great wave of benevolent enthusiasm, as the 'thirties began, Finney swept into New York City.[31]

CHAPTER II

THE NEW YORK PHILANTHROPISTS

1830–1831

In 1830—as now—New York was a subject for prayer, "eventually to be the Babylon or the Zion of the United States." But, in 1830, the city was divided against itself, a contrast of sooty black and burning white. Five Points and the Sink were in their evil flower, and theaters openly encouraged prostitutes to solicit business among their patrons. But once a year New York was Zion. Thousands of the godly assembled every May for the annual conventions of the national benevolent societies, which had already grown "beyond the most sanguine expectations of their founders." At these "anniversaries," delegates from the nation met to report the year's progress, to lay their plans for next year's assault upon the wicked and to appropriate their funds, "revenues such as kings might envy." Their councils formed a state within a State—"immense institutions spreading over the country, combining hosts"—and their united forces made an empire, "a gigantic religious power, systematized, compact in its organization, with a polity and a government entirely its own, and independent of all control." [1]

There were eight large societies—"the Great Eight"—whose objects were promoting home and foreign missionary enterprise, distributing Bibles and religious tracts, financing Sunday schools, promoting temperance, and saving the sailors. There were innumerable lesser societies, to promote peace among nations, to reform prisons and abolish imprisonment for debt, to stop the carrying of mails on the Sabbath, and the wearing of corsets. Indeed "you can scarcely name an object for which some institution has not been formed. . . . It may be said, without much exaggeration, that everything is done by societies." [2]

The discovery of the "Principle of Association" was still new; most of these societies were less than ten years old. But their memberships were growing by the hundreds of thousands, including both sexes and all ages. The American Temperance Society, a product of the Great Revival, had developed State societies, city societies, and township societies. New York State Society, the largest federation, boasted two thousand locals in 1833, with young men's societies, infant societies, and female auxiliaries; and during the year it printed eighty-nine million pages of propaganda. Sanguine hope pervaded the movement. "The intimate connection of temperance with revivals" made the downfall of liquor and the conversion of the nation a single object, to be attained within a decade or so, and to be followed shortly by the conquest of the world.[3]

Except for the temperance society, the benevolent societies both in purpose and in method were inspired by British originals. At that time, England exercised "a vast power over the public mind of this country and especially over the northeast portions of it. An intense and immediate sympathy binds them together," so closely, said a Southerner, that "the inhabitants of the Northern and middle states are more familiar with the daily press of England than with that of their own country south of the Potomac." [4] In moral even more than in literary matters, the United States was still a British province, and British devices in benevolence were eagerly imitated. Indeed British precedent was the highest authority throughout the benevolent empire, and the American anniversaries exhibit a pathetic dependence upon the approvals of the British leaders.

Like the British benevolent societies, the societies in America had no formal connection with the churches. Exceptional denominations— notably the Methodists and the Episcopalians—"which cared more for their sectarian peculiarities and less for the great and substantial interests of society" had their own benevolent organizations; but the Great Eight and the host of lesser societies, like their British models, were free of ecclesiastical control. Their non-denominational character, however, was simply a device to avoid wasteful duplication of sectarian effort. Among the sailors and the heathen, the children and the wicked, churches worked together through the "benevolent system" rather than apart through their denominations. Non-sectarian control was thus an expression of interchurch unity. The whole benevolent empire was a part of the church community; it was "a religious enterprise."

Despite its non-denominational organization, however, the benevolent empire was dominated by "New-School" Presbyterians, liberals of the Great Revival. Among other denominations it was charged that "Presbyterians are rapidly advancing their interests, under the sanction of national societies, which, though under their own immediate control, are so directed as to excite public liberality"; and among the godless the "Presbyterian Idol" was a popular bugbear:

> "Whether it gain its notoriety
> Under the name of Tract Society
> Or Foreign Missionary Board
> The Idol still must be adored."

Jealous sectarians insisted that "these great national societies should assume their proper denomination, and be declared Presbyterian, as they really are in effect." But Presbyterian leadership came about through no such sinister motives. It was the natural result of the "disinterested benevolence" which overflowed among converts of the Great Revival.[5]

The rulers of the benevolent societies, the presidents, vice-presidents, auditors, and life-members were comparatively few in number. One finds such names as Thomas Smith Grimké, Gerrit Smith, Anson Phelps Stokes, and William Jay repeated again and again, but most frequently appear the Tappans. The leadership of benevolent societies was exercised through a series of interlocking directorates composed of a relatively small number of prominent clergymen and philanthropists; and of the latter the six Tappan brothers were the most notable in America, princes in the empire of benevolent societies.

In New York, Arthur and Lewis Tappan, wealthy merchants, sustained in a large and liberal manner the cause of temperance, Sunday schools, tract and Bible distribution, Sabbath observance, and education. Lewis Tappan, the lesser of the two brothers, was careful, exact, and systematic. Even his enemies praised "his determined benevolence . . . his immovable decision of character . . . work done and done thoroughly, everything cared for and everything provided"; but his determined rectitude was given a different name by some of his exacerbated merchant associates. He made an ideal treasurer or auditor in the societies for which he labored. He played the part of Martha to his brother, taking over much of the detail of their large silk importing business, in 1828, in order to free Arthur's energies for his work in "the great system of benevolent institutions," which owed "its expansion and power, in a great degree, to his influence."[6]

Before Finney's arrival in New York, in 1830, Arthur Tappan's benevolent activities—if we except his founding of the New York *Journal of Commerce* [7]—were confined largely to generous contributions to the existing benevolent societies. His income, which was very large for his day, was derived from a business built up on the principles of one price to all customers and quick turnover at a small profit. The times favored the principles. In 1830, New York merchants were notorious for their shifty ethics and higgling habits, and Tappan's single price for all, backed by his rigid and unyielding probity, made money.

In character, Arthur Tappan was an embodiment of the sterner virtues—"Such integrity, conscientious fidelity and true independence; such simple, unwavering directness in duty; such sincerity, exact truth; absence of all self-seeking; a benevolence most prodigal in its outlay, yet wholly unostentatious . . . with a sense of justice so quick and intense, that it seemed equally a principle and a passion." [8] Personally he was reserved, grave, taciturn, even abrupt, with a gloomy solemnity of manner that matched the rancorous temper of his crusades against the pleasures of the godless, such as the theater, intemperance, and immorality. But his rigidity of conduct and his deep jealousy and hatred of natural man were somehow joined with an impulsive and winning generosity, an unwearying pity for the unfortunate of whatever rank, and an humble devotion to the welfare of the poor. The world to Arthur Tappan was a habitation of pain. He suffered from chronic headaches, from which hardly a moment, never a day, was he free.

When Finney began his ministry in New York, the Tappans attended his preaching and enlisted in his cause, supporting his views from the outset. The New York religious papers refused room to Finney's new theology and the Tappans formed among their wealthy merchant associates an "association of gentlemen" to establish a weekly of their own, the *New York Evangelist*. One of the group of professional reformers created by the benevolent society movement, Joshua Leavitt by name, became greatly interested in the project. He was a Yale graduate and an ordained minister; and to him the labors of Finney were the final, practical expression of the doctrines of his teacher, Nathaniel Taylor, a "portentous union between the New Divinity and the New Measures." After editing earlier issues as a labor of love, Leavitt resigned his position as secretary and agent of the Seamen's Friend Society, to become editor of the *New York Evangel-*

ist. Protected from New York Calvinists by the wealth and vast
prestige of the Tappans, he began an able propaganda for Finney's
theology and for benevolent reform.[9]

Under Finney's influence the benevolent activities of the Tappans
gained momentum. "Believing that the accumulation of property for
selfish purposes is repugnant to the gospel; that every person is a
steward," they and their associates in philanthropy entered "into a
solemn engagement not to lay up any property we may hereafter acquire . . . but consecrate the whole of it to the Lord, deducting sufficient to supply ourselves and families, in a decent manner, as becomes
those professing Godliness." [10] Heretofore benevolence had been
their pastime; it now became their vocation.

In May of 1830, the brothers conferred with their fellow philanthropists regarding the state of the unchurched poor in New York,
"suffered to live in this Christian land like heathen, feeling excluded
from our houses of worship," where the best pews were owned by
individuals and a few long benches were provided for the poor. "The
fact is our churches are rich; a repelling distinction is made between
the rich and poor; those in humble life do not feel at home in the
churches; the preaching is not adapted to their capacities or their
spiritual wants." They agreed that charity missions would not do. "A
chapel is necessary, a settled minister, a regular church, a Sunday
School; and those individuals who would exert a salutary influence
over their brethren in humble life, must sit down with them and become members of the same church and congregation." [11] The Tappans
and two others pledged the sum necessary to carry on the experiment for a year, secured the Rev. Joel Parker from the revival center
of western New York as minister, and opened a hall for services on
June 27, 1830. The Tappan families sat humbly with the poor of the
first ward, where the hall was located, and their quiet, unflagging
work made the church a success. After much opposition, the New
York Presbytery granted the congregation a special status with entire
freedom of action, and it was installed as the First Presbyterian Free
Church of the city. The movement spread. A second Free Church
assembled in a lecture room of Rutgers College, and congregations
increased so rapidly thereafter that at least six additional free churches
were installed in a few years, the Tappans leading the departures
from church to church in order to help the young congregations to a
self-supporting basis. For all of them the revival area of western

New York furnished the ministers. Thousands of "the neglected, the poor and the immigrant . . . those who have been almost entirely overlooked," were thereby churched.[12]

Arthur Tappan was not satisfied. The free church movement, though it provided religious opportunities for the families of the poor, did not touch the large floating population of New York, "20–25,000 strangers who are in our city, many of whom I *know*, traverse our streets on the Sabbath, for the want of an invitation to go to church," and unattached men, coming to New York from country towns where they were church members. In New York "they have no seat that they call their own . . . and they soon become habituated to idle away the Sabbath, and they die in impenitence and their souls are lost." Tappan suggested a large hall "in a central part of this city, to accommodate 5 or 6,000 persons. . . . There is another consideration; such a building is much needed as a place of meeting for our annual societies, and for want of such a central house many hundred Christians are prevented attending most of these annual meetings." Such a hall "might by the blessing of God, be the means of salvation to many a thirsty soul who would otherwise perish eternally." [13]

The New York churches responded generously to the plea. Chatham Street Theater was leased and fitted up, the churches paying half the expense, and the Tappans and their "association of gentlemen" paying the rest. Finney, who had returned to western New York after his sojourn in New York City, was persuaded to return as the settled minister. The congregation was established, in 1832, as a free church, and until Broadway Tabernacle—"the largest Protestant house of worship in the country"—was built for Finney, Chatham Street Chapel was the capitol of the new empire of expanding benevolence. Here vast congregations of delegates, meeting each year during the first two weeks of May, concentrated the organized power of the benevolent system. Through the rest of the year Finney conducted perpetual revival among the common people of the city and perpetually renewed the enthusiasm of the wealthy philanthropists in the great cause of reform.

The acceleration of the Tappans' benevolent enthusiasm worked by Finney's ministry did not always result so favorably as in the free church movement. Lewis Tappan was deeply interested in Sabbath observance and did much to finance the campaign, in 1830, for stopping Sunday mails. The campaign was a failure, and the anniversary report of 1831 showed a disastrous falling off in membership and contributions. Nevertheless Lewis Tappan, who was corresponding secretary for the national society, insisted with "determined benevolence"—or "irascible stubbornness"—that the society take the ground that churches should not be piped with gas, if they pretended to be Christian churches, because supplying gas would involve work for the gas companies on the Sabbath. The society did not follow him.[14]

In the temperance society, Arthur Tappan expressed indignation that "the mixture of waste liquids, logwood dyes and cheap French brandy" sold as wine for use in the sacrament should be permitted on the Lord's table. He proposed a resolution that only "pure wine" should be used for communion, but the society refused to sustain him. Undeterred, Tappan secured a ship-load of "burgundy wine, warranted pure, imported expressly for sacramental purposes." With more zeal than knowledge of the process of fermentation, this wine was "confidently recommended as the simple juice of the grape, such as was used in primitive times before 'alcohol' was discovered or manufactured." The year 1830 was not characterized by a keen sense of humor. Prominent New Yorkers were greatly exasperated with Tappan, but that did not disturb him. Quite the contrary! Lewis Tappan wrote that his brother loved "unpopular causes: the more unpopular they were the more they secured his patronage."[15]

A still more unpopular cause was an outgrowth of Arthur Tappan's labors in the First Free Church, close to "the Five Points and . . . some other of the abodes of moral death." Here were centered the houses of prostitution, and he turned to their reform with bitter zeal. On the model of the London Magdalen Society, he organized the Magdalen Society of New York and persuaded it to found an "Asylum for Females who have Deviated from the Paths of Virtue." His co-worker was a serious, godly young Presbyterian clergyman, John Robert McDowall, who had first encountered prostitution at the door of a mission Sabbath School near Five Points. The evil roused in him the horrified fascination peculiar to a certain type of reformer, and he set himself to explore the subject of its foundations. He "visited many of the brothels, conversed closely and feelingly with the women," and embodied his observations in a pamphlet entitled *The Magdalen Report,* to which he persuaded Arthur Tappan and two doctors of medicine, Brown and Reese, to set their names. Claiming the sacred British precedent, McDowall explained that just as the

British and Foreign Bible Society was "the blooming daughter of Sabbath Schools; so the Magdalen of New York was developed by the labors of the Sabbath School in this city." Assuming that "every tenth female in our cities is a prostitute," and that a prostitute's "feet go down to death . . . for in about five years they are carried to the grave and their places are filled by a new class of unfortunate, guilty females," McDowall computed that among New York's two hundred thousand "the number of females in this city who abandon themselves to prostitution is not less than ten thousand!! . . . ten thousand harlots in this city!" and that the number of yearly "seductions" to their ranks was therefore two thousand. The report then proceeded with damnatory but intimate gusto to details.[16]

This publication produced a storm. The newspapers raved with wounded civic pride, and even the righteous were shocked. Dr. Reese published a card denying any part in the authorship, though Dr. Brown and Arthur Tappan honorably stood by poor McDowall. But reform ended in disaster. McDowall persisted in "exposing this vice by detailed narration and pictorial exhibition," and he was suspended by his presbytery. *The Magdalen Report* was pirated, large numbers of copies were sold to the curious, and Tappan's conscience —never the opposition—drove him to publish a letter regarding the report, regretting that "the language is in some instances indelicate, and the details too minute." The final disaster was the closing of the "Asylum for Females who have Deviated from the Paths of Virtue," because, as Tappen admitted, it was a waste of moral effort and produced no "fruits of repentance" in the unfortunate inmates. There was no general interest in the asylum, and the die-hards of the movement were unable to collect sufficient funds to reopen it. Mrs. Leavitt, Mrs. Tappan, and the wives of several other Free Church philanthropists formed a Female Benevolent Society to care for the few forlorn unfortunates left in the asylum when it was closed.[17]

But neither opposition nor failure discouraged Tappan; his unyielding determination never recognized failure in well-doing. Two years after the closing of the "Asylum for Females who have Deviated from the Paths of Virtue," Tappan and his friends proposed another society for moral reform. They were done with asylums: "An asylum . . . is not the Gospel mode of converting sinners. Did Jesus Christ say 'Go ye into all the world and build *asylums* for every sinner?' Never! . . . . The word of God is the 'sword of the spirit,' and if properly wielded by Christians would subjugate more sinners . . . in three months than all the asylums on earth would ever rescue from damnation." Finney also advocated the reproving word as a weapon for moral reform: "converting these abandoned people to God by *preaching*." This new society had no British precedent; it was a pure American product, a child of the Great Revival; for its program was not to reform prostitutes but to denounce prostitution. They named it "The Society for Promoting the Observance of the Seventh Commandment." [18]

The course of the movement against prostitution vividly illustrates a fundamental quality of American reform in the 'thirties. Revivals occasionally did save sinners deep in their sins, but their greatest execution was among earnest young people predisposed to morality and reform, who were sinners by courtesy only. Conversion involved a change of attitude for most of them, rather than a change in pattern of life. "The intimate connection of temperance with revivals has been sufficiently admitted," and the temperance reform partook of the same nature It increased among teetotallers by taste and training rather than among topers. To them the cause justified its existence when it moved temperate people to denounce intemperance. The Society for Promoting the Observance of the Seventh Commandment also fulfilled its purpose when moral people were persuaded to denounce immorality. And the greatest benevolent society of the 'thirties, the American Anti-Slavery Society, was to achieve its end by persuading citizens in the non-slaveholding North to denounce slavery in the slaveholding South. Its first concern was not the abolition of slavery; it was "the duty of rebuke which every inhabitant of the Free States owes to every slaveholder." Denunciation of the evil came first; reform of the evil was incidental to that primary obligation.[19]

Arthur Tappan's next benevolence was a novelty in education—college training for Negroes. In 1828, when Lewis Tappan took over the details of their business, Arthur purchased a summer home in New Haven, next door to Nathaniel Taylor. Here he spent his weekends, commuting more or less regularly to New York. At New Haven he met a home missionary to the Negroes, a lovable young idealist named Simeon S. Jocelyn, whose devotion to the welfare of the colored race attracted him greatly. With generous zeal Arthur Tappan entered into Jocelyn's plans to uplift the Negroes of New Haven; on occasion he attended service at Jocelyn's Negro church and talked with the members of the congregation. Out of this association grew a more ambitious plan, to establish a college at New Haven for the Negroes of the nation.[20]

With characteristic energy Arthur Tappan proceeded to make the plan a reality. He purchased several acres of land in the southern part of the city for a campus, and together with his brother Lewis, he pledged a large contribution for college buildings. To provide teachers, he secured promises from several of the Yale faculty to serve in the college when it should be organized.[21]

He made generous provision for publicity. Conferences with influential citizens of New Haven and with officers of Yale College assured local support. State-wide publicity was obtained through a public hearing before a committee of the Connecticut Legislature. The chief speaker on this occasion was Benjamin Lundy, the pioneer abolitionist, whose address in support of Negro education was well received. To provide national publicity, a convention of representative Negroes was arranged. Through his colored friends, Jocelyn secured the appointment of delegates, and Tappan provided funds for the expenses of the convention. It met, in June of 1831, in Philadelphia, the stronghold of the race.

Though the convention was called to discuss the Negro college, it is far more significant for another reason. It was the first of a movement, the Annual Conventions of the People of Color, the beginning of organized activity for the Negro race in America. One of the many speakers on the program was a youthful editor from Boston, William Lloyd Garrison, who was having a hard time starting an antislavery paper in that city. Tappan it was who urged him to come and paid his expenses to Philadelphia. To Garrison, the convention was a godsend. He improved the occasion by telling his colored hearers that it was their sacred duty to subscribe to antislavery periodicals in general and to his weekly, the *Liberator,* in particular; and his hearers did their duty. From the delegates to the convention and their colored friends, he secured a list of subscriptions which was to be the main support of his *Liberator* for years to come.[22]

The convention enthusiastically approved the Negro college. An appeal for endowment funds was signed by prominent philanthropists of Philadelphia, among them Ezra Stiles Ely, who expressed his "confidence in the wisdom and perseverance of Arthur Tappan, in his efforts to promote the welfare of our colored brethren." [23]

In a manner dear to reformers of the 'thirties, both Tappan and Jocelyn regarded the college not only as an institution for the education of Negroes, but also as the minor premise in a syllogism of reform. By turning out graduates "as good as the best," the college was to demonstrate that the Negro race itself was capable of improvement. It followed by corollary that the Negroes now in slavery could be rendered fit for freedom. A safe and salutary basis for the abolition of slavery was the syllogism's grand conclusion. Hitherto the stock objection to all plans for the abolition of slavery had been that they made no provision for the necessary consequence of emancipation, a mass of pauper freedmen who were deemed incapable of self-control or improvement. The final answer to this objection was to be the Negro college. It was to be at once a demonstration of the Negroes' capacity for improvement and a training school for leaders of the prospective freedmen.

This plan was conceived as an alternative to another antislavery program then popular, that of the American Colonization Society, which proposed to eliminate both slavery and the free Negro by deporting the entire race to its "native home," an unhealthful strip of jungle on the coast of Liberia in Africa. Agents of the society advocated this program in the North as an antislavery measure, but in the South it was urged as a safeguard for slavery. By removing the free blacks who formed a disturbing element in every slaveholding community, the plan promised to make slavery itself more permanent and stable. This simultaneous appeal both to slaveholding and to antislavery interests was subserved by the pronouncements of the national officers of the society, who alternately disavowed hostility to slavery and advocated emancipation together with colonization for the Negroes.

By 1830, the colonization program had become so popular that its support was advocated in Congress itself. At the same time, however, opposition was fast arising. Some of its opponents, like Lewis Tappan, regarded its ambiguous attitude toward slavery as "a piece of malignant jesuitry." A larger number had come to realize the futility of the colonization scheme as an antislavery measure. Even to deport annually the slaves' natural increase, declared Benjamin Lundy, would exhaust each year "the wealth of a Croesus. We might as well bail dry old Ocean with a thimble." A few who, like Jocelyn, had sympathetic contact with the free Negroes themselves, were pitifully aware of their fear that adoption of the colonization program would mean expatriation for themselves and their families. Still other reformers were discouraged by the meager results obtained after a decade of expense and effort. By 1830, this opposition had become formidable.[24]

Condemning the plan of the American Colonization Society to exile the emancipated Negroes to Africa, the founders of the Negro college accepted the only alternative, which was to educate the freedmen for citizenship in America. "We owe it to the cause of humanity, to our country and to God," said Tappan. "The motives which should induce the Christian and all the friends of humanity to make untiring efforts to . . . raise them from the depths of their degradation and misery are irresistible." For the realization of this program the Negro college was to provide the leaders; and the founders of the college announced to the citizens of New Haven: "In connection with this establishment the abolition of slavery in the United States will be advocated." [25]

Filled with impractical enthusiasm, Jocelyn began plans for the college buildings. In his mind the college expanded, not only to educate the Negroes of America for freedom, but to train leaders for the Negroes of the West Indies as well. For the antislavery movement in England had gone far; immediate abolition of West Indian slavery was impending; and where but in New Haven could a college be found to educate leaders for this new host of freedmen? The Negro college, Jocelyn told his fellow townsmen, would be a training school for the Negro race in the Western world. His fellow townsmen did not hear him gladly.

CHAPTER III

THE BRITISH EXAMPLE

1831–1832

Simeon Jocelyn was not the only one to heed the British movement for immediate emancipation in the West Indies. Charles Stuart, fresh from three months of revival in "the glorious Finney's Holy Band," had marked it down as early as 1829. A Jamaican by birth, he had more than a casual interest in its progress. Moreover, as a disciple of Finney's revival in benevolence, he had more than an ordinary inspiration toward reform. Deciding that his duty led him across the water, he wrote a parting admonition to Weld, "beloved brother and son and friend," and sailed in the summer of 1829 to offer his services to the British antislavery cause.[1]

In the nation as a whole, however, the progress of the movement was noticed only in a small way before 1830; but the parliamentary debates in August of that year put it on the front page of the great daily newspapers. Everywhere men were asking what it signified to America. Would this country follow the British example in reform, asked a Southern editor, or "are we after all to lose the race for human liberty and advancement?" If we do not follow, a New York daily concluded, "we shall be decidedly the most despicable nation on the face of the earth." The example alone was potent; and John Quincy Adams wrote James Monroe that the influence of British emancipation "may prove an earthquake on this continent." With interest painful or exultant, Americans followed the struggle in parliament and the agitation in the empire. By the close of 1830 it was apparent that the onslaught upon British slavery in the West Indies would succeed, and thereby set a new precedent for American reform.[2]

The British movement for emancipation had started in 1823, when the successful Society for the Abolition of the Slave Trade was enlarged under the name of the Society for the Mitigation and Gradual Abolition of Slavery throughout the British Dominions. Its purposes and program were expressed in its name, but it was familiarly known as the Anti-Slavery Society. Several leaders of the earlier movement carried over to the new: the venerable Thomas Clarkson, and his co-worker, the most illustrious personage in the benevolent empire, William Wilberforce—"a name," said the *New York Evangelist*, "with which there is probably associated more of love and veneration than ever fell to the lot of any single individual throughout the civilized world." [3] The brilliant and caustic essayist, Sir James Stephen, and the indefatigable Zachary Macaulay, father of the historian, were also veterans of the slave-trade struggle, only less widely known in the United States than the first two. In parliament were Thomas Folwell Buxton, who succeeded Wilberforce as parliamentary leader of the antislavery members, and Henry Brougham, one of the most brilliant orators of the century. Even at this distance these names make one of the most picturesque groups in humanitarian history; but a hundred years ago they were honored in this country North and South as the immortals of the benevolent empire.

The British crusade had a realistic program. Parliament was sovereign in the West Indies over the self-governing colonies as well as over the crown colonies, and the Anti-Slavery Society proposed to abolish slavery by procuring the votes of a majority in parliament. In the United States the situation was quite different. In general slavery was an affair of the States in which it was permitted by law; and effective agitation against it was limited to securing majorities for abolition in the slave-State legislatures or persuading individual slaveholders to free their slaves. This difference in the situations of the two countries, British critics of American slavery seldom realized; and, with disastrous effect upon the movement in the United States, Americans frequently did not realize it either.

Before 1826, the Anti-Slavery Society in England advocated gradual emancipation with no success whatever. Against determined opposition, the society lobbied measures through parliament looking forward to the ultimate abolition of slavery, and these measures were then transmitted as orders in council to colonial governors and legislatures. But fierce resistance to regulation developed in the crown colonies, and the colonial legislatures were uniformly recalcitrant. Measure after measure, pressed with difficulty through parliamentary opposition, proved abortive in the West Indies; and the great assemblies of the antislavery host at Manchester, Glasgow, Leeds, London, and elsewhere—with lords, dukes, earls, and royal hignesses in great profusion as chairmen, vice-presidents, and patrons—expressed growing exasperation. The pamphlet literature, reflecting this, began as early as 1824 to question the possibility of ultimate emancipation unless a definite term should be set to the institution of slavery by parliamentary fiat. Gradual emancipation was characterized as something "half-way between now and never." "Gradual emancipation means step by step," wrote a reviewer, "but the planters will not take the first step towards emancipating the negroes."

In 1825, the movement waxed in growth and boldness. A periodical was published, the *Anti-Slavery Reporter,* and pamphleteering sharpened in tone. That same year radical antislavery speakers began advocating a change in the antislavery program from gradual to immediate emancipation. It was admittedly the counsel of despair, a sign of complete loss of confidence in the policy of gradualism, a realization that from the legislatures of Jamaica and Barbados, in a state of mutual exasperation as great as their own, no coöperation in gradual emancipation could be expected. By March of 1826, petitions for immediate emancipation began to arrive in parliament, and the radical program gained progressively in adherents.

During the remainder of the decade, while propaganda increased in volume and bitterness, colonial legislatures remained obdurate, "carrying intractibleness to the verge of insanity" toward orders from the home government for amelioration. In order to justify the desperate policy of immediate emancipation, it was gradually translated by propagandists into a philosophy of human rights, the natural and immediate right of the slave to freedom as a human being. Even the right of planters to indemnity was denied on grounds of abstract justice. The entire question came up before parliament in the great debate of July, 1830.

The debate brought the British agitation to America, where the proceedings of parliament were copied in scores of dailies and weeklies. Phrases and extracts from the speeches gained a national currency. The high moment of the debate was the speech of Henry Brougham, who "excelled in the lofty strain of vehement indignation." Brougham had been a late convert to the desperate doctrine of immediate emancipation; though, as early as March of 1828, he had declared that unless the colonial legislatures changed their tactics, something far more drastic than orders in council would have to be tried. For up to the present, he said, "the progress of the colonies was so slow as to be imperceptible to all human eyes save their own."

But, in the debate of 1830, Brougham was for immediate abolition both in policy and in principle. "Tell me not," he cried, "of the property of the planter in his slaves. I deny the right . . . I acknowledge not the property. . . . In vain you tell me of laws which sanction such a claim! There is a law above all the enactments of human codes—the same throughout the world, the same at all times—it is a law written by the finger of God on the heart of man; and by that law, unchangeable and eternal, while men despise fraud, and loath rapine, and abhor blood, they will reject with indignation the wild and guilty phantasy that man can hold property in man!"

To the agents of expanding benevolence in the United States, this was deeply moving logic; and on every level of opinion it gave cause for reflection. Northern newspapers pointed the obvious conclusion from British precedent, "that this kind of reform needs to begin in our country. The doing away of our slavery is called for by every notion of humanity, justice, consistency, patriotism, national honor and internal prosperity," said a New York daily. "We suggest to the *National Intelligencer* [the national organ of the Whig party] to take up this view of the subject, and to call upon the people of Virginia to begin this reform. . . . Let this position be taken and we will vouch for the coöperation of the North." [4] Many other Northern papers burst forth with like opinions.

The religious weeklies and monthlies were more profoundly affected. It was evident, wrote one essayist, that the "exertion of the moral power of reason and justice will . . . abolish slavery in the British islands forever. Can nothing, we are led to inquire, be done in the United States to free our country from the sin and shame of slavery? The answer is obvious. Let all who are opposed to the system . . . unite in associations for the abolition of slavery; let them be active and constant in their exertions for this great object, never appalled by opposition, never discouraged by defeat. In one word, let them use the same efforts which have been made in Great Britain to make the public understand the true nature of slavery and they cannot fail to produce effects as glorious as those which have been already obtained in Great Britain." [5]

British antislavery leaders marveled that American reformers had not taken such action long before. They wrote urgently to friends in this country, advising prompt action; they sent thousands of their more effective pamphlets; and in the annual letters to corresponding denominations in America, they called on their brethren in the faith to begin antislavery organization without delay.[6]

Charles Stuart, "incessantly engaged in the sacred pursuit of negro emancipation" across the seas, laid it upon his disciple, Theodore Weld, to do likewise in America and at once to save this country from perdition. "Never have I found such burning cause for gratitude to God," he wrote, "as in the fact that while we continue guilty of slavery, He can refrain from fairly breaking up the earth beneath our feet, and dashing us into sudden hell." He sent Weld copies of the tracts which he had written, as well as numerous other abolition pamphlets: "I beg your prayerful perusal of them. . . . I long to hear of your being engaged in the sacred cause of negro emancipation." Weld complied. He mastered the British propaganda and diligently sifted the pamphlets and newspapers of this country for facts and arguments against slavery. Before the end of 1830 he had laid the foundation for his future rôle as encyclopedist of the antislavery movement.[7]

But it was not merely to master antislavery lore that Stuart exhorted him. "I want to have my Theodore's soul engaged," he wrote; and Weld was ready to obey. Indeed, his whole life had prepared him to espouse the antislavery cause. His years of discipleship, of "indivisible existence" with his mentor, made Stuart's mandate the law of his will as well as of his mind; and his long service to Finney, high priest of expanding benevolence, gave to Stuart's appeal the sanction of religious authority. With evangelistic fervor Weld made the antislavery cause his own.[8]

To the New York Association of Gentlemen, the British example appealed with thrilling force. "Let us imitate our British brethren and open the flood gates of light on this dark subject," said their organ, the *New York Evangelist*. Early in 1831, Lewis Tappan summoned Weld from Oneida Institute to join in a discussion upon the subject of slavery and its abolition. There were others in their councils: George Bourne—"Father" Bourne they called him—the first immediate abolitionist in America; Joshua Leavitt; Simeon Jocelyn from New Haven; and William Goodell, editor of the *Genius of Temperance*.[9]

Their antislavery inspiration was various. In part, at least, it was drawn from the old abolition tradition. Like Father Bourne, most of the group had been concerned in antislavery agitation before. To none of them was the cause a new one; it was an expression once again of the traditional hatred of slavery which had been a part of religious benevolence for a generation.[10] Their immediate urge, however, was the British precedent; and for that inspiration, Weld was probably the spokesman.

To his knowledge of British propaganda, Weld united extraordinary personal gifts. Everybody who spoke of him remarked his persuasiveness and charm. In presence, said a contemporary, he was "a very manly, noble-looking man." Indeed, Whittier's shy maiden sister Elizabeth was overwhelmed by "the magical power and richness of his voice, the benignity of his manner, and the Godlike attributes of his very presence. It was," she wrote in her diary, "as if an archangel had entered our home!" Possibly she was a prejudiced witness, but to Lyman Beecher, himself the most popular preacher of his day, Weld was "logic on fire. . . . As eloquent as an angel and powerful as thunder!" In the whole benevolent system no orator approached him in effective conviction.[11]

Weld had one attribute inimical to fame. His friends called it modesty, but Weld himself believed it to be pride. "It is the great besetment of my soul," he declared, "the poisoned thorn that festers and corrodes. I am too proud to be ambitious, too proud to seek applause, too proud to tolerate it when lavished upon me,—proud as Lucifer that I can and do scorn applause and spurn flattery." He made it a principle never to accept an office of authority or honor; nor would he speak at anniversaries or conventions, or even attend them. "The Stateliness and Pomp and Circumstance of an Anniversary," he declared, "I loathe in my inmost soul." He would not lecture in the larger cities or permit his words to be reported in the antislavery press. Though the tracts which he later wrote were the most powerful in the movement, they were printed either anonymously or under the names of other writers. Even his letters from the field he refused to have published; the few that saw the light were usually printed without his consent and over his indignant protest. By his own action he thus prevented any tribute to his achievements, or public recognition of his authority.[12]

Whether it was pride or modesty that prompted it, his horror of publicity lost Weld his place in history; and even in the days of his power it was a trial to his colleagues. But every one admired and loved him. In the antislavery discussion of 1831, whatever the decisive inspiration may have been, Weld's "sagacious, active, far-reaching mind," his unique knowledge of British antislavery doctrine, and his greatness of heart and flaming zeal for abolition, must have exercised a powerful influence to action.

The Association of Gentlemen's plans enlarged with discussion, and—an outcome inevitable in the 'thirties—they envisaged a National Anti-Slavery Society on the British model. A committee was formed comprising Weld, Lewis Tappan, Leavitt, Jocelyn, and Goodell, to consider the matter; and toward the last of June, 1831, this committee reported for immediate organization. They submitted to the Association of Gentlemen a scheme for an "American National Anti-Slavery Society . . . upon an enlarged and extensive plan," and it was approved. "Men of wealth and influence" in the city pledged their support. "Success to it!" cried the *New York Evangelist*.[13]

Simeon Jocelyn returned to New Haven full of sanguine and ill-considered dreams. Too full of hope to keep silent discreetly, he told his fellow townsmen of the new organization. What could be more fitting, he asked, than that the projected American National Anti-Slavery Society should make its headquarters at his projected Negro college, the future center of Negro culture not only for the prospective freedmen of this country, but also for the prospective freedmen of the West Indies? But New Haven citizens did not want their city to be a center for the Negroes of the new world. During the last weeks of summer, hostility toward a Negro college grew more and more vocal until, on September thirteenth, the mayor and council were forced to call a mass meeting in order to discuss the question. By overwhelming majorities the assembled citizens condemned the scheme "to establish a college in this city for the education of the colored population of the United States and the West Indies." Even more strongly did they resent the fact that "in connection with this establishment the immediate abolition of slavery in the United States is not only recommended and encouraged by the advocates of the proposed college but demanded as a right." They resolved to oppose both the college and the American National Anti-Slavery Society "by every lawful means in our power." This ended the Negro college.[14]

Heartbroken though he was at the destruction of his years of labor, Jocelyn addressed a public letter of forgiveness to his fellow citizens. Regarding some young Negroes whom he had enrolled in the projected college, he communicated with his friend President Storrs of Western

Reserve College, who wrote, after consultation with his board of trustees, that "the board will rejoice to . . . receive the colored youths whom you mention, to all the privileges of this college." [15]

After the mass meeting a mob gathered and damaged Arthur Tappan's summer home; but neither mobs nor mass meetings could break Tappan's iron heart or turn his unbending will from doing good. Why was it, he asked with bitter indignation, that in this country " 'pale faced' human beings arrogate to themselves the right to trample underfoot their fellow men because the color of their skin is different?" England made no such distinction of privilege. It was a "prejudice that exists in this country alone." Even New Haven editors remarked the contrast. "Compare the events here recorded," wrote one, "with the doings . . . in England. . . . Let them weigh the authority of the names there quoted and compare the spirit of the addresses there delivered with the spirit which ruled the New Haven meeting on Saturday." England had spoken, "declaring the voice of the British people in favor of complete and immediate emancipation." [16]

Provincial and prejudiced though New Haven might be, however, the lesson of its action could not be ignored. The North was not yet ready for antislavery organization. After all, the British movement had not yet succeeded in abolishing slavery, and American organization could not point to the British example until West Indian emancipation was a published triumph. The American National Anti-Slavery Society was therefore temporarily suspended, but there was much to be done. For two years the Association of Gentlemen—known informally as the New York Committee—wrote and published in order to build foundations for a national antislayery movement and waited upon the news from London. Not until the autumn of 1833, when the news arrived that West Indian emancipation was law, did formal organization again go forward.

During the two intervening years one danger rose to threaten the infant movement. The American Colonization Society made a determined effort to capture British sanction for its program in America. Early in 1831, Elliot Cresson, the ablest of the colonization agents, journeyed to England and eloquently presented the colonization cause. In America, he said, "one hundred thousand slaves are ready to be given up if means can be found for sending them to Africa"; and he proceeded to canvass the philanthropic public for the means. Not

all of the British abolitionists approved his mission, but he encountered no serious opposition until he chanced upon Charles Stuart, who
had apparently formed his opinion of the colonization cause before
he left the United States. Abandoning his agency for the moment,
Stuart devoted his every effort to blasting Cresson's mission and
the claims of the American Colonization Society to antislavery sympathy.

In England, Stuart had recommended himself well. To his audiences
in the provinces, "he talked like himself, feelingly and affectionately";
and though his eccentric manner and appearance precluded any large
success, he was loved and respected for the goodness of his heart and
his selfless devotion to the cause. But as a writer he had rendered
a real service. An outline of his "Bible argument" against slavery
was used as an agents' handbook, and his tract, *The West Indian
Question,* was one of the most famous pamphlets in the British
propaganda. His indictment of the Colonization Society consequently
received a consideration which an unknown writer could never have
secured.[17]

Stuart wrote a succession of pamphlet philippics against colonization and spoke on every occasion against Cresson's mission. By the
autumn of 1831, he had won over the *London Times* and had persuaded the chairman of the Anti-Slavery Society's Agency Committee, James Cropper, to condemn the colonization plan. Wilberforce
joined Cropper in a public indictment of Cresson's mission, and by
the spring of 1832, the American Colonization Society was in bad
odor not only among the abolitionists but in the public press as well.
For the approaching struggle between colonization and abolition in
America, Stuart had assured to American abolitionists the approval
of the British immortals.[18]

CHAPTER IV

Organization

1833

Arthur Tappan's next reform—an interim activity—was a project to promote higher education in the West. He had long been a patron of the colleges. As director and contributor to the American Education Society, he had assisted many young men of limited means who were preparing to enter the ministry; and when the funds were lacking to care for several scores of indigent students at Yale, he had assumed their tuition charges. Before 1830, he had aided sundry struggling young colleges in the West to the extent of tens of thousands of dollars; but his favorite among them was Oneida Institute in western New York. George W. Gale, who had converted Finney, organized this school for Finney's converts on the manual labor plan, a scheme like that of reformatories to-day. During the school term, from spring to fall, the students labored a part of each day on a farm, thereby earning the larger portion of their board, and in the long winter vacation most of them taught school to earn their tuition. Gale was a man of zeal, and a vigorous, practical farmer. Prices for farm products were good, and the plan succeeded. To Tappan's Association of Gentlemen, the manual labor plan promised a solution of the problem of higher education for the plain people; and in the 'thirties such a prospect was a signal to act. A Society for Promoting Manual Labor in Literary Institutions was organized, with Joshua Leavitt as secretary and Lewis Tappan on the board of managers, and application was made to Weld, most famous of the Oneida students, to be the society's agent to the nation.

If the agency alone had been offered, Weld would probably have refused. He had resolved to accept no engagement which would interfere with his education for the ministry, and hitherto he had declined all such appointments. But Arthur Tappan and the Association of Gentlemen also offered him a commission to select a site for a "great national Theological Seminary on the Manual Labor Plan"; and the two commissions together promised so much to Weld's fraternity of converts that he broke his resolve and accepted the double appointment.

The seminary was greatly needed. Five years had passed since the beginning of the Great Revival, and many of the ardent host, their literary preparation completed, had long been eager to begin their theological training. It was necessary to provide educational facilities for them right speedily, or they would fall away. So Weld started out, in the autumn of 1831, to find a site for a seminary, and to spread throughout the nation the new evangel of education by manual labor.[1]

Weld had many adventures. He spoke to State legislatures, colleges, mass meetings, and churches. He was nearly drowned and all but battered to death when his stage was upset while fording a stream in flood. At Nashville, Tennessee, he met and added to his ardent host, Marius Robinson, an able young man just graduated from the University of Nashville. At Huntsville, Alabama, Dr. Allan, a notable slaveholding Presbyterian minister, was his host for a month. A casual discussion of slavery, begun at the dinner table, prolonged itself for a week and ended with the conviction not only of Dr. Allan but also of his neighbor, James G. Birney. Weld enlisted Dr. Allan's two sons in his fraternity of converts and journeyed on, but Birney's deep conviction gave him no rest. Abandoning a prosperous legal practice, he accepted an appointment from the American Colonization Society, which was the only antislavery agency then available, and began his life of labor for the slave.[2]

On the Western Reserve in Ohio, at Cleveland, Weld made another antislavery convert, an old friend and fellow laborer in Finney's Holy Band, the Rev. John Keep. At Hudson, the seat of Western Reserve College, he had an experience of still greater import to the antislavery cause. Here he addressed the public in the interests of temperance and manual labor; but in conference with the college faculty, he followed Charles Stuart's mandate and agitated "the sacred cause of negro emancipation." Elizur Wright Jr., graduate of Yale, a mathematician of parts and an indefatigable idealist, pledged his life to the cause, and others of the faculty were profoundly stirred. Weld moved on to his next appointment, but the discussion which he had precipitated among the faculty assumed each day "a far deeper interest." Beriah Green, a sober, plodding radical, shortly "came out nobly, and preached three sermons on three successive Sabbaths" for the slave.

Then President Storrs himself lifted his voice for the slave. Storrs was the ablest educator in the West, with a national reputation for scholarship and eloquence. "There does not live," said Wright, "a man whose whole character is so adapted to the exigencies of the anti-slavery cause." [3]

These three reformers then set themselves to convert the college and the Western Reserve, but straightway they encountered opposition. The local press was induced to close its columns to their arguments, and friends of the college angrily demanded that they cease their agitation. In order to silence them, Wright asked Weld's aid: "It may be of use to some friends of our college here, who are prodigiously afraid we shall run our ship on the breakers, to know where their powerful friends in N. York stand." At Weld's behest, Arthur Tappan wrote a letter "just like himself" to the three, praising their stand for abolition and promising his aid "in scattering light over the 'Reserve.'" "Mr. Tappan's letter was just the thing we needed," Wright told Weld. "There is perhaps no man for whom the people of the Reserve entertain a more profound respect. Light flowing from such a source will be doubly valuable." Greatly heartened, the three reformers extended their labors east and west of the college; and during commencement week of 1833, they organized an antislavery society "out of the very 'bone and sinew' of our community," the first organized effort for abolition on the Reserve.

But the most significant experience of Weld's whole mission was the outcome of his quest for a site on which to build a theological seminary. The quest was a joint affair. A few of his fraternity wanted him to choose a location somewhere in "Little Greece," between Utica and Syracuse in northern New York. But malaria was epidemic there, and one of the fraternity had heard "reports decidedly unfavorable to the salubrity of that country." He feared "that in the publick mind at least—if not really—that circumstance will be an objection to Greece as the site for a school." [4] Several others of the ardent host, notably H. B. Stanton, wanted the seminary to be at Rochester; but Westerners did not agree. "I doubt not Rochester may have some facilities," one of them wrote Weld, "but I feel sanguine in the belief that if you would come over and view the land in its length and breadth . . . you would be at once in favor of locating the great institution in the Valley of the Miss[issippi]. You are well aware of the fact that this western country is soon to be a mighty giant that shall wield not only the destinies of our own country but of the world! 'Tis yet a babe. Why not then come and take it in the feebleness of its infancy, and give a right direction to its powers, that when it grows up to its full stature we may bless God that it has such an influence? What could be better calculated to do this than an Institution of the character we contemplate? . . . I hope and pray you will not take any decisive step until you come to Cincinnati and see for yourself." [5]

By coincidence a site for a theological seminary in Cincinnati was already available. Some years before a tract of land had been donated for a seminary campus by two merchants named Lane; a charter had been secured from the Ohio Legislature under the name of Lane Seminary; and a small amount of money had been collected from local philanthropists. In 1830, the agent for the project, the Rev. F. Y. Vail, had applied to Arthur Tappan for an endowment. At that time the seminary consisted of some woods and one foundation for a building; but Rev. Mr. Vail "knew how to elaborate a thing and make it grand," and though he did not get any money, he succeeded in rousing Tappan's interest. The next year Vail returned to the attack, and Tappan, now pledged in any event to finance a theological seminary, referred him to Weld. Vail thereupon added his words to those of the Western faction of Weld's fraternity. "You ought not to fix upon your location for this institution until you have paid a visit to the great valley," he wrote. "We only need to have your plan and efforts identified with our own, in order to secure the influence of New York and make it strictly a national institution." Weld visited the site in the lovely, wooded Walnut Hills above Cincinnati, and reported favorably on Lane Seminary for the national manual labor institution. [6]

Arthur Tappan made the project his own. A princely endowment was pledged and notable scholars were appointed to the faculty. For president Tappan selected the famous Lyman Beecher, and in the face of New England's protests, induced him to accept. Rejoicing that his fraternity of young converts now had an opportunity for theological training, Weld sent them word that the appointed day was here. By some strange fate, this host of Finney's converts was to confront Beecher as Finney had done in 1827. Once more Finney's new measures, now in antislavery guise, were fated to rouse Beecher's ire; once again there was to be a dispute, a defeat, and a separation. [7]

Before he went west, Beecher had engaged in the antislavery controversy. He was a good abolitionist. Benjamin Lundy, the pioneer abolitionist, visiting Boston in 1828, had found that "friend Lyman

was very warm-hearted in the cause and encouraged him to do all
he could to get up Anti-Slavery Societies and flood the whole country
with abolition tracts." With equal warmth he had encouraged young
Garrison when beginning his work in Boston. But with characteristic
breadth, Beecher was also a good colonizationist. Toward all forms
of antislavery agitation his attitude was like his theological position: a
"great . . . assimilation . . . into one grand brotherhood . . . overlooking or winking at the differences of what are styled the 'minor or
non-essential parts of the faith.'" So when Garrison attacked the
motives and methods of the American Colonization Society, Beecher
in the name of the "grand brotherhood" of antislavery effort, organized a protest.[8]

When the parliamentary debates of 1830 were published in the
United States, Garrison, then only twenty-four years old, was in
Baltimore helping Lundy with his *Genius of Universal Emancipation*.
Lundy was well considered by the British abolitionists, who sent him
their papers and pamphlets and kept him informed of the progress of
the cause in England. Upon Garrison these British contacts had a
revolutionary effect. His ardent, suggestible imagination seized upon
the abstract absolutes of the radical pamphleteers of immediate abolition, and he made them his own. Unfortunately his formal education
had been meager, and he possessed no background of general knowledge to balance the radical doctrine of the British extremists. To him
the gradual abolition of slavery in the West Indies was not a parliamentary policy urged in vain upon the West Indian legislatures; it
was, as many British agitators argued after 1828, simply theory without sound logic, a wicked compromise with the natural right of man
to possess his body. It was therefore bound to fail, Garrison concluded, whether tried in Pennsylvania, Georgia, or the islands of the
sea. Neither did Garrison realize that immediate emancipation was a
parliamentary policy of last resort, adopted after every moderate
device had failed. To his naïve, youthful mind it was not a policy at
all but a principle with proper logic to back it up, and therefore right
and bound to be successful wherever tried.[9]

Along with the doctrines, Garrison adopted the style of the last
and extremest propaganda of the British movement, tainted with a
savage bitterness of invective which nearly a decade of frustrated
effort had aroused. Garrison's "harsh language" was after the British
mode; the terms of opprobrium which he used so indiscriminately

were "epithets which have from the same source, and with similarly false imputation been transplanted to America and there applied to men whose virtue and philanthropy had never before been called into question." [10]

The sharpness of Garrison's attack on slavery was increased by an incident before his departure from Baltimore. Having spoken his mind in the *Genius of Universal Emancipation* regarding a ship owner whose captain had contracted with a planter to move his slaves to a new plantation in Louisiana, he was imprisoned for libel. Seven long weeks he lay in the Baltimore jail until Arthur Tappan, who did not know him but had heard of his imprisonment, ·sent to his friend Lundy the money necessary to secure Garrison's release.[11]

His sojourn in jail was only the conclusion of a series of disasters. He had quarreled with Lundy, and their paper had failed to interest an indifferent public. Moribund when Garrison was arrested, it shortly died. He came north from his imprisonment burning with indignation. "The detestation of feeling, the fire of moral indignation and the agony of soul which I have felt kindling and swelling within me," he cried, "reach the acme of intensity." In Boston he started a weekly, the *Liberator,* in which he tried to express his feeling toward slaveholders, but without entire success. "The English language is lamentably weak and deficient in regard to this matter. I wish its epithets were heavier. . . . I wish it would not break so easily . . . I wish I could denounce slavery and all its abettors, in terms equal to their infamy." But in the columns of the *Liberator* he did what he could, and he had a genius for quotable invective.[12]

Even before founding the *Liberator,* Garrison had advocated the organization of antislavery societies on the British model. Referring to the British program for the West Indies, he declared that Englishmen had long passed the point of fearing immediate emancipation. British reformers, he said, had no patience with the argument "against an immediate abolition of slavery that it would not be safe or expedient to make an ignorant and degraded set of men free, without giving them any previous cultivation." Their position was that the abolition of slavery "is a question of right, not expediency; and if slaves have a right to their freedom, it ought to be given them, regardless of the consequences." Such doctrine did not take well among Bostonians, despite Garrison's assurance that "calling for the immediate abolition of slavery may be reckoned a very large majority of the wisest and best men in Great Britain . . . including Clarkson,

Wilberforce, Brougham . . . and the most eminent clergymen of all denominations. . . . These are convinced by sad experience that the doctrine of gradual abolition is a cheat—a lie—a delusion: and that it will be always in the future tense." He concluded that the policy of gradual abolition anywhere in the United States would be equally delusive, and that therefore his hearers should begin on the sound British ground of immediatism.[13]

After a year of intermittent agitation, Garrison called a meeting, November 13, 1831, to organize the New England Anti-Slavery Society. Fifteen men responded, and to them Garrison described "what the abolitionists of Great Britian had done since . . . they had put their movement on the ground of immediate, in distinction from gradual, emancipation. He wanted societies formed in America upon the same principle, and could not be satisfied with any scheme of gradualism." Failing to secure endorsement of his position, he called another meeting for December 16, but only ten people appeared. Upon this handful, Garrison forced the true British doctrine; though David Lee Child, Ellis Gray Loring, and Samuel E. Sewall declared at the time that they would refuse to sign a constitution containing the word "immediate." As Tappan had learned a few months before at New Haven, people were not yet ready for antislavery organization; certainly not on the basis of Garrison's application of British policy to the totally different political situation in America.[14]

Besides editing the *Liberator* and attempting to organize Boston for immediatism, Garrison added his voice to the growing reprobation of the American Colonization Society. Inspired by Charles Stuart's exposure of colonization in England, he wrote a tract of his own, *Thoughts on African Colonization,* filled with charges couched in his usual style against the motives and characters of the members of the American Colonization Society.[15]

Lyman Beecher, good abolitionist and also good colonizationist, deplored the widening breach between the two causes. He visited Garrison and labored with him in vain. He wrote urgently to other abolitionists, advising "as a motive for union, the unseemliness of discord among the brethren." Surely the controversy was unnecessary. "Are colonization and abolition opposed to each other after all? . . . The good men of both parties have the good of the slave . . . at heart. Now then is not union among good men desirable?" Union between abolitionists and colonizationists was more than desirable.

It was necessary. "The door of immediate and unconditional emancipation is closed and barred" by a resentful South. "What shall we, philanthropists? Run from Dan to Beersheba and rail against the slaveholder, taking care, however, to keep clear of his territories?"

As an alternative, Beecher proposed a plan of assimilation for abolitionist and colonizationist, "a plan which precisely meets the difficulty. It unties in a manner the hands of the master . . . and it points both the liberated slave and the free black to a place of refuge from the tyranny of prejudice . . . and the means of an honorable, an affluent and a happy independence." The plan was simplicity itself: "Let the abolitionist press abolition, not seek to destroy the colonizationist, and the colonizationist, let him press still harder colonization. . . . Let there be harmony and love and benevolence after this sort, and who need care for nullification or tariff or abolition in opposition to colonization? Oh yes, Union, this blessed union of all the good! The gates of hell even shall never prevail against it." [16]

Like Beecher's "famous technic" of "Evangelical Assimilation of Calvinism and New Theology," this plan for assimilating the conflicting programs of colonization and abolition was unworkable. Arthur Tappan, fully aware of this, was deeply troubled. That a man as influential in the East as Beecher should oppose the abolition program, was a serious handicap to the maturing plans of the New York Committee; but that Beecher as president of Lane Seminary should take such a stand, threatened a more serious disaster. For Tappan had already come to an understanding with Theodore Weld that the seminary was to be not only a center of learning to the West, but also a forum for abolition propaganda. Now this program was indeed doubtful of success.[17]

Late though it was to save the situation—Beecher had already left for Cincinnati when his plan was published—Tappan sent a brilliant article to Beecher's periodical, *Spirit of the Pilgrims,* to show the irreconcilable differences between abolitionists and colonizationists. "Justice to those denominated Abolitionists," he wrote, "entitles them to be heard, and the reasons why they can not unite with Colonizationists should be stated through the medium of your very respectable publication." Tappan then wrote to Beecher at Cincinnati, begging him to reconsider his position; but Beecher replied: "I am not apprized of the ground of controversy between the Colonizationists and the Abolitionists. I am myself both without perceiving in myself any inconsistency. . . . I trust God has begun by the instrumentality of both a great work which will not stop until not only the oppressed here are free, but Africa herself shall have rest in the Lord along her extended coast and deep interior." It was doubtless with a heavy heart that Tappan paid the amounts he had pledged to Beecher's salary.[18]

Meanwhile young men gathered at Cincinnati "as from the hives of the North." Most of them were from western New York. H. B. Stanton and a few others from Rochester floated down the Ohio from Pittsburgh on a raft. More than a score came from Oneida Institute. Even more arrived from Utica and Auburn, Finney's converts all. From Tennessee came Weld's disciple, Marius Robinson, and across the Ohio from Kentucky came James Thome, scion of a wealthy planting family. Up from Alabama journeyed two others of Weld's disciples, the sons of the Rev. Dr. Allan. From Virginia came young Hedges; and from Missouri, Andrew, of the famous family of Benton. From the South came another, James Bradley, a Negro who had bought his freedom from slavery with the earnings of his own hands. Most of these students were mature; only eleven were less than twenty-one years old; twelve of them had been agents for the national benevolent societies, and six were married men with families. The theological class was the largest that had ever gathered in America, and its members were deeply conscious of their importance. "Oh Christians!" wrote a student, "Pray for us! We are set upon a hill; and we feel ourselves in solemn and responsible circumstances. . . . The western states are looking to us!" Beecher surveyed them with swelling pride, "the most talented, spirited, heroic phalanx I ever met!" How little he realized—how soon he was to know—that this was the very "host of ardent, inexperienced, impudent young men" of his prophecy, who would pour out from the great revivals "as from the hives of the north, to obliterate civilization, and roll back the wheels of time to semi-barbarism!"[19]

While the students were gathering at Cincinnati, the New York Committee was completing the foundation for a national antislavery society. They established a central bureau in charge of Weld's convert, Elizur Wright Jr., from Western Reserve College. They corresponded with known abolitionists, urging them "to have a number of Sectional Societies formed, which may form a National Society by delegation." They launched a newspaper, the *Emancipator;* they sent agents to spy out the land as far west as Ohio; they published and distributed editions of antislavery pamphlets by earlier American abolitionists; they republished British pamphlets of proved effectiveness. They presented four searching questions to the secretary of the American Colonization Society as to its attitude toward slavery and toward free Negroes, and published his equivocal answers in an extra number of the *Emancipator,* distributing thousands of copies.[20]

Arthur Tappan wrote with businesslike thoroughness to prominent reformers of the day, putting before them the plans for a national society and asking their coöperation. He urged "the expediency of forming an American Anti-Slavery Society and of doing it now. The impulse given to the cause by the movement in England would, it appears to me, aid us greatly here." The old Pennsylvania Society for the Abolition of Slavery, responding heartily to Tappan's invitation, distributed the pamphlets of the New York Committee and pledged friends of emancipation around Philadelphia to a national agitation.[21]

Day by day the New York Committee scanned the news from London. Early in 1833 they learned that a bill for the emancipation of West Indian slaves would probably become a law within a few months. The time had come to revive their projected American Anti-Slavery Society. Certain friends of the cause in Philadelphia had suggested that city as an expedient place for a national antislavery convention, and Tappan wrote to the Pennsylvania society asking them to prepare the way. But furious opposition to the project arose in Philadelphia. Even abolitionists declared it unwise, and the *Presbyterian* said indignantly: "The attempt talked of *in this city* to break down the American Colonization Society by the formation of a National Anti-Slavery Society should be met . . . by a consolidation of all our forces." The Pennsylvania Society's enthusiasm thereupon diminished, and after a summer of hesitant consideration they had not yet decided on their course. But West Indian emancipation was imminent and the New York Committee could not wait. They resolved to hold the convention at Philadelphia on October twenty-fifth, and Tappan notified the Pennsylvania society to that effect; whereupon they came to a decision. They discovered "solemn convictions as to the propriety and wisdom of the movement at this particular juncture." They advised the New York Committee to "make haste slowly" by agitating "through the medium of State and other limited bodies," before organizing "any national movement." But their advice was too late. Five days before they came to a decision, news of West Indian emancipation had arrived, and the New York Committee had gone forward with organization.[22]

The last weeks of the summer had been full of suspense to the New York philanthropists. With increasing excitement, "when observers trembled at the result," they had followed the antislavery measures in parliament from resolution to committee, from committee to bill, and finally, near the end of August, from bill to law. The day of triumph was come, "the greatest event in history since the founding of Christianity." Abolitionists were certain that "future generations of Britons will look back to the abolition of slavery as the brightest and most Godlike act in the annals of their country." The day had come for this country to organize in like fashion, with like assurance of success; for "when the British King put his name to the statute for abolishing slavery in the colonies, he signed the death warrant of slavery throughout the civilized world." A day or two after the news from London, a notice appeared in the New York papers calling a meeting of "The Friends of Immediate Abolition in the United States," to be held on October second at Clinton Hall. The public proving hostile, the place of meeting was changed to the lecture-room of Chatham Street Chapel. Here with a mob rioting outside, the Tappans formed the New York City Anti-Slavery Society.

The address of this epochal society began, like Garrison's New England society, by claiming the British precedent of immediate abolition: "By the epithet *immediate,* we mean emphatically to mark our dissent from the project of gradual abolition—a plan that, on the testimony of Wilberforce and Clarkson, and the unanimous consent of the philanthropists of England, has been the virtual means of preventing the abolition of slavery in the British possessions for nearly half a century. . . . In contrast with this, the world knows that the doctrine of immediate emancipation has availed more the past six years in England than fifty years of previous discussion of the delusive dream of gradual abolition." So much was conceded to British doctrine in order to claim the British precedent. But the remainder of the address was in a different tone.[23]

The New York philanthropists, unlike Garrison, were practical men, aware that in a union of sovereign States, immediate emancipation could not have the meaning which it had in an empire ruled by a sovereign parliament. Therefore, while adopting the British motto of immediate emancipation, they interpreted the motto to suit their needs. Any measure, they declared, is immediate "if it be promptly commenced with the honest determination of urging it on to its completion. . . . A protracted campaign may intervene between the decree and its accomplishment." That is, measures were immediate whenever they were honestly begun. Thus the longest stretch of gradual abolition was immediate if its beginning was "immediately prosecuted." Gradual abolition had been a failure in the West Indies, not because it was gradual abolition, but because the planters had never begun. But gradual abolition in the Southern States would be immediate just as soon as measures looking toward abolition were begun. "In fine, it is *immediate* emancipation which is gradually accomplished." [24]

The committee, aware that common minds would marvel at their calling this sort of emancipation immediate, grandly declared: "We see no absurdity in the use of immediate as applied to these measures, nor do we transcend the ordinary force of language when we call an important and complex public measure an immediate one, if it be promptly commenced." But an almost unanimous outburst of condemnation North and South showed that their peculiar understanding of immediate emancipation did truly "transcend the ordinary force of language." It could hardly have been otherwise. "Men at the North and men at the South," wrote Lyman Beecher's daughter, Catherine, "understand the language used in its true and proper sense; and the Abolitionists have been using these terms in a new and peculiar sense, which is inevitably and universally misunderstood." [25]

Even those who were aware that the motto of immediatism was adopted merely to secure the sanction of the British precedent, felt that the New York Committee had followed "the British example, beyond the limits their example could be imitated by Americans!" In taking over the motto of immediate emancipation they were "led by . . . a blind imitation of their predecessors in England" into a position which William Ellery Channing justly characterized as disastrous. For however carefully abolitionists might "explain the word immediate so as to make it innocuous," they would be judged by the word, and not by the explanation. "It is a fatal mistake," Channing declared, "for a party to choose a watchword which almost certainly conveys a wrong sense and needs explanation." [26]

But the real tragedy of immediatism was that the motto did not win for the movement the prestige of the British triumph. There were several reasons for this, an important one doubtless being that Arthur

Tappan's name was already odious—"a running title to volumes of recorded sneers and sarcasms." But there can be no question that the most important influence preventing their identification with the British movement was William Lloyd Garrison's unhappy notoriety.[27]

Garrison's reputation in the North was not a product of successful propaganda among the subscribers to his newspaper. They were too few. In 1831, the first year of its existence, the *Liberator* secured only fifty white subscribers; and although the fame of Garrison quickly spread over all the land, by 1833, white subscribers numbered less than four hundred. Even by the standards of the time this was insignificant: among the professional reformers of the benevolent empire a far larger patronage was considered the minimum of success. While the *Liberator's* total subscription list of 1833 was many times four hundred, the other subscribers were Negroes, secured by Garrison's appeal through the First Annual Convention of the People of Color to free blacks in the Northern cities. The largest total of subscriptions came from Philadelphia, where Negroes were most numerous. New York followed, with Boston third in the total number of subscribers.[28]

Though Garrison's editorials were addressed to the white abolitionists of the North, his appeals for aid were addressed to his subscribers. The *Liberator* did not belong to the white population, he wrote: "they do not sustain it." Instead "the paper belongs emphatically to the people of color—it is their organ." But at that time the people of color belonged to a subject race, inarticulate and powerless, and oppressed in most Northern States by special disabilities in the law. In public affairs their opinions went for nothing, and as their organ alone the *Liberator* would never have been known. Nor did it win its fame as the organ of the abolitionists of the North, though it was popularly so regarded. Abolitionists who mattered were white; and few of them subscribed. The truth is that the *Liberator* was made famous not by its Northern supporters but by its Southern enemies.[29]

According to the journalistic practice of the day, the *Liberator* was mailed to an exchange list of more than a hundred periodicals (one hundred and fifty by 1837) throughout the country. Northern papers merely returned the courtesy; but Southern papers did otherwise. The period was crucial for the slave régime. The very year that the *Liberator* began, a bloody insurrection of slaves in Southampton

County, Virginia, revived a terror throughout the South which had never died since the massacres in Hayti a generation before. The agitation in England for complete equalization of the races in the West Indies added a fear that such an example in liberation would provoke other uprisings. Everywhere in the South there was a reaction toward suppression, such a reaction as had been recurrent with every slave outbreak in the past, but never so strong as now. Public fears centered upon the secret circulation of inflammatory propaganda on the plantations. There was none such, but legislatures and governors expressed their fears in regulations and messages. Georgia made the circulation of abolition publications a capital offense, and the legislatures of Virginia and North Carolina held long and solemn council over a pamphlet by David Walker, a Boston Negro who dealt in old clothes and prophecies. "Our brethren of the South," wrote a timid abolitionist to Arthur Tappan, "are in a state of phrensy on this subject and ready to catch at any thing which they may be *told* militates against the enjoyment of their constitutional rights." To Southern editors, scanning the exchanges for items to supply their readers' "state of phrensy" with the food they craved, came the *Liberator,* loaded with quotable invective.[30]

American opinion, in 1831, had much dignity and little humor, but that dignity had a quality of juvenile self-importance peculiarly intolerant of criticism and rebuke. Nowhere in the nation was this sensibility so tender as in the South, the home of Southern chivalry and the duelling code. Upon this sensibility, already exacerbated by the events of 1831, fell Garrison's unmeasured diatribes on slavery. As Southern editors quoted from the *Liberator* week by week in their exchanges, Garrison's fame increased. Grand juries indicted him, State legislatures passed resolutions, and governors demanded his suppression by the Massachusetts authorities. Northern newspapers were moved by the Southern furor to notice Garrison, to reprint some of his more pungent utterances, and to express a concurrent indignation. By 1833, Southern resentment had reached a level of hysteria, and Garrison's name was known throughout the North.[31]

His was not a discriminating notoriety. To the millions, Garrison's doctrines were unknown; his editorials were seldom published in exchanges, only isolated phrases from his vitriolic pen. He was simply a notorious name, a term of opprobrium, a grotesque of abolition fanaticism. Inevitably the Northern public identified the New York movement, not as an extension to America of the glorious triumph of British abolition, but as an agitation at one with that of the fanatic Garrison.

Possibly the New York Committee would not have disavowed Garrison had nothing else occurred. That the South should hate him was regarded as only natural; and the sinister quality of his fame throughout the North was not yet perceived. After all he had won publicity of a sort, and abolition, it was believed, "has nothing to fear but from indifference." [32] Garrison's "trumpet voice has roused the nation," as the abolitionists put it; and to many of the leaders, even such notoriety as his was not to be despised. But other things happened which not only enhanced Garrison's reputation but so identified him with the British precedent that for the time his disavowal was out of the question.

Though all the abolitionists revered the British antislavery leaders, probably none but Garrison had thought of capitalizing that reverence in his own behalf. None of the others, it is true, had his advantages. Thanks to the furor in the American newspapers, his name was not unknown in England. If he could only get across the ocean, Garrison was aware that as the representative of American abolitionism, he would be so honored by the leaders of the British cause as to unite his name with the British precedent itself. [33]

But Garrison had no money for a voyage to England; and since he was not regarded among American abolitionists as their leading representative, he had no prospect of collecting funds in that capacity for his expenses. But he provided himself with a money-raising cause. Piecing together Jocelyn's broken plans for a Negro college, he published a prospectus for a "Manual Labor School for Colored Youth," and proposed an agency to Great Britain to raise fifty thousand dollars for its endowment, himself to be the agent. With considerable caution he sounded out the New York Committee on his project; but the Committee was of the opinion that instead of a new school, "it would be cheaper and better for the cause to cast Satan out of the old ones." The committee also remarked that facilities for the education of Negro youth were now available. They refused to sanction the mission, and they declined to contribute to its expenses. [34]

Garrison then turned for official sanction to the board of his own organization, the New England Anti-Slavery Society, and for expense money he applied to his subscribers, Negroes of the Eastern cities.

The board approved his mission, and his colored subscribers and their friends contributed enough money to purchase a one-way fare to England.[35]

Garrison reached London in May, at the moment of victory for the abolition of West Indian slavery, and the British abolitionists welcomed him in a mood of exalted enthusiasm. His peculiar temperament found nothing incongruous in this ovation. Abandoning his Negro school entirely—it had accomplished its purpose—he stood forth as the accredited ambassador to England of abolition in America, and took the seat of honor in the antislavery host. Garrison was a young man of pleasing appearance, a passable platform manner, and considerable personal charm. His reverence for the British founders of his antislavery creed perhaps added to his bearing a modesty not always apparent to his associates in the United States. The orthodoxy of his antislavery doctrine doubtless delighted his British hosts, imitation being always an acceptable form of flattery. Everything contributed to make him for the time a notable figure in the world's eye.

As ambassador of American abolition, Garrison spoke his mind on American slavery and its Northern supporters before cheering audiences in Exeter Hall; and New York papers reported his words, frothing with indignation. He raised his voice against the American Colonization Society's claim to antislavery sympathy; and the British public, won to the same position by Charles Stuart's labors two years before, applauded him heartily. He visited the aged Wilberforce who laid upon his young shoulders the mantle of abolition. He discussed with Buxton and all the heroes of the British cause the prospects of agitation in America. He outlined, and they agreed to, a plan of material aid for the American movement. As a climax to his mission, a "subscription breakfast" was given in his honor and leaders of the British cause spoke memorable words in his praise.[36]

The lofty rôle of ambassador from the abolitionists of America, Garrison maintained to the very end. When the time came for departure, instead of stepping out of his rôle and begging money for a passage home, he borrowed it from Arthur Tappan's protegé, the Rev. Nathaniel Paul, a colored American who was actually collecting money for a Negro school. This money, advanced from Paul's collections, Garrison "was requested by Mr. Paul to pay immediately into the hands of Arthur Tappan" upon his arrival in America. Even his own Negro school in the end received attention—though not from

him. It was Charles Stuart who rescued it from oblivion, and successfully presented its claims to the generosity of the British public.
Finally, everything said and everything provided for, Garrison departed in a blaze of glory, reaching America on the very day that
the New York City Anti-Slavery Society was organized.[37]

After the mob at Clinton Hall, Arthur Tappan and the New
York Committee had decided to put off the organization of a national
society until spring. The notice for the original date, October twenty-
fifth, "was so imperfectly given," wrote Elizur Wright, "and the
friends in Philadelphia were so little prepared for the meeting, that
it was necessarily postponed." [38] Meanwhile the occasion which had
made that date timely, the news of British emancipation, had gone by;
and it was now too late to associate the foundation of a national
society with that tremendous event. The expedient thing was to wait
until the time of the anniversaries next May, when thousands of
delegates from the benevolent empire would be gathered at Chatham
Street Chapel in New York.

But when Garrison learned after his arrival in this country, of the
committee's changed decision, he censured it in the strongest terms.
It was not only that they were publicly committed to hold the convention that year: Garrison declared that if they did not hold it they
would stand accused of cowardice in the public eye. With an insistence
almost frantic, he demanded a reversal of the committee's decision and
an immediate call for a convention.[39]

It is probable, however, that the true reason for Garrison's insistence was not the one asserted. The promise he had made to Nathaniel
Paul, to deposit with Arthur Tappan the money he had borrowed for
his passage home, had not been kept. Though Paul's draft on Tappan
for the loan was now due to arrive at any time, he had not only made
no provision for its payment, but he had mentioned it to nobody. Indeed, there was no provision which he could make. His own purse was
empty, the *Liberator's* finances were desperate, and for the moment
the sources of munificence in Boston were dry. His one hope of relief was the immediate organization of a national society to which he
could appeal for funds.[40]

But even if his financial obligations were put off, for Garrison, a
meeting next May would probably be too late. His recent acclaim in
Great Britain would then be an old story, and his appeal for relief
might not even be considered. Whatever the exigencies of the anti-

slavery cause, therefore, Garrison demanded an immediate call for a national convention; and such was his prestige at the moment that he overpersuaded Arthur Tappan and got his way.

The New York Committee mailed invitations to a hastily made list of names, summoning "the friends of immediate emancipation to meet . . . on the 4th of December to form a NATIONAL ANTI-SLAVERY SOCIETY." The Committee regretted the briefness of the notice; but "the public expectation is already excited, and the friends of our cause are to some extent committed to such a movement in the present year." Other causes just as "feeble and obscure . . . have been the means, under God, of immense benefit to the human race. Especially is this true of the National Anti-Slavery Society of Great Britain." The call closed with a warning: "To avoid interruptions in our meetings, we wish this to be considered confidential." With characteristic tenacity, the Tappans called the convention to meet in Philadelphia.[41]

Although the Pennsylvania Society for the Abolition of Slavery was still convinced that it was *"unwise* to urge by a National Convention the principles of *immediate emancipation* before the people at large are informed of our meaning of the terms," [42] its members were asked to join the new organization, and a committee waited upon one of its officers, Robert Vaux, inviting him to preside at the convention. When he refused, Weld's convert, Beriah Green of Western Reserve College, now president of Oneida Institute, declared that they could provide presidential timber themselves, and he was elected to the office *pro tempore*. Arthur Tappan, of course, was elected president of the society.

As national conventions went in the benevolent empire, the meeting was a convention only in name. The shortness of the notice, the unseasonable time of the year, and the muddy winter roads had prevented all but a handful of reformers from attending. Few of them represented societies; the greater number were correspondents of Arthur Tappan. Some, like George Bourne, were ardent abolitionists of the old school. A few of the Pennsylvania Society came—Atlee, Coates, and Lewis—and Negro delegates were there in some force. Theodore Weld, an abstainer from conventions "on principle," would not come; but he wrote from Lane Seminary pledging his efforts and prayers to the cause, and he was elected to the board of managers of the society. In all there were only sixty in attendance—a committee rather than a convention of delegates. As a representative gathering to establish an antislavery movement throughout the nation, it was a fiasco.[43]

But for Garrison personally the meeting was one of the great occasions of his life. With the glory of his British ordination still about him, he seemed to the delegates—pledged as they were to the British precedent—like a Moses from Sinai, bearing the tablets of the law to his people. His face still shone with the reflected glory of his triumph overseas. He had breakfasted with Buxton; he had communed with Henry Brougham; Wilberforce himself had summoned him and blessed his labors in America. The delegates saw in him their ordained priest, the vicegerent of the British movement in America. Speeches were devoted to his praise. Resolutions were passed in his honor. "He has won the confidence of the people of England," said Lewis Tappan. "We ought to put that honored name in the forefront of our ranks." They did so. As Leonard Bacon, leading clergyman of Connecticut, scornfully remarked, Garrison was "the man whom they assembled a national convention to glorify." [44]

He retired from the session and wrote a Declaration of Sentiments to which the convention listened with reverent attention and adopted with hardly a change. It was the first time in the new movement that an antislavery society had uttered a declaration without claiming the British precedent; for Garrison, always ready to think well of himself, had accepted the investiture of the British precedent, and he felt no need to refer to its greatness to enhance his own.

Here began the Garrison legend—consolidated by later events—that he was the leader of the antislavery movement in America. The members of the convention left Philadelphia pledged to maintain the legend against all detractors; [45] and they did their work so well that for a time abolitionists everywhere not only accepted the popular identification of the national movement with Garrison and his works, but acclaimed it as a truth!

His reputation thus established, Garrison cashed it in. At a meeting of the executive committee of the new society immediately after the adjournment of the convention, "called," said Garrison, "for the purpose of hearing my statements respecting the embarrassments of the Liberator, I stated that . . . relief should at once be given to the Liberator; otherwise the paper must inevitably go down. I remember that all who were present expressed deep sympathy," but nobody offered anything more substantial. However, Garrison had a scheme:

"I stated that Mr. Knapp and myself had on hand about $1,000 worth of anti-slavery publications . . . which, inasmuch as we could not dispose of them, were a dead weight sinking us to earth." He proposed that the society purchase enough of these unsalable pamphlets to relieve the *Liberator;* "but several of the committee raised some *constitutional* or rather financial objections to the purchasing of the publications alluded to, inasmuch as the Parent Society was then destitute of funds. . . . At last, on motion, it was voted that the Society purchase of Garrison & Knapp, publications to the amount of $440—to be paid for as soon as possible." With unspeakable relief, Garrison then turned to Arthur Tappan and told him "that it would not be necessary to raise the whole sum of $440, inasmuch as I owed Rev. Mr. Paul, then in England, $200 . . . and which I desired and was requested by Mr. Paul to pay immediately into the hands of Arthur Tappan." The Society could now owe Arthur Tappan the two hundred dollars, he informed the perplexed president; Tappan in turn could owe it to Paul, and he himself was thus cleared of all indebtedness. The remaining two hundred and forty dollars of the society's pledge, Lewis Tappan generously advanced to Garrison out of his own pocket. "This arrangement," Garrison declared, "saved the life of the Liberator." [46]

Though Garrison's elevation in the new society enabled him to discharge his debt to Nathaniel Paul (at least so far as his conscience was concerned), and to save the *Liberator,* it did no sort of benefit to the cause. Indeed, it was a disaster second only to the endorsement of immediate emancipation; for his notoriety fixed upon the society a "vague and indefinite odium" which hampered its growth from the beginning. Moreover the manner of his exaltation began in the anti-slavery movement a disposition to glorify men instead of measures, which Weld acutely called one of "the greatest perils of the anti-slavery cause." Such eulogies as those to Garrison, Weld prophesied, were bound in time to stir "one of the basest sediments at the bottom of Human Depravity." Such fulsome honors to "the individual instead of the cause" would inevitably provoke rivalries for priority between the "idolatrized leaders," and rivalries such as these were sure to cause factional strife. " 'He that flattereth his neighbor spreadeth a net for his feet.' We abolitionists have dreadfully entangled our own and each other's feet. Murderous friendship!" [47]

For all his elevation, Garrison never justified his priority by leadership. Indeed, he had no qualifications for leadership. His one office in the society, secretary of foreign correspondence, was soon resigned; and so long as the national organization held together he was never asked to fill another. He was so little a leader that even in the New England Anti-Slavery Society his journal was endured as its official organ for but a brief, unhappy period. He was equipped by taste and temperament for free-lance journalism and for nothing else. As a journalist he was brilliant and provocative; as a leader for the anti-slavery host he was a name, an embodied motto, a figurehead of fanaticism.

CHAPTER V

Hostility

1834

In 1834, the American Anti-Slavery Society began its formal agitation. Throughout the North the general tone of response was riotous hostility. In speeches, resolutions, editorials, and mobs, public opinion expressed its enmity to "Garrisonism" and to immediate emancipation. Northern papers joined the Southern press in an almost unanimous condemnation of the agitation. Mobs of grown men bent on violence, quite different from the usual gangs of mischievous boys, sought the lives of the agents. In New York, Lewis Tappan's house was gutted, and the store was preserved from a like fate only because Arthur Tappan had armed his "veritable army of clerks," and announced his unyielding determination to meet violence with violence.[1]

Leonard Bacon, Congregational clergyman and friend of Beecher, pronounced this hostile response a natural sequel of immediatism. Summarizing the events of 1834, he remarked that while few would oppose the sort of immediate emancipation that leading abolitionists "of logical and calculating minds argue for under these names . . . the public understands them as demanding immediate and complete emancipation in the obvious meaning of the terms; and . . . denounces them as visionary and reckless agitators. Hence it is that even in those States where the hatred of slavery is most pervading and most intense, the call for an immediate abolition meeting is so often the signal for some demonstration of popular indignation." Lyman Beecher's daughter, Catherine, put the blame for these demonstrations upon the abolitionists themselves. So long as they preached immediate emancipation "in a new and peculiar sense which will always be misunderstood," what else could they expect? "They are guilty of a species of deception, and are accountable for the evils that follow." Nor could they hope to secure a quiet hearing until they "cease to . . . urge their plan as one of immediate emancipation, and teach simply and exactly what they do mean."[2]

59

The movement made slow progress in the field. Proponents of antislavery doctrine discovered that "the mass of people found their objections to immediate emancipation in a misconception of what it means. . . . If this were corrected, thousands would find themselves enlisted under the banners of abolition who now feel themselves against it." But even after abolitionists had explained what immediatism did mean, it still seemed to many antislavery men that the explanations "have not removed the serious objection that to the general public their principle would produce a precipitate action." Some of these antislavery men, such as Channing, the New England liberal, did give the abolitionists aid and comfort, though they remained outside the organization. Allied with them were "a large number of men . . . who have been driven to give up their 'gradualism' and their Colonization as a remedy for slavery, but who cannot give up their grudge against Garrison!" There were others, however, protesting Garrison and the motto of immediatism, who felt bound to join anyhow, like William Jay, son of the great jurist, and Gerrit Smith, a public-spirited millionaire of western New York. Here and there "visionary and reckless agitators, ultras of the time," joined the society because of its very ill repute. Doctrinaire abolitionists of the old school, "persons with whom all temperate reasoning . . . is thrown away," subscribed to immediatism with enthusiasm.[3]

This motley association was not a national movement; the New York Committee had certainly hoped for more. Somehow the revival fire that burned so fiercely in their hearts had not spread to the nation. Instead, the agitation had lighted fires everywhere of a different kind. Over one such fire kindled in Utica, the greatest city of the Great Revival, burned an effigy of Beriah Green, president of the Anti-Slavery Convention; while the City Council pronounced the agitation "highly inexpedient." Nowhere in the nation were communities being roused from their indifference toward slavery to a denunciation of slaveholders. Everywhere communities were losing their indifference, it is true, but their denunciation was directed toward abolitionists and not toward slaveholders.

To conciliate the North and to convert it to "immediate emancipation gradually accomplished," the society propagandized the cause through pamphlets and journals, and through traveling agents. The most widely circulated pamphlets of these earlier years derived their importance from the fame of their authors rather than from their contents. Contributed by a rising young poet, a noted author, and two wealthy philanthropists, they were important to the cause of immediate emancipation rather as testimonials of belief than as sources of inspiration to the unconvinced. They advocated the safety and rightness of immediate emancipation, and their contemporaries marveled that they did so, but were not themselves inspired.[4]

The two journals of more than local fame were the *Liberator* and the *Emancipator*. Until it was edited by Joshua Leavitt some years later, the *Emancipator* was no more than mediocre. Its early editors, first C. W. Dennison, then William Goodell, were not competent to do more than conduct a recording organ for the American Anti-Slavery Society. The *Liberator* was brilliantly edited, but its prescription for conciliating and converting hostile communities was ever stronger doses of "the hateful bitterness and personality which season . . . the acrid and virulent tone of its writing." Garrison may have been only a figurehead in the national society, but as editor of the *Liberator,* he was no silent image. He continued to address his public in such words as to renew weekly his peculiar repute in the public mind.

During the first year of the new society's existence, Arthur Tappan, its president, in closest touch with its many activities, came to realize acutely the true and fatal significance of Garrison's name to the movement. He acted upon his realization with characteristic promptness. In the closing months of 1834, his brothers in Boston, John and Charles, united with Congregational ministers in organizing a moderate abolition society along the lines laid out by Lyman Beecher, which they called the American Union for the Relief and Improvement of the Colored Race. The Rev. Baron Stow, a member of the board of Garrison's New England Anti-Slavery Society, was a vice-president, and the society claimed the support of the poet Whittier and other prominent abolitionists. Arthur Tappan published in the New York *Journal of Commerce* a letter declaring his allegiance to the new organization to which he subscribed five thousand dollars. The society was expected to rid the antislavery movement of Garrison's reputation. It advocated "a conciliating spirit, a Bible spirit," and expressed its belief "that the hopes of the friends of the peaceful abolition of slavery in the United States depend upon securing the concurrence of slaveholders, procured by an appeal to their human and Christian principles." Its founders had high expectations. "Thousands among the best men in the land," they declared, "stand aloof

. . . ready and solicitous to combine their exertions for the welfare of the colored people, as soon as they can see how to act." Garrison naturally expressed bitter hostility, though Arthur Tappan journeyed to Boston especially to procure his silence.[5]

The movement was ill-starred. Lewis Tappan, more tenacious of his opinions than Arthur (it took another year of Garrison's editorials to alienate him), refused his support, and wrote sympathetically to Garrison. Even the *Emancipator,* pointing out the obvious fact that "Mr. Garrison is not . . . the leader of the Anti-Slavery Society," could see no point in a new society organized "because the leadership of Garrison is objectionable to some." He had, the editor declared, no leadership to eliminate. More unfortunate was the program of the society, which was to send an agent to the South to study slavery as it was, to begin the education and industrial training of Negroes, and to gather statistics regarding the condition of the free blacks. Such a program made as little appeal to the 'thirties as did asylums to reform prostitutes.[6]

The society maintained agents for a while, published a book by their traveler to the South—an acute and penetrating survey—and flickered out. Tappan withdrew from the movement when he saw that the society could not win the abolitionists' support and appealed to Garrison himself. He rebuked him for his "severe and denunciatory language," and expressed his earnest desire "to see this corrected," and his hope "that argument will take the place of invective." Tappan's desires were not realized. Garrison's style did not change nor did his reputation grow more tolerable. The *Liberator* became a greater incubus upon the cause with each week's issue.[7]

However eloquently the written propaganda might advocate immediatism, it could do no more than convert here and there a thoughtful soul; and it was not of such that kingdoms in the benevolent empire were made. In the 'thirties a national benevolent society was never based on the thoughtful, and therefore isolated, individual but on the local church communities. How otherwise could there be local societies meeting in the churches? How county societies and State societies? And how, without organized church communities, could there be an American Anti-Slavery Society which was truly what it claimed to be, "one of the noble sisterhood of Christian charities?"[8]

To inspire zeal in unfriendly church communities was a task beyond pamphlets and journals. It was a task for agents of the spoken word to whole communities, rather than for authors who could address individuals only. But such a task demanded revivalists in benevolence, who would preach abolition as "a glorious cause, allied to revival," and none such were available. Whittier tried an agency, but he was too gentle for the needs of such work and he soon returned to his pen. Garrison made one trip into the West, where he collided with his reputation, was burned in effigy, and returned to the *Liberator*. William Goodell, sincere but dull, spoke at intervals without any success whatever. Beriah Green labored faithfully in western New York against increasing resistance; but he was a college professor, with the "interminable House that Jack Built style" of his kind, and his agency was not long continued.[9]

Two agents who came over from Great Britain to aid the cause, fared no better. Charles Stuart was the first to arrive, with a thousand dollars for Garrison's abortive Negro college. He straightway began an agency at his own charges. But his British origin did not contribute to his effectiveness, and his eccentric manner and appearance were probably as much an obstacle to success as they had been in England. Garrison's friend, George Thompson, was the other British agent. His eloquence, Garrison had told the British leaders, was the most valuable contribution they could make to the cause in America. Financed for a three-year mission, Thompson began an agency which ended in a crescendo of violence a few months after his arrival. With some difficulty he was smuggled on board ship ahead of a mob and returned to England.[10]

Of all the agents who entered the field in 1834, only Amos A. Phelps met with more than moderate success; but he was "one great, clear, infallible argument—demonstration itself," and no firebrand. It was at Cincinnati, and not in the East, that agents were to be found fiery enough to inspire communities with the spirit of the Great Revival itself.[11]

CHAPTER VI

The Lane Debate

1834

At Lane Seminary, though Lyman Beecher still declared that he had never known "such power for intelligent and strong action condensed in a single class," his pride became tempered with doubt. "As the offset of so much good," he remarked, was "the independence inseparable from such mature age and power of mind. Unaccustomed to the discipline and restraints of college life . . . they have not regarded our advice as we hoped they would and think they ought to have done." Instead, as the perplexed president observed, they followed rather the advice of a student, Theodore Weld. Beecher admitted that "the young men had, many of them, been under his [Weld's] care" long before they came to Lane. But he noted with concern that their respect was not the ordinary deference of college men for a leading student. "In the estimate of the class he was president," Beecher wrote. In the eyes of his fellow students "he took the lead of the whole institution." In fact, "they thought he was a god." [1]

Weld himself wrote home that he had "never been placed in circumstances by any means so imposing." That exhaustless vitality—"all awake . . . scarce keeping still a minute together," which so much impressed Harriet Beecher—had ample occupation. Besides being a student of theology, he helped to administer the manual labor department, which included printing, coopering and cabinet-making shops, and a large farm; he also taught a class. But Weld was not inflated: modesty was an essential part of his nature. His devoted humility disarmed even President Beecher. He never trespassed upon the president's prerogatives, and Beecher himslf testified that in the months of strain that followed they never quarreled. [2]

During the first term, in August of 1833, an event occurred which consolidated Weld's leadership among those students who had not been under his care before. The terrible epidemic of cholera reached

Lane, and "all at once . . . from being a seminary of learning it was converted into a hospital of sick and dying." Weld organized the well to care for the sick, and for fourteen days set them an example of devotion. "The Lord sustained me throughout," he wrote to a relative. "I had not, during the whole time, scarcely a single sensation of fatigue or the least disposition to sleep, though in more than one instance I was without sleep forty-eight hours in succession." Those students not members of Weld's ardent host were strangely moved. One wrote: "Such coming together, such tenderness, kindness and love I never saw. . . . None seemed desirous to leave the place. . . . And though they knew not but the next hour they themselves might die they hesitated not to accompany their brethren to the very face of death and door of heaven." When the epidemic was over, all the students in the seminary were a united band.[3]

Before this, Weld had redeemed his promise to Arthur Tappan to discuss the abolition of slavery. For months he and a few others "had been prayerfully investigating the subject" with increasing interest. The young men of Lane Seminary had the common opinion of Garrison and of immediate emancipation. By the body of students "abolitionism was regarded as the climax of absurdity, fanaticism and blood," and abolitionists shared the invidious reputation of Garrison, of whom one student wrote: "We had accustomed ourselves to regard him with suspicion . . . and to treat as incendiary, or idle words, whatever he chose to say." Among them were no abolitionists except the few whom Weld had been quietly proselyting. One of these was William T. Allan of Alabama, at whose home Weld had argued the question of slavery with Birney. With Allan he labored, as he had many times labored with young men convicted of sin; and "after some weeks of inquiry and struggling with conscience, his noble soul broke loose from its shackles" and he was converted to abolition.[4]

This little group Weld organized for more extended effort. "Those of us who sympathized together in an abhorrence of slavery selected each his man to instruct, convince and enlist in the cause. Thus we carried one after another, and before ever we came to public debate, knew pretty well where we stood." Even then, Weld wrote, "a majority were still opposed," though general interest increased until February, 1834, when it was resolved to discuss publicly the merits of the question. The students applied to President Beecher for permission to hold the discussion, and with thoughtless enthusiasm he not only assented but offered to participate. Upon second thought, how-

ever, and after listening to comments of certain friends of the seminary, he moderated his enthusiasm, advised the students to postpone
the discussion, and finally, when the faculty decided not to forbid the
debate, he sent his daughter, Catherine, to represent his interests.[5]

In substance the discussion was a protracted meeting, a revival in
benevolence; it was a debate only in name. For eighteen nights, with
deepening emotion, these young men prayerfully considered their
duty to the colored race, not in the spirit of debate but in the spirit
of an inquiry-meeting in Finney's revivals. "When the debate commenced," wrote Stanton, "I had fears that there might be some unpleasant excitement, particularly as slaveholders and prospective heirs
to slave property were to participate in it. But the kindest feelings
prevailed. There was no . . . denunciation." Indeed, the spirit was
not argumentative. "There has been no struggling, no quibbling, no
striving to evade the truth," another student wrote, "but on the other
hand candor, fairness and manhood have characterized the debate." [6]

The meeting began with a consideration of the question: "Ought
the people of the slaveholding states to abolish slavery immediately?"
For two evenings William Allan, "born, bred and educated in the
midst of slavery," presented immediate emancipation as its remedy.
He defined immediatism in terms of the New York Committee's
interpretation: "By immediate emancipation we do not mean that the
slaves shall be turned loose upon the nation nor that they shall be
instantly vested with . . . political rights and privileges." Instead he
advocated "gradual emancipation, immediately begun."

As he proceeded, a profound sense of personal guilt for the system
of slavery developed among his hearers, and during the seven evenings
thereafter all of them, particularly the Southerners, added their testimony to the cruelties of slavery. The substance of this testimony was
made up partly from personal observation, and partly from the folk-
tales of the antislavery tradition, retold throughout antislavery literature from the earliest Quaker pamphlets to the writings of Bourne.
The young men repeated these tales as hearsay reports of cruelty on
distant plantations; and the familiar properties of these legends—the
heavy, perforated paddle through whose holes spurted blood and flesh,
the tanned skin of the slave flayed alive, the red-hot tongs, and the
child born dead—were displayed with such effect that one student
wrote home: ". . . the facts developed in the debate have almost

curdled my blood. . . . Facts are the great instruments of conviction on this question." [7]

The testimony of James Bradley, the former slave, himself an authentic document for the antislavery case, was a fact of another order, as were the keen observations of James Thome regarding the coercion of intelligent mulattoes in Kentucky who, like Bradley, were often far more capable of freedom than their masters. Also of a different order were pitiful tales of the internal slave-trade, of which all who had lived observantly in the border States had sad personal knowledge. Of a different order, too, was the thrilling eloquence with which Weld closed the question of immediate abolition. "He . . . uttered no malice; sharpened no phrase so that its venomed point might rankle in another's breast. . . . His great soul was full of compassion for the oppressor and the oppressed. . . . Nobly simple in manner, free from thought of self, he touched the springs of the human heart." On the ninth evening a vote was taken; it was unanimous for immediate abolition. "The Lord has done great things for us here," wrote Weld to Tappan.

The remaining nine evenings looked to a foregone conclusion. The subject was the Colonization Society: Was it such as "to entitle it to the patronage of the Christian community?" The students made a noble effort to be impartial, but their previous vote had given a hostage to the opposite cause. As Stanton said, they now considered the Colonization Society "not like blinded partizans, but like men whose polar star was fact and truth, whose needle was conscience, whose chart was the Bible," and whose north was the New York program of "immediate abolition, gradually accomplished."

At her father's behest, Catherine Beecher presented his famous plan of assimilation for abolitionists and colonizationists, "which attempted to prove that colonizationists and Abolitionists ought to unite their efforts and not contend against one another." It was accorded a respectful hearing and was answered to the satisfaction of the students point by point. None defended it. More substantial were complete files of the *African Repository,* a profusion of colonization pamphlets lent by friends in Cincinnati, and a statement from a Cincinnatian who had paid a visit to Liberia. This material the students examined and condemned. Huntingdon Lyman of Louisiana naïvely remarked: "We are astonished at the result of our own investigation. . . . Now we perceive that we have been deceived by a specious exterior." Almost unanimously they voted colonization down and organized an antislavery society.[8]

The effect of this revival in benevolence was more than a change of opinion; for scores of the students it meant a change in their lives. Some unnamed, average student wrote to a friend describing his deep inward transformation: "I came here strongly prejudiced against antislavery principles and determined to exert all my influence to maintain the sound ground of colonization in opposition to them. . . . I professed, however, to be a lover of truth, and determined to examine the arguments of my opponents with candor and impartiality. . . . I now feel an impulse strongly urging me to do something . . . and hope soon to manifest that I am in earnest by taking part in elevating the colored in and about Cincinnati." Upon another student, Augustus Wattles, the impulse to do something was so imperative that he shortly requested permission from the president to leave the school and devote his life to educating the poor blacks of Cincinnati. Forgetting his exasperation for the moment, Beecher wept with him, blessed him, and let him go.[9]

Devotion was in the air. Wattles' school was swamped with colored applicants, and another student, Marius Robinson of Tennessee, took honorable dismissal to go down into Cincinnati and help him. Still another student withdrew to free the slaves upon whose hire he was subsisting at Lane, and to find work so that he could support them while they received a common-school education. "We have vowed unto the Lord," wrote Lyman of Louisiana, "to use our personal exertions and whatever influence we have or may acquire to raise up the free black population, and to persuade our fellow-men to love them as they do themselves."

To elevate the free blacks of Cincinnati the whole converted seminary turned their efforts. Students subscribed some hundreds of dollars among themselves and equipped a library, a reading room, and a hall. Several evening classes were established for adults, as well as a course of lectures on useful subjects. Every Sunday three large Sabbath Schools gathered in different parts of the city. "System and order is the salvation of our time," remarked Weld, and he organized the students into sections so that they could teach in rotation, thus performing "an immense amount of labor among them without interruption of our studies." [10]

This solid, practical application of radical doctrine warmed Arthur

Tappan's heart, and he straightway sent Weld a thousand dollars for incidental expenses. Soon afterward certain young ladies from New York appeared in Cincinnati, their expenses all paid, their board provided for, to teach the colored girls and women of the city.[11] In addition, Tappan wrote to Weld: "Draw on me for whatever is necessary for the schools, teachers, house-hire, books, etc." Determination to raise up the free blacks grew, and the earnest students established social clubs, temperance societies, an employment service, outdoor relief, and a "freedom bureau" to assist free blacks to purchase the freedom of relatives still in bondage.

The Lane debate reverberated throughout the nation. To the May meeting of the American Anti-Slavery Society, James Thome and H. B. Stanton went as delegates. Stanton was the better orator, but Thome was an exhibit, a *bona fide* Southerner converted to abolition, and he made the great speech of the year. On the subject, "The Southern Slave Kitchen, the Sodom of the Nation," he spoke with impressive eloquence: "Oh! the slave kitchens of the South are the graveyards of the mind. Every countenance of their miserable inmates is the tombstone of a buried intellect, and the soulless eye is its dreadful epitaph!" Among the abolitionists of the East there grew a hope that with the winning of Thome and his Southern brethren of Lane, the conversion of the South had begun. Thome's visit "constituted a new era. . . . Mr. Thome is the first, but we trust he will not be the last *Kentuckian* . . . to plead the cause of the colored man." [12]

Another Kentuckian shortly followed Thome. James G. Birney had been working as agent for the Colonization Society ever since he had been converted by Weld two years before. Revolted by the measureless invectives of Garrison and interpreting "immediate emancipation" to mean immediate, he had published in the organ of his society, the *African Repository,* a series of articles against abolitionists, which attracted wide attention. Just before the Lane discussion he had moved his family to Danville, Kentucky, and echoes of the debate came clearly to his ears across the river. He journeyed to Cincinnati to talk to Weld and the converted students who, as Huntingdon Lyman said, "expounded unto him the way of God more perfectly." Weld explained the inner meaning of immediate abolition, and Birney yielded as he had yielded to that magnetic voice before. He left Cincinnati an immediate abolitionist. In his diary he recorded his conversion. "I have seen in no man such a rare combination of great intellectual powers with Christian simplicity," he wrote of Weld—"the most simple hearted and earnest follower of Christ that I have known. . . . He must make a powerful impression on the public mind of this country." He returned home to write a public letter repudiating the Colonization Society and advocating immediate abolition. Accepting a secret agency from the American Anti-Slavery Society, he began his labors in Kentucky for the cause.[13]

While the students' vow to raise up the free blacks prospered, their other vow, to persuade their fellow men to love the blacks as they did themselves, revived bitter issues in Cincinnati. Five years before, the city authorities had despaired of controlling the constantly augmenting Negro population and determined upon the heroic measure of wholesale deportation. This proved to be impossible to enforce; and the next year, in 1830, the exasperation of the whites broke out in a series of bloody riots, the scars of which were still unhealed in 1834. Of all Northern cities, Cincinnati could least endure to be asked to love the Negro as itself. Ugly rumors spread about the city that social amalgamation between students and Negro families had gone far, and those strange, secret race repugnances in the American tradition woke and blindly stirred. "Cincinnati was never so convulsed before," remarked an apprehensive trustee of Lane Seminary. Violence seemed imminent; and though it was avoided for the moment by the summer vacation and the scattering of faculty and students, friends of the seminary were seriously concerned.[14]

Lyman Beecher journeyed east to attend the New York anniversaries. He called on the Tappans and assured them that though he could not agree with everything the students had said in the debate, nevertheless "he would insist on free discussion and on the insertion of its recognition in the laws" of the seminary. But when Beecher visited the anniversaries, he found that the debate had stirred the entire college world. Previously Western Reserve, Andover, Amherst, Miami, and Center College were the only other institutions of importance that had harbored active antislavery societies, and other schools had little cause for uneasiness. But after the picturesque and widely published discussion at Lane, similar discussions—as similar as college students could make them—were to be expected everywhere. To meet this crisis in higher education, the presidents and college representatives who were attending the anniversaries called a conference. Here Beecher—if he attended—turned his coat; for the conference "unanimously agreed that the times imperiously demanded that all anti-slavery agitation should be suppressed," and they sent copies of their resolution to every college in the country.[15]

Upon receipt of these resolutions, the executive committee of Lane Seminary's board of trustees passed some striking regulations. They resolved to abolish the students' antislavery society, to place the movements of the students and their occasions for discussion under the censorship of the board, and to invest the trustee's committee with summary power of dismissal. Asa Mahan, a Presbyterian minister who had once been a member of Finney's Holy Band, protested against the resolutions with all his power. He was almost the only one of the twenty-five trustees familiar with the students, and he knew that the young men were too devoted and too mature to endure such regulations. He wrote to Beecher in moving terms, urging him to return at once and "save the school from dismantlement." [16]

Instead of hastening home, Beecher stayed away. "I hope you will all be patient and take no course till after my return," he wrote the students on the ground. "In the meantime pray much, say little, be humble and wait." In the end "God will bring us over shoals and difficulties into a broad place." But that fall when the students gathered for the next term, they found Beecher still absent and the rules in force. The intent of the rules, admitted both by trustees and faculty, was to abolish the abolition society, to expel Theodore Weld and William Allan, who was president of the society, to end all projects to raise up the free blacks in Cincinnati, and to stop all discussion on the subject of slavery. Almost to a man the students arose and shook the dust of the seminary from their feet; nor could Beecher, when he arrived, cajole them into returning as long as the faculty held the position "that the exciting nature of any question is good ground for forbidding its discussion, and that the unpopularity of moral action warrants its total discontinuance." [17]

The board's action provoked a storm of popular condemnation throughout the North. The trustees were astonished, and Beecher wrote a bitter public statement which closed with the following melancholy tribute to Weld: "In our opinion, all our difficulties were originated and continued by the instrumentality of an influential member of the Abolition Society. . . . But while we feel called upon to say this, justice and affection require us to render at the same time a willing and melancholy homage to the talents and piety and moral courage and energy of the individual, while we lament that want of early guidance and subordination which might have qualified his mind to act safely by consultation in alliance with other minds, instead of relying with a perilous confidence in its own sufficiency. . . . While our high expectations and warm affections have been disappointed in him . . . it is not without hope and daily prayer that the past may suffice and that wiser counsels and more auspicious movements may characterize his future course." [18]

In his empty seminary Beecher reflected gloomily upon the disaster. The students, that "set of noble men" whom, he had told Weld, he "would not at a venture exchange for any other," he had lost forever; but even in his days of pride they had never been truly his own. They were, he had long since learned, converts of the Oneida revivals, children of Finney's spirit and never more than stepchildren to him. As the months passed, his rancor did not diminish. The students had refused to conform to the prejudices of respectable people, and he could not forgive them. "He-goat men," he called them, "who think they do God a service by butting everything in the line of their march which does not fall or get out of the way." [19]

Anti-Slavery reformers Beecher had known in the East as had no other man of his time. He had dealt in turn with the colonizationists, with Lundy, and with Garrison; and he had labored to enlist them all in a union to free the slave. But in those quiet months a conviction grew upon Beecher that Weld's abolitionism was of a more dangerous kind than these, part of a larger creed which he had opposed before. He remembered his conflict with Finney who, like Weld, had refused to conform his "new measures" to public approval, and had manifested instead "a self-sufficient and daring state of mind which is incorrigible to argument and advice." He remembered that Weld was Finney's disciple, that his own students had been Finney's converts, and that even the New York philanthropists were a part of Finney's congregation. Remembering these things, alone in his day he discerned the true impulse of the antislavery movement, not in the noisy futilities of the Boston reformers, but in the expanding benevolence of the Great Revival. "Abolitionists," he concluded, were "the offspring of the Oneida denunciatory revivals." [20]

Within Beecher's family the great debate went on. His children had been educated by controversy within the household: "Opinions were canvassed without ceremony. . . . All propositions must be discussed . . . every mind must be expected, in supporting its opinions, to exert itself to the utmost." The documents of the Lane debate—the faculty statement, the students' statement, and newspaper comment—went to those away from home; and at their gatherings Weld spoke through the lips of the children who had heard him to those who had not.

Only Catherine, the eldest, stood steadfast by her father. The others maintained for a time a troubled neutrality and then went over to the abolition cause. For two of them, Henry Ward and Harriet, the debate was to have more than a personal significance. Henry Ward entered the theological department of Lane the autumn that the rebels left, and made one of the tiny residue of students in that black winter; but Harriet had been at Lane during the whole debate. She heard the heartrending stories that the Southern students told of cruelty and wrong, and she heard Weld's moving plea for the abolition of slavery. Decades later, when she was challenged to prove that the events of *Uncle Tom's Cabin* could have been real, she turned naturally to the book in which Weld had retold those stories, *Slavery As It Is;* and from its pages she quoted her evidence that Uncle Tom was true.[21]

CHAPTER VII

THE LANE REBELS

1835

Of the fifty-three students who had signed the public statement of their case in the fall of 1834, some went home and others shifted to distant schools, but many of them stayed to teach the free blacks of the city. Weld supported them by drafts on Arthur Tappan, and friends rose up in Cincinnati to give them shelter. A brilliant young lawyer there, Salmon P. Chase, profoundly stirred by the debate, persuaded his brother-in-law to put at the students' disposal a large rambling house near Walnut Hills. Here during the winter, the boys alternately taught each other and visited their classes of blacks in the city.[1]

Arthur Tappan brooded over their forlorn condition and propounded various plans for their relief. He asked Finney to go out and take charge of them at least for the winter; but Finney, deep in the completion of his Broadway Tabernacle, flatly refused. Tappan discussed with his friends in New York a new institution on a larger scale than Lane, where free speech would be assured; but before his plans matured, the students had voted to move to Oberlin College, and Tappan loyally seconded their decision.[2]

The claims of Oberlin were presented to the Lane rebels by its founder and factotum, the Rev. John J. Shippherd, an uneducated, impractical visionary, whose glowing descriptions ignored the fact that Oberlin at that time possessed almost nothing but disadvantages. It consisted of a few crude shacks deep in a woods clearing a few miles from Western Reserve College, the institution to the support of which Presbyterians of northern Ohio were already definitely committed. While Shippherd was prepared to admit that Oberlin's location was unfortunately close to Western Reserve College, he disclaimed any hostile purpose. "Providences too numerous here to mention indicated clearly that we could not obtain a location so eligible as this," he said. "We concluded to risk the *appearance* of opposition and locate on the spot." The chief providence was its undesirability for settlement, due to its tenacious clay soil and heavy forestation. Prospective settlers had refused to purchase sites in that locality, and so nearly waste was the land esteemed that the company exploiting the Western Reserve had let Shippherd have the Oberlin site without a cent paid down and without security for future payments.[3]

When Presbyterians of northern Ohio asked with some asperity how another college of their denomination on the Reserve could be justified, Shippherd answered that he was an enthusiast for the manual-labor plan of education, and in his judgment other schools had incorporated that system "only with partial success." In none of them were the students' expenses even half provided for; whereas he believed that the manual-labor device in his plan would cover most of their expenses. "We felt therefore bound to build."

Shippherd failed to convince northern Ohio of Oberlin's right to support, and he was put to desperate expedients to keep the institution alive. He offered "perpetual scholarships" for $150 apiece, promising the student purchaser that this amount invested in buildings, grounds and equipment would care for him during his entire course. "And when he graduates [he can] sell the same scholarship, not diminished but increased in value." He proposed to "obviate the necessity of raising large sums for the establishment of Professorships" by persuading teachers to donate their services, the college guaranteeing to provide them a subsistence. This he said could easily be done "through the cheapness of living at Oberlin." Meanwhile, no college students had yet enrolled.[4]

By the winter of 1834, the rickety project was about to go to pieces. As a last recourse, Shippherd resolved to appeal to Eastern philanthropists, and he went to Columbus to catch the eastbound stage. Here he chanced to learn that a whole schoolful of young men—with wealthy Eastern friends—were at large in Cincinnati. He straightway hurried south to snare them for Oberlin.[5]

To the Lane rebels Shippherd described his "forest bivouac" in such glowing terms that the whole group agreed to enroll in the spring, provided they could designate Oberlin's president, faculty, and rules. Asa Mahan must be elected to the office of president, Theodore Weld and John Morgan, a former member of the Lane faculty, must be given professorships, and Negroes must be admitted to the student body. Shippherd, claiming power from the trustees "in fact and form plenipotentiary," generously consented to the appointments and also pledged the college to debar no student on account of his color.

When Weld was offered his professorship he refused, proposing instead Finney, who, he told Shippherd, was "in too great a prostration of health for evangelism or pastoral work. Teaching theology," said Weld, "would be a needful rest to him." Shippherd and Mahan went to New York and explained the situation to Arthur Tappan. His response was prompt, for Oberlin offered at one stroke a refuge for his homeless protegés, a school for Negroes, and a nursery for abolitionism. With all his resources he proceeded to bring the college into being. He canvassed his wealthy friends for contributions, he pledged tens of thousands on his own account, and lent Oberlin thousands more. He went again to Finney and with an insistence that would not be denied, persuaded him to go.[6]

With a student body, a set of rules, a president, a faculty, and an endowment all provided through the Lane rebels, Shippherd asked the trustees to approve his promises; but some of them raised objections. Possibly without meaning to do so, he had misrepresented his own powers and the sentiments of the trustees. Toward abolitionism and the education of free Negroes, most of them had the prejudices of their time. They were farmers, ministers, and merchants of a rural community, part of the general public which believed that immediate abolition was a dangerous heresy and that Garrison was its genius. Despite Shippherd's pledge, they refused to approve the rule that Negro students would be admitted. Students in the Academy and townspeople in the colony were of the same mind. Even to save Oberlin from destruction, they would not admit Negroes.[7]

But on the board of trustees itself there was a powerful advocate for the other side. Rev. John Keep, president of the board—one of Weld's converts to the cause—had already proved himself a devoted abolitionist; and it is probable that his influence with his colleagues changed the votes of enough of them to secure reconsideration of "the odious resolution" denying Shippherd's pledge to Weld. Once again the question of admitting Negro students was proposed, but this time the trustees divided on the question. John Keep cast the deciding vote, and thereby opened Oberlin not only to Negroes but to the Lane rebels as well.[8]

At Oberlin the Lane rebels gathered for the spring term of 1835, bringing with them Asa Mahan and John Morgan. Then Finney ar-

rived to command once more his ardent host, now matured and experienced in reform. He traversed with them the events of the years
of their separation since the Great Revival. He praised their works
for the free blacks of Cincinnati. He justified the abolition creed
which they had received from Weld, but he warned them, as Tappan
had warned Garrison, "to avoid a censorious spirit" in their pleas
for the slave. "A denunciatory spirit," he told them, "is unchristian,
calculated to grieve the Spirit of God . . . and is injurious to the
. . . slaves themselves." Before they parted he revived them again
and gave them over once more to Weld's leadership in reform.

Late in August, Weld, now agent of the national society, summoned thirteen of their number to Cleveland, and after drilling them
for two weeks in antislavery lore, sent them out to convert Ohio.
Then he visited Oberlin to claim still more of his old classmates. For
three weeks he taught them in turn in his "abolition school," the by-
product of which was the conversion of the entire community to
immediatism. From this band of young men the national society
drew more and more of its agents of agitation as their resources
increased, until thirty of the fifty-four who had signed the students'
statement at Lane were pioneering the North for immediatism. Until
Weld's Seventy were chosen in 1837, the Lane rebels formed the
bulk of the antislavery staff in the field.[9]

They preached the New York doctrine. "We did not wish [the
slaves] turned loose," Thome told an Akron audience, "nor even to
be governed by the same Code of Laws which are adapted to intelligent citizens. I was replied to by a lawyer. He expressed his
astonishment at the disclaimer I had made. Said he didn't know but
that he was ready to go all lengths with me; but he protested that
I was a *new* abolitionist and had disowned every distinguishing
feature of modern abolitionism."[10]

But before so moderate a definition of immediatism could be cred-
ited, the Lane rebels had to earn a quiet hearing. Their initial task was
the conciliation of communities made hostile by Garrison's methods
and by the popular misconception of immediatism. They conciliated
hostility by enduring it with steadfast meekness; for only after the
mobs were spent would people listen. Their task of conciliation was
"a dispiriting experience," marked by "harsh words . . . stale eggs,
and brick-bats and tar," and sometimes by "indignities too gross to
be printed"; and in their letters from the field they frequently voiced

their loneliness and despair. But after violence had worn itself out, the agents had their reward. "Never have I found an unattentive audience, once they are persuaded to listen," reported one, and the foundation of an antislavery society, he declared, was his sufficient reward. "However terrible the strain," wrote another, "we rejoice that we are doing our part toward the moral conquest of the world." [11]

Only fiery zeal inspired by the Great Revival itself could so endure and achieve. Rather than agents, the Lane rebels were evangelists of abolitionism, and their power to move communities was one with the power of Finney. Together with Weld, their leader, they precipitated another Great Revival in the nation, a revival in abolitionism.

CHAPTER VIII

WELD'S AGENCY

1835–1836

Late in 1834, as field agent for the national society in Ohio, Weld entered on his mission with consuming zeal. His concern was not organization merely, but conviction. He asked for "hearts and heads and tongues—for faith and works"; enlistment without them was "an imposition upon abolitionists and a mockery of the slave's wrongs." His appeal was the intimate personal challenge of the evangelist: "If your hearts ache and bleed, we want you, you will help us; but if you merely adopt our principles as dry theories, do let us alone: we have millstones enough swinging at our necks already. Further, if you join us merely out of a sense of *duty,* we pray you keep aloof and give place to those who leap into our ranks because they can not keep themselves out; who instead of whining about duty, shout 'privilege', 'delight'!" [1]

Weld preached the New York doctrine, "immediate abolition, gradually accomplished"; but he presented it as a principle, "rarely appealing to sympathy and never descending to popular trickery and . . . declamation." He even refused to quote instances of cruelty to slaves, because "however numerous or well authenticated, they would be either scouted as incredible or met with the cry 'exception' . . . . Treatment, however bad, is but an appendage of slavery." His points of emphasis were "the inflictions of slavery on *mind*—its prostration of conscience . . . its destruction of personality—its death-stab into the soul of the slave."

To Weld the evangelist, the economic aspect of slavery appealed not at all. Its function as a system of control and protection for a barbaric race he ignored. "As a question . . . of national economy I have passed it with scarce a look or word, believing that the business of abolitionists is with the heart of the nation rather than with its purse strings." For his mission was to persuade Northern communities to denounce slavery as a sin, not to reform slavery as a system. [2]

Weld's methods were the "New Measures" of Finney in the Great Revival, the form and spirit of a protracted meeting. "In most places," he reported, "I have lectured from six to twelve times—sometimes sixteen, twenty and twenty-five, and once thirty times." To the Boston abolitionists this method was as extraordinary as it was beyond their capacity to imitate. They thought it a personal peculiarity of Weld's, "his manner of executing his work"; but it was simply the manner of the Great Revival. Each night Weld spoke from two to five hours, never exhausting his subject nor his hearers. "It may seem extravagant," wrote one of his audience, "but I have seen crowds of bearded men held spell-bound by his power for hours together and for twenty evenings in succession." His eloquence was of the order called in his day "terrific," with much fine language and startling effect; but it was charged with a sincerity and conviction which few could withstand. "No one, not even Wendell Phillips so moved his hearers to the cause," said one who knew his work; and even in distant New England he was reckoned "one of the most powerful advocates of truth and liberty the world has ever witnessed . . . of all the young men in the land . . . without a compeer." [3]

Beginning in the autumn of 1834, Weld labored for over a year to conciliate hostility and procure a hearing across the State. His repute as a temperance orator served usually to open the Presbyterian church to his first lecture in each locality, but the riot which attended his stand for immediatism often closed the church to later meetings. Stores, halls, and warehouses thereafter accommodated his audiences until he convinced the community that immediatism was reasonable. Then interest in his message replaced violence, and "his extraordinary mental powers . . . his irresistible eloquence, his excellent humility, and his high moral heroism" made the remaining lectures unfailingly successful. [4]

The preliminary period of violence was usually more annoying than dangerous. Rowdy youths outside the lecture-room made an uproar which Weld overcame by raising his splendid voice above the din. Outrages were committed, but they were usually puerile: "Peaceable horses tied to the posts were assaulted—snuff and sand thrown into women's eyes—innocent and unsuspecting sitting hens disturbed in their nests and the eggs thrown into meeting—cannons are fired and *Rum* drinked—yes, even there!" For such disorders Weld expressed a patient contempt. "I beg the audience will be composed," he told his nervous hearers as an egg broke upon his face. "He wiped it away calmly . . . and proceeded as deliberately as if he had paused to take a draught of water." [5]

But at any moment the mob could become dangerous. Many times Weld was stoned, even while he spoke from the pulpit. At Circleville a large stone crashed through the church window: "one so well aimed," wrote Weld, "that it struck me on the head and for a moment stunned me. Paused for a few moments till the dizziness had ceased, and then went on and completed my lecture. Meanwhile some of the gentlemen had hung their cloaks up at the window so that my head could not be so easily used as a target. The injury was not serious, though for a few days I had frequent turns of dizziness." The most dangerous moment was likely to be at adjournment when the speaker must face the mob outside. Usually a bodyguard of young men assured his safety, but there were not infrequent nights after the first lecture when not even a bodyguard was converted to the cause. Then Weld folded his arms, and fixing his eyes steadily upon the leaders sometimes walked through unscathed. "The Lord restrained them," he wrote after one such deliverance; "not a hair of my head was injured." [6]

Often disturbances had a more serious purpose. Citizens called mass meetings, and after angrily resolving that no abolitionist should speak in their town, adjourned to fill the church where Weld was to lecture. For hours Weld would meekly endure "bedlam broke loose," until a moment of quiet gave him a hearing. Invariably his eloquence captured his audience. Once a disturbance of this sort lasted until it was too late to speak. Then lifting his mighty voice, Weld informed his hearers that he would speak the next night—and the next. "He should . . . continue to plead for constitutional liberty . . . until liberty or he was defunct." [7]

Usually after the second night—though sometimes not for a week—the violence died. Then Weld reaped his harvest. Again and again audiences of hundreds rose unanimously for immediate abolition, not alone the restless reformers of the 'thirties, but the sober, substantial business and professional men of the community. To Presbyterian ministers he appealed with special power; and as his fame increased through central Ohio, clergymen from distant points gathered to hear his words, and "went back right," to convert in turn their fellow clergymen in the Ohio presbyteries. Like Finney,

Weld was powerful with lawyers, and occasionally secured an initial hearing by challenging any lawyer in the community to meet him in debate. Invariably he converted his opponent as well as his audience.[8]

In his closing lecture Weld asked converts to immediate abolition to stand. Local enthusiasts among the audience, like "personal workers" in the Great Revival, urged their neighbors to rise. Occasionally the "personal workers" took over the meeting. At Steubenville, Weld remarked a young lawyer, Edwin M. Stanton, who sat in the front seat facing the pulpit. "I said at the end: 'Friends, will all of you who believe . . . please rise to your feet?' Stanton sprang to his feet and turned to the audience with uplifted hands, which rose in a body in response to his lead." [9]

Always the mass of Weld's hearers, usually the whole audience, rose to its feet. More than once several hundred people thus unanimously expressed their conversion to the cause. Opponents became partisans. Anti-abolitionists "foremost in threats and bluster before the commencement of the course"—ringleaders of the riots—"pledged themselves to the principles of *immediate* abolition." Southerners who had migrated to Ohio added their testimony. Even slaveholders visiting relatives in the community rose to confess their guilt and promised to amend their ways. Refractory editors, too much prejudiced against abolition to be capable of conversion, nevertheless expressed admiring regard for the man: "However individuals may differ with him as to the most advisable method of abolishing slavery . . . all without exception agree that he fully maintains the character of a man of talent, a gentleman and a christian." [10]

Among his converts Weld seldom organized a society, preferring to leave that task to local initiative while he journeyed on to face the mob in the next town. Advice and guidance, however, he imparted with liberal pen. At Jefferson, for instance, a young lawyer convert, Joshua Giddings by name, organized a local society, and with the aid of his partner Wade, faithfully extended its bounds throughout the county. Out of this contact grew a friendship which, seven years later, when Giddings was in Congress and Weld was head of the national antislavery lobby, was to influence powerfully the antislavery agitation in the House of Representatives.[11]

After several months of agitation, spokesmen for Weld's multiplying societies urged him to form a State society. He summoned the delegates to meet in the city of Zanesville, notorious for its anti-abolitionism, and went ahead "to prepare the way for the Convention. Zanesville was locked up. Could get no place to lecture, not a shanty even. Putnam, on the other side of the river, was a little better, and I could get *one* public room. Lectured. A mob from Zanesville came, broke the windows, doors, tore off the gate, and attacked me, when I came out, with stones and clubs. This continued until the trustees of the room shut it up. Then adjourned to a private room. In short every kind of outrage was committed." But Weld pursued his dauntless course unmoved. A night came when the mob listened, and the next evening Weld addressed them from the pulpit of a church. Zanesville called him back across the river, and on the sixteenth night, hundreds pledged themselves to immediatism. The way for the State convention was prepared.[12]

Over a hundred delegates attended. Birney journeyed north to represent his short-lived Kentucky State auxiliary. From Oberlin and the Negro schools in Cincinnati came the Lane rebels. Quakers and old-time abolitionists, John Rankin and his sons among them, occupied the seats of honor; but most of the delegates were Weld's own converts of that year. The convention pledged the West to the New York doctrine: "By immediate emancipation we do not mean that the slaves shall be . . . turned loose"; they must be subjected instead to "the salutary restraint of laws appropriate to their condition." With true revival ardor, the members of the Convention dedicated their efforts to the sacred cause, and organized the Ohio State Anti-Slavery Society.[13]

At the end of the year 1835, Weld brought his agency in Ohio to a close. He had visited fewer than two score villages and towns, and only a few thousand had heard his voice. But as in the Great Revival, each converted community was a center of contagion. His converts continued the work, spreading abolitionism through towns and countryside near their homes. Already they had organized many local societies, one numbering four thousand members. But the movement was still only a beginning, insignificant in size when measured against the State's population. It was a movement of communities rather than of individuals, however, the first in the antislavery agitation and the first promise of success for the cause.[14]

Weld's agitation in Ohio ripened to harvest during the next year. Shortly after his departure Birney moved to Cincinnati and founded a newspaper, the *Philanthropist,* which served as the organ of the

State society. At the second State convention, in Granville, Weld's work was consolidated by the Lane rebels in a permanent organization, and hundreds of delegates pledged their efforts to extend the agitation. In the years that followed, Weld's agency unfolded in a progressively enlarging movement whose influence made Ohio's part a distinctive one in the next three decades of the nation's history.[15]

Early in 1836, after "some irruptions into Vermont," especially around Middlebury, where his friend Charles Stuart had been laboring, and where "the field was already ripe for the harvest," Weld began the abolitionizing of western Pennsylvania. The reputation he had made in Ohio preceded him, and everywhere he was accorded a respectful hearing. Churches competed for the honor of entertaining him, and the daily papers reported his words. Never before had such success attended his efforts. In Pittsburgh, before he began to lecture, there was hardly an abolitionist in the city; but after he left, a visitor reported that he had "never found so many abolitionists in any other place in proportion to the number of inhabitants as we find in Pittsburgh." His converts established a weekly, the *Christian Witness,* and organized the Anti-Slavery Society of Western Pennsylvania, long the only auxiliary in the State. Even after abolitionists of Philadelphia had formed an eastern branch society, the western branch continued to dominate Pennsylvania abolitionism.[16]

Weld's thrilling triumphs in Pennsylvania roused leaders of the movement throughout the East, and a determined effort was made to secure his services there. His name was put on the program for the next anniversary of the national society, but Weld refused to go. "An anniversary," he said, "is an element I was never made to move in. My heart never was in that way of doing things and never can be." The executive committee of the society then appointed him to explain the antislavery movement to the Rhode Island Legislature and also to speak before committees of the legislatures of Connecticut and Pennsylvania; but he would not. "Legislators in this cause," he told the leaders, "are no more important than any other man." Nor would he answer calls to speak in the Eastern cities, no matter what the occasion. "We must leave the great cities alone," he said. "I have no right to go on [East] when the pressure for labor upon me back here in the country is importunate and imperative." [17]

At least, the New York executives wrote him, he could report his achievements to the antislavery press. This Weld flatly refused to do, however great the pressure. Even his closest friends were vexed. Stanton wrote: "Do you think it possible for an individual to go thro' the United States in this age of free enquiry . . . and produce in the public mind 'an intelligent, rational, abiding Excitement' . . . and at the same time, entirely screen himself from public observation through the medium of the press?" This was exactly Weld's intention, however; and, the historian is moved to add, he succeeded.[18]

In the early summer of 1836, Weld turned western Pennsylvania over to his agents and journeyed to western New York. Here abolitionists had not only failed to conciliate hostility; they had provoked still fiercer resistance. Four months before Weld's arrival, their first State convention had been driven out of Utica by a mob, and of late, agents in the larger centers had been completely silenced. Weld was faced with the dangerous task of reopening the agitation.[19]

He began a protracted meeting for immediatism in Utica, in the very church from which the convention had been driven. His increasing fame secured him a respectful hearing, and he captured the city. Hundreds were turned away nightly from the crowded church; and after the sixteenth lecture, when he pledged his hearers to immediatism, a host of converts responded. "Now the intellectual and moral, perhaps the numerical strength of the city are ours!" wrote an exultant abolitionist. "Not a dog wags his tongue mob-like against us. . . . Mr. Weld is one of the most astonishing men of the age." [20]

From Utica Weld started out through the homeland of the Great Revival. Buffalo and Rochester he won with ease; but thereafter he encountered a deepening hostility. Town by town the mobs grew more respectable and more dangerous. At Lockport county officials led the rioters, and they ceased their disorders only when they found that they must kill Weld in order to silence him.[21] At Troy, hostility became invincible.

Here was stationed Dr. Beman, in whose church Finney had preached during the Great Revival. Like all of Finney's colleagues he was an abolitionist; but his tone was pugnacious and irascible, and his agitation had only increased hostility throughout the city. When Weld came he found the entire community already provoked against his cause, ready for any extreme of violence toward his person. The mayor expressed public regret that he did not have the power to remove Weld bodily from the city, and the public crier with his bell summoned a mob: "All you who are opposed to amalgamation meet in front of the courthouse!" At Weld's first meeting, rioters led by a city official invaded the church and surged up the aisles toward the speaker. Three times they attacked the pulpit and were thrice repulsed by his fighting bodyguard of young men, with casualties on both sides. The frightened mayor, repenting his heated words, called the city council to his aid, and after the meeting the city fathers escorted Weld to his lodging amid a shower of stones.[22]

Weld chose to remain in the city and face the mob till violence was exhausted and he could get a hearing; but it was a perilous business. When he appeared on the streets, surrounded though he was by a bodyguard, mobs gathered to stone him. After a few days of this, his entire body was "one general, painful bruise," and several times he narrowly escaped more serious injury. Despite the pleas of his friends and the protests of the authorities, he determined to remain until either his life or mob violence had ended. He cancelled engagements to lecture elsewhere, and in a mood for heroic martyrdom wrote a farewell letter: "Let every abolitionist debate the matter once and for all, and settle it with himself . . . whether he can lie upon the rack—and grasp the fagot—and tread with steady step the scaffold—whether he can stand at the post of duty, and having done all and suffered all . . . fall and die a martyr 'not accepting deliverance'. . . . God gird us all to do valiantly for the helpless and innocent. Blessed are they who die in the harness." [23]

Violence did not die nor did Weld. The city authorities finally offered him the alternative of voluntary or forcible removal, and he departed, having failed for the first time to conciliate hostility and win a hearing for immediatism.

Weld's agency in New York continued only a few months after his departure from Troy. His title of honor, "the most mobbed man in the United States," was dearly won. Scores of outrages on his person had taken toll of his vitality, and it was long before he recovered from the effects of the battering he had received at Troy. Excessive use was breaking his voice, and incessant labor was exhausting his health; but his inspiration and his faith had never burned so high. The last months he spent in New York were the most successful of his agency. Thousands pledged their faith to immediatism, consolidating their efforts in a State society which was the most powerful of the auxiliaries, the center of abolitionism in the North.[24]

Toward the close of his agency, Weld paused to survey his work. Notable though it was, he thought of it only as a beginning. In Ohio, Pennsylvania, and Vermont he had opened up the way for others; in New York he had revived an agitation suppressed by violence; but nowhere did he lead the movements he initiated. He was a pioneer. His genius resided in his evangelism, his power to make missionaries of his converts. Wherever he spoke he established nuclei for societies rather than societies themselves. With characteristic humility Weld depreciated this pioneering: "If these are the first fruits what will be the harvest? If this is the growth of the border, what the teeming product of the field? And if the gathering of handfuls wakes up such loud acclaim what will be the song when the morning stars break out together and all the sons of God shout long and loud for joy?" [25]

CHAPTER IX

"GARRISONISM"

1836

In 1836, the prestige of New England was at its brightest. "It is the emporium for all that is good and great in America," an abolitionist wrote from the wilds of Ohio, "and the light there will shine even to the West." New England's priority was hardly questioned in projects of moral reform. Indeed, before the antislavery agitation began, a Yankee prophesied that New England would begin it; and when it did begin, "the Spirit and the men of New England must take the lead." Though its abolitionists numbered hardly more than one fifth of the national society, their doings were followed with a solicitude far beyond the measure of their proportion. Their importance was a dogma of the age.[1]

Probably nowhere in the nation were there so many reformers ripe for abolition doctrine as in New England. Remotest from slavery in distance and economic interest, they were the most "deeply impressed with a sense of the duty of rebuke which every inhabitant of the free States owes to every slaveholder."[2] At the sound of antislavery agitation in 1832, this abolition sentiment crystallized into organization, first in Boston, then in Lynn, next in smaller towns in the central New England area.

Usually these individualists did not merge with the "system of benevolent operations, well digested" in the Congregational churches. Mostly they were radical minorities in the church and the community, abolitionists by temperament and conviction, who did their own thinking and walked by themselves. Their central auxiliary was the New England Anti-Slavery Society at Boston, which was founded by Garrison and grew in his image. To its meetings societies rather than delegates repaired to exchange their views. Observers from elsewhere invariably remarked the absence from its proceedings of the usual business of central societies: reports from local societies, details of the year's efforts in the field, and plans for future operations.

Instead, the sessions were occupied with the elucidation of points of doctrine and with speeches. Elsewhere in the benevolent movement a central auxiliary served a system of organized local communities; but the New England organization was primarily an association of independent abolitionists for mutual self-expression.[3]

Even in central New England, where distances were small, the population dense, and traveling easy, such a loose organization of independent minds made for friction. For meeting place they depended upon the local church—which in central New England was usually Congregational—however small their minority in the congregation. As a matter of right their traveling agents made the pulpit their forum and even expected to address the Sunday congregations in the interest of their cause. Pillars of the church, who listened patiently to agents advocating clothes for the heathen and "bethels" for the sailor, drew the line at abolition; and Congregational ministers whose pulpits were thus invaded nursed a growing hostility toward the antislavery cause.[4]

In Rhode Island and southern Connecticut another kind of antislavery movement gathered way, a true community movement, the single-handed achievement of the Lane rebel, H. B. Stanton. Commissioned by the national society in July, 1834, for a year and a half, Stanton campaigned Rhode Island for abolition, closing his agency at Providence with a convention of four hundred delegates. This convention—said to be the largest ever assembled in the State— organized a State society and pledged their communities to the cause with a unanimity and enthusiasm which "surpassed the most sanguine expectation" of the national society.[5] From Rhode Island, Stanton carried the antislavery revival first into Connecticut, and then into Massachusetts itself, where he addressed members of the State Legislature with telling effect for the cause.[6]

Among the Methodists of the New England conferences a second community movement gathered headway. Its leader was Orange Scott, a presiding elder and the most successful revivalist of his faith in New England. He was bluff and rude, with "an undisciplined mind, warmed up with a heated fanaticism"; but he had a lion's courage and a martyr's sincerity. At a meeting in 1834, he heard Stanton, fresh from the Lane debate, denounce slavery as a sin; and he rose from his seat in the audience to pledge his life to abolition. Out of his meager salary he purchased numerous antislavery pamphlets which he distributed among his colleagues. He persuaded the editors of *Zion's Herald,* the journal of New England Methodism, to publish his utterances, and in its columns he waged fierce controversy with the anti-abolition forces of his church.[7]

Scott preached the New York doctrine. More downright than the casuists of immediatism, he frankly admitted that his brand of immediate emancipation was gradualism under another name; he understood immediatism to mean *"that at the earliest possible period consistent with the best good of the slaves, they should be fully emancipated.* With respect to that period there are different opinions." His entire doctrine was marked rather by vigor of statement than subtlety of thought; and when the controversy in the church journals became involved in the intricacies of the "Bible argument," his store of learning soon ran out. The newspaper controversy was taken over by the venerable Timothy Merritt, beloved "father in the spirit" of the New England conference, while Scott devoted his efforts to platform agitation. A thoroughgoing abolitionist, Merritt learnedly exhibited the sinfulness of slavery, but only as a legal relationship. "Whether slavery . . . should at once cease, I am not so clear," he wrote; "but the *right* to hold men as goods and chattels, subject to sale and transfer at the will of a master, *should cease and be discontinued instantly and forever."* [8]

To this moderate interpretation of immediatism, a large majority of the New England and New Hampshire conferences heartily subscribed. Methodists outside New England united against them, but with steadfast courage they defended their faith against their bishops, the national Methodist press, and even the general conference of the church. Viewing the American Anti-Slavery Society as "an important link in the great chain of operations of the Presbyterian and Congregational churches," they organized sectarian antislavery societies, so that they could "do their benevolent works in the name of their own denomination and proper character." In every antislavery conference they organized a Wesleyan Conference Society, and in the heart of the enemy's country, at New York City, they founded a journal, *Zion's Watchman,* and established a national Wesleyan headquarters. With picturesque zeal they campaigned among the ministers of the Northern conferences until the great division in the church a decade later.[9]

In New England their agitation was a triumph. The Methodist

strength was in the rural towns and countryside, away from the prosperous centers dominated by the Congregational churches. Here solid
congregations went over to the abolitionists. Baptists were moved to
emulate their Methodist brethren, and the two denominations made
up the strength of the movement. More than two thirds of all the
abolitionists in New England were either Methodists or Baptists,
and an even larger part of the effective local organization was made
up of Methodist and Baptist congregations.[10]

In 1836, most abolitionists still considered Boston "the most important part of the field." For Bostonians believed that in projects
of moral reform "Boston rules Massachusetts, Massachusetts rules
New England and New England rules the nation"; and nowhere
was this conviction deeper than among the abolitionists. Of them all,
Garrison had the surest faith in Boston's moral primacy, especially
in the antislavery cause; but in point of fact Boston abolitionism was
in a bad way.[11]

In sharp contrast to the Lane rebels, who first encountered hostility
and then secured a hearing, Garrison first secured his hearing and
then encountered hostility. In issue after issue of the *Liberator,* "his
rancorous denunciations and his brawling, ferocious abuse" raised
new opponents and embarrassed faithful friends. Upon the latter
fell the burden of excusing his violence and propitiating his victims,
a task which Garrison made more onerous by his growing tendency
to advocate incidental causes along with immediatism. But these
vagaries of his reforming spirit were minor irritants; the head of his
offending was his promiscuous vilification of all individuals, institutions, and beliefs with which at the moment he did not agree.[12]

From the beginning of the agitation, Garrison's "proneness to
denunciation" had impeded the efforts of Boston abolitionists to extend the bounds of their society. "His spirit," they found, "affects
too much . . . the reputation of the society," [13] not only among
prospective converts but also in the minds of clergymen to whom
agents of "Garrisonism" applied for the use of their pulpits. There
were objections and refusals; and leaders of the movement belatedly
realized that their "chief task" was "to labor . . . for the purifica-
tion of the New England churches," if their agents were to get a
hearing. This meant that they must abolitionize the Congregational
churches; for the Methodists insisted upon "doing their work in their
own peculiar manner" through societies of their own, the Baptists

were too decentralized to canvass as a church, and other creeds were inconsiderable.

In 1834, Amos A. Phelps, spokesman for the Boston society, appeared before the Association of the Congregational clergymen of Massachusetts and eloquently presented the claims of immediatism. He was too late. Two years before, Lyman Beecher had convinced the Congregational churches of New England that "union, blessed union" between colonizationists and abolitionists was desirable; and the association would concede to Phelps only "that the principles and objects of the American Anti-Slavery Society, so far as they do not come into collision with those of the American Colonization Society, meet with our approval." [14]

However unsatisfactory this statement was to orthodox abolitionists, it implied a not unfriendly attitude and opened the way for further discussion. The discussion, however, was continued by Garrison, who described the statement as a cowardly and time-serving attempt to avoid a positive pronouncement and accused the Association of a "pro-slavery subservience" to the wishes of slaveholders. Further attempts to win the Congregational churches consequently encountered a less friendly attitude, and thenceforth they lived in the outer darkness of Garrison's disapproval.

Beecher's plan of union continued to exercise the Congregational clergy, and a year later, in 1835, it was embodied in formal organization, the ill-starred American Union for the Relief and Improvement of the Colored Race, which so bravely attempted a dispassionate and unbiassed survey of the Negro race in freedom and in slavery. It came to nothing, but for the time it disabled Congregational opposition to the abolitionists, pledged as it was to a peaceful union of all opinions to free the slave. Its failure, however, added bitterness to the growing hostility toward Garrison.

Meanwhile (1835–1836) in central New England, resistance to the Boston agitation increased. Agents were put in the field, itineraries were arranged, and meetings were well advertised; but more and more Congregational ministers denied their churches to "Garrisonism," often thereby closing their communities to the antislavery word. The agents protested; abolitionist minorities in the churches made trouble; and the *Liberator* dredged the language for epithets to characterize the offending clergymen. Such tactics did not open more churches; it increased rather than diminished the friction. One act of war led to another, and by the beginning of 1836 the heated editor of the *Liberator* was insisting that churches must open their pulpits to antislavery agitation, whatever their beliefs. If they expressed their unwillingness to do so, then "the wishes of pastor and churches are to be disregarded." [15]

Before the controversy began, Garrison's religious views had been what Benjamin Lundy termed "ultra-orthodox"; but as his rancor toward the churches rose, his reverence for their claims declined. To justify his changing views he borrowed some of the heresies rife in the 'thirties, weaving them with self-righteous logic into his indictment of the churches. In an editorial upon Lyman Beecher's famous sermon in praise of the Sabbath, Garrison contended that the Sabbath was an outworn superstition. As various denominations failed to measure up to his standard of antislavery action, one by one they roused his ire. The Methodist church was "a cage of unclean birds and a synagogue of Satan"; the Presbyterian church was anathema; the Congregational ministers stood "at the head of the most implacable foes of God and man," toward whom "the most intense abhorrence should fill the breast of every disciple of Christ." Finally, when every creed had been denounced, he concluded that ecclesiastical institutions themselves confined the soaring spirit.[16]

Once he had tasted the heady wine of anarchism, Garrison drank deep. Not only churches but other institutions as well were useless. By 1836, Garrison had "renounced all allegiance to his country and had nominated Jesus Christ to the Presidency of the United States and the World." [17] His new beliefs he advocated with vigor and eloquence in the columns of the *Liberator*.

His novel heresies completed Garrison's alienation from orthodoxy. Methodists and Baptists, most orthodox of denominations, could not be expected to connive at such doctrine, and their defection left to Garrison only a fraction of the New England abolitionists. Clergymen of every creed publicly condemned "the sins of William Lloyd Garrison . . . his crusade against the churches—against the constitution and union of the United States—against civil government itself, with all its rights and powers"; and Garrison retorted with intolerant bitterness in the columns of the *Liberator*. The "blackhearted clergy," convinced that Garrison was a man "of whom honest men may well speak in terms of honest indignation," needed only leadership to crystallize its resentment into positive action against "Garrisonism" and all its works. That leadership was supplied by Lyman Beecher himself.[18]

In the West, Beecher continued to advocate a union of all opinions against slavery but with considerably less effect than in New England. Colonizationists and abolitionists heard him unmoved and continued their fratricidal strife. But he persevered, lifting his voice above the rising fury of the antislavery controversy wherever he could find an audience.[19] In 1836, he appeared at the Presbyterian General Assembly in Pittsburgh to urge his plan upon the delegates of that slavery-ravaged session.

Though the national antislavery movement had made its beginning among Presbyterians, the subject was not agitated in the Presbyterian General Assembly until the session of 1835. The principal agent in the agitation was the ubiquitous Theodore Weld. He was not a delegate to the assembly; he attended as a lobbyist for immediatism, seeking "opportunity for free personal conference" with the delegates regarding their attitude toward slavery, "and this as often as possible." He found the field ripe to the harvest. Delegates from the Great Revival area, many of them old friends, turned abolitionist as soon as immediatism was shown to be harmless. Abolitionists of the old tradition were quickly won to the new. At a series of antislavery meetings which Weld organized in a Pittsburgh church, the converted delegates successively pledged "their open advocacy to the cause," and persuaded their hearers to follow their example. When the assembly closed, Weld reported that the number of delegates "decidedly with us on the subject of slavery" was forty-seven, "nearly *one fourth part of the* Assembly!" [20]

With true revival zeal the newly converted delegates carried the antislavery gospel home to their churches. "It looks as if the Presbyterian Church were becoming an Abolition Society," said a bystander; but such was not the case. Most of the converts were from the New-School synods of Ohio, western New York, and Pennsylvania; and their agitation did not extend beyond their own faction. But their effective labors in the New-School synods throughout the year 1835 promised to add in future sessions of the assembly the bitterness of sectional strife to the doctrinal dispute between New- and Old-School factions.[21]

When the new assembly gathered, in 1836, it was at once apparent

that to the issue of Calvinism was joined the issue of immediatism.
"The whole General Assembly is secretly heaving under the apprehension that slavery may divide this body before its close," wrote a
delegate. Southern Calvinists expressed their conviction that abolitionism was a natural child of New-School heresy, and Northern
advocates of Finney's theology replied that bigotry and slavery were
inseparable.[22]

Into this conflict of irreconcilables came Lyman Beecher to plead
for union between the warring delegates. "These silken ties," he
said, "these soft but mighty bands which have held Christians of
the North and of the South together are beginning to break. Well
may panic go through the hearts of those that love the land."[23]
Could something not be done to save the Union? Union itself would
save it. Most of the delegates were opposed to the principle of slavery; if the end which they all sought w?? its abolition, why should
they so bitterly debate the means? Let them forget their differences
and unite in common cause, and Heaven soon would bless their union
with triumph.[24]

His plea for fusion, far from winning the church to peace, was
treated with angry disdain by abolitionists and colonizationists alike,
and Beecher realized at last that his blessed union was a pitiful futility. For the moment he lost that "benevolent and enlarged feeling"
which had so long enabled him to be at the same time Calvinist and
liberal, abolitionist and colonizationist. He became simply an angry,
vengeful old man. Impotent to harm abolitionism in the West, he was
still a prophet not without honor in his own country. From Pittsburgh he went straight to Connecticut, where ministers of the Congregational church were in session, in order to stir up the Eastern
clergy against Garrisonism.[25]

Beecher's hatred was not simply toward abolitionists, "the offspring
of the Oneida denunciatory revivals."[26] It also included the revivalists who inspired the abolitionists. Standing before the Congregational Association, he demanded that the Congregational churches
of Connecticut forever close their pulpits to revivalists. He admitted
that his present attitude was inconsistent with his entire career. "But,"
he said, "I wish to confess my sin. I was wrong. . . . The system
of evangelism . . . is as if a man should sit down and attempt to
eat enough to last a whole year." It was against evangelists, however,
rather than the system of evangelism that his anger burned. At last
he expressed the resentment he had hidden during the years since

Finney had evangelized his own church in Boston: "The influence of the evangelist is to break up the order of Christ's house. . . . In the church the pastor is the sun, the source of light and center of sweet influence. This is God's established order of things. Break up this and we have . . . the miseries of hell." No champion of evangelism showed his head; the association took unanimous action against revivalists among their churches.[27]

Then Beecher demanded action against the Great Revival's product, the abolitionists; but to this demand the association raised objection. The difficulty was not with the sentiment, but with the statement of condemnation. It would not do to mention abolitionists by name; the resolution simply proposed closing the churches to "itinerant agents and Lecturers" who advanced "sentiments . . . of an erroneous or questionable character." The objection was that this statement was ambiguous: "The objects which it aims to exclude might be confounded with other objects" worthy of a hearing. But after "explanations and interpretation," Beecher persuaded the doubtful clergymen that no acceptable reformer need be denied a hearing, and the association gave this resolution a unanimous vote as well.[28]

In the General Association of Massachusetts a few days later, Beecher's task was easier. Here he spoke to fellow-citizens of the Boston abolitionists, and by them his measure against Garrisonism was acclaimed with relief. What opposition there might have been from lovers of free speech, from friends of reform, or even from honest abolitionists among the clergy was either shamed into silence by memories of Garrison's achievements in heresy and abuse, or prevailed upon by Beecher's powerful influence to approve the action. Both the resolution excluding evangelists and the one against abolitionists were passed without a dissenting vote.[29]

Some general action by the Congregational churches condemning the Boston abolitionists was inevitable; but that the action should close the churches to their agents, and by unanimous vote as well, was fatal to the Boston movement. Its accomplishment was an extraordinary tribute to Beecher's adroitness and prestige. "Indeed," said William Goodell, "we know of but one man in the nation who could have procured its unanimous adoption . . . Lyman Beecher."[30]

To the New York executives this was catastrophe. Repudiation in New England, "the conscience of the nation," was to their minds the worst disaster that could strike the cause. Massachusetts and Connecticut Congregationalists were lost, but the rest of New Eng-

land might be saved. They hastily summoned Weld and Stanton to
New Hampshire, where the Congregational Association was about
to assemble, in order to prevent Beecher from carrying his vengeance
further. Weld and Stanton succeeded; but the saving of New Hampshire was poor consolation for the loss of Massachusetts and Connecticut.[31]

Congregational repudiation speeded the collapse of Garrison's support in New England. Reaction in Boston was so strong that not a
church would open its doors to the next session of Garrison's society.
Several abolitionist clergymen escaped the odium of Garrisonism
by condemning Garrison and his heresies in a public statement, the
Clerical Appeal. Claiming that their sentiments were shared by
nine tenths of their fellow-workers in Massachusetts, they called upon
abolitionists everywhere to repudiate Garrison and his *Liberator*.
Raging with wounded vanity, Garrison demanded that the officers
of the national society "punish this sedition and chastise" the authors
of the document; but this they refused to do. Maddened by their
"studied silence . . . respecting the Clerical Appeal," he wrote them
again. "What is the meaning of it?" he asked. "I maintain, with all
seriousness and earnestness, that you are both bound to meet these
aspersions promptly, and in an official capacity; and should you refuse
to do so, I for one shall feel that you will have greatly misapprehended
your duty, and need to be admonished by abolitionists universally."
He warned them that their silence, "if it be continued longer, will
. . . call for a plain rebuke through the columns of the Liberator."
Undisturbed by his threats of excommunication and abuse, however,
the leaders refused to break their "studied silence"; though they did
inform him by letter that in their opinion the charges in the Clerical
Appeal were true.[32]

But neither his proscription by the Congregational churches nor
the alienation of his colleagues touched Garrison's conviction of his
grandeur. He had no inkling that his conspicuousness in the movement was the work of those who called all abolitionists by his name
in order to bring opprobrium upon the cause. The term "Garrisonism"
was anything but an epithet of infamy to him; it was solid proof of
leadership. Every such effort North and South to identify immediatism by his name only fed his self-esteem. Thus he viewed the Congregational resolutions as more than an assault upon his leadership.
As the founder and embodiment of abolitionism, he considered his

proscription by the clergy to be a proscription of the cause itself. "It is becoming more and more apparent," he wrote, that clergymen are "blind leaders of the blind, dumb dogs that cannot bark, spiritual popes—that they love the fleece better than the flock—that they are mighty hindrances to the cause of freedom." Abolitionism was not safe so long as clergymen were in control. *"The cause must be kept in the hands of laymen, or it will not be maintained."* [33]

Garrison's terror of "the black-hearted clergy" was as much a delusion as was his certainty of his own primacy in the cause. From the beginning the movement had been inextricably bound up with the churches. The churches were its forums and the homes of its local organizations; from the churches it drew its justifying inspiration. It was an aspect of the churches, non-sectarian in organization but evangelical in character—a part of the benevolent empire. Everywhere in the organization clergymen were in control. Even in Garrison's own New England Anti-Slavery Society, clergymen composed nearly two thirds of the delegates in the typical session of 1835. In every aspect, the agitation was "a moral movement—a religious movement" drawing its life from the churches; and Garrison's "anti-clerical" obsession made him an enemy of the antislavery impulse itself.[34]

Amid the disintegrating elements of New England abolitionism, some still lingered in Garrison's train. His personal following was not inconsiderable. A few like Garrison had been dazzled by "the simplicity and beauty and consistency of the doctrine that all government, whether civil or ecclesiastical, conflicts with the government of Jehovah, and that by the Christian no other govt. can be acknowledged." Garrison did not originate his heresies. He merely caught up those "ultra views" of the 'thirties that rationalized his obsessions; and among abolitionists who were progressing toward the same opinions, his leadership was still unchanged.[35]

Not all such followers were insignificant. There was Edmund Quincy, finished product of the Boston aristocracy, who left all to follow Garrison; and there was Wendell Phillips, "abolition's golden trumpet"; and there were others as able and devoted. But there were more who followed Garrison despite his heresies. They knew the man himself, the austerity of his life and his singleness of purpose. They knew that the harshness of his writings was derived from his righteous absolutes of faith, never from vindictiveness; and that his intolerance was for the principles that he hated, and not for the men who followed them. For all his "I-ness"—his obsessive self-importance—Garrison was truly what his followers believed him to be, the embodiment of devotion to a cause.

Still to the public of the 'thirties, Garrison's harsh and intolerant style made up the man himself. If the hateful self-portrait which Garrison's own words depicted in the *Liberator* had been true, its effect could not have been more ruinous to the antislavery cause; for it was this picture that counted as Garrison with the public, and not Garrison himself. In the Eastern mind, he continued to be the incarnation of fanaticism, inimical to every institution of religion and the State.

The time had passed, however, when he could be "cashiered or voluntarily leave the ranks." The Garrison legend had been too long believed. To the thousands of distant abolitionists who knew nothing of his heresies, he was still "abolition personified and incarnate," and these would not sanction his repudiation. Though the Massachusetts society split apart and the movement in New England fell into hopeless disrepute, Garrison still remained a hero to his disciples and the legendary figure of abolitionism to the nation.[36]

CHAPTER X

Revival Triumphant

1836–1837

At the antislavery offices on Nassau Street in New York City, Elizur Wright and his helpers worked throughout the year 1835, directing pamphlets to the nation. Only a few were printed to sell; most of them were distributed gratis "by strewing the wayside, the parlor, the bar room, the stage coach, the rail car and the boat deck," and by sending them haphazard through the mails to such addresses as could be secured from published lists. A few thousand were sent regularly to governors, judges, lawyers, editors, and legislators, but most of them were mailed in large bundles to clergymen and postmasters, accompanied by letters requesting them to distribute the contents throughout their communities.[1]

Governors, judges, Congressmen, and the like were poor prospects for printed propaganda, and clergymen frequently notified the New York office that they had destroyed the bundles entrusted to their care. Where the pamphlets were distributed, results were never commensurate with the effort. The motto of immediatism was so hard to understand, so difficult to explain, that the printed word was a poor medium of propaganda. Even in communities hostile to slavery, pamphlets proved to be irritants rather than aids to inquiring prospects. Angry protests were the most common response; pamphlet conversions were seldom reported.

In the South the pamphlet campaign was disastrous from the beginning. Everywhere resentment developed, and, in July, Charleston citizens broke into the mails and burned the pamphlets in the public square. Their action was widely imitated. Southern postmasters, upon intimations from Washington authorities that this one kind of mail might be destroyed, removed the pamphlets from the mails as they arrived. On a hint from the postmaster general, the New York postmaster publicly declared that he would no longer forward antislavery matter to the South; and the New York office thereupon announced that "out of regard for Southern feeling," pamphlets would no longer be mailed to Southern addresses.[2]

This action marked the collapse of the pamphlet program against slavery, which proposed to win the South by appealing to the conscience of the slaveholders. The entire movement would soon have ended had a realistic program of reform been required for its existence. Its basis, however, was denunciation and not reform. "The question is not so much, how shall we abolish slavery, as how shall we best discharge our duty . . . to ourselves"—a sufficient reply to all but the most pragmatic inquirers.[3]

In the North, even where the doctrine of immediatism was actually understood, the pamphlets were likely to start controversy. With increasing frequency questioners asked: "How much emancipation does 'immediate' mean?" "After you have abolished negro slavery, what will you do with the negroes?" In time these questions were all merged into one: "What is your plan?"[4]

For a time the stock answer was that first the slave must be freed. "Whatever else may be substituted in place of slavery, whether apprenticeship, servitude for years, villeinage, copyhold or progressive . . . enfranchisement, is matter for separate consideration." Critics naturally replied that substitutes for slavery were not matters for separate consideration, but were bound up with the practicability of immediate emancipation. Some abolitionists were inclined to shift the responsibility to the Southern states: "We don't pretend to tell the states how. . . . They have got it to do. And as soon as they get ready to do it, I have no doubt there will be fifty ways proposed." But this was an equivocation, not an answer: it implied no plan at all. For even if abolitionists converted slaveholders to the principle of immediatism, the question would remain: ". . . has our apostle of freedom one word of . . . instruction to give them?" and the answer must be, "None is known—nothing is proposed."[5]

To some, the New York doctrine of immediatism, with its equivocal acceptance of a plan of forced labor, for a time provided an answer. The slave might be freed from slavery, and "all necessary restraint imposed without holding him as a chattel." But as the controversy developed, this doctrine soon became untenable. It involved simply "the substitution of one type of slavery for another," the condition of slavery under another name. If this was their plan, abolitionists were "*gradualists* in fact though immediatists in language, liable to all the absurdity of 'immediate emancipation—fifty years hence.' " And if abolitionists were really gradualists, why cling to immediatism? [6]

The tragedy of immediatist doctrine was that it led to an inescapable dilemma. Either immediate emancipation meant that it was the "duty of every slave-holder . . . to emancipate his slaves at once without regard to the peculiar circumstances of the case and without inquiring as to the probable consequences which may result from the act," or it meant the substitution of one form of slavery for another. The first was "nothing less than insanity," and the second was not immediate emancipation. William Jay naïvely stated the dilemma: "Abolitionists are constantly called on for a plan of emancipation. They have little encouragement to respond to the call. If they propose the simple plan of proclaiming by act of the State Legislatures the immediate and unqualified abolition of slavery, they are denounced as reckless incendiaries. If they intimate that abolition does not necessarily inhibit all compulsory labor . . . they are reproached with wishing to substitute one kind of slavery for another." What therefore could they say? There was no reply.[7]

The dilemma of immediatism did not by any means disable the pamphlet controversy. Protagonists of immediate emancipation still wrote on, defending every statement in the gospel of abolition with all the brave confidence of professional reformers. At each anniversary of the American Anti-Slavery Society, "with its bustle, its excitement and its enjoyment . . . clergymen and others, who visited the city to be present on these interesting occasions," enlarged on each success of the year just closed and painted every failure in the colors of a moral victory. What else was there to do? By 1836, the doctrine of immediatism had become so much a slogan of antislavery orthodoxy that it could not be abandoned without ruin to the cause. To admit that immediatism was simply "gradualism under another name" would identify the whole abolition doctrine with the futile gradualism professed by the entire North and much of the South, a gradualism "in favor of present slavery but opposed to future slavery . . . of abolishing slavery by not trying to abolish it . . . of abolition never begun and never finished." [8]

The alternative to immediatism gradually interpreted was immediatism literally interpreted, the radical British doctrine with which Garrison had begun and in which he persisted. However, most good abolitionists "knew of no such abolitionism as this, although they knew that many persons really supposed there was." They agreed with Benjamin Lundy that an immediatism which involved "turning the Slaves loose without any restriction whatever," regardless of consequences, was one which "no person of sane mind will advocate." But Garrison continued to advocate it throughout his career. His concern was not with programs but with principles: "Duty is ours and events are God's. . . . All you have to do is to set your slaves at liberty!" [9]

In the West, the Lane rebels had revived a third alternative to the doctrinal dilemma. Preaching abolitionism as a great revival in religious benevolence, they had argued from the first that slavery was not only an evil but a sin, and on that account ought immediately to be abandoned. This was the doctrine with which the national agitation had begun; but in the propaganda for the nation, at least, it was not widely emphasized, partly because many abolitionists contended that slavery was an evil and not a sin, and partly because the conversion of the South was hopeless so long as the sin of slavery was maintained. In the West, however, its efficacy for the conversion of the North was once again demonstrated. At one stroke it cut through the dilemma of immediatism; for as the South itself admitted, "if slavery be adjudged a sin, if it be condemned by the revealed word of God, then in Christendom it cannot continue to exist." It also freed the agitation from the need for a plan, since sins required no plan for their abandonment. [10]

The success of the Lane rebels raised champions for their doctrine. Prominent abolitionists, especially among the clergy, aware that "matters were tending to a disastrous result," urged the sinfulness of slavery upon the antislavery host. In many of the State conventions of 1836, there was acrimonious debate between proponents of "slavery an evil" and "slavery a sin"; and some time during the autumn of that year the doctrine of the Lane rebels became the leading tenet of the official gospel of abolitionism. [11]

Though the doctrine offered an escape from the dilemma of immediatism, it raised new problems of its own. The controversy shifted from the realities of policy and legislation to the wilderness of "the Bible argument." Learned inquiries into the legal status of Bible slavery displaced studies of the free Negro and his capacity for improvement. "The Bible argument" was interminable. Nothing and everything could be proved to the bewildered layman by properly used "proof-texts." On the other hand, in the North, it aroused an unexpected interest. Weld wrote an official summary of the Lane rebels' argument, but that was only the beginning of a new pamphlet controversy. Notable theologians, North and South, wrote extensively on the doctrine for the religious journals and for the press, and new dignity was added thereby to the antislavery cause. More important still, while "the Bible argument" came to no possible conclusion, at least it did not produce dilemmas of doctrine.[12]

While propaganda by the written word led to futility and disaster, propaganda by agents expanded into triumphant revival. Since the Lane rebels had been dismissed from the seminary "and God thrust them out, full of philanthropy and zeal, to awaken a slumbering nation," [13] they had become to the antislavery leaders the hope of the cause. Their agitation was subject to none of the dangers of pamphleteering. It did not depend for success on triumphs of controversy, but rather upon repetitions of doctrine, always to fresh hearers. In the hands of agents, doctrine became dogma; an unchanging immediatism was the basis of their gospel.

Their immediatism, however, was more than the Jesuitical "gradualism in a British cloak" of the New York doctrine. It was an immediatism of repentance from sin. By making the sin of slavery "the standard to which the Abolitionist is to rally," Weld's agents made the antislavery cause "identical with religion; and men and women are exhorted by all they esteem holy, by all the high and exciting obligations of duty to man and God, by all that can warm the heart and inflame the imagination, to join the pious work of purging the sin of slavery from the land." [14]

By 1836, the failure of pamphleteering and the sucess of revivalism had become so evident that the national society decided at its annual meeting in May to abandon the pamphlet campaign, to reduce printed propaganda to a minimum, and to employ all available resources in enlarging Weld's ardent host. The number of the expanded band was to be seventy, the number sent out in Bible times to convert the world to Christianity. Their name too was to be "the Seventy," and they were to be spread over the North to convert it to immediatism.[15]

Weld was appointed to select the new recruits, and Stanton and Whittier were employed to aid him. First they commissioned afresh the Lane rebels; and then, when the fall term began, they visited the colleges of the North, "winnowing the nation" for "men of the most unquenchable enthusiasm and the most obstinate constancy." In the main they chose students from the seminaries, though they also selected several experienced ministers. Only a few were not clergymen in standing or in preparation. They well maintained the level of the Lane rebels. "No body of men," wrote an editor, "has exhibited better specimens of intellectual and moral worth." [16]

By November, nearly the whole of the Seventy had been found. The Lane rebels at once began their campaign, but the new recruits were assembled at New York City for training and inspiration. Simeon Jocelyn, Charles Stuart, Stanton, the Tappans, and even Garrison addressed them, but Weld was "the central luminary around which they all revolved." Gaunt and battered, his ragged voice seeming "as if every sentence that was uttered sounded the knell of departing life," he never spoke with greater power. Day and night for two weeks, "scarcely allowing . . . time to eat," he filled the Seventy with facts and fervor. "All imaginable objections to our cause were ingeniously presented and as conclusively shown to be futile." The fire of pentecostal zeal came upon the new recruits, and they pledged their lives to immediatism. Observers were profoundly stirred. "Probably a more important convention has not been held since the beginning of our holy enterprise," wrote one. "Their deliberations . . . will result in consequences of the greatest moment to our country, to humanity and to religion." [17]

The price of their inspiration, however, was Weld's mighty voice. Shortly after the close of the convention he collapsed, burnt out. His "set purpose . . . as soon as the convention was over, to lead the battle in the Great West, especially in Ohio, Indiana, and Illinois," was abandoned; and for a time it was doubtful whether his health would ever be regained. However, a few weeks of rest restored a measure of his strength, and he returned to his labors with unabated zeal; but his voice was never entirely recovered. For years he could not speak at all to public assemblies; and when he finally did, it was not with his former power. But at abolition's focus in the New York office, where he now labored, his "sagacious, active, far-reaching mind" proved of even greater value than his voice had been; and abolitionists were moved "to praise God that his usefulness was turned into another channel." [18]

Before the agents' conference, the plan had been to send the Seventy into districts where no antislavery effort had yet been made, namely, southern New York, western Ohio, Kentucky, and the "Great West," Michigan, Indiana, and Illinois.[19] But after Weld's collapse the plan was changed. It may have been that without Weld's leadership the boldness for such an enterprise was lacking. It is also probable that requests for the services of the Seventy by the older State auxiliaries were too insistent to be denied. Moreover, conservatives on the New York Committee may well have argued that the extension of the movement had gone far enough, and the time had come to draw the areas already canvassed into a functioning organization. In any event, it was decided to assign the bulk of the Seventy to areas within the State auxiliaries.

With this decision the extension of the antislavery movement largely ceased. The agitation became intensive rather than extensive in character, advancing through the growth of local societies rather than through the conquest of new communities. But even this agitation the Seventy found hazardous enough to try their devotion. They lived again the troubles and the triumphs of the ardent host. "Many pens and tongues have been sharpened against them," wrote Timothy Merritt. "They have been mobbed and lynched. They have been branded in the forehead and in the back as 'traitors, madmen, incendiaries, and fanatics.' We pray God that none of these things may move them to anger or retaliation; and we trust that in due time they will reap if they faint not." [20]

The sending out of the Seventy was followed by a reorganization of the American Anti-Slavery Society. Its extraordinary growth, in 1835 and 1836, had already put a heavy burden on the New York Committee, and the mass of detail involved in maintaining the Seventy and in following up their achievements added much more to the burden. The campaign for petitioning Congress was also developing unexpected volume and importance. It is not impossible, too, that the increasing embarrassment of Arthur Tappan's business affairs limited the time that he could give to the cause. Whatever the deciding factors, the New York Committee reorganized the society and put a staff of professional executives in charge.

To head the administration, the committee selected their premier example of the reformed slaveholder, Weld's convert, James G. Birney. The Lane rebel, H. B. Stanton, was appointed secretary in charge of finances, and Weld himself enlisted after his strength was regained. Joshua Leavitt abandoned the *New York Evangelist* and took over the *Emancipator,* and Elizur Wright, of course, retained his post. During the ensuing years, others came and went on the executive staff, the poet Whittier, and Amos A. Phelps from Boston; but the four, Birney, Leavitt, Stanton, and Weld, remained to the end.[21]

The conjunction of so many elements of the Great Revival in the antislavery agitation was more than coincidence. The personalities— the Tappans, who had been the financial angels of the Great Revival; Joshua Leavitt, who had been its editor; Weld and Stanton, who were its evangelists; and Birney and Wright, Weld's converts—were identified too closely and too intimately with the Great Revival and its sequels to make their antislavery association a chance regrouping. Even more significant was the society's new program and its greatest achievement, the sending of the Seventy; for the teacher of the Seventy was Weld; their method was the evangelism of the Great Revival; their doctrine was a doctrine of sin; and their program was to convert congregations of the North to the duty of testimony against the slaveholders of the South. In leadership, in method, and in objective, the Great Revival and the American Anti-Slavery Society now were one. It is not too much to say that for the moment the antislavery agitation as a whole was what it had long been in larger part, an aspect of the Great Revival in benevolent reform.

For two crucial years the Seventy labored among the older auxiliaries, spreading the gospel of immediatism between the centers already organized, renewing the fervor of the faithful, and producing everywhere they went "a great concussion in the earth and heavens, portentous, we trust, to their passing away." In due time they reaped a noble harvest, but only occasionally did the newspaper public mark their progress. For Weld, now back in the New York office, advised that "everything in the shape of agents, papers &c be poured into the *country,*—the country, the villages and the smaller cities of the interior." He directed the agents to "let the great cities alone. They must be burned down by back fires. The springs to touch in order to win them lie *in the country.*" With statesmanlike acuteness Weld perceived that the cities of his day were trading centers for a rural nation, dependent on the countryside for their support. Opinion in the cities, he believed, was predisposed to echo the rural mind. To the rural communities the Seventy were accordingly assigned, and there they toiled to build county and township organizations, district by district, away from the cities and the public press.[22]

Their fields of labor were subject to constant scrutiny. They were often reassigned to different fields "according to their various adaptations . . . as the ever varying exigencies of the cause demand, as a general will dispatch batches of troops to different parts as the battle waxes or wanes." One who had been a leader in the antimasonic warfare was shifted from a field where many free-masons resided; a former colonization society agent was moved to a locality which was a colonization stronghold; a famous debater was shifted to a district where the former agent had been worsted in debate. Agents whose health could not sustain the exigencies of lecturing in the field were replaced, and others whose degree of success did not warrant their support were dismissed.[23]

A corps of workers was finally secured whose capacity and devotion were unsurpassed. Their labors are recorded nowhere in history; they worked in the rural counties, unnoticed and unknown. Despite their anonymity, however, they so inspired the local organizations in the larger State auxiliaries that, by the end of 1837, a network of communities, fired with the spirit of the Great Revival itself, was ready at hand to maintain the petition struggle in Congress which was already gathering way.

CHAPTER XI

THE RIGHT OF PETITION

1836

In the spirit of the old antislavery tradition, the constitution which the American Anti-Slavery Society framed, in 1833, pledged abolitionists "to influence Congress to . . . abolish slavery . . . in the District of Columbia." Influencing Congress meant sending petitions to Congress, a measure which the older antislavery societies, before 1830, had made their chief concern. But "their voice," wrote Whittier, "was too faint to be heard amidst the din of party warfare, and the petitions too few and feeble to command attention" until 1828. In that year a quickening antislavery sentiment greatly increased the number of petitions, especially for the abolition of slavery in the District of Columbia; and in 1828–1829 a nation-wide movement to petition Congress on the subject was so successful that the House of Representatives was forced to act. A committee reported that emancipation in the District was inexpedient, and after an acrimonious debate, the report was adopted. To the rising antislavery sentiment throughout the North, however, this defeat was merely technical. Slavery in the District was an inconsiderable part of slavery in the nation, and its abolition had only a symbolic value. Its existence had a greater practical value, for so long as it remained, petitions for its abolition were in order, and petitions raised debate. The lesson of 1828 was clear. Thenceforth a means of agitation was available to which the nation would listen. Slavery in the District was the Achilles' heel of the entire institution.[1]

The decade of the 'thirties was the golden age of Congress. In the Senate, Clay, Webster, and Calhoun were in their gigantic prime. In the House, John Quincy Adams, "Old Man Eloquent," was bringing his long life of public service to its glorious climax. Among the representatives were three future presidents, Pierce, Polk, and Fillmore, besides a group of orators as brilliant as any in our history. These men were made greater by their time. Never before or since has the floor of Congress been so much the rostrum of the nation; never have party issues—nullification, the tariff, internal improvements, and the bank—been more living; never did party spirit burn so high. To the nation, news of Congress was the most vital of the day. Whittier's insistence on petitions as "the first measure of our cause" was sound statesmanship; for if petitions should provoke a discussion of slavery on the floor of Congress, the whole nation would give ear. Agitation could find no better forum.

It was not until 1835, however, that petitions again reached Congress in sufficient volume to provoke discussion; but with the beginning of 1836 they headlined the news. It was a presidential year, and Calhoun, developing his theme of Southern sectionalism on the floor of the Senate, saw in the petitions an opportunity to exploit them for his ends. They represented, he said, a purpose novel and sinister. "They do not come as heretofore, singly and far apart, from the quiet routine of the Society of Friends or the obscure vanity of some philanthropic club, but they are sent to us in vast numbers from soured and agitated communities." [2] They were the instruments, he charged, of a Northern conspiracy to attack the peculiar institutions of the South, and he moved against their reception. The motion provoked an intermittent debate which continued for weeks. Calhoun lost his motion, but the debate had a greater propaganda value than his defeat. The abolitionists were highly edified. "Slaveholders," wrote an editor, "are prime agitators."

It was in the House, however, that the petitions furnished abolition's golden opportunity. There Calhoun's motion not to receive antislavery petitions was echoed by his henchmen, and after a recurring debate of weeks, "worth a thousand dollars to the cause," the whole question of reception, along with the accumulating petitions, was referred to a special committee, which recommended that "all petitions relating . . . to the subject of slavery or the abolition of slavery, shall, without being either printed or referred, be laid upon the table, and . . . no further action whatever shall be had thereon." When the vote was taken, John Quincy Adams rose, and instead of voting, pronounced the measure "a direct violation of the Constitution of the United States, the rules of this House, and the rights of my constituents," while Speaker and members vociferated, "Order! Order!"

This was the famous Pinckney gag. In various forms it was re-

peated session by session until 1840, when it was made a standing rule
of the House. Abolitionists naturally charged that petitions which
were denied a hearing by rule were not petitions; and thereby they
secured their first real issue, a chance to identify abolitionism with
the constitutional right of petition.

Before the passage of the gag rule, Northern opinion had been
overwhelmingly unfavorable to the abolitionists. Convinced that their
doctrine was literal immediatism and that Garrison was their chief,
most of the thinking public outside the circle of the Lane rebels'
labors had no basis for any other conclusion. Now, however, the
movement stood for something more than Garrisonism and immediatism. Thousands felt that "if the issue of the question is to be . . .
'Slavery or the right of petition,' they have but one course to pursue,
however unpleasant it may be." [3] Many of these joined the American
Anti-Slavery Society, and many more, "inimical to the object of the
petitioners," furthered the petition campaigns, "preferring that the
object of the petitioners should be attained rather than that the sanctuary of all our rights should be violated." [4]

As to the manner in which the sanctuary of their rights had been
violated, abolitionists were by no means agreed. To Weld, official
spokesman, it was a clear case: "the right of petition ravished and
trampled by its constitutional guardians, and insult and defiance
hurled in the faces of the sovereign people"; but many others considered the denial rather virtual than explicit. Alvan Stewart, a lawyer by profession and the legalist of the New York State Society,
believed that the violation of the sanctuary began with the Patton
gag, which was passed the following year, on December twenty-first,
"the longest night in the darkest year of American liberty." He persuaded the State society to this view, but most of the county societies
resolved that even the Patton gag was only a "virtual" violation.[5]

The Atherton gag of 1839 was regarded merely as a reënactment
of the Patton resolution; but, in 1840, when the gag was made a standing rule of the House—with the addition of Calhoun's previous proposal that antislavery petitions be not even received—many conservatives conceded that Congress had at last "formally denied" the
right. As late as 1842, however, an antislavery mass meeting in New
York resolved that even the standing rule was no more than a "virtual crushing of the right of petition," and not a formal denial.[6]

The case was not simple. The Constitution of the United States provided that "Congress shall make no law . . . abridging . . . the right of the people . . . to petition the government for a redress of grievances." But the Constitution also provided that "each House may determine the rules of its proceedings." It was clear that somewhere in the progress of a petition through the House, the rights of the petitioners ceased and the rights of Congress began. Where in the progress did the gag rule come? Did it infringe upon the rights of the petitioners, or was it a legitimate exercise of Congressional right?

The right of petition, all agreed, included the right of the people to frame and entrust petitions to their representatives. It also included the procedure by which they were presented to Congress. By a rule of the House, members were required to present petitions by title: they rose and stated briefly the subject of the petitions, and by custom added such details as the place from which they came, and the number of signatures. This was the process of presenting petitions. Any rule hindering the progress of abolition petitions up to this point would admittedly be in direct violation of the Constitution.

After the petitions were presented the question was, must they be received? Here arose the first debate on the right of petition. Did "the mere fact of presenting a petition impose the obligation of receiving it?" Before 1840, majorities in both houses voted that it did. In vain Calhoun argued that precedent, both in the British parliament and in Congress, was against them, that the highest authority was against them, that even their own rules of procedure were against them. Logic, precedent, authority, and rules may have been with Calhoun, but expediency was not. Franklin Pierce pointed out that refusal to receive abolition petitions "might be construed into a denial of the right of petition," and thus enable the abolitionists to "make up a false issue before the country." He advised his colleagues to yield the point of reception in the interests of peace, and they did so. "The right of petition," said James Buchanan, "was thus solemnly recognized." [7]

After the petitions were received, they were before Congress for disposal. At the pleasure of the members they could be read, printed, discussed, referred to a committee, laid on the table, rejected, or granted. Did the right of petition extend to the procedure of disposal? There were various opinions. "Some gentlemen think they should be received and laid on the table; and some think they should be referred to a committee with instructions to receive and report on them. Then

there were other gentlemen who were of the opinion that the petitions should be heard at the bar of the House." [8] Amid the confusion
of opinions a majority in the House finally determined upon the gag
rule, by which abolition petitions were received and then automatically
laid on the table.

The Senate, after long debate, developed a smoother procedure.
When an abolition petition was presented, the chairman assumed
that the question of its reception was raised and some member moved
to lay the question on the table. "Their craftiness," wrote an abolition editor, "rendered the violation of our rights . . . more complicated than it was in the House." Abolitionists contended nevertheless
that "there *was* a violation of the right of petition." "But," asked
James Buchanan, "with what justice? . . . Their prayer . . . was
considered, discussed and rejected. . . . After these solemn proceedings had taken place, were the Senate bound, whenever a new
petition of a similar character was presented, again and again, on
each succeeding day, to discuss and decide" the subject once more?
Turning from the Senate, where they "should have had to prove in
the first place that there was a violation of the right," abolitionists
concentrated their whole petition campaign upon the House, exploiting the gag rule as a self-evident denial of the right of petition.[9]

The situation that prompted the first gag rule, in May, 1836, was
not simply hostility to the prayer of the petitioners. Even without
the antislavery petitions to clog its schedule, the House was in desperate straits. Since 1830, its numbers, and even more its business,
had greatly increased, but no provision had been made to care for
the added load. Its rules were antiquated, and its oratory was interminable; but such checks on the flow of speech as there were, members fiercely resented. The debate-closing motion—the previous question—Adams declared positively unconstitutional; and Patton is
reported to have wept when, after proposing his gag rule, for the first
time in his life he felt obliged to move the previous question. Innovations, such as an hour rule for debate, were opposed by a large
majority, and on even the most pressing measure no vote was taken
until all had been said. Into this congestion the abolitionists poured
their petitions.[10]

On petition days the call for petitions was by States, beginning
with Maine and proceeding geographically through the Union. This
put the antislavery stronghold in a favored place. From Vermont to

Ohio progress ceased while members from those States reduced the bundles from their antislavery constituents. Time, however, went on; petition day passed, and members from below the antislavery belt, their hands filled with petitions, were often left uncalled. For a time they cared for their more pressing petitions by persuading friends from States first called to present them; but the practice grew to such proportions that the Speaker was forced to forbid it.[11] Temporary relief was secured by suspending the rules and beginning with Wisconsin instead of Maine, and then the call was made to begin with Maine and Wisconsin on alternate days; but these expedients only put off the evil day when the offending States were called. Other more desperate devices were proposed, namely, the devotion of a part only of each petition period to abolition petitions, and the shortening of the petition period itself; but these the House very properly refused to approve.

Not only the numbers of the petitions but also their subject robbed the schedule. There was an evil magic in slavery's very name, and "tid-bit debates" were incessant. Throughout the struggle the Speaker usually did what he could to limit discussion, but a time came in nearly every session when he "was compelled to bow his head to the howling hurricane. . . . Every man seemed to grow into vast, pyramidal altitude in his own mind, and speak he must or the country would be ruined."

It was not the immediate flood, however, but the prospective deluge of abolition petitions that the gag rules had in view. Petition floods were no new thing. The National Bank, the campaign to stop the Sunday mails, Georgia and the Cherokees, the tariff, and the currency question had all produced their inundations, some spontaneous and some inspired. But these floods had their periods; the petitioners wanted either a high tariff or a low, either a charter for the Bank or its denial. A report was made or a bill was passed or lost, and the flood receded. But no such action dried up the antislavery petitions; every resolution denying their prayer increased their volume but the more. To meet this situation, already intolerable and steadily growing worse, the successive gag rules, therefore, not only denied the petitioners' prayer—a measure which would have ended petitions on any other subject—but in effect also warned the petitioners themselves that additional petitions on the same subject would do no good; they would be neither read, printed nor referred.

At the beginning of almost every session of Congress after the
first gag rule was passed, resolutions were offered proposing some
form of gag; but with perennial optimism they were always voted
down. Weeks of raging debate "sprung" by the petitions would then
ensue, proving session by session that the House could not do business without self-protection. Then, and not until then, the House
would resolve once more to reject the prayer of the petitions already
presented,[12] and to gag those yet to come. In defense of the gags it
was urged that this procedure fully secured their rights to the petitioners. During the weeks of debate, their prayer was considered and
discussed, and then by resolution rejected. What more could any petition secure? The gag rules simply provided that petitions for the
same object received thereafter were to be tabled without debate. They
would thus be "presented like any other petitions; from the statement
of their contents it is seen that they relate to subjects which have
been fully considered by the House, and on which a majority of the
House have definitely formed an opinion . . . and they are at once
laid upon the table . . . from which they can be lifted at the pleasure
of the House." [13] Except insofar as the gags assumed for each petition that the tabling motion had been made, this practice was no novelty. Every flood of petitions for some popular cause had been so di-
verted in the past. The gag rules simply expedited that procedure
"without in any wise infracting the legitimate limits of the right of
petition, the freedom of debate or the constitutional rights of the
members of this body." [14]

This was the logic which made thoughtful abolitionists regard the
gags as only a "virtual" and not an actual denial of the right of petition. Fortunately for the antislavery cause, the logic was a little too
involved for the average understanding, and the Northern public
never thought it through. To them it was enough that by gagging in
advance all petitions upon slavery, the House presumed to dictate to
the North "the subjects upon which the people may or may not petition." The House had an admitted right to gag petitions one by one
as they were presented; but to gag them by "prospective action"
through a general rule was a denial of right so clear to the average
man that argument was needless. In the House, however, this point
against the gags was seldom urged even by the most militant champions of petitions; for, said a member, "if we have a right thus to
dispose of single petitions, have we not an equal right, by rule, to

dispose of a class of petitions all relating to the same subject in the same manner?" [15]

The conclusive argument for the gag rules, however, was not their constitutionality but their necessity. Without the gags the House was helpless. Members pointed out that while they had no right to bring up measures once rejected by the House, petitions were restrained by no such rule. No matter how recently the House had taken adverse action on their prayer, with every new petition the House must once more hear and once more act. The case for the right of petition implied, therefore, "a regular, recurring reconsideration" of the object of the petitions as each one was presented. "Here then the right of the House to regulate its own proceedings is annulled by the right of petition"; for if each petition must be heard, then the House could do nothing but hear petitions. The question of disposal would "be renewed again and again. . . . Thousands of petitions relating to the same object must be read"; for no restriction governed either the length or the number of petitions presented. "The whole time of the House and the whole business of the nation may be suspended by the discussion or the decision of them in detail, in settling, one by one, memorials without number." [16]

It is not easy to see what else besides the gags could have protected Congress. The usual procedure, tabling the petitions by separate motions, had been so abused that the gags had displaced it. The Senate's procedure broke down in the House, and reference to committees had been a failure. Opponents of the gags continued to urge one or the other of these devices on the House, promising on their behalf an early end to agitation and a subsidence of the petition flood. But the House well knew that whatever was done, petitions would continue; and any plan which assumed that they would not, was bound to be a failure. [17]

It is a singular fact that during the whole course of the struggle no one referred to the experience of the British parliament with antislavery petitions a few years before. The petition deluge in that country began to embarrass the parliamentary schedule as early as 1830; and after three years of experiment a procedure was devised for their disposal which was so successful that it continues to this day. It was based on the parliamentary practice of grouping petitions into two classes: private petitions, which prayed for some benefit peculiar to the petitioners; and public petitions, which prayed for some public action in which the petitioners had no individual concern. Under the new procedure, private petitions were to be presented by members of parliament as before; but all public petitions—which included antislavery petitions—must be submitted to a select committee, which classified them and at intervals reported to parliament their substance, their number, and the number of their signatures. This device enabled parliament to treat antislavery petitions as propaganda for a cause rather than as prayers for the relief of the petitioners themselves, and its success was due to that distinction. Its adoption, however, depended upon a classification of petitions not yet developed by Congress. In the House every petition was still regarded as a private petition, whose right to separate consideration was therefore sacred.[18]

Indeed, the whole case for the right of petition was based upon the assumption that all antislavery petitions were private, though their substance was repeated a hundred thousand times—and not only their substance. After the petition campaign was well begun, not one abolition petition in a hundred was more than a list of signatures pasted to a printed form run off literally by the million on the antislavery press. Still each one of this multitude, it was contended, merited reading and disposal for itself alone.[19]

All of these considerations closely limited whatever rule of disposal the House could devise. The rule must treat all petitions as private petitions with right to separate presentation; before 1840, at least, it must provide reception for each petition; and it must protect the legislative program of the House majority. Except for the gag rules, no device was proposed which would do all this and nothing more.

It was not only the case for the right of petition that displayed this peculiar legalism. The substance of the petitions themselves had few friends among their champions. When the debate began, only one member of the Senate, Thomas Morris of Ohio—a "lone and humble individual . . . opposed by the very lions of debate"—stood for abolition in the District of Columbia; on the same subject in the House, William Slade of Vermont was in a "glorious minority of one." Whether petitions were received or rejected, heard or tabled, slavery in the District would remain; and Millard Fillmore impatiently termed the whole question "a mere abstraction." [20]

As the years went on, petitions multiplied their prayers. They demanded the abolition of the slave-trade between the States and of slavery in the territories; they prayed that Arkansas and Florida be denied admission to the Union as slave States; and they developed ingenuity in petitioning for objects not directly covered by the gags. But their prayers were as far as ever from being granted, and no member who presented them expected favorable legislation on their objects. Year after year, however, they continued to present them, and session by session they contended for their rights against the gags. Nothing in the stakes of victory explained their persistence. "Was the miserable farce of receiving these petitions and then immediately rejecting them a thing worth contending for?" asked a partisan of the gag. "Surely not!" [21] Deeper causes moved the House. Behind the windy, unreal issues of constitutional abstractions were the living issues of party malevolence and sectional conflict.

In 1835, when the struggle began, Andrew Jackson was President, and the Democrats controlled the House. Between them and the minority Whigs there raged intense partisan warfare. The Whig minority "was tyrannized over, and they were naturally in a refractory, restless and perturbed condition, and if they could not be heard orderly they would do so disorderly." To raise disorder, no better weapon than abolition petitions could have been devised. Northern Whigs presented them as an obligation to their constituents and, on the same ground, waged war for their hearing. To the charge of obstruction, they replied that they were fighting for the constitutional right of petition; and however weak their claim might be, there was sufficient public sentiment in the North to support them. Southern Whigs were not so consistently partisan. A "little band of loyal Whigs" fought the gags beside their Northern colleagues, but the rest of the Southern Whigs merged with the Democrats. The latter were mostly for a quick ending to the obstruction and an early gag; but abolition petitions were irritating to the South, and Southern Democrats often felt constrained by the sentiments of their constituents to add their words to the disorder. Still, the Southern champion in the contest was a Virginia Whig, Henry A. Wise, a brilliant but erratic obstructionist; and between his efforts and those of the arch-obstructionist, John Quincy Adams, the House was kept in an uproar session after session for weeks at a time.[22]

Considered as a party device, therefore, the petition campaign was one of obstruction. The Whig case for the right of petition, with its fictitious issue that the House must receive and discuss petitions it had "predetermined to reject," and its corollary, that petitions had rights superior to the necessities of legislation, was typical obstructionist doctrine. The mere mass of the Whigs' petitions (the number presented by Democratic members was negligible) was enough to clog the wheels of legislation. The discussions of slavery constantly "sprung" by petitions were even more time-consuming, and the debate for the right of petition was interminable. Except for the panic session of 1837, when petitions were withheld by common consent, the controversy hampered every session of Congress from the beginning of the struggle to the end of the decade. Thus from the angle of House politics the gag rules were passed to prevent obstruction by the opposition. Their movers, Henry C. Pinckney, John M. Patton, and Charles G. Atherton, were Democrats; and their purpose, to use Adams' pungent phrase, was that "the House should not act the tragedy of *Agitation,* but the pantomime of *Hush,*" in order that the Democratic majority might get the business of the nation done.[23]

In 1840, the Whigs elected the President and captured the House. Petitions having served their turn, the Whigs found that the right of petition was not so mandatory over the House business as it had seemed before. Even the antislavery champions for the time were not so sure. William Slade admitted—temporarily—that "this House, as well as every other legislative body, may entertain the question of reception," and John Quincy Adams himself for the moment did "not deny the right of the House to refuse to receive a petition when it is first presented." The House then passed a gag which not only shelved abolition petitions but denied their reception, and the rule was made a standing rule of the House. At the first session of the next Congress (the twenty-seventh) the Whigs went even further. By a strict party vote they passed a rule denying reception, not only to abolition petitions, but to all other petitions that did not refer to the party program for the session. But these Whig inconsistencies came too late to affect the issue. In the North the petition campaign was in full swing, battle lines had long been drawn, and the right of petition, both among its champions in the House and among the abolitionists in the North, was no longer an argument but a creed. It was now a sectional as well as a party issue, dividing its champions by Mason and Dixon's line.[24]

Throughout the North abolitionists continued to maintain that either actually or "virtually," their constitutional right of petition had been denied, and as a whole the North believed them. Their cherished sense of oppression, however, was based on the denial of a hearing rather than upon the denial of a right. Anti-Slavery petitions were true public petitions, framed for agitation, not for redress of grievances. "The gag rule," wrote an editor, did not "prevent our writing, signing, and sending petitions to Congress, but it prevents their being *heard* when they get there." For antislavery purposes such a petition "is no more a petition than the blank paper would be on which it is written." What abolitionists demanded was "the right of being *listened* to by their own national rulers," not the consideration of their prayers. As prayers the petitions were worthless; emancipation by petition was a hopeless cause, and abolitionists before long knew it. But as instruments of agitation, petitions were priceless. Throughout the struggle "no other human instrumentality" had so "compelled the country to consider and discuss the great question now at issue between Freedom and Slavery." Indeed, the Southern leaders claimed that the whole case for the right of petition was "a false issue" behind which abolitionists sought to introduce in Congress "an offensive discussion of the tenure upon which we hold our slaves under a pretense of petitions for redress of grievances." [25]

The right of petition may have been a false issue, but abolitionists convinced the North that it was a true one. To the newspaper public their case was clear because it was so simple. The House rule, refusing to hear petitions on slavery even before they were presented—what could it be but a denial of the right of petition? Ignoring the explanations of the experts—ignoring even the doubts of abolitionists—the greater part of the newspaper public honored the abolitionists while they opposed them, as champions of the rights of the free as well as of the slaves.

In this public error there was an ironic justice. The public had erred in their understanding of immediatist doctrine, and that error formed an insuperable obstacle to antislavery success in the North. Now the public erred in their understanding of the right of petition, and on that error the antislavery forces built an agitation which swept the nation. The scales were evened and more than evened for the abolition cause.

CHAPTER XII

PETITION STRATEGY

1837

Amid the cross-currents of factional disputes and constitutional claims for petitions, the sectional conflict in the House gathered momentum year by year. At the beginning of the struggle most of the Southern members argued that the House should not receive abolition petitions. Coming from communities already inflamed against abolitionism, they spoke for their constituents; but many, themselves slaveholders, had a personal as well as a political interest in their cause. "It exacts some patience in a Southern man," said Preston, "to sit here and listen day after day to enumerations of the demoralizing effects of his household arrangements *considered in the abstract*—to hear his condition of life lamented over" by Northern abolitionists.[1] But this union of personal and political interest in the fight against petitions prejudiced their case; for it was clearly not the number of petitions but their substance that roused the South. Behind their case against reception grew the fixed resolve that no stricture on slavery should have a hearing in the House, either in petitions or in debates; and to this end the gag rules were only instruments.

Already a minority interests in the House, Southern members determined to meet the antislavery agitation at the threshold: "If we yield one inch we are gone!"[2] Aggression, they decided, was their best defense, and on every subject involving slavery they took the highest ground. The effect of this was to identify the gag rules with their program of aggressive defense, and thereby to give the rules a meaning in the struggle which at first they did not deserve. As the fury of the contest grew, however, they ceased to be simply an instrument of the majority, and became a part of the challenging policy of the South, the basis of the system of coercive silence by which the Southern leaders "enslaved the North" on the subject of slavery.

On the Northern side of the House there was no such community of feeling toward the gags. Northern Democrats supported them, but even among the Whigs opposition to them was more apparent than real. More than one member defended the right of petition rather from expediency than from conviction, "particularly if he was pretty hard run in his district . . . and more especially if he had been making a loud oratory for the right of petition as a great and fundamental doctrine of the constitution." In the North the right of petition was cheap ammunition. No Northern interest was involved, and many members, especially from northern Ohio, New York, and southern New England, came to Congress pledged in advance to oppose the gags. Other members, when the legislatures of their States began sending resolutions to Congress protesting against the gags, were constrained to speak for their State, whatever their personal convictions. In consequence the whole debate on the Northern side took a forced, *ex parte* course, unusual even in Congress. "No man believes here," said an indignant Southerner, "that the right of petition is or ever has been in danger by the action of this House"; and many Northern members merited his rebuke, despite their public creed.[3]

The charge, however, was not always true. There were some members, particularly from the antislavery strongholds, who firmly believed that the gag rules violated the right of petition. Most of them were antislavery Whigs, and during the long campaign of obstruction, the right of petition became to them a weapon of sectional warfare in which they had a partisan faith. They were true sectionalists: on the slavery issue they would not be gagged. From the first, William Slade of Vermont conscientiously fought the gags, and in later years Joshua Giddings of Ohio, Seth M. Gates of New York, and a handful more joined him in the struggle. All were abolitionists; most of them were from districts into which Theodore Weld had carried the antislavery revival; and three of them at least—Giddings, Gates, and Andrews—were Weld's own converts. But the genius of their cause was John Quincy Adams.

One petition day in January, 1837, a day or two after the Pinckney gag had been renewed, Adams rose from his seat in the House and addressed the Speaker, James K. Polk. " 'Sir,' he said, 'my old petition, presented the other day, being presented before this rule was adopted, does not come under this rule.' 'But it does,' said Mr. Speaker Polk." Adams appealed to the House, which sustained the Speaker. "The old gentleman surveyed his file of petitions;—he turned an eye upon the House; he gave a dreary look up to the Speaker's chair . . . 'Give me back my old petition then,' he said. The Speaker sent the boy with it. He then re-presented it again and made a statement of its contents, and reiterated that the petitioners avowed they would present this petition every year. The House heard him quite quietly. The old gentleman then branched off. He got upon the abolition principle. 'Order, *order*, ORDER,' screamed a hundred voices from every part of the House. Not at all disconcerted, Mr. A. sent up this petition and drew forth another from his prodigious file . . . He stated the contents. 'It was for Liberty'; the House budged a little, 'it was for the human race'; the House budged more; 'it was to relieve the wrongs of the African'—and 'order, *order*, ORDER,' stopped him there." During the remainder of the morning hour and until three o'clock that afternoon [4] Adams continued to present petitions, "dodging points of order, creeping through this rule and skipping over that . . . all the while flourishing away in tit-bit speeches, which were so short and so quickly said that, though they were out of order, nobody could call him to order; and when they did, he would say, 'My speech is done.'

"At last he came to a petition from certain Lutheran ministers in New York, praying that Congress would frame laws to carry out the principles of the Declaration of Independence in the District of Columbia, 'This says nothing of slaves,' said Mr. Adams. . . . 'It does not come within the rule.' 'But it does, though,' said Mr. Speaker Polk," and Adams appealed to the House. The Speaker put the question: whether or not "such a memorial comes within the rule. 'But what is the memorial?' asked Mr. A. 'You have not read it. The House has not seen it.' . . . He compelled the Speaker to read the petition so that the House might know on what they were to vote. And there he sat, half rabid and half laughing. . . . He had had his way even with the opposition of two hundred to one!" [5]

This was Adams in action. His plan was to present abolition petitions in such numbers and "with comments so marked and aggravating" as to make the gag rule ridiculous and excite champions of the Southern cause to war. Enjoined by the rule from reading the petitions themselves, he "wantonly tortured the feelings of [the Southern members] by the minuteness with which he . . . dwelt upon the contents of offensive petitions and the names and character of those who signed them." It did no good to hurry him, for "if any impatience is manifested he speaks still more deliberately and stands immove-

able as a pillar until he has completed his task"; while attempts to in-
terrupt his course usually ended in disorder. Possessed of few of what
were deemed in his time the necessary elements of oratory, Adams'
stinging tongue was master of every tone of passion, from vindictive spite to the noblest heights of feeling—"today growling and
sneering at the House . . . and anon . . . lashing the members into
the wildest state of enthusiasm by his indignant and emphatic eloquence." No man however placid could sit unmoved under the lash
of his vituperation, and none of his antagonists had the skill or the
hardihood to balk him in his course against the gags. Whether rated
as only "a mischievous bad old man," as Calhoun called him, or
"fierce as ten furies, terrible as hell," as he seemed to Andrew Johnson, Adams was the nemesis of the Southern conspiracy of silence,
the bane of the slavery cause.[6]

In his public utterances Adams grounded his agitation directly
upon the right of petition. Before the Pinckney gag was passed, he
had "deprecated all discussion of slavery and its abolition in the
House," and on every occasion he professed his opposition to the
abolition of slavery in the District of Columbia. He contended, therefore, that the object of his efforts was to secure the rights of the
abolition petitions and not their substance. "It is the right of the petitioner and the duty of the House," he said, "that when a petition is presented to it the House should inform itself upon what that petition
contains, should then consider and then answer it. . . . When you
assume that the right of petition does not give that right . . . decent
language will not express what you do." With passionate consistency
he presented his "prodigious file" one by one, for he "felt it due to
the petitioners generally to present them singly," however numerous
or however similar their substance. Every petition that came to his
hands he presented to the House—prayers for his own expulsion, for
aid to crack-brained inventions, for the annexation of Canada and
the protection of maniacs from their delusions. When objections were
raised against receiving such petitions, he replied that in his judgment "the right of petition was co-extensive with the liberty of
speech." "That," Underwood of Kentucky said with scorn, "was
the *ne plus ultra* of the right of petition." [7]

Doctrine such as this was dogma to support his war against the
gags, and not Adams' real position. A statesman as well as a warrior,
he recognized in practice the right of the legislative program to pro-

tection; he contended only that protection should be extended to the rights of the petitioners as well. At crucial moments he admitted that a general rule for the disposal of petitions—"a decision in advance of the disposition to be made"—was within the power of the House, provided that the disposition included a decision on the petitioners' prayer. Indeed, he once proposed a general rule of his own, that all petitions not acceptable to a majority of the House be rejected without reading or discussion. Under the press of legislation in the short session of the twenty-seventh Congress he went even further; he procured the passage of the famous "Adams gag"—infamous to abolitionists—by which all petitions were to be deposited directly with the Speaker, to be disposed of according to the Speaker's judgment.[8]

For these measures Adams can be charged with no more inconsistency than was inseparable from his position. In the petition struggle he waged war for an abstract right, the claims of which were, therefore, absolute; but in practical affairs he conformed those claims without hypocrisy to the exigencies of events, as any statesman would. His real inconsistency was a deliberate one, not of belief but of purpose; for Adams was a sectionalist, the most zealous of them all, and his fight for the right of petition cloaked a determination to further the antislavery cause by agitating the forbidden subject on the floor of the House "in every mode his ingenuity could devise." [9]

When Adams first opposed the gag, in 1836, he was careful to base his objections on constitutional grounds; but even thus early in the contest his protest was really an antislavery gesture. During the debate which preceded the gag, he had condemned "the new pretensions of the slave representation in Congress of a right to refuse to receive petitions"; but he confided to a friend: "I did not and could not speak a tenth part of my mind. . . . I did not, for example, start the question whether by the law of God and of nature men can hold property in man. . . . Had I spoken my mind . . . the sturdiest of the abolitionists would have disavowed the sentiments of their champion." Convinced that the gag rules were merely symptoms of a "deadly disease, seated in the marrow of our bones—and that deadly disease . . . Slavery," he determined to devote the remnant of his life to antislavery agitation in the House. It was a momentous decision for a man nearly seventy years old to make. Indeed, he wrote in his diary, "were there in the House one member capable of taking the lead in this cause of universal emancipation, which is moving onward in the world and in this country, I would withdraw from the contest, which will rage with increasing fury as it draws to its crisis, but for the management of which my age, infirmities and approaching end totally disqualify me. There is no such man in the House." [10]

Despite his self-depreciation, Adams of all men in his day—of all statesmen in our history—was best fitted to lead the antislavery cause in Congress. To qualities of astuteness, obstinate will, and upright devotion to the public good—the traits of his family line—was joined a fame in public service matched by few statesmen of his time. "Ancient, venerable, time honored . . . the coeval of the Constitution, its illustrator and guardian . . . the glory of three ages," Adams was a legend of public honor. After his defeat for a second term as President, his humble acceptance of a place in the lower House had filled the nation with "the moral grandeur of the spectacle. . . . Where but in our own free land could such an event take place?" it was asked, as "the venerable Ex-President . . . came forward, a true republican, to devote his last days like his first to the service of his country." But all of that prestige Adams needed for his struggle in the House. Against a majority so hostile to the agitation that it would censure Giddings on a pretext, contemptuously denying him the right to speak in his own defense, hardly Adams was safe; and only his great name saved him from a like humiliation when he was put on trial.[11]

As necessary to his safety as his great name was Adams' abiding contempt for his antagonists. It sprang from a spirit embittered by a decade of mortifications and betrayals. His presidential term, far from crowning his lifetime of public service with honor, had been a history of treacheries; and the campaign of 1828 against his reëlection—the most scurrilous in our history—had consisted largely of slanders against his character. Moreover, his defeat and Andrew Jackson's victory meant to Adams that every measure of his Federalist faith was lost forever. After the election he had made his disregarded way back home, determined on a "complete retirement— as much so as a nun taking the veil"; [12] and in "a life of almost total solitude," the lonely old man remembered in his diary the baseness of his enemies and the ingratitude of his friends, against all of whom he pronounced his bitter reprobation.

Though a sense of duty constrained him to return to public life as representative of his Plymouth neighbors in the House, Adams' contemptuous appraisal of his colleagues was unchanged. To his jaundiced eye the brilliant Congress of the 'thirties, "the cream of the land—the culled darlings of fifteen millions," was conspicuous only for its "exceeding mediocrity; and this universal mediocrity is the basis upon which the liberties of this nation repose." [13] Memories of shameful betrayals and sordid acts against his administration and the country's interests colored his contempt with animosity. But without the contemptuous aversion for his antagonists which charged his every thought, in the struggle that followed he never could have battled as he did against their united will. A moment's desire for their approval, a moment's fear of their hostility, and he would have lost the cause.

Adams' aversion for his colleagues intensified an isolation in the House established already by his prestige and his probity. Too great to follow others and too upright to play the game of party chief, he walked alone. Giddings remarked that in the House, Adams "consults with no one, takes the advice of no one, and holds himself accountable to no one but the nation." [14] If the antislavery cause in Congress had called for party leadership, he never would have served its needs. What it called for was a will unflinching and tireless, a temper indomitable against assault, and "an over-ruling consciousness of rectitude" in isolation and defeat. These qualities Adams personified as no other has in our history. "If he could be removed from the councils of the nation or silenced upon the exasperating subject to which he seems to have devoted himself," said one of his opponents, "none other, I believe, could be found hardy enough, or bad enough to take his place." But he could not be removed, silenced, or ignored. Never absent from his sentinel's place "on the watch tower of the nation," he sat year after year through Congress after Congress, "enfeebled, but yet . . . never tired,—worn out, but ever ready for combat," directing his war against the gags. "Astute in design, obstinate and zealous in power and terrible in action," he was "an instrument well fitted to dissolve the Union." [15]

Adams' set purpose was to stimulate antislavery feeling in the North by "springing" debates on slavery under cover of the demand for the right of petition. Essentially a policy of irritation, it depended for its success upon his capacity to provoke Southern members into a defense of slavery. But it was a dangerous game and, astute politician though Adams was, more than once he skirted the edge of disaster. In the early years of the struggle, he was obliged to disclaim any cause other than the right of petition, and he carefully avoided any official relation with the abolitionists, advising them that "the cause itself would be more benefited by such service as I could render it in discharge of my duty in Congress than by giving notoriety to any action in support of the societies." [16]

During these early years, his arraignments of slavery in the House conformed in tone to what public opinion at the North would endure. It was here that the greatest danger lay, for at any point Adams knew that he could go only "as far upon . . . the abolition of slavery as the public opinion of the free portion of the Union will bear . . . but one step further, and I hazard my own standing and influence there, my own final overthrow, and the cause of liberty itself." The danger was enhanced by his irascible temper. "Upon this subject of anti-slavery," he wrote in his diary, "my principles and my position make it necessary for me to be more circumspect in my conduct than belongs to my nature. I have therefore already committed indiscretions." None of them proved fatal, however, even though Democratic papers in the North denounced him in unmeasured terms.[17]

Another source of danger was the urgency of his abolitionist friend, Benjamin Lundy. During the crucial years, 1837 and 1838, they saw much of each other; and it is probable that the persistent little Quaker lost few opportunities to advise a bolder course in the House. "He and the abolitionists generally," Adams wrote in his diary, "are constantly urging me to indiscreet movements, which would ruin me and weaken and not strengthen their cause. . . . I walk on the edge of a precipice in every step that I take." [18]

As the sectional issue gathered momentum, however, Adams grew more daring. With increasing boldness he swept "all the strings of discord in the House." By the end of the decade his position was so secure that he ceased to render any longer the lip-service to the rule that he felt compelled to yield before. He told the House that hereafter he would obey the gag only as he was compelled by "actual physical force," and he defied his enemies to silence him in any other way. "There are ways enough to get at the subject," he said. "I could bring it into this House tomorrow." And despite the gag, he did. He no longer claimed that his cause was the right of petition only. Casting circumspection to the winds, he admitted to the House that his warfare was in the cause of freedom. To the North he declared that the remainder of his life was consecrated to the overthrow of slavery. "Whether it shall be done peaceably or by blood," he said, "God only knows. But it shall be accomplished, I have no doubt; and by whatever way, I say let it come." [19]

Adams' agitation dramatized the antislavery struggle in the House. His plot, it is true, was the struggle for the right of petition; but the slave power was the villain of the piece, and when abolitionists had won the right to denounce slavery on the floor of the House, the curtain fell and the play was done. At times during the long contest he staged pure farce;[20] but underlying every scene was the tragic theme of rights denied and souls enslaved by the powers of evil. As the drama moved toward its climax, the number of petitions grew; but with each session an increasing proportion of them went to Adams. As the abolitionists devoted more and more of their resources to swell the petition flood, Adams' leadership in the movement became more conspicuous. Before the decade ended, the mere volume of petitions entrusted to his care made him the greatest spokesman of the cause.

CHAPTER XIII

THE PETITION FLOOD

1837

It was the multitude of the antislavery petitions that sustained the battle for their rights. Even with a majority in the House opposed to their reception, they were too numerous to be tabled without confusion; and their unremitting volume—their "perpetual repetition of the same thing" [1]—overwhelmed every device for their disposal. But a mere fraction of these petitions were circulated spontaneously by their signers. Nearly all were inspired by such an organization for propaganda as had never before existed in our history. That organization, however, was not easily or suddenly accomplished. Its devices were discovered by trial and error in the local societies, and its structure was developed by degrees within the State auxiliaries.

In New England the propaganda for petitions originated in 1833 with Whittier, whose impulse doubtless came from his membership in the Society of Friends, which for a generation had petitioned Congress annually for abolition of slavery in the District. Furthermore, Whittier was one of the few politically minded abolitionists, a hardworking, conscientious party man. He caused his own Essex County Anti-Slavery Society to appoint name-getting committees in every town in that county; he advocated the measure in a pamphlet which the national organization circulated widely; and on every antislavery occasion he pressed the organization of petition campaigns. It was long before his words were effectual. Not until the annual meeting of 1835 did the New England Anti-Slavery Society promise "individually to . . . get petitions, with as numerous signatures as possible, presented to Congress at its next session." An enemy of the cause remarked the fact that this resolution changed "the purely religious movement of Mr. Phelps and others" into one for "political action." [2]

In the West, the line that there was in the East between the old and new efforts did not exist; and the new societies organized in 1833, turned as a matter of course to the familiar business of circulating petitions. The Lane students sent from Cincinnati a monster petition for the abolition of slavery in the District, and Weld wrote into the constitution of the Ohio State Anti-Slavery Society a section pledging its members to petition Congress early and often. One evening of his famous course of lectures was devoted to the power of Congress over the District, the responsibility of the North for slavery there, and the duty of every abolitionist to petition for its removal.[3]

Among Western abolitionists, petitioning proved popular. On the subject of slavery in the District, "all classes, Abolitionists, Colonizationists, Mongrels, and Nothingarians can agree." Moderates everywhere urged the petition campaign: "Here is the place to begin; and we beg, in the name of suffering, bleeding humanity, that those who are now expending their strength and ingenuity against Colonization would occupy this field. We are sure they would have scores of helpers where they now have one."[4]

The American Anti-Slavery Society did not take up petitions in a serious way until December, 1834, when it sent out a printed form-petition and requested all the auxiliary societies in the nation to circulate it, or others of their own, within their bounds. The measure was one of duty rather than hope. During the previous session the House had effectively buried such abolition petitions as were presented by referring them to the standing committee on the District—"the tomb of the Capulets," in Adams' phrase—where they were never heard of more. But, said the *Emancipator*, "if Congress can *bury* 10,000 names this year, let them have 20,000 next year, and 40,000 the next, and so on till at length some member is obliged, at least, to pronounce a decent funeral oration." The following year, 1835, Dickson of New York, a thoroughgoing abolitionist, made such an effective oration over these petitions that the hopes of the antislavery leaders rose. Thousands of broadsides were straightway sent to the mailing list of the society: "The subject has been brought up before Congress during the session just closed in such a manner that it will naturally be called up at the next session. . . . Let every one who means to do something BEGIN NOW!"[5]

The response for the next (the twenty-third) Congress, however, barely met the expected twenty thousand names; and during the following session (1835–1836) the petitions submitted to Pinckney's select committee bore only thirty-four thousand names instead of the forty thousand hoped for. Newspapers called to mind the last great petition campaign in England, when ten times as many names had been procured in ten days, and "sneeringly reported" that the petition campaign in this country was a failure.[6] But it had just begun. The Pinckney gag had passed, and the antislavery host was all aflame:

> "What! Our petitions spurned! The prayer
> Of thousands, tens of thousands, cast
> Unheard beneath your Speaker's chair?"

Despite this increased sentiment, however, it was not yet effectively organized. Responsibility for petitions, during the summer and autumn of 1836, was still left largely to the State and local societies. The New York office sent out petition forms, but these were not often used. Most of the memorials originated in the local societies among which they were circulated, and their management was a local concern. Though the number sent to the next Congress increased five-fold, the increase was not in proportion to the effort. Petitions were everybody's and nobody's business, and their circulation was usually started too late to reach the current session of Congress.[7]

Moreover, while petitions in the West were regularly circulated by volunteers from the ranks, in the East agents were usually hired to do the work, and their methods did not always honor the cause. The agents were paid to get names, not converts; and respectable citizens, discovering too late that they had inadvertently signed abolition memorials, petitioned Congress to erase their names, which had been secured, they declared, through "mis-statement and . . . false representations," by "emesarys . . . who go Skulking through our Country and villages, Sowing the Seeds of discord and Strife in Sted of Bringing the gospul."[8]

The language of the local petitions was not always discreet. Most of them were designed to secure signatures rather than to impress Congress; and "the foul stain of legalized plunder" was regularly fixed with many a rhetorical flourish upon "the villainous enslavers of souls." Congressmen informed their constituents that petitions thus "disfigured by . . . extravagant statement and harsh allusion" could not be presented. "I beg of you," Caleb Cushing wrote Whittier, "if any petitions are to be sent to me, that they may be . . . free of the bitter language good Mr. G[arrison] cultivates in the Liberator." The signatures themselves were frequently exceptionable. The charge was made on the floor of the House that half the names on the petitions submitted to the twenty-fourth Congress were forged; but the local character of the petition campaigns made a check on fictitious signatures impossible.[9]

The most serious consequence of unorganized petitioning was that thousands of respectful and *bona fide* petitions were never presented to Congress. Petitions with the names attached were ordinarily sent to the petitioners' own Congressmen: "Thus," the antislavery leaders hoped, "each member will be made aware of the feelings of his own constituents." But the members had feelings of their own. Most of the senators simply would not present them, and among Democratic representatives only the handful from antislavery constituencies would put them before the House. "If you could see for yourself," Cushing wrote Whittier, "you would understand why it is that we shall discharge this part of our duty *with a heavy heart*." Even Whigs—before petitions became weapons of party warfare—did not present them willingly. "Too many . . . truckling to the aristocratic lords of the slaves," would not present them at all. Nobody knew how many petitions were thus lost to the cause, but it must have been a large proportion of the total number sent to Congress.[10]

It was clear to the antislavery leaders that such haphazard methods could not be continued. In 1837, at the May meeting of the American Anti-Slavery Society, the newly elected executive staff was ordered to begin a petition campaign for the nation.

Sometime in May the staff laid plans for the petition campaign. It was a prodigious undertaking. Indeed, outside the field of politics, it was the greatest project in propaganda that had ever been conceived in our history. Only a part of the staff, however, were free to undertake it. Birney could not be counted on for any help at all. The public representative of the society, endowed with a "weight of character, dignity, courtesy, and Christian spirit" which commanded "the confidence of all parties," [11] he appeared with distinction before State societies, legislative committees, and churches; but these duties seldom left him time for anything else. Joshua Leavitt and Elizur Wright, too, had little time for petitions. Leavitt had the *Emancipator* to get out, and Wright was corresponding secretary for the society. With his own hand he wrote the correspondence of the movement, directions to the Seventy, letters to auxiliaries, and answers to inquiring individuals from the field. He also wrote the society's reports and had charge of its mailing list. His official duties often kept him at his desk far into the night and more than once he broke under the strain. Only occasionally could he help with petitions.

Almost the entire management of the campaign, therefore, fell to Stanton, Whittier, and Weld, the same trio that had selected the Seventy. Stanton was now financial secretary to the society, and his duties in that position alone would have been enough for an ordinary man; but Stanton was a driver, with a genius for organization and an extraordinary capacity for detail. His efforts in the petition campaign probably counted for more than those of either Whittier or Weld, especially since Whittier was frequently prostrated by nervous headaches, and Weld had just recovered from a breakdown. With such handicaps their achievements were almost incredible.

To them all Weld set a standard of devotion. He refused to take either a title or a salary. He slept in a little unplastered garret in the Negro section of New York, and he charged to the society only the trifling expense of his vegetarian diet and the cheap, rough garments that he affected. At the antislavery office he labored from early morning until late at night, a humble unpretentious figure, but a dominant one in the movement. "I have always refused all office," he wrote a friend, "and worked in the ranks as a common soldier; and yet in reality did actually control and give shape to a thousand things with which I seemed to have nothing to do. This has arisen from the fact that those around me and most intimate with me have always had unlimited confidence in me, have probably overrated my talents . . . and freedom from unworthy motives." He looked backward over the antislavery movement to its beginning and found nowhere "a contradiction of my will, plans, suggestions, &c &c, by any person or persons with whom I was ever associated. . . . It was so at Lane Seminary, and it is so now. And yet so far from having a desire to be looked upon as a leader, to *be* a leader, I have always loathed and spurned it." [12] But however much he despised its honors, even now, voiceless, worn, and ill, working patiently at his desk in the New York office, he still dominated the movement.

Before they began their campaign, this committee of three surveyed the field, a network of over a thousand antislavery societies with more than a hundred thousand members. New York led the State societies with twenty thousand, largely west of Utica and along the Erie canal, though a few thousand were scattered up the Hudson. Ohio reported nearly fifteen thousand, in the Ohio River towns and among the eastern and northern counties of the State, the area of Weld's agency. Third in number was Massachusetts' eight thousand —Methodists and Baptists mostly—with Pennsylvania close behind, few in numbers around Philadelphia (where most of the "modern abolitionists" were Quaker women), strong in Pittsburgh and the western counties. Next was Vermont, the only State society that controlled its legislature, with a membership of nearly six thousand. Around Rhode Island and southern Connecticut were Stanton's four thousand. The Maine and New Hampshire societies together reported four thousand more. West of Ohio the movement was only beginning. There were a few Quaker abolitionists in Indiana; but the Oberlin Volunteers were working in the northeastern counties, and in Michigan they had won close to a thousand to the cause. In Illinois, Elijah Lovejoy, his martyrdom only six months away, was venturing abolition doctrine in the *Alton Observer,* and two college presidents were speaking boldly for the cause, George W. Gale—now president of Knox College—and the president of Illinois College, Edward Beecher, Lyman's son. A third who had been a college president, Dr. David Nelson, was continuing in Illinois an agency for the national society which he had courageously begun at Marion College, in Missouri. This heroic handful even then were planning a State society.

By 1837, this network was more than numbers. During the previous year, the Seventy had been consolidating organization everywhere in the rural districts behind the cities, drawing together local organizations into new county societies, and inspiring old and new alike with the spirit of the Great Revival. Thousands were now incipient revivalists in benevolence, ready to "make themselves useful in the highest degree possible" for the cause. The antislavery movement was at last a true community movement, "one of the noble sisterhood of Christian charities." [13]

The committee on petitions proceeded to build an organization. Hired agents were no longer necessary. Volunteers were now ready everywhere to circulate petitions themselves, if they only had the petitions. The committee's task, therefore, was *"to get petitions thoroughly circulated through the country.* The great barrier to the accomplishment of this has heretofore been the *lack of names* in the several towns of the free States. To remove this," the committee asked abolition agents and secretaries throughout the North to name two persons in every county to receive petition blanks and to lead

the county campaigns. The county leaders were asked in turn to
recommend two trustworthy persons in every township. This list
of names the committee then checked by personal correspondence
and sent each one a bundle of petition blanks with minute directions
as to their circulation. After they were signed, the petitions were to
be returned to the county officers, who checked and counted the names
and reported their number to their State society or to the New York
office. If the local Congressman could be trusted, they were sent to
him; if he was "a truckler to Southern power," the petitions were sent
on to a central office, either State or national, where they were checked
again and mailed to a dependable Congressman in Washington.[14]

The petitions themselves were mere sentences, brief and to the
point. "Congress," remarked the committee, "is more powerfully
moved by large numbers than by strong arguments." But there was
a more potent reason for brevity. Under the gag rules, petitions
could be presented by subject only, and anything more than the simple
statement of their prayer never would be heard.[15] The first of these
sentence prayers was for abolition in the District of Columbia, "the
Thermopylae of Slavery." Next were two prayers against the annexation of Texas, one conservative and one radical; a prayer to abolish
the interstate slave trade; another to forbid slavery in the territories;
and a prayer to refuse statehood to Florida so long as slavery was
permitted within its boundaries. "We suggest that all the petitions
should be circulated at the same time," advised the committee. "Generally those who would sign one would sign all," and the number of
abolition petitions would thereby be multiplied by five. The variety
of forms might increase "the burden of explanation and argument,"
but this, the committee declared, was anything but an obstacle. It
was "the greatest benefit of the plan. It brings into the field a new
class of labourers who carry our principles home to places and minds
that would never be reached by our publications and lecturers. . . .
The circulators of memorials . . . will be among the most important
of the agencies for the overthrow of slavery."

Those appointed to the work were enjoined not to be weary in
well-doing. "Let petitions be circulated wherever signers can be got.
—Neglect no one. Follow the farmer to his field, the wood-chopper
to the forest. Hail the shop-keeper behind his counter; call the clerk
from his desk; stop the waggoner with his team; forget not the
matron, ask for her daughter. Let no frown deter, no repulses baffle.
Explain, discuss, argue, persuade." Petitions were placed in stores,

banks, and barber shops; they were passed around at hustings, at church fairs, at log-rollings and camp-meetings. But most of them were carried from door to door and from farm to farm by devoted volunteers.

Nearly everybody signed the petitions against the annexation of Texas. Thousands of Texas memorials were then in circulation, and a majority of those who signed the ones presented by the abolitionists probably did not think of them as antislavery petitions at all. For signatures to the remaining petitions, the central committee urged that applications should "not be confined to abolitionists. All who hate slavery and love the cause of mercy . . . should put their names to them without regard to their views of abolitionism." [16]

But, by 1837, antislavery petitions, like every abolition measure, bore the double stigma of Garrisonism and immediatism; and many, refusing "to distinguish between the devil and those who do his works," would not sign, however strong their antislavery sentiments. "We set down everyone without exception as an Abolitionist who signs an abolition memorial," said such a one. "This is the touchstone by which they are designated from others holding a different creed." Southerners wrote to their Northern friends and relatives, begging them not to sign abolition memorials. There were anti-petition mass meetings. In Pennsylvania a state-wide convention of the "Friends of the Integrity of the Union" was called "to quiet the South" by "an unmeasured condemnation" of antislavery memorials. In the face of opposition such as this the volunteers sometimes found the circulation of petitions "the most odious of all tasks." The petitions themselves bear evidence that they neither faltered nor wearied of well-doing. "But oh Lord, sir!" [17]

Their hardest task was to convert doubters to the right and expediency of abolition in the District of Columbia, "the test question" of the movement. To aid them, Weld wrote *The Power of Congress over the District of Columbia,* published first as a series of articles in William Cullen Bryant's paper, the New York *Evening Post,* and broadcast in pamphlet form by the thousands among the volunteers. Weld argued that "the *real question* at issue" was this: *"Is the Abolition of Slavery within the appropriate sphere of legislation?"* He concluded that it was, because *"slavery . . . is the creature of legislation."* Indeed, "wherever slavery is a legal system, it is so only by statute law." [18] If slavery was thus a municipal institution sustained only by statute, then it was within the appropriate sphere of legislation and subject to Congressional repeal. Thus did Weld add to the antislavery creed the municipal theory of slavery, the basis four years later of his antislavery lobby in Washington, and still later the basis of Republican party doctrine.

For some prospective signers of petitions, a case for abolition in the District was not enough: the right and expediency of abolition itself had to be proved. Demands from the field for antislavery tracts in quantity reached the New York office for the first time in the movement. The demand, however, was no longer for the newspapers and short appeals that had hitherto made up the pamphlet propaganda. What the volunteers wanted were solid treatises upon antislavery doctrine. Of the two such tracts already published, Weld's *Power of Congress* was well enough, but it covered only a limited field, and his *Bible against Slavery* appealed only to the pious. What the volunteers needed was information as to the character of slavery and "practical arguments" for its immediate abolition. To this end Weld now turned his pen.

A year before, when Weld had summoned the Lane rebels at Oberlin to join the Seventy, Thome had been too ill to come. "I am afraid," wrote Streeter, "that if he attempts to lecture . . . he will . . . perhaps induce pulmonary consumption, terminating in death." Streeter suggested that Thome be sent to the West Indies to examine the results of immediate emancipation there. "Will it not be for his health and at the same time . . . advancing the cause of emancipation? . . . The wounded soldier must prepare ammunition for those who can fight." Thome and another invalid abolitionist, Kimball of New Hampshire, were accordingly sent to the West Indies to find out how immediatism was working in practice. Kimball was too sick to do much (he died soon after his return), but Thome found just what he was looking for. He brought Weld a great mass of material to prove that immediate emancipation was a success; and in his clear and emphatic style, Weld made of it *Emancipation in the West Indies,* by Thome and Kimball. This pamphlet effected a revolution in antislavery doctrine. To such as were anxious to believe, it proved by example that immediate emancipation was safe, practicable, and efficient. Word went out from headquarters that the New York doctrine, with its difficult subtleties of "immediate emancipation, gradually accomplished," need no longer be believed. The official plan became an immediatism by which "slavery is abolished; free laborers take the place of slaves; and all the difficulties involved in the perplexing processes of gradualism . . . are avoided. All this may seem wild," remarked an antislavery editor, "but it will seem so only because . . . people have not yet examined the question of immediate emancipation in the light of . . . the work of Thome and Kimball on the West Indies, just published." [19]

For information as to the character of slavery, Weld turned to Southern sources. All the Southern newspapers at the New York Commercial Reading Room he secured as they were removed from the files. He and his staff of assistants searched these thousands of papers daily for six months, "marking and cutting out facts of slaveholding disclosures." To supplement these "incontestable facts of cruelty and horror," Weld appealed to the abolitionists themselves. "A multitude of facts never yet published, facts that would thrill the land with horror, are now in the possession of abolitionists," he wrote. "Shall such facts lie hushed any longer, when from one end of heaven to the other, myriad voices are crying, 'O Earth, Earth, cover not their blood.' The old falsehood that the slave is *kindly treated,* shallow and stupid as it is, has lullabied to sleep four-fifths of the free North and West; but with God's blessing this sleep shall not be unto death. Give facts a voice, and cries of blood shall ring till deaf ears tingle." Abolitionists over all the North responded nobly to his call. Facts of the sort Weld wanted came pouring in, and he embodied them with his newspaper clippings in a terrible tract which he called *Slavery As It Is,* the handbook of the antislavery impulse for more than a decade.[20]

Such solid treatises as these embodied the whole antislavery doctrine. To a considerable extent they took the place of antislavery agents, especially in the areas already canvassed. Systematic provision was made for their circulation. Weld and Whittier were directed to prepare a standard "school district" library to sell for five dollars, and two "county libraries . . . put up in suitable cases" at ten and twenty dollars respectively. State societies urged the libraries upon their auxiliaries, and county societies in turn recommended "to each township Anti-Slavery Society, and immediately . . . to supply themselves with anti-slavery libraries." The antislavery society's pamphlet printing thereupon increased once more; but it was now largely self-supporting, a product of demand from the field rather than gratuitous distribution from the center. Antislavery libraries went out to the local societies by the thousands, and the petition volunteers prepared them-

selves to convert their neighbors to the reasonableness of abolition itself, if conversion would secure a signature.[21]

Among the volunteers, the society's chief dependence was the
women. Petitions were well within women's powers. Indeed, said the
Emancipator, "if the ladies of this country really take the business in
hand, *it will go.*" The parent society itself urged women's participation: "Female Societies probably did more for the abolition of slavery in Great Britain than those of the other sex. They scattered anti-
slavery tracts . . . they circulated petitions. . . . Let the female sex,
then, throughout the land, emulate . . . their sisters over the
ocean." [22]

The times were propitious for such appeals to be heard. The "deep
slumber" which, from the time of Adam's fall, "for nearly six thousand years . . . has rested upon the minds of the better part of crea-
tion," was passing, and women were beginning to find minds of their
own. Throughout the benevolent empire, women were forming auxiliaries to do their part in saving the nation and mankind—though there
was some question "whether it was quite *delicate* for a lady to join a
temperance society." [23] Women's freedom had progressed furthest in
western New York where, thanks to Weld's wise strategy, men had
ceased to question women's right to speak in mixed assemblies. "There
is a revolution going on in the female mind at the present day," one
of the sex observed, "out of which glorious results may rise !" [24]

But these freedoms were scattered seeds as yet, barely sprouting
in a wilderness of tyranny. At law, Blackstone's dictum that "the very
being or legal existence of woman is suspended during marriage"
was still authority. A woman's personal property was still absolutely
her husband's, and even over the children of her body she had no
rights at law. By nature and by divine command, woman was conceived to be forever subject and inferior to man; and her interference
by petition in "the external and political duties of society," Caleb
Cushing prophesied, would be at the sacrifice of "all that delicacy and
maternal tenderness which are among the highest charms of woman.
Hers be the domain of the moral affections, the empire of the heart";
let her "leave the soul-hardening struggles of political power to the
harsher spirit of man, that he may still look up to her as a purer and
brighter being, an emanation from some better world, irradiating
like a rainbow of hope the stormy elements of life." [25]

In 1836, when Pinckney reported that on the petitions submitted to his committee women's names preponderated, it was considered a reproach even by some among the abolition host. That woman should "so far unsex herself as to be meddling in man's affairs, interfering by petition and recommendation in matters of legislation and national concerns," was deemed unscriptural. In Congress the tone of comment, especially from the South, was one of outraged propriety. Partly this was to bring the petitions themselves into disrepute; but the reprobation clearly expressed more than a sectional bias. Even Northern members were truly "pained to see the names of so many American females to these petitions. It appeared . . . exceedingly indelicate that sensitive females of shrinking modesty should present their names here as petitioners"; and Arthur Tappan's own brother Benjamin told the Senate that such "intermeddling in men's affairs by females" was unbecoming: "Nature seems to have given to the male sex the exclusive powers of government, by giving to that sex the physical strength and energy which the exercise of those powers call into constant and active exertion. To the female a more delicate physical organization is given; and she need not repine that she has not the iron nerve of her protector, man; he has the storms of life to encounter; she has the calm and sunshine of domestic peace and quiet to enjoy." For himself he was opposed to the reception of such memorials. However, petitions from women were never refused upon that ground alone. Whatever its opinions, Congress had discretion; and whether women's petitions were condemned as the work of "devils incarnate," or merely deplored as the mistaken efforts of "blessed, pious old maids," they were never denied reception. But Adams was almost alone in defending the right of women to be heard by petition on the floor of Congress; and in the North, petitions sponsored by "bustling and obtrusive companies of females" endured the stigma not only of Garrisonism and immediatism but of impropriety as well.[26]

Against every obstacle, however, with unfaltering devotion women carried their petitions from door to door. "If the lady of the house on whom these 'female brethren' call declines to give her name, they demand the reasons . . . and proceed to exercise the inalienable right of free discussion, concluding their tirade with a request that the domestics be called to give their signatures."[27] Their devotion attracted others to the task. Women's auxiliaries multiplied, and the number of volunteers was many times increased. Secretaries corresponded with their sisters, exchanging experiences; a corporate feeling arose; and, by 1837, a national system of female societies was in being to support the petition campaign.

During the summer of 1836 the female antislavery societies of New York, Boston, and Philadelphia simultaneously planned a national executive committee to coördinate their petitions and direct the campaign. In order to make the committee a representative one, they decided to call a national convention of women delegates to meet in New York at the time of the benevolent anniversaries next May. "Some societies would doubtless prefer the organization of a National Ladies' Anti-Slavery Society," the Boston secretary wrote, "while others would prefer that no change should take place. . . . In this last way we might, perhaps, avoid the charges of deserting our natural sphere (if it were worth while to do so). . . . But these are all matters of comparative indifference." The main thing was to call the convention, which met while the American Anti-Slavery Society was in session, May 9 to 12, 1837.[28]

"Petitions to Congress," the convention resolved, "constitute the one central point to which we must bend our strongest efforts." Lydia Maria Child proposed a systematic plan for a national campaign, essentially the same as the one developed by Weld, Stanton, and Whittier. Three divisions were set up, with headquarters in Boston, New York, and Philadelphia, and a central committee of three women was appointed for each division. Through the antislavery offices, local committees were to be appointed, one woman for each county in her division.[29] These county representatives were then to name a woman in every town in their county (the Seventy had promised to assist them here), who would receive petition blanks from the national antislavery office. After the petitions had been circulated, they were to be checked by the county leaders and rolled up into county memorials, which should go to division headquarters by November at the latest. Here the signatures would be counted and recorded, and the petitions would then be sent to Congress. State by State, the delegates "pledged their hands to this work, never to be withdrawn till they can be raised in joyful thanksgiving to Heaven for the gift of complete and entire success."

A public appeal to all the antislavery women of the North was ordered, whose "first and most important object" was "the obtaining of petitions." Citing the British precedent, the appeal described what women could do for the cause: "When the celebrated petition of

British women was brought into Parliament, one of the members arose and said, 'We can delay no longer. When all the maids and matrons of England are knocking at our doors, it is time for us to legislate.' That petition was signed by 800,000 women; and it effected the redemption of 800,000 slaves! . . . Be not persuaded that your petitions are useless because they are signed by women." [30] Nor should women be easily discouraged in the task of obtaining signatures. A hard-won signature "answers a three-fold purpose. You not only gain the person's name, but you excite inquiry in her mind and she will excite it in others; thus the little circle imperceptibly widens until it may embrace a whole town." The convention then adopted a resolution of thanks to John Quincy Adams "for having defended so wisely and so well the right of women to be heard in the halls of legislation," [31] and went home to rouse their sisters throughout the North.

Petitions, "the only mode of access . . . women . . . have to Congress," opened a way toward citizenship. It was not a wide way nor did it lead far; but to the women of that day it meant revolution. The mere exercise of their right of petition inaugurated "a new era of the world, so far as respects the dignity of their character, and the power and extent of their influence on the moral destinies of the human race." Upon that right, which woman's "physical weakness renders so peculiarly appropriate that none can deny her its exercise," the women of the new era built a mighty organization, the first corporate expression of women's will in American history and the first organized stage in their century-long struggle for civic freedom. [32]

Like the Great Revival the new movement among the women released a prodigious impulse toward antislavery effort. Women of all ages and every social level united in the circulation of memorials. Lucretia Mott and Lydia Maria Child commanded the forces in Pennsylvania and Massachusetts. In the ranks labored the youthful Susan B. Anthony, an indefatigable volunteer, [33] and Elizabeth Cady, Stanton's bride-to-be. Their very names make the petition movement and the woman's rights movement a continuity.

Over half the memorials that poured into Congress were signed by women. "We are aware," they told their rulers, "that scenes of party and political strife are not the field to which a kind Providence has assigned us," but they were bound nevertheless to supplicate for the oppressed. Nor would they ever cease their importunities. "We respectfully announce our intention to present the same petition yearly," they declared in thousands of repeated forms, "that it may at least be a Memorial to us that in the holy cause of Human Freedom 'we have done what we could.' " What women did was to sustain the greater part of the campaign. "There would be but few abolition petitions," said a weary Congressman, "if the ladies . . . would let us alone." [34]

Throughout the year of 1837 petitions signed both by men and by women poured into the central offices to be counted, checked, and entrusted to "safe men" in Congress. Through the New York office flowed nearly half of the total, and Weld, Whittier, and Stanton were swamped. "By the time Congress meets," Whittier wrote his sister, "there will be petitions enough to break all the tables in the Capitol, ready for delivery." His expectations were more than fulfilled. When Congress assembled, thousands of petitions had already been delivered, and they continued to arrive "in almost incredible numbers. . . . In the House of Representatives, the time of several clerks is wholly occupied with them alone. They are stowed away in the antechambers by waggon loads, and ere long there will be almost a sufficient quantity to erect a pyramid that shall vie with the proudest on the plains of Egypt as a great moral monument to the expressed will of a free people." [35]

Though a "continued stream, constantly flowing in upon Congress" was maintained throughout the remainder of the decade, the petitions were hardly as important to the cause as the volunteers' agitation in the field. Even where "they met with . . . heartless refusals," said a county leader, "they believe they accomplished much good by conversing with those who are opposed to our principles and measures." [36] Indeed, to volunteers inspired by the proselyting spirit of the Great Revival, their labor brought "its own recompense in the opportunity which it furnishes the friend of the slave to plead his cause in the presence of those who seldom hear it advocated." In this respect, the volunteers not only extended the work of the regular agents, but they did a work which no other agency could accomplish. For their house-to-house agitation brought to bear *"a neighborhood influence"* upon the unconverted "for which nothing can be made a substitute . . . as information is thus carried where our editors and lecturers are utterly unable to penetrate." [37]

It was a humble, unpublished agitation which the volunteers conducted, without stated times or places, and recorded nowhere in detail
except upon the petitions themselves. But so effective were their
labors that after only three months of organized petitioning, they
were officially pronounced to be "rendering to the cause a service by
no means inferior in importance to that which is rendered by our
traveling agents." [38]

In 1838, the financial stringency which followed the great panic of
the previous year obliged the society to dismiss many of the Seventy.
Stanton, Weld, and Whittier exhorted the petition volunteers to fill
the gaps: "Every man and woman must be an agent. . . . We must
make the most of our abolitionism by bringing it all into use." The
volunteers more than filled the agents' places. Annually the number
of petitions and the number of signatures on each petition increased
—an accurate measure of the rising antislavery sentiment in the
North and a tribute to the volunteers. For wherever the volunteers
had been "faithful in the discharge of their duties"—always careful
to "answer all the questions and make all the explanations" that
doubters required—it was often remarked that the next year not only
the doubters but also their families and their neighbors signed. That
the petitions might never be heard did not matter. It was enough that
"although not read in the halls of Congress, their voice has gone out
in all our land and roused the vital energies of thousands who have
been sleeping the sleep of death." [39]

Toward the close of the decade, antislavery organization further
declined, and feuds between the "idolatrized leaders" marred its
unity; but the petition movement waxed greater year by year. By the
end of the decade, every agent for the national society had been
either dismissed or transferred to the State and county societies, and
the petition volunteers, a host of thousands, possessed the field. In
1840, the year that the American Anti-Slavery Society ceased to exist
in everything but name, Adams noted in the House "a greater number of petitions than at any former session." [40]

CHAPTER XIV

Decentralization

1838

The transfer of antislavery effort from traveling agents to petition volunteers did not enlarge the area of the movement: it merely continued the intensive agitation which the Seventy had begun. The "neighborhood influence" exerted by the volunteers was local in its nature. Only a few of the petitions were circulated far from home, and they seldom inspired antislavery organization in areas not yet canvassed. But within the restricted limits of their own towns and counties, the volunteers so increased petition effort that, by the summer of 1838, the centralized organization for petitions established by Weld, Stanton, and Whittier no longer sufficed, and control of the campaign everywhere was transferred to the local auxiliaries. In central and southern New England, responsibility was shifted to town societies; in Pennsylvania, the central offices gave over the entire campaign to the county societies; while the New York State society abandoned its control and advised the county auxiliaries to send their petitions directly to Congress. The office of the national society still supplied blank petitions to enquirers, but it closed its correspondence with the county agents, and withdrew from active leadership.[1]

Once the campaign had rightly begun, central offices were no longer necessary. One petition campaign was much like another. The petitions themselves were almost the same, and the volunteers, once they had done their job correctly, needed no further direction. Moreover, though central control had at first been necessary, it had proved expensive, not only on account of the labor involved, but also because postage had to be paid on petitions sent to the central offices; and postage was then many times as costly as it is to-day. Petitions sent to Congressmen, on the other hand, went free. Economy as well as efficiency argued for local control, and it was established. Thereafter most of the petition blanks were printed on local presses; they were circulated in the neighborhoods; and when they were done, they were sent directly either to John Quincy Adams or to some other Congressman friendly to the cause.[2]

Throughout the campaign, Congressmen who refused to present petitions from their constituents were the special objects of antislavery censure. Politically minded volunteers summoned all true abolitionists to make reprisal: "Those who said . . . it was not expedient for them to attend to our petitions," should learn that it was not expedient for abolitionists to give them office. But Congressmen who "voted away the rights of the people" by voting for the gags were the blacker traitors. "One right still remains to the people," abolitionists angrily declared, "viz: to vote them away." [3]

Prevention, however, was better than punishment. Volunteers began to question candidates for Congress as to their views upon the subject of the right of petition, abolition in the District and the like, and published their replies in the local papers and the antislavery press. "Righteous and renovating political action" of this sort was a success. Most of the Whig candidates—and here and there a Democrat—promised to present petitions, and a considerable number of candidates came out against the gags. Some of the State societies took up the questioning of candidates, first the Rhode Island auxiliary and then others in New England; but the larger State societies usually left this task to local enterprise. Even in New England the effectiveness of the measure depended upon the local constituencies rather than upon the State societies. It was, of course, entirely outside the province of the American Anti-Slavery Society.[4]

Still more a local matter was the questioning of candidates to the State legislatures. Like the questioning of Congressional candidates, the practice arose out of antislavery memorials to the State legislatures, praying for the repeal of the "black laws"—discriminatory laws repressing free Negroes—and demanding legislative resolutions to Congress on antislavery subjects. These petitions were part of a movement which had begun in nearly every Northern State before 1830, and had united with the antislavery impulse during 1835 in a flood of State memorials which paralleled the deluge that inundated Congress. Throughout the remainder of the 'thirties, the State petitions kept Northern legislatures in an uproar. Members who refused to present them were proscribed; candidates were questioned; and one by one representatives from antislavery areas were whipped into line.

The success of such measures encouraged a few of the forward-looking leaders to propose a larger program. They first suggested independent candidates, and later they advocated an antislavery party. But antislavery groups almost without exception repudiated any such design. Their political measures consisted only "in petitioning Congress and choosing public officers to those ends,"[5] and in the "righteous renovation" of their State legislatures. "The Anti-Slavery reformation is emphatically a religious enterprise," they declared, "and prominent measures for its accomplishment ought to be of a consistent character." They insisted upon a local course toward local candidates: ". . . we will vote for no man who does not vote against slavery."

Though the control of petitions had passed to the local societies, the executives of the American Anti-Slavery Society still did what they could to further the campaign. Every year they sent out a broadside of instructions. They continued to furnish applicants with blank petitions, and they distributed new petition forms when new issues arose. As far as their shrinking means allowed, they sent timely documents to the town and county supervisors on their list. Birney and Lewis Tappan opened a correspondence with antislavery congressmen, who kept them informed of the needs of the cause in Washington. Though petitions were now supposed to be sent directly to Congress, the thousands that still came to the New York office were checked and mailed to Washington as before.[6]

The rulers of the State societies, on the other hand, did not surrender their leadership so willingly. As spectators instead of leaders in the movement, they became critical. They regretted the emphasis upon the gags. It seemed to them that thereby "the struggle has been removed from its proper ground. Instead of a struggle for the slave it has been a struggle for the right of petition." Others resented the abandonment of oratory for memorials. "We do not rely upon [petitions] as the great means for accomplishing the overthrow of slavery," resolved a conference of conservatives, "but still place our main dependence upon *the truth,* faithfully proclaimed." To some of Garrison's followers—especially those who had joined their leader in refusing to "acknowledge allegiance to any human government"— petitions were illogical. "I, for one, am sick of this *praying to men,*" said one of them. "Let abolitionists call upon God!" The petitions themselves, they declared, were useless. What could be hoped from Congress, "a thing of tail, nearly all tail, with a little popularity-hunting head? . . . It will abolish slavery at the Capital when it has already been doomed to abolition and death everywhere else in the country." [7]

But defeatism reached its nadir at the center of State abolitionism, the New York antislavery office at Utica. Here its president, Alvan Stewart, repudiated petitions utterly. Though abolitionists had presented more petitions to Congress than had been presented since the foundation of the government, what had been the result? Nothing but insults to the petitioners. "We might as well send the lamb as an ambassador to a community of wolves," he declared. "I would not lift my hand to sign a petition to Congress, to be insulted by that body." [8]

Meanwhile, in disregard of these defections, the petition campaign approached its climax. Volunteers by the thousands bombarded their neighbors with antislavery arguments. Petitions by the tens of thousands piled up on the desks of their State and national representatives. Local societies adopted constitutions pledging their efforts to one end only, the circulation of petitions. And numerous memorials from the antislavery areas were appearing in the House with the significant caption: "None of the signatories is a member of any abolition society." The antislavery impulse was getting out of bounds. [9]

A complete program for State societies involved a weekly newspaper, a headquarters office, and agents in the field. Funds to support the program were supposed to be pledged by the county societies, and by them assessed upon the township locals. As long as the county and township organizations were primarily "societies for mutual inflammation," whose chief task, in Senator Preston's words, was "preaching up to nightly crowds a crusade against slavery," the system worked well. Lecturers from the State societies were helpful adjuncts to local meetings, and the State anniversaries provided opportunities for local leaders to express themselves before a larger audience. But when the county societies made petitions their chief activity, the system broke down. The circulation of petitions and the election of "safe men" to Congress and the legislatures were measures for which State aid was not necessary or even desirable. Support for the State societies fell away and pledges went unpaid.

Some of this was due to the pecuniary pressure that followed the panic of 1837; but most of it was the decentralizing consequence of the petition campaign. Everywhere the decline in State support was greater than the financial stringency. Numerous county societies refused to send any of their collections to the State headquarters, and resolved instead "that the first claim that the anti-slavery enterprise makes to the money of the abolitionists of this county is in behalf of the county." Some county societies went so far as to forbid financial agents of the State societies to raise money within their borders.[10]

By the summer of 1838, several of the State societies were close to bankruptcy. The Eastern division of the Pennsylvania society had suspended every activity except its journal, the *Pennsylvania Freeman;* the New York State society maintained its ten agents and the *Friend of Man* by running heavily into debt; and the Ohio society was in no better case. But county societies were withdrawing moral as well as financial support, and the larger State societies were falling apart. The immediate points at issue were various. In Massachusetts it was Garrison's leadership, and in New York it was the amount of political action proper to abolitionists. It was pure sectionalism in Ohio, and in Pennsylvania it was no reason at all. But whatever the issues, the divisions were there. In Massachusetts the western counties—and numerous conservatives on the seaboard—formed a league against Garrison's heresies, which they called the Massachusetts Abolition Society. The New York society put off the inevitable for a year by carrying the movement to the counties in a series of regional conventions, but it finally split apart. In Ohio, Joshua Giddings' partner, Wade, advised against disunion, and for the moment his influence held off separation; but a year later the Western Reserve was operating as an independent entity. The Pennsylvania society, a union of the eastern and western branches, consummated in 1837 by a thousand enthusiastic delegates, died so quietly that its passing was not even marked by an obituary.[11]

All this occurred while the antislavery issue sharpened daily. It agitated churches, legislatures, lodges, and conventions. The subject "occupies and absorbs the minds of nine-tenths of the folks one meets," wrote a diarist. "All other topics run into and are swallowed up by this troubled reservoir of party spirit and infuriated patriotism. What a happy country to be so well looked after by its citizens!"

In the national organization another decentralizing tendency appeared. Despite its name, the American Anti-Slavery Society did not control the movement. Every State auxiliary claimed exclusive jurisdiction within its boundaries and each State antislavery newspaper competed for subscribers with the *Emancipator*. During the first years, financial agents of the national society operated at large; but as early as 1834, solicitors for the national and the State societies collided in New England, and it was decided that thereafter national agents should collect funds within a State society's territory only "in concert with the . . . society in that state, as far as practicable." But the practicability of concert was interpreted differently by State and national officers, and at the national anniversary of 1837 a new plan was enacted which provided that State societies should each pledge a definite amount to the parent society, either to be paid directly from their treasuries or to be collected by national agents operating within the State society boundaries. The plan satisfied the parent society, but not the State organizations. To collect unpaid balances on State pledges, the executive committee sent their premier solicitors, Stanton and Gould—another Lane rebel—and after them the gleanings were slight indeed. The State societies rebelled, and at the national anniversary of 1838, their delegates closed every State auxiliary in the nation to financial agents from the parent society. Thereafter the American Anti-Slavery Society depended for its support upon the prompt payment of pledges by the State societies.[12]

This resource was bound to fail. It was not only the financial depression and internal disunion that embarrassed the State societies; the decentralizing tendency had sapped their loyalty as well. "A dollar spent at Utica is worth three spent at New York," said Alvan Stewart. The State program was definite, immediate, and local; the national society's program was general in character, and it was far away. In any case the State program was bound to receive first consideration, but decentralization had so reduced their incomes that of all the pledges made by auxiliaries in 1838, not one was paid in full, and on some pledges nothing was paid at all.[13]

Meanwhile the New York office itself declined. The executive committee of the American Anti-Slavery Society, like others in the benevolent empire, was not a representative board elected from the State organizations. Its significant members were the remnant of Tappan's Association of Gentlemen, wealthy philanthropists of New York City. Though the annual assembly of the antislavery host returned them year after year to their places on the board, it was not because they truly represented the movement; it was because they were wealthy and prominent philanthropists. The source both of their philanthropy and of their prominence, however, was their wealth; and the panic of 1837 had so reduced the latter that their contributions to the antislavery treasury nearly ceased. Without the respect which had been inspired in previous years by their munificence, the board was in no position either to discipline recalcitrant State leaders or to hold together the disintegrating auxiliaries.[14]

On the shrunken board, Arthur Tappan, bankrupt and despondent, still served the cause, but he no longer dominated its policies.[15] Lewis, however, was made of tougher fiber. Though his own church associates turned against him, after he had lost his fortune, he stubbornly maintained his course.[16] From 1838 onward, his was the dominating personality on the antislavery board. But Lewis Tappan's dictatorial, irascible temper was not the one best fitted to resist decentralization. Conciliation was foreign to his nature. The self-regarding attitude of the New York State society he treated as a personal affront; and he refused to make an expedient adjustment to the growing independence of the other State societies. He was even more impatient with men than with measures, and his frank hostility to Garrison antagonized even the conservatives in the Massachusetts Anti-Slavery Society. He was openly intolerant of Garrison's subsidiary enthusiasms, and his opposition to one of them, the cause of woman's rights, became the ostensible issue that finally divided the society.

CHAPTER XV

THE WOMAN QUESTION

1838–1839

In early years men had spoken at antislavery meetings for women, but never had women spoken either at meetings for men or at "mixed assemblies" of both sexes. Even among the emancipated females of the Boston society, none had dared to "so far forget themselves as to itinerate in the character of public lecturers and teachers." [1] In 1836, when Weld offered Lydia Maria Child an appointment to the Seventy, all of the Boston abolitionists except her husband opposed a "female itineracy"; and though Weld insisted that it was "wrong to let any foolish scruple stand in the way of doing so much good," they would not admit its propriety. [2] The first women who dared to speak in public for the slave were two timid, diffident daughters of an aristocratic slaveholding family, Sarah and Angelina Grimké.

The Grimké name was a great one in South Carolina, and the Southern background of the sisters made their antislavery agency notorious. But even in their home in Charleston they had been exotic figures. A son of the house, Thomas Smith Grimké, graduate of Yale and secretary for a season to its president, was a naturalized Northerner and a stranger in the land of his birth. He was one of the most famous of the rulers in the benevolent empire, and the very year that the cholera epidemic ended his life (1834), he had planned to examine in all its bearings the subject of slavery and its abolition. Several years previously he had moved his sister Sarah to question the authority of the Anglican Church, and during a sojourn in Philadelphia she had become a Quaker. Sarah converted her younger sister Angelina to the Quaker creed, and the two women left the "ungentle, uncongenial air" of Charleston for Philadelphia. [3]

Except for their Southern origin, the two sisters were not uncommon types among the women of their day. Touched by the reforming spirit of the 'thirties and free from any need for self-support, they sought vaguely and unskilfully to do something for the world. In the Society of Friends, Sarah's conscience compelled her to "exercise the gift of speech" in the Quaker meetings. She continued to speak and pray "through an intensity of suffering . . . for nine long years," until the ruler of the Yearly Meeting bade her be silent. Angelina, a restless, soul-searching pietist, taught school and visited the poor; but she did not like children, and she was too self-centered to enjoy social work. "What then am I to do?" she asked. "The door of usefulness in our Society seems as if it was bar'd and double lock'd to me. I feel no openness among Friends; my spirit is oppressed and heavy laden and shut up in prison." [4]

Sometime in 1835, Angelina came upon some pamphlets issued by the American Anti-Slavery Society and escaped from her prison into the antislavery movement. "The door of usefulness among *others* seems to have been thrown open in a most unexpected and wonderful manner," she wrote her sister. "What have we done with the talents committed to us? I sometimes feel frightened to think of how long I was standing idle in the market place." She made her testimonial of conversion to immediatism, which she entitled *An Appeal to the Christian Women of the South,* and promised Elizur Wright to speak for the cause among the women of the North. [5]

When the name of Angelina Grimké came up for confirmation as agent, the agency committee for the national society, unwilling to take the responsibility for "the employment of female itinerants in the cause of abolition," referred the matter to the executive committee. After long debate the perplexed board passed the question back to the agency committee "with power," and it was finally decided "that it is expedient to appoint females." Angelina Grimké received her appointment; both she and Sarah attended Weld's Convention for the Seventy, and the sisters began to speak among the women's auxiliaries around New York City. [6]

Their New York agency made a considerable stir. Some opposition was expressed to their employment, even among abolitionists; and clergymen especially questioned their scriptural right to speak in public places. But the New York officers ignored the objections and advised the sisters to go on quietly with their work, which had been difficult enough without the opposition. "It is a hard place to labor in," wrote Sarah. "Ten thousand cords of interest are linked up with the southern slaveholders." But Sarah's unhappy platform style and Angelina's inexperience were probably the real obstacles to their success. [7] Weld took them in hand. For months he tutored Angelina in the elements of public speaking and trained them both in antislavery lore. Their lectures began to attract more favorable attention, and in the spring of 1837 they accepted a call to speak in New England.

In Massachusetts the sisters were a sensation. At first they addressed only women's auxiliaries; but "one brother wanted to come," wrote Sarah, "and another thought he had a right, and now the door is wide open. Whosoever will come and hear our testimony may come." Within a few weeks they were speaking regularly to "promiscuous assemblies." It was not only because of their romantic repudiation of slavery that men as well as women flocked to hear them. Neither of the sisters was beautiful, but they were obviously ladies of refinement and distinction; and under Weld's tutelage Angelina had become an orator of considerable power. "Never before or since have I seen an audience so held and moved by any public speaker," said one of her listeners. "She really seemed to be an angel of light." [8]

In New England as in New York, some conservatives among the clergy murmured objections, but at first everybody was too eager to hear them to pay much attention to their critics, and even clergyman went to hear "Carolina's high-souled daughters." Weld wrote them to be of good courage: "I would that every anti-slavery woman in this land had heart and head and womanhood enough, and leisure withal, to preach. . . . God give thee a mouth to prophesy. . . . If the men wish to come in, it is downright *slave holding* to shut them out." He told them to ignore the murmurs and to continue in their course. [9]

But Garrison advised a different course. The time was only a few years past when he would have been the first to condemn the sisters for their forwardness; [10] but his opinions had changed with his environment, and his suggestible, expansive mind now viewed the "ultra" doctrine of woman's rights as one bound up with the cause of human freedom. In his rancorous, provocative manner, he denounced the conservatives—especially among the clergy—and pronounced the Grimké sisters to be pioneers in the movement to free humanity from the bonds of family, church, law, and government.

Early in 1838, the Massachusetts legislative committee on antislavery petitions announced a series of public hearings on the subject of slavery, and Stanton called on Angelina to tell her that she should be among the speakers. "I treated it as a jest," said Angelina, "but after he left, felt to my great surprise that I *must* do it. I could hardly believe my own feelings." She applied to the Boston abolitionists to have her name put on the list of speakers, only to find that unlike Weld, who advocated the practice and advised silence as to the theory of woman's rights, the Boston radicals advocated the theory but were not entirely convinced as to the practice. "They all flinched," wrote Angelina, "except F. Jackson." Scorning to deal further with "Abolitionists who were only right in the *abstract* on Woman's rights and duties," Angelina applied to the chairman of the legislative committee himself, who courteously appointed a time for her to speak. After it was arranged that she should appear, the Boston abolitionists decided to approve it.[11]

Angelina's three appearances before the committee in the crowded State House hall were a triumph. "All agreed, pro-slavery and anti-slavery," Weld heard, "that Angelina's lecture before the legislature had been done more for the abolition cause in Massachusetts than any or all other means together for the whole season." For a time she was a national figure, and the sisters' antislavery meetings were thronged.[12]

Meanwhile, however, clerical opposition to their agency had become formidable. The publicity which Garrison had given to woman's rights as a part of his anarchic creed inevitably drew the Grimké sisters into his feud with the Congregational clergy. Upon their devoted heads descended all the hostility which Garrison himself had earned in New England. Congregational pulpits resounded. "The term Female Orator," said one minister, "has a sound too nearly allied to another that may not be named. And all approaches to the character of a female public speaker proportionally detract from the honor appropriate to females." The conclave of Massachusetts ministers, which the year before had ruled abolition agents out of their churches, resolved—once Garrison had made the Grimkés' cause his own—to condemn "the mistaken conduct of those who encourage females to bear an obtrusive and ostentious part in measures of reform."[13]

The Grimké sisters were overwhelmed. "Was it *right* for us to come to Massachusetts?" asked Angelina. "Am I in my right place and doing my appropriate work?" They were doing their proper work, Garrison told them, but if they expected to continue, they must defend their right to do it. Though they now had crowded audiences, it was only because "it was a new thing under the sun to see a *woman* occupy the place of a lecturer, and the people were very anxious to hear and see for themselves." But once the novelty had worn off, the question of right would arise. If the sisters were to continue their agency, they must defend the rights of woman! Garrison's counsels unhappily prevailed. Angelina planned a course of lectures on woman's rights, to be delivered in Boston, and Sarah began a series of letters on the same subject in the Boston *Spectator*.[14]

Garrison's provocative measures, it seemed to Weld, had done the cause of woman's rights an irreparable injury and a needless one. "Nothing more utterly amazes me," he declared, "than the fact that the conduct of a great moral enterprise should exhibit so little of a wise, far-sighted, comprehensive *plan*." That the sisters had been advancing the cause of woman's rights by their antislavery lectures was "almost plain enough to be self-evident. Why my dear sisters," he wrote the Grimkés, "the best advocacy you can make is just what you are making day by day. Thousands hear you every week who have all their lives held that a woman must not speak in public. Such a practical refutation of the dogma as your speaking furnishes!" Reasonable men, he told them, would never deny the right of an intelligent woman to speak "if they first witness the successful practice rather than meet it in the shape of a doctrine to be swallowed." But to advocate the doctrine before the practice had made it acceptable, was to ruin the whole cause. "If instead of blowing a blast through the newspapers, sounding the onset and summoning the Ministers and Churches to surrender, you had without any introductory flourish just gone right among them and lectured when and where and as you could find opportunity, and paid no attention to criticism, but pushed right on without making any ado about 'attacks' and 'invasions' and 'opposition,' and let the barkers bark their bark out, within one year you might have practically brought over . . . the very moral elite of New England. . . . Your specimens of female speaking and praying will do fifty times as much to bring over to woman's rights the community, as your indoctrinating under your own name through the newspapers those who never saw you." [15]

Whittier wrote the sisters in a somewhat sharper tone: How could they, at a time like this, forget "the great and dreadful wrongs of the slave in a selfish crusade against some paltry grievance . . . some trifling oppression, political or social," of their own? He told them frankly that in their course toward woman's rights they appeared to be "abandoning in some degree the cause of the poor and miserable slave." But both his words and Weld's were wasted. Every point that they made, the Boston radicals answered to the sisters' satisfaction. "Your habits of reasoning greatly expose you to fallacies," Weld wrote the Grimkés. "They are highly analogical, not analytical"; and the sisters found a more congenial atmosphere among the Boston abolitionists than among the leaders in New York. Sarah finished her letters on woman's rights; and though Angelina did not give her course of lectures, she spoke on occasion for her sex.[16]

Weld finally removed Angelina from the controversy very effectually by asking her to marry him. Immediately she recanted, and assured him that he need no longer have any "fears relative to those whose influence I was measurably under." Sarah too came over to their view that however important the cause of woman's rights might be, it was unfortunate "that this or any other extraneous doctrine should be made an apple of discord" in the antislavery movement. Garrison raged at their defection, but to no avail. "They wanted us to live out W. L. Garrison," wrote Sarah Grimké "not the convictions of our own souls. . . . I do not think I love Garrison the less for what he has said; his spirit of intolerance towards those who do not draw in his traces and his adulation of those who surrender themselves to his guidance have always been exceedingly repulsive to me. . . . But nevertheless I honor the stern principle which is the basis of his action."[17]

The net result of the woman's rights controversy was to reduce the antislavery influence of the Grimké sisters' agency and to retard materially the actual progress of woman's emancipation. Garrison, however, was convinced that the honors of the controversy remained with him. He now claimed to be the champion of the rights of women and the hope of their cause, and many of the antislavery women believed him.

At the next anniversary of the American Anti-Slavery Society, in 1839, delegates from the State societies listened to Lewis Tappan's annual report, which enlarged upon the difficulties of the national agitation and concluded that "the cause divided by State action does not present so commanding a front as if all its resources were concentrated in the national association." The delegates could hardly be expected to accept this statement calmly. After an angry discussion, they resolved that the report should be received as the opinion of the executive committee only, and not as the report of the American Anti-Slavery Society.

Of all times for Lewis Tappan to vent his irritation toward the State societies, this was the most inopportune. For Garrison had come to the convention with a host of delegates in order to capture the organization, and Lewis Tappan needed the support of every State society in the convention to resist him. Garrison's raid was well conceived. The Boston radicals were there in force, but many of his delegates were women from New England, who had stopped off at New York instead of going on to Philadelphia, where the Anti-Slavery Convention of American Woman was holding its third anniversary.

Doubt was cast upon the women's right to participate in the convention, so a resolution was proposed that hereafter women delegates should have votes as well as men. Among the regularly constituted delegates a majority was against the measure; but the women insisted upon casting their ballots for the resolution in advance of their right to do so, and their votes gave it a majority. The New York leaders protested, but the disgruntled delegates from the other State societies would not uphold them, and the women got their votes.[18]

Even with the women's votes, however, Garrison could not muster a majority. The New York philanthropists, unpopular though their measures might have been, were not so bad as Garrison, and they were returned to power.[19] But in anniversaries to come, the strength of Garrison promised to be greater. The action granting suffrage to women had virtually consolidated the American Anti-Slavery Society and the Anti-Slavery Convention of American Women; and at the coming anniversary of the society, in 1840, both organizations could meet as one.[20] If Garrison should again try to capture the national organization, a combination of the women's votes and those of Garrison's friends might give him a majority. It was all too clear, therefore, that if Lewis Tappan and his friends wanted to retain their power, they must seek support among those who believed that the participation of women in men's affairs was "a moral wrong—a thing forbidden alike by the word of God, the dictates of right reason, the voice of wisdom, and the modesty of unperverted nature." [21]

Thus it was that the point at issue between the handful of "Garrison men" and the withered remnants of the New York Committee became the "woman question." To Garrison the question was defined in black and white: he was the champion of the women's cause and his opponents were its enemies. But in point of fact the question was not so clear. Throughout the controversy in New England, though Garrison and his followers had defended women's rights in theory, in practice they had proved to be "Abolitionists who were only right in the *abstract* on Woman's rights and duties," as Angelina Grimké said. They had consistently opposed the enlistment of New England women in the public agitation, and on occasion they had even doubted the propriety of the Grimké sisters' agency. On the other hand, among Garrison's opponents all who had been executives in the New York office, save two, were on the women's side. Birney, a Southern gentleman of the old school, and Phelps, a conservative Congregational clergyman, were opposed; but Weld, Whittier, Stanton, Wright, and Leavitt were champions of the rights of women in fact as well as theory. Though they deprecated Garrison's agitation of woman's rights, it was because his agitation did harm not only to the cause of the slaves but to the women's cause itself. Indeed the most unfortunate aspect of the whole affair was the identification of the rights of women with the Boston abolitionists. Over the cause of women's rights they cast the same odium of narrow fanaticism and brawling intolerance which had cursed the antislavery agitation from its beginning.[22]

By the summer of 1839, the American Anti-Slavery Society had clearly ceased to embody a movement; it was fast becoming an organization without a constituency; in a year it was to be little more than a name. Even now its paramount issue involved only a petty squabble between two factions for priority.[23] To such a level had the greatest in "the noble sisterhood of Christian charities" descended.

CHAPTER XVI

Collapse

1839–1840

Among the causes for the decline of antislavery organization, the localizing tendency of the petition campaign was clearly paramount. But there was another weighty factor, less material and more obscure, a change in the spirit of reform. By 1839, the Great Revival had burnt out, and "a fearful declension of evangelical piety" pervaded the nation. The homeland of the Great Revival itself had sunk so low in spiritual grace that western New York came to be known as the "burnt district" of Presbyterianism. At Utica, a church which had experienced one of the greatest of revivals held a "seeking meeting." The congregation sang:

> "Where is the blessedness I knew
> When first I saw the Lord?"

and the minister preached from the text: "How can we recover the brightness of that rising?" But the spiritual feast was over. Even the greatest of all revivals was subject to the laws of its kind; it declined, and "the Holy Spirit in a great degree departed from the church." [1]

With the passing of the Great Revival, the antislavery impulse itself was altered. There was no lessening of its power. On the contrary, slavery was rapidly "becoming the question of questions," and the year 1839 marked a climax of excitement on the subject. But the impulse no longer expressed itself in a benevolent effort "to bring all enslavers to immediate repentance for the sin of slaveholding." The hope that somehow abolition doctrine would penetrate to repentant Southern ears was failing, and in its stead there grew a hatred of the sinner as well as of his sin, a sectional hostility toward slavery and the South. [2]

This hostility had been deepened by violence. Though mobs in the North had nearly ceased, Southern irritation had grown more pronounced; and near the border, two antislavery centers had recently been demolished. In the West, at Alton, Illinois, close to the boundary of Missouri, an abolition press had been destroyed and its editor, Elijah Lovejoy, had been killed; and in Philadelphia a large assembly hall, financed by antislavery contributions, had been stormed by a mob and burned to the ground. Only less provocative than this border warfare was the growing violence of Southern opinion. Slavery, it was proclaimed, was not an evil but a positive good—"the most safe and stable basis for free institutions in the world." Moreover, Southern churchmen were no longer content merely to deny that slavery was a sin; they now contended that it was "a merciful visitation; it is the Lord's doing, and is marvellous in our eyes." Acts and words such as these were provoking in the North a denunciation of slavery more in the spirit of anger than of love.[3]

Finney, high priest of the Great Revival, had long feared this outcome. Denunciation would serve the cause, he said, only as it was uttered in a spirit of loving reproof. But denunciation "in a censorious spirit" such as he was now hearing, would carry the nation "fast into a civil war. Unless the publick mind can be engrossed with the subject of salvation, and make abolitionism an appendage . . . the church and world, ecclesiastical and state leaders, will become embroiled in one common infernal squabble that will roll a wave of blood over the land. If abolition can be made an appendage of a general revival of religion, all is well. . . . I fear no other form of carrying this question will save our country." But the decline of the Great Revival and the rise of Southern resentment made inevitable what he had feared. The antislavery impulse ceased to be a missionary movement to save the slaveholders—"the bewildered Southern brethren in the Lord"—from their "state of desperation," and became a drive for petitions to support a sectional war.[4]

The decline of the Great Revival and the rise of sectionalism did not limit its effect to the slavery issue. As the spirit of expansive benevolence faded, sectarianism in the churches gained in strength; and the benevolent empire, whose existence depended upon nonsectarian coöperation, became to the orthodox first an object of suspicion and then a menace to the faith. When the Presbyterian Church finally cast out the New-School faction in 1837, it also proscribed three of the greatest societies of the Great Eight—home and foreign missions, and education—and established sectarian societies of its own.

From the effects of this Presbyterian proscription, the benevolent system never recovered. Most of the lesser societies, unable longer to claim interdenominational sanction for their operations, speedily collapsed; and, by 1839, even among the Great Eight some were bankrupt. Only those societies which had large financial resources or embodied some important ecclesiastical function were assured of survival. The remainder, deprived of their status as members of the interchurch community, had small prospect of continued existence.

Even more disastrous than the collapse of individual societies was the decline of the interdenominational unity which had made the benevolent empire possible. Its passing ended the dream of "a union of Churches for the conversion of the World," which for more than a decade had inspired religious liberals throughout the nation. Though fragments of the system continued to survive, they never recovered the unity which gave to the benevolent movement of the 'thirties its peculiar strength and its millennial promise.

Though the antislavery impulse had largely ceased to operate through societies, the New York committee still carried on. The antislavery libraries sold well, and for some tracts there was an unprecedented demand. Weld's book, *Slavery As It Is,* was one of the nation's best sellers of the year. Weld was still book editor to the national society, but since his marriage he had worked in his little country home up the Hudson, "far from the world and yet most effectually and usefully in the mind of it—monk and hero all in one!" With the aid of his wife, Angelina, and their devoted sister, Sarah, he wrote editorials for the New York papers and reports for the society. Late in the year he planned what was to have been his greatest work, an examination of the North's share in sustaining slavery. Weld was convinced that although slavery was a municipal institution only, it was nevertheless maintained by the political, financial, and commercial power of the North. He proposed to prove that it was the duty of the North to discontinue all support of slavery, and thereby bring it to an end.[5]

Weld wanted facts. He secured five agents and put them to work in Boston, New York, and Philadelphia to collect information. At his rural home he collated the information as it arrived and developed his program for a separation of the North from slavery. The pamphlet was never printed, but two years later its doctrine and its facts were to have momentous results in Washington.[6]

Aside from the dissemination of pamphlets, the society's program for the year was a failure. Encouraged by the promise of a donation, the largest ever pledged to the cause, the executive committee had selected twenty agents to campaign the Far West, the only part of the North left open to their operations. But either the promised donation did not materialize or the committee had counted too much on State pledges. By November the treasury was exhausted, and the agents still in the field were dismissed. Only two continued to speak for the national society, and they collected their own expenses.[7]

The American Anti-Slavery Society, in fact, was starving to death. During the summer of 1839, Birney had made the rounds of all the State headquarters, but they still refused to admit financial agents to their locals and they would not pay their pledges. Stanton sent a "financial circular" to all the local societies, pleading for donations to the parent organization; but the State leaders forbade their locals to respond, and insisted that all "financial correspondence" between the parent society and the locals should cease. Lewis Tappan applied for contributions to an antislavery convention at Albany, and then he called a special meeting at Cleveland (October twenty-third) in order to save the society, but the money secured was inconsiderable. No other sources of income were apparent, and the society's treasury was bare.[8]

In the *Emancipator,* Leavitt tried desperately to recapture the lost antislavery impulse. Hoping that it might now be made to operate through political action, he advocated an independent antislavery party; but except for a few radicals in western New York and handfuls here and there, the whole body of abolitionists condemned his "monstrous suggestion . . . that a religious society should . . . seek to build up political parties on geographical distinctions, and to array one section of the country against another." Even the New York Committee reproved him, and Lewis Tappan published a condemnation of his course. But Leavitt was intractable, and Stanton supported him. Internal dissension was thus added to the troubles which the New York Committee already had to bear.[9]

Several of the leaders had long been aware that something was radically wrong with the society. Its preposterous doctrine of immediatism, its futile program for converting the South by propaganda which was debarred from Southern territory, and its incubus, the

putative leadership of Garrison, were any one of them enough to
discredit it. The marvel was that it had lasted so long! Apprehending
something of these obstructions, Birney unselfishly proposed an entirely new movement, to be captained by William Ellery Channing,
the New England liberal. Either at Birney's suggestion or on his own
initiative, Channing talked over the prospect of antislavery organization with John Quincy Adams and published a plan for a society to
take the place of the existing organization—a society which would
condemn immediatism and advocate the amelioration of slavery and
its gradual abolition. But Channing's substitute society was never
organized. The death blow to the American Anti-Slavery Society was
dealt not by Channing but by John Quincy Adams himself.[10]

The years that had changed the means of agitation from revivals
to petitions had also seen a transformation in Adams' leadership.
At first only the unofficial representative of the agitation in the
House, with the concentration of abolition effort on the petition campaign, he had become the genius of the antislavery cause. Adams'
authority had no name; never before or since has there been anything like it in our history. He was the representative, not of the
Old Colony in Massachusetts, but of the nation; and his constituency
was the antislavery host throughout the North.

Adams fully realized his position. His vast correspondence and
the thousands of petitions that burdened his mail were enough to inform him daily of his leadership. Indeed, for more than a year he had
regarded the antislavery movement as being "almost exclusively committed" to his trust. "With a sacred sense of duty" he assumed the
rôle of spokesman for the cause; and when it became apparent that
the antislavery societies had ceased to represent the antislavery impulse, he proceeded to read them out of the movement.[11]

Early in 1839, in an address "more to the Abolitionists of the North"
than to his hearers in the House, Adams condemned the abolition
creed, and a month later he proposed an antislavery program of his
own, the limitation and gradual abolition of slavery by constitutional
amendment. Then he wrote a public letter to his larger constituency
——"the Citizens of the United States, whose Petitions, Memorials
and Remonstrances have been intrusted to me"—which doomed the
American Anti-Slavery Society to collapse.[12]

"Let me ask those of you, my friends," he said, "who believe the
immediate emancipation of the slaves of this country [to be] a
practical thing, whether the success of your moral suasion upon the

minds of the slaveholders hitherto has been encouraging to your hopes or expectations. . . . Have you converted many to the true faith of immediate emancipation without indemnity? Is the temper with which your arguments are *received;* nay, is the temper with which they are *urged,* of that character which conciliates acquiescence and ripens hesitancy into conviction? With what feelings towards you is the heart of the slaveholder impressed? With what feelings are your hearts impressed towards the slaveholder? 'Do you gather grapes of thorns, or figs of thistles?' "

Their doctrine of immediatism itself he termed preposterous. "In what page of the volume of human nature they found the recipe for this balm to the sore of slavery, or in what cell in the imagination, I know not. FRANKLIN, it is said, made the discovery that an effusion of oil will soothe the mountain waves of a stormy sea; but no philosopher has yet appeared to make the experiment of pouring oil into the summit of a smoking crater to extinguish the volcano within. . . . What then is the meaning of that *immediate* abolition which the Anti-Slavery Society has made the test of orthodoxy to their political church? A moral and physical impossibility."

Over the perplexities and the controversies in the abolition ranks moved Adams' terrible pen. He mocked their reverence for the British precedent of immediatism—"the Keystone in this divine argument, as placed in its eternal home by the parliamentary liberation of the slaves in the British colonies." He remarked their differences over the woman question, political action, and Garrison's heresies, which had "eminently concurred not only to counteract their influence upon the main objects of their association, but to make them unpopular and even odious, not only in the South, but in all parts of the Union." He concluded that so long as this kind of antislavery organization represented the antislavery cause, emancipation "in this Union, or even in the District of Columbia, is as far beyond the regions of possibility as any project of the philosophers of Laputa."

This was more than an indictment of the American Anti-Slavery Society. To the host of petition volunteers which Adams now commanded, it was an interdiction, and it was so intended. Most of the abolition leaders were stunned to silence, but a few were moved to reply. Old slanders against Adams were recalled, old lies retold:

"He that played Sir Pander
While wages were to be had,

And saved slave-trading Andrew,
Now rails at them like mad;
And turning to us he modestly says,
'Your language is too bad.' "

But this was the buzzing of flies against the eagle. Adams was now so much an antislavery hero that most of the leaders themselves could not but admire him; and even Garrison's radicals refused to vote at his behest for "the impeachment of John Quincy Adams." Thoughtful abolitionists everywhere began to calculate the value of antislavery organization.[13]

In New York the executive committee drearily faced the end. They resolved that so long as the State societies maintained their ban "there is no alternative before us but that of bankruptcy." After one last ineffectual appeal to the State societies for aid, they called a special meeting of the American Anti-Slavery Society (January 15, 1840), in order to decide its fate. Only a handful responded, and the result of their deliberations was "practically a decision of bankruptcy." In consideration of the New York Committee's financial straits, the meeting agreed to permit agents of the parent society to raise ten thousand dollars within State boundaries; but toward a permanent change in the existing arrangements, Lewis Tappan could muster hardly one fifth of the convention. The delegates appointed a committee "with power," to decide the fate of the society—Birney, Lewis Tappan, and Gibbons (a "Garrison man")—and adjourned.[14]

For the moment the antislavery journals put aside editorial discretion and frankly discussed the crisis. "It cannot be denied," wrote Whittier, "that in some parts of the country there is a jealousy and fear with respect to the powers lodged in the hands of the Executive Committee and an unwillingness to sanction its proceedings, which will be likely to increase instead of diminish." This being the case, "it is easy to perceive that the Committee cannot adopt *any course* of efficient action without misrepresenting a part of its constituents. . . . It is a painful position for these faithful laborers in the cause; and a sense of their past services and unswerving integrity for the last seven years . . . should prompt abolitionists in all parts of the country to relieve them." The measure of relief that Whittier proposed was the payment of the committee's debts and the dissolution of the society.[15]

Ohio agreed with Pennsylvania. "What . . . is the use of the national society?" asked the *Philanthropist*. "Annually it is convened at New York; discusses ambiguous points in its own constitution; is agitated by the discrepant views of its members on topics not immediately connected with the antislavery cause; considers proposed amendments; votes that it will not be held responsible for the reports of the Executive Committee; excludes this Committee from the wide field of antislavery operations; and leaves it without providing it . . . resources." Like Whittier, the *Philanthropist* recommended that the parent society "quietly dissolve itself" at the next anniversary.[16]

Both editors were nevertheless convinced that "the committee at New York is composed of men whose services we cannot afford to lose." They proposed that the committee conform to the changed realities of the antislavery cause by becoming once more "a central point of influence and correspondence," as it had been before the American Anti-Slavery Society was organized. New York and the Massachusetts conservatives concurred,[17] but not Garrison. He had other plans for the society.

In the committee on the fate of the society, Gibbons spoke for Garrison; but Lewis Tappan, realizing that the organization had become "a stench in the nostrils of the nation,"[18] came to the conclusion reached by Whittier and his editorial brethren. Disregarding Gibbons' irate protests, Tappan and Birney reported that the parent society should either be given the right to operate where it desired or be dissolved.[19] The first, everybody knew, would never be granted; the second was not choice but necessity. With this report as its authority, the executive committee thereupon proceeded to liquidate the American Anti-Slavery Society.

Assured that they need no longer fear the encroachments of the New York Committee, most of the State societies came nobly to its aid in clearing up its financial obligations. Garrison's organization, of course, refused to do anything, but the Massachusetts Abolition Society, which also claimed jurisdiction over Massachusetts territory, invited Stanton to tour the State. Throughout the North, pledges were made good and the more pressing debts were paid. For its larger obligations, the committee gave over its stock of antislavery books and pamphlets. The remaining property of the society was transferred to Lewis Tappan and another as trustees, to be applied upon debts not yet due. Prepared for the final dissolution, the committee awaited the anniversary of May, 1840.[20]

It was not Garrison's intention, however, that the American Anti-Slavery Society should dissolve. He regarded it as his own society, the child of his inspiration; and even its members, he reasoned, had no right to end its existence. He determined to save his society.

Garrison was perfectly aware that during the past year his support had largely evaporated. Indeed, except for the handful of "Garrison men" and certain of the former delegates to the Anti-Slavery Convention of American Women, he had no support worth mentioning anywhere in the organization. Among the delegates from the nation at the coming anniversary, he knew that he could expect nothing like a majority. He therefore decided to import a majority of his own! A steamboat was chartered and stationed at Lynn harbor, and citizens of Lynn were offered an outing to New York at nominal cost, on the understanding that they would cast their votes at Garrison's direction. "A large portion of the town of Lynn" [21] responded, and were appointed "delegates." Similar methods were employed elsewhere, though the remainder of the "delegates" did not travel so picturesquely. More than five hundred of those who were enrolled in the anniversary of 1840 came from Massachusetts.

It was fortunate for Garrison that he had planned so well. Friends of the New York Committee had "drummed up recruits from all quarters," Garrison wrote his wife, "by the most dishonorable means." But their means fell short of the wholesale methods of the Bostonians. On a preliminary issue, the appointment of a woman to the business committee of the convention, women delegates and the town of Lynn joined hands. The New York Committee lost by a moderate majority (560 to 450), and rather than remain to be humiliated, they withdrew from the anniversary and the society. "It was our anti-slavery boatload," Garrison boasted, "that saved our society from falling into the hands of the new organizers, or more correctly, disorganizers." [22]

At last Garrison controlled "our society." Apparently he looked upon the antislavery boatload as an army of crusaders who had cleansed his own organization of rebels to his authority; and although their withdrawal left only Garrison's following as the convention, in his self-approving view this was as it should be. Nor was he disturbed when almost all of the State auxiliaries withdrew from the society. In his judgment, he was the society! But the departure of the New York Committee and the withdrawal of the auxiliaries left the American Anti-Slavery Society with little more than its name.

CHAPTER XVII

RESIDUES

1840–1841

After the convention in New York there was another in London, a World Anti-Slavery Convention, called at the suggestion of the New York Committee by a group of prominent British abolitionists, the Executive Committee of the British and Foreign Anti-Slavery Society.[1] The convention proposed to consider the state of slavery in every land, especially in America; to examine the results of abolition in the West Indies; and to formulate a program for universal emancipation throughout the world. The venerable Thomas Clarkson promised to act as chairman, and "the friends of the slave of every nation and of every clime" were asked to send delegates.

When the invitations reached the Massachusetts Anti-Slavery Society, Garrison advised the appointment of women. It was true that the invitations stated explicitly that "gentlemen only were expected to attend. But," as one of the Massachusetts delegates later told the World Convention, "we neither did nor could regard this as of any consequence. We deemed the question of who should sit in the Convention would be determined by the Convention itself, not by any self-constituted Committee." Several women were accordingly appointed. Numerous other societies in America also appointed delegates. The New York Committee selected Birney, and after a futile attempt to persuade Weld to go, they also appointed Stanton, who made a honeymoon of the trip with his bride, Elizabeth Cady. Most of the delegates sailed for London in April, but Garrison and a few others delayed their departure until the May anniversary was over.[2]

When the World Convention assembled, the women from Massachusetts were not seated with the delegates, and the male representatives of Garrison's society made formal protest. Their hosts were much embarrassed. "The document calling for this Convention had no reference to, nor did the framers of it ever contemplate that it would include females," said the secretary. Most of the Americans also were embarrassed. Champion of woman's rights though he was, Stanton kept silent; but Birney publicly regretted that the question had been imported across the Atlantic. It had, he said, caused trouble enough at home. British delegates earnestly besought their Massachusetts guests to pass the question by. "This is very unlike the meetings we have hitherto held," said one unhappy host. "I do hope that our American friends, considering what a small minority they are, will withdraw the motion. . . . Will they on a minor question—the admission of female delegates from a small section of the American continent—run the hazard, the fearful hazard, of exciting a spirit which may tarnish the whole procedure in which we are engaged?" But the champions of Garrisonism refused to yield. After a day of discussion, they pressed the question to a vote and were defeated by "an overwhelming majority."[3]

Five days later Garrison arrived. He refused to join the delegates, and for the remaining three sessions he glowered at the convention from the gallery. Not until the sessions had adjourned did he have an "opportunity to relieve his full heart." At a farewell party to the foreign delegates "he opened his mouth," wrote Elizabeth Cady Stanton, "and forth came, in my opinion, much folly. . . . He was received with many cheers, but oh! how soon by his want of judgment did he change the current of feeling in his audience. A general expression [?] of disappointment was visible among the English ere he had spoken long. The Chairman . . . was obliged to call him to order," and finally told him to take his seat.[4] For Garrison alas! could no longer hope to be honored as the ambassador of American abolitionism to the world. The British immortals now knew better. He still had some friends left in England, but his course both at the World Convention and in America had alienated the confidence of his hosts. To them, at least, he now seemed anything but "abolitionism personified and incarnate."[5]

In a striking manner the Americans at the World Convention made up a microcosm of their antislavery organization at home. The little group of "Garrison men," with their strident agitation for a measure not connected with the antislavery cause, had few friends among the other delegates from America. But these in turn were divided on other issues; and none of them recognized the authority of the delegates appointed by the New York Committee. It was clear to their British hosts that antislavery organization across the seas had fallen upon evil days.[6]

Meanwhile Garrison's exultant followers in America—the "old organization" they called themselves—had elected an executive committee for the renovated American Anti-Slavery Society. The new committee's program was much more modest than the old. It included no such measures as the antislavery libraries, agencies, petition campaigns, and correspondence which, even during its final year, had busied the days of the New York Committee. Its function now was to maintain the appearance rather than the reality of a national organization, in order to prove the supremacy of Garrisonism in the antislavery cause. To establish this claim only two things were necessary, a weekly newspaper—which they named the *National Anti-Slavery Standard*—and conventions in New York once a year.[7]

Funds were wanted at once to launch the *Standard,* and an appeal for support was published to the nation. But, as might have been expected, almost no one responded. Since the debâcle of the last anniversary, nearly all the State auxiliaries had withdrawn, and Garrison's Massachusetts society had financial burdens of its own. Moreover, philanthropists who had contributed to the old régime would not give a penny to the new. England, however, was wealthy; and to such British abolitionists as were not aware of recent happenings overseas, the American Anti-Slavery Society might still be a name of power. An agent, John A. Collins, was accordingly dispatched across the ocean to solicit funds.[8]

Collins first applied to the Executive Committee of the British and Foreign Anti-Slavery Society for a donation; but in answer he was told: "the course recently pursued by the American Anti-Slavery Society has alienated their confidence." [9] In the field his efforts were further hampered by Weld's old mentor, Charles Stuart, who appointed himself agent and pamphleteer to the opposition. But in the provinces the name of Garrison was still one to conjure with; and there Collins procured funds enough to save the *Anti-Slavery Standard*. More important than the money were the contacts which he formed. A system of regular contributions was arranged which measurably secured the future.[10]

With Lydia Maria Child as editor, the *Anti-Slavery Standard* made a brilliant beginning; but Garrison's constant interference was too much to be borne. After two years of service, Mrs. Child resigned in disgust, and her husband took her place on condition that he be let alone. Freedom for his followers, however, was a privilege which Garrison could promise but never fulfill. After a year of friction,

David Lee Child also resigned, and the editorial chair was taken by one of those who were willing "to live out W. L. Garrison." Thereupon the editorial troubles of the *Standard* ceased, but its distinction ceased as well. It became simply an echo in New York of Garrison's words in Boston. It was anything but the organ of a national movement.[11]

Once a year the Boston abolitionists invaded New York to hold the anniversary of the American Anti-Slavery Society. They printed no reports—there was nothing to report—and they discussed not at all the questions of budgets, pledges, and support which had concerned anniversaries in the past. Instead they elucidated points of doctrine and made speeches. Their doctrine now included no plan for emancipation. "To be without a plan," they said, "is the true genius and glory of the Anti-Slavery enterprise!" But their doctrine did include much that angered their contemporaries. They argued that the Constitution of the United States was "a covenant with death and an agreement with hell"; and the churches, they contended were no better. On the other hand, their speeches, sometimes shocking and sometimes thrilling, but seldom dull, grew famous. Wendell Phillips spoke in polished periods amid hisses and applause, and Frederick Douglass uttered mighty words for freedom. The curious public thronged the anniversaries, and they were charged admission at the door. But only a handful of those who sat in the assemblies were members of the American Anti-Slavery Society; almost none were delegates. Indeed, there was no system of societies from which delegates could come. Behind this pretense of a national organization there was a total membership of only six hundred souls![12]

The antislavery impulse had departed, and hardly more than the name of the older movement still existed. But to Garrison the name and the impulse were still the same: he controlled the one and he was convinced that he embodied the other. At an anniversary meeting he proposed a resolution: "That indifference to this movement indicates a state of mind more culpable than was manifested by the Jewish nation in rejecting Jesus as the Messiah, eighteen hundred years ago"; and his loyal followers voted the resolution through.

Since the schism in the Massachusetts Society, these followers of Garrison had come to constitute a fraternity—almost a secret society —based upon the knowledge, mutually shared, that Garrison was not the egregious fanatic of his public reputation, but a single-minded hero—"the only man who *would do to tie to,*" as Thomas Wentworth

Higginson said. Their faithfulness was astonishing but not incredible. Garrison's conviction of his own significance gave to those who shared it that unclouded sense of right which has been one of the chief consolations of religion through the ages. To others, his integrity and consistency were enough to hold their loyalty. But all told, they were few. So far as their influence goes in history, their primary function was to sustain the legend that Garrison and the abolition cause were one. The popular tradition that Garrison had first inspired the antislavery impulse, they kept alive by constant iteration; and though they were now even further than before from the actual center of the movement, they still maintained that Garrison was its chief. Thus they claimed for him the glory of each victory that others won in the antislavery struggle; and hostile publicists, ready to damn the antislavery cause with every odious epithet, gladly ratified their claim. In time, sheer repetition made their legend of Garrison's leadership a part of our tradition.

Not all of those who ratified the legend were hostile to the cause. Notables of New England, knowing Garrison as a voice at their literary afternoons in Boston rather than as the evil genius of the antislavery movement, found in his lofty qualities of consistency and devotion a character not incongruous with the legend. Moreover, even the greatest of them knew little enough of the Methodists and Baptists who formed the bulk of New England abolition, and they knew even less of the tens of thousands of abolitionists who made up the movement in the nation. Thus, with no basis for a sounder judgment, they accepted Garrison at his own valuation, and embalmed the legend of his leadership in the New England literary tradition.

The Boston abolitionists made the Garrison legend history; but this was their only great achievement. As advocates for a reputation, Garrison's followers were unique; but as factors in the antislavery impulse—at least throughout the decade of the 'forties—they and their leader were even less than negligible; they were "dead weights to the abolition cause." [13]

After the anniversary of 1840, the New York Committee and their friends—the "disorganizers," as Garrison called them—reorganized as the American and Foreign Anti-Slavery Society. For a time they hoped that they could nucleate antislavery organization throughout the North. Several of the State societies and scores of county societies affiliated with them, and plans were laid for a national organization. But the larger State societies continued to hold aloof, and many leading abolitionists refused to join. "I totally dissent from the foundation principle on which the society is based," said Weld, "a denial of the equal membership of women." But he dissented just as strongly from the agitation of woman's rights by Garrison's society: "The agitation of that question in connection with abolition societies and their operations I believe always has been, and must be, only evil, and that continually, on the slave's deliverance." Gerrit Smith would not join because he feared that "Old and New Anti-Slavery Organization . . . will be the occasion of keeping up and aggravating their quarrels"; and Whittier wrote that though his abolitionism grew daily stronger, his "faith in . . . organization is not of the 'saving' kind." It soon became apparent that, even with Garrison removed, there was not sufficient unity among abolitionists to bring them together in a national organization.[14]

But the principal cause for failure was named by the delegates themselves at the first anniversary of the society in 1841. There was now no place, they said, for a national organization. The antislavery impulse was not with them. State and county auxiliaries soon withdrew; Birney and Stanton, the secretaries, resigned; and even Leavitt admitted failure. But Lewis Tappan, a host in himself, still persisted. Gathering around him the faithful remnants of the New York Committee, he labored ceaselessly for the cause. He maintained an enormous correspondence, especially with the British leaders; he raised money for antislavery objects; he crossed the seas as ambassador for the slave; and he was instrumental in founding the *National Era*, the paper which later became the organ of the antislavery host. As the moving spirit of the New York Committee, he continued to make history until he retired.[15]

The most pathetic residue of antislavery organization was the little group which had attempted to turn the antislavery impulse toward political action. In 1840, they organized the Liberty Party and nominated Birney for president; but among the millions who cast their ballots in the national election, they won him barely seven thousand votes. "May God forgive the thousands of Abolitionists," said a disillusioned campaigner, "who . . . by their votes have bolstered up the tottering fabric of slavery."[16]

CHAPTER XVIII

THE TURNING POINT

1842

The antislavery impulse had passed to the thousands of petition volunteers, and its center was now at Washington. Years before, when the petition struggle first began, abolitionists had recognized Washington's strategic importance to the cause. At the May anniversary of the society in 1837, a Congressional lobby was projected, and Weld was appointed to "repair to the city of Washington, when the discussions of Slavery shall come up," in order to advocate the cause among the Congressmen. But Weld refused to go, and the project was abandoned. It was not until three years later that a lobby was again proposed, this time from Ohio. Thomas Morris, the one abolition senator, suggested that delegates be chosen by each State auxiliary to form an "Anti-Slavery Congress" in Washington, to hold daily meetings and publish a daily journal of their proceedings during the regular Congressional session. His proposal was badly timed: antislavery leaders were then too much occupied with factional feuds to take united action on anything. Some months later, when Senator Morris's proposal was renewed, the antislavery movement had split apart; the fiasco of Birney's Liberty Party campaign had broken the hearts of the political abolitionists; and the antislavery treasuries were exhausted.[1]

To Joshua Leavitt belongs the credit for keeping the project of a Washington lobby alive. He was a shrewd, resourceful Yankee, with an eye for essentials which was rare among his antislavery colleagues. During the years of disunion and decline, though he fought the battles of the New York Committee in the antislavery press, he had never staked his abolition faith upon their side of the controversy, and their defeat had not unduly cast him down. In the kaleidoscope of the following months, every shift of organization found him searching for the antislavery impulse. He sought its reincarnation in Birney's Liberty Party, and he hoped that it would embody itself in the American and Foreign Anti-Slavery Society. When it would not, Leavitt, admitting failure, took up the search again.

In January, 1841, he went to Washington as correspondent for the *Emancipator,* and in the House of Representatives at last he found abolition's center. He heard Adams, Giddings, Gates, and Slade present petitions, and he saw the petitions themselves, huge piles of documents stacked in the corridors. After the years of disunion in antislavery organization, of failing resources and frustrated plans, what he saw must have been a revelation. Here was a plethora of resources, the contributions of the antislavery thousands in the field. Leavitt was inspired!

His first efforts at Congressional reporting were unhappy. From sheer ignorance of the rules he scolded antislavery members for not doing with petitions as he would have done in their places. The members were justly incensed. "Must I be driven to the conclusion that you are predisposed to censure me and my abolition friends in Congress?" asked Slade; and Giddings wrote him in similar vein. But Leavitt was willing to learn. He made his peace with the indignant Congressmen, and they took him into their antislavery circle.[2]

Leavitt shortly discovered that although the members of the group were "as sincerely opposed to the domination of the slave power" as himself, they were also loyal Whigs. They reasoned that the platform of their party, properly considered, was hostile to Southern interests and favorable to the North. Thus, instead of attacking slavery itself, they advocated the Whig platform, "thinking it better to aim first at specific points of policy . . . beneficial to free labor—or rather to the North, as a bank, tariff &c." They argued that the effect of this strategy would be to drive Southern Whigs out of the party and make it a Northern, sectional organization. Only thus, they declared, could opposition to slavery be made a political issue.[3]

To Leavitt this strategy of economic interests seemed doomed to failure. "It is vain to think of harmonizing the North in favor of a restrictive policy or an artificial credit system," he told Giddings. "We must have a leading object in which we can all harmonize." Such an object was slavery. Indeed, Leavitt declared, "there is no object but slavery that can serve our turn." He urged it, however, not as an economic but as a moral object, "the greatest of evils and the prime cause of other evils." He pressed it on grounds of expediency as well as of principle: "I regard it as the dictate of sound wisdom to make opposition to slavery the *leading object* of public policy. I feel so sure I am right, that I cannot be satisfied without doing all in my power to bring the people to my view." [4]

Leavitt, characterized by Gates as a "most inveterate, upandicular man," had a reformer's fixed tenacity. Throughout the summer of 1841, "with his iron pen, invincible zeal, indomitable courage, untiring faith and indefatigable labors" he besieged the Congressmen with his views. When he returned to Washington in the fall, he found them entirely persuaded, ready to abandon their strategy of economic issues and make slavery the "leading object" of their endeavors. Setting at defiance Whig party discipline and the Whig program for the session, they announced that they were "determined to carry the war in upon the enemy—to shift the plan of campaign and attack slavery at every point." [5]

This decision was a momentous event in antislavery history. Previously the Whig service to the abolition cause had been incidental to the course of party opposition. Despite its antislavery animus, the Whig campaign for petitions had been obstructive only, and attacks on slavery had not been sanctioned by the party leaders except as incidents of the petition struggle. But with the decision of the antislavery Congressmen to make slavery the object of their strategy, slavery itself was bound to become an issue. The antislavery impulse at last was to have an unequivocal voice in Congress.

The antislavery Congressmen began their warfare by taking over the Washington end of the petition campaign. In the directions for the campaign of 1841, the New York Committee informed the petitioners that when they forwarded memorials to their favorite congressman they should also "address another letter to the Hon. Seth M. Gates, M.C., stating the . . . person to whose care it is sent." No longer could the "truckler to Southern power"—the Congressman who would not present memorials—remain anonymous. Hereafter he would be checked in Congress by his colleagues. Wise of Virginia pointed out to the House that the petition system was now complete, from the "letter from A. Tappan and J. Leavitt, in which those two highly distinguished individuals made their appeal to all abolitionists throughout the Union," to the final provision that petitions "be forwarded to the Hon. Seth M. Gates, the agent of the Abolitionists on the floor of Congress." [6]

For their aggressive warfare in the House, the insurgents constituted what Giddings liked to call "a Select Committee on slavery."

Like a regularly constituted committee, they planned a program of bills and resolutions of a kind that would open the discussion of slavery "in a shape in which *the* gag or any gag which it is possible for Congress to pass cannot touch them." [7] For each of these occasions, judiciously distributed throughout the session, one or more of the "select committee" would prepare a speech; and these speeches, polished after their delivery by the members themselves, would be published in the official records, to be scattered North and South.

But there was a difficulty. The subjects which they had in mind for bills and resolutions—such as the interstate slave trade, the annexation of Texas, and the admission of Florida—could not be adapted to antislavery purposes without considerable investigation; and the antislavery members, all of them practising lawyers and several of them senior members of important committees, had no time to spare for research. What they needed was an organization for collecting and abstracting information and opinions: in short, an antislavery lobby.[8]

The New York Committee—now the Executive Committee of the American and Foreign Anti-Slavery Society—made an effort to supply their need. Through the columns of the antislavery press they appealed "to the friends of the Constitutional right of petition throughout the United States" for funds to support an antislavery delegation to Washington. They had in mind a group of antislavery leaders. "The known presence of such persons, for two or three weeks at the beginning of the session, could not but be felt, with the most beneficial effects, among the members of Congress." But the credit of abolition organization was now so low that the appeal had no success at all. Among the thousands of friends of the right of petition throughout the United States, none came forward with funds for the lobby.[9]

Nevertheless the antislavery lobby was established, not from outside of Congress but from within, one of the strangest lobbies in history—a lobby contrary to the course of nature! On their own account Giddings and his colleagues made contributions and pledges to a common fund; they rented rooms in a house conveniently near the Capitol; and for a lobbyist they turned to Weld. In moving terms they called on him to come to Washington at their expense and help them.[10]

Such a summons Weld felt that he could not ignore. "This request, coming in the shape and with the apparent earnestness that it does, impresses me with the responsibility involved in the decision," he wrote. "These men are in a position to do for the A. S. cause by a single speech more than our best lecturers can do in a year." Moreover, the political antislavery men themselves could learn a lesson from these Congressmen. "The fact that men NOT *sent* to Congress by the 'third party' [Birney's Liberty Party] are ready to take such ground, will more than all things else open the eyes of abolitionists, who far and wide are getting so intoxicated with third partyism, and relaxing their grasp on the conscience of the South and North." Besides, he noted, "nobody beyond the persons concerned will know my business." This sort of lobby just suited Weld: it was anonymous. "On the whole, the more I look at the subject ·the more I feel as though I *dare* not assume the responsibility of refusing to comply with such a request." He went to Washington.[11]

The insurgents, Weld found, were a homespun group of heroes. Their antislavery inspiration had for the moment lifted them to leadership, but they were singularly ill equipped to wage a factional war. Giddings, Gates, and Slade were the leaders, and Giddings was their chief. He had real force of character and a driving sense of duty; but his capacity was commonplace, and he had none of the adroitness necessary to a successful party leader. But he was a determined fighter, and he never failed to throw himself into every breach in the Southern wall of silence around slavery. He was almost the only member in the House whom Adams loved.[12]

In contrast to Giddings' rough readiness for action, Gates, though staunch enough in the faith, was as "timid about speaking in public as J. G. Whittier." For service in Congressional warfare he was useless. Whether he would "have sufficient self-possession to speak extemporaneously is doubtful," Weld feared. "If not, he will write and read." [13]

Slade was a thoroughgoing abolitionist, and if the notion took him, he could be more dangerous in debate than any of the others; but he could not be counted on. A Yankee character, eccentric and independent, he would make no promises of coöperation beyond financial contributions. On the other hand, his colleague from Vermont, General Mattocks, promised Weld to "vote for anything . . . no abolition is too ultra for me; but as to speeches, I never made one in my life!" [14] Andrews of Ohio, a man of ability and an eloquent speaker, had a weak throat, and the Washington climate had reduced his voice to a whisper. Others—Borden of Massachusetts, James of Pennsylvania, and a handful more—were earnest abolitionists, but nonentities.

Still, though they were now insignificant—"members of a select committee about which little is said and little is thought"—many of them probably felt with Giddings that their "select committee" was one "which in the future history of our government will fill a larger space than that of any other select committee of this or any former Congress." But this sense of the historical importance of their mission, as well as a conviction of its righteousness, they needed to sustain them in the trials to come. For their decision to defy the party leaders by making slavery an open issue involved political isolation as a sure consequence and political annihilation as a possibility not at all remote. Such a decision was not one to be lightly taken. It may well be that without the inspiration of the antislavery impulse which Leavitt had brought them, the decision would not have been taken at all! It is worth noting in this connection that all of the group were "professors of religion," and five were elders in the Presbyterian Church. Several were "revival men"; Gates particularly, Weld found, "seems to have felt *much* of the power of the gospel." Indeed, the Great Revival had no small part in the origin of their zeal. Giddings, Gates, and Andrews were Weld's own converts to abolition, and others without doubt had felt his inspiration in some degree.[15]

The rooms which Giddings had rented for the lobby were at Mrs. Sprigg's boarding-house—"the Abolition House," it came to be called—directly in front of the Capitol and overlooking the park. At first only Giddings, Leavitt, Gates, and Weld lived there, though none of the other boarders were hostile to the cause. "They treat brother Leavitt and myself exactly as though we were not fanatics," Weld told his wife, "and we talk over with them at the table and elsewhere abolition just as we should at home." As opportunity offered, Slade and five or six more of the antislavery members shifted their quarters to the Abolition House. Mrs. Sprigg, a good Virginian, was apprehensive "that the character of her house would be hurt by it and that members of Congress would shun her. We have feared so too," said Weld. But it was not so. He remarked later that "this house is at this present moment, as Giddings tells me, the only boarding house in Washington which has *all* its rooms and beds occupied, and this too, notwithstanding she has *not,* as most of the other boarding houses have done, *lowered* her *prices* at all." One precaution Mrs.

Sprigg did take. Several of her servants were slaves; and fearing that it was "quite unsafe to have slaves in such close contact with abolitionists . . . she has taken care to get *free* colored servants in their places! *Stick a pin there!*" [16]

Indeed, the tolerance that Weld experienced everywhere in Washington was an agreeable surprise. He had come prepared for indignities—possibly arrest and imprisonment; but he found that even slaveholders, in private at least, were not unfriendly. "I may be called before the legal authorities to account for the Abolition books that are in my possession," he told his wife, "but I do not feel that I am in any special peril. I have been, you know, for months together in hourly danger of assassination. When I ran the danger, I felt it; but my duty not to heed it was plain, and I never lost a moment's sleep on account of it. . . . We are not the agents God has chosen for the deliverance of the slave if fear of *anything* swerves us from duty." [17]

For the first two days after his arrival Weld counseled with the insurgents, and on the third Giddings took him for a passing glance at the President's New Year's reception in the White House; and after "looking with sadness and pity at the pomp and tinsel, fashion and display of magnificence," they went to pay their respects to John Quincy Adams. "Found him and his wife living in a plain home, plainly furnished, and themselves plainly dressed—the old gentleman *very* plainly. When Mr. Leavitt introduced me, Mr. A. asked, 'is it Mr. Theodore D. Weld?' Yes. 'I know you well, sir, by your writings.'" He inquired after Weld's wife whom he had met, and introduced him to Mrs. Adams. "In doing it," Weld wrote his wife, "I was glad to hear him call her 'my dear,' as I think you told me they lived unhappily together." [18]

"By the way," Weld added: "Mr. A. says that since he has seen you, he has found that you and he are 'blood relations,' as he called it. . . . Mr. A's great grandmother (I think that is it) was . . . a Smith and she was a sister of your great grandfather Smith. Now I confess this scrap of genealogy is the only one that ever gave me any real pleasure. Father and J. Q. A. are second cousins, SO YOU AND I MUST BE ABOUT SIXTH COUSINS!!" [19]

Weld settled down to work. He had an alcove in the Library of Congress, secured for him by Giddings; here he arranged the mass of material he had brought to Washington and began his researches.

The most promising item on which to hang antislavery resolutions was the *Creole* case. An American vessel in the coastwise trade, the *Creole* had been seized on a voyage to New Orleans by some slaves on board, and had been brought by them to the British port of Nassau in the Bahamas, where those of the slaves who were implicated in the rising were taken into custody pending a determination of their status. The United States authorities had claimed them both as felons and as slaves, and Southern newspapers clamored for their blood. The case was ideal for antislavery propaganda. What was the status of slaves in an American vessel on the high seas? If "slavery . . . can exist only by force of positive municipal law and is necessarily confined to the territorial jurisdiction of the power creating it," then the slaves on the *Creole,* once the ship entered upon the high seas, "ceased to be subject to the slave laws of such State, and thenceforth . . . are amenable to the laws of the United States," which, since slavery was "an abridgement of the natural rights of man," could not establish slavery.[20]

This case embodied in striking form the municipal theory of slavery, upon which Weld had based his argument five years before in his tract, the *Power of Congress over Slavery in the District of Columbia.* Resolutions were drawn to embody the theory, and the council of insurgents urged Giddings to present them. After some demur he consented.[21] Their presentation was to have been the opening move in the program of aggressive war upon slavery; but before an opportunity arose to put them before the House, Adams himself opened the war.

A day or two after the *Creole* resolutions had been framed, Adams and his wife entertained some of the insurgents at dinner. "It was a genuine abolition gathering," said Weld. "The old patriarch talked with as much energy and zeal as a Methodist at a camp meeting. Remarkable man!" They discussed their plans for war upon slavery in the House, and Adams claimed a place for himself upon their "select committee." He did more. Either in collusion with the insurgents or on his own account, Adams decided to begin the war himself. The next day in the House he opened an attack upon slavery exceeding in boldness anything he had ever done before. Weld, duly warned by Adams that he intended to "set them in a blaze . . . took care to be in the House at the time." Adams first presented a Southern petition asking for his removal from the committee on foreign relations on account of his antislavery opinions, and then demanded to be heard in his defense. Despite the slightness of the pretext, the Speaker ruled that his request was in order as a question of privilege; and Adams proceeded, not in his own defense but against slavery. "He lifted up his voice like a trumpet, till slaveholding, slave trading and slave breeding absolutely quailed and howled under his dissecting knife. . . . A perfect uproar like Babel would burst forth every two or three minutes. . . . 'I demand Mr. Speaker that you *put him down.*' 'What, are we to sit here and endure such insults?' . . . Whenever any of them broke out upon him, Mr. A. would say, 'I see where the shoe pinches. Mr. Speaker it will pinch *more* yet!' 'I'll deal out to the gentlemen a diet that they'll find it hard to digest!' 'If before I get through every slaveholder slavetrader and slavebreeder on this floor does not get materials for bitter reflection it shall be no fault of mine!" The next Monday Weld was back in the House, but the question of privilege was tabled, and Adams went on presenting abolition petitions.[22]

Whig leaders, however, were furious. It was not only that Adams' insurgency had interrupted the legislative program of the Whig majority; his open attack upon slavery had disturbed the harmony of Northern and Southern interests upon which the party's existence depended. A caucus of Southern members decided that on the first pretext that offered, Adams should be censured; and Northern leaders concurred in their decision.[23]

The opportunity was not long in coming. Among his petitions a day or two later was one from citizens of Haverhill, Massachusetts, praying for a peaceable dissolution of the Union. Adams moved that it be referred to a select committee with instructions to deny the prayer of the petition; but the Whig leaders judged that its presentation could be made a sufficient occasion for party discipline, and a resolution of censure was accordingly proposed.

This was a party move—"a family quarrel in which Whig met Whig." It was a censure for insurgency, not for presenting a petition for the dissolution of the Union. The Whigs initiated it, and the Democrats "stood by . . . without taking part in the conflict." [24] But on that very account the attempt might be successful: Adams stood alone. The antislavery insurgents hastily gathered at the Abolition House and appointed Weld and Leavitt to call on Adams and proffer in behalf of the group "any assistance in their power." Adams was greatly affected. Weld lingered a moment. "I . . . offered him my services to relieve him from the drudgery of gathering the requisite materials for his defense. He replied, 'I thank you. I accept your offer gratefully.'" Weld dropped everything on which he was engaged and set to work on Adams' memoranda.[25]

The trial began auspiciously for the antislavery cause. "All the galleries were crowded excessively," wrote Weld. "Some of the most distinguished members of the Senate left their own hall and crowded into the aisles of the House." After the opening speech, Adams rose to reply. "And such a reply! He never spoke better. The personal invective and bitterness in which he sometimes indulges in his controversies with slaveholders was all laid aside. For half an hour he breasted the torrent of excitement with a calm fearlessness and majesty that furnished the highest illustration of the moral sublime that I ever witnessed in a popular secular assembly." [26]

Day by day the trial went forward, and night after night Weld and the old warrior counseled together upon the program of defense for the morrow. To the House, Adams spoke of the weeks that would be necessary to lay his case before them; but he told Weld that he did not expect the House to let him occupy the floor for more than a few days. He proposed to make his defense an occasion to "take up nearly all the relations of *slavery* to this government," and he laid out for Weld a program of research which occupied him incessantly.[27]

To Weld, Adams' exhaustless vigor was a marvel. "The energy with which Mr. A. speaks is astonishing. Though seventy-five years old, his voice is one of the clearest and loudest in the House, and his gestures and bodily action when warmly engaged in speaking are most vigorous and commanding. Last Friday, after he had been sitting in the house from 12 o'clock till 6, and for nearly half that time engaged in speaking with great energy against his ferocious assailants, I called at his house in the evening, and he came to meet me as fresh and elastic as a boy. I told him I was afraid he had tired himself out. 'No, not at all,' said he, 'I am all ready for another heat.' He then began and went through with the main points which he designed to push in his speech the next day, and with as much rapidity and energy of utterance and gesture as though he had been addressing the house. I tried to stop him, telling him he would need all his strength for the next day; but it was all in vain. He went on for an hour, or very nearly that, in a voice loud enough to be heard by a large audience. Wonderful man!" [28]

On the fourth day of the trial, Weld noted that "the slaveholders seem to see plainly that the tide is beginning to turn against them

with power." Weld, of course, interpreted the change in terms of the
battle in the House; the result of Adams' eloquence, which "has been,
with occasional exceptions, when Mr. A. has momentarily lost his
temper, perfectly confounding." But what Weld saw was probably
the reflection in the House of the tide of public sentiment in the
North. Adams himself told his opponents to read "the public presses
of the North upon this very transaction—from New York, or even
from Philadelphia northward—and see the opinions which they had
already expressed regarding it." [29] With hardly an exception, editors
of every political faith condemned the attack upon Adams in the
strongest terms. It soon became apparent that, even if the vote of censure could be secured, its effect would be a political disaster of the
first magnitude. On the sixth day of the trial, therefore, the resolutions of censure were laid on the table. "The triumph of Mr. A. is
complete," Weld wrote exultantly. "This is the first victory over the
slaveholders *in a body* ever yet achieved since the foundation of the
government, and from this time their downfall takes its date. It will
be as certain as that of Haman. . . . Let us thank God that the counsel of Ahithophel is turned headlong." [30]

But the victory was not yet complete. Something, it is true, had
been gained for insurgency. A few days later Giddings presented another petition for the dissolution of the Union, and in Adams' very
words he moved to refer it to a select committee with instructions to
deny the prayer of the petitioners. An effort to censure him was not
supported. "The slave-holders had been so horribly burned by the
hot iron before," Weld wrote, "that they took especial care not to
make any more errors." [31]

Still freedom to denounce slavery on the floor of the House was
not by any means assured. Though Adams had taken on his own
shoulders the first backstroke of party discipline, he had not come off
unscathed. In the cloak rooms of the Capitol, men said that Adams
had purchased his escape from censure by a promise to withhold additional petitions for the dissolution of the Union and to cease his
open war upon slavery in the House. The Whig leaders were not
yet reconciled to insurgency, and they struck back once again.[32]

After waiting vainly for Southerners to open the case of the
Creole, Giddings presented his own resolutions on the subject. He
was straightway censured by his angry Whig colleagues, who re-

fused him the right even to speak in his own defense. He immediately resigned his seat in the House and went back home to stand for reelection in his district.[33]

The issue between party regularity and party insurgency now was joined, not for Giddings only but for the other antislavery congressmen as well. If the Whig party leaders could secure the defeat of Giddings in his district, insurgency was doomed. But if they failed, and Giddings was reëlected, insurgency would receive its vindication. Giddings himself left Washington quite hopeful: "The whole of our Northern Whigs are deeply with me in feeling," he believed. But no sooner had he gone than pressure was exerted to prevent organized aid from Washington in his behalf. A caucus of Northern Whigs arranged by Gates was called off by party whips, and Gates was unable to assemble another. A few of the Ohio delegation "were spunky for a day or two," Gates wrote Giddings, "but they are afraid. . . . The Lord send you deliverance, for your Whig colleagues won't. . . . You are getting no help from here." [34]

To the opposite side, however, unstinted aid was sent from Washington, "and by persons, too, who would be ashamed to see their baseness exposed." [35] Inspired invectives against Giddings appeared in the Cleveland *Whig;* word was passed around his district that Giddings was at outs with his party; and aspirants to political place or to federal patronage were warned to treat his candidacy coldly. The whole weight of party interest and partisan loyalty were thrown against his campaign for reëlection.[36]

To Giddings' antislavery colleagues in Washington, the contest seemed a desperate one. Impotent to help—though the issue of the contest might involve their own political future—they could only wait and hope. Adams particularly felt the suspense. Unable to restrain his tears when Giddings bade him good-bye, he grew ill with worry. Even the newspaper correspondents who were on the insurgents' side "seemed to feel that their all depended" on Giddings' reëlection.[37]

But as a matter of fact the outcome had been decided years before. For Giddings' district on the Western Reserve had heard Weld preach the abolition revival; and the issue there was not between Giddings and his party: it was between party regularity and the antislavery impulse. With the whole weight of his party against him, Giddings was reëlected by a larger majority "than that of any other representative in the present or any other Congress." Insurgency was triumphant! In the face of his victory, Whig leaders were confounded. Wise of

Virginia, spokesman for the Southern Whigs, declared it to be "the greatest triumph achieved by a member of the House!" and Giddings returned to Washington immune to party discipline.[38]

After his return, certain die-hard Whigs declared that, if Giddings brought up the *Creole* case again, they would censure him once more; but they were unable to do so. In his initial speech, Giddings argued powerfully and at length on the municipal theory of slavery, the *Creole* case, and the right of free discussion in the House. When the die-hards tried to check him, a Northern colleague warned them that it could not be done. "The gentleman from Ohio," he said, "had come here determined to deliver a speech on the subject of abolition—he had come here fully charged with the subject; and they could not stop him." It was not for want of a majority that the Whig leaders permitted him to continue. "I have no doubt," said a member, "that he could be at this moment censured by a most decisive vote for everything and anything he might do here." His immunity from censure was probably due not only to the support of his constituents but also to the need for his vote. He was endured as an abolitionist in order to secure his support on party issues. Giddings' immunity, it was found, also applied to his antislavery colleagues; and their freedom to denounce slavery on the floor of the House was never again put in serious jeopardy. The Southern conspiracy of silence on slavery was broken.[39]

This victory, and its sequels, changed the whole aspect of the antislavery agitation in the House. Heretofore slavery could be discussed only under cover of other questions, and especially in connection with the right of petition. Now, however, slavery was open to direct attack, and petitions were no longer essential to the agitation. Though the issue of the right of petition still had sufficient momentum to convulse the House, and finally, two years later, to break down the standing gag, its importance was only historical. It was no longer needed as a cover for attacks upon slavery.

But in a far greater degree the victory for insurgency changed the aspect of the slavery issue in the nation. Throughout the agitation heretofore, the question of slavery had never been a party issue. Both the Democratic and the Whig parties were national organizations, dependent upon a harmony of Northern and Southern interests for their support. Whatever platforms they might frame, neither party could adopt a sectional issue; and slavery, of all issues the most clearly sectional, was thus excluded from party politics. But now the slavery question was outside the control of the Whig party leaders : it was an issue in the House. Its insurgent spokesmen made up an antislavery bloc within their party, a rallying point for the antislavery host throughout the North. At any time thereafter, endorsement of their program could be made a test question for Whig candidates in the antislavery belt ; while on the hustings, aspirants for office would be free to denounce slavery without sacrificing party regularity. Such operations were bound to enlarge the bloc in Congress and deepen sectional hostility. Inevitably the time must come when this broadening impulse would escape its party bounds and divide the nation. The victory of insurgency was thus a true turning point in history, the nucleus of a new movement in national affairs.

CHAPTER XIX

The Broadening Impulse

1843–1844

Between these momentous events, Weld pursued his researches. By nature he had rare powers of concentration. "Long, protracted investigation seems to rouse rather than fatigue him," Stanton said of Weld. "He will dig a month with the patience of a Cornwall miner into a musty library for a rare fact to elucidate or fortify a new proposition." [1] He lacked the mastery of his material that could have come only from a thorough education, but perhaps this was not needed for the sort of work he was doing. He searched for arguments to support a partisan cause, and no excess of learning tempered his conviction of their conclusiveness.

Adams still used him liberally, especially to find material "to counteract the project now started again for the annexation of Texas." Others of the antislavery circle had him at work on the recognition of Hayti, the taxation of the North in the interest of the South—"all those aspects of public life which involve support of slavery." The facts which his agents had collected during the last year of the American Anti-Slavery Society, to show the dependence of slavery upon the North, he now found invaluable; and he supplemented them daily from the material that was brought to his alcove in the Library of Congress. As each emergency came, he presented a documented case to the Congressman chosen for the occasion. [2]

During the last weeks of his stay Weld began another kind of work. As his acquaintance among the Northern Congressmen extended, he had advocated the antislavery cause—"for I feel a necessity laid upon me, yea a woe unto me if I do not!" [3] Indeed he put "the importance of personal intercourse with the members who are abolitionists and those who are inclining to abolition" above every other object of his mission. Accordingly, as the session advanced and calls for his services diminished, he devoted an increasing proportion of his time to solicitation for the cause. [4]

The effect of his lobbying can only be conjectured. Even for a super-lobbyist such as Weld, Congressmen in the 'forties were but indifferent prospects. "Public opinion is not brought here in any man's pocket," wrote a correspondent. "You might as well attempt to bring the North wind or the tide. . . . The dullest representative has all his faculties constantly intent on the remembrance and perception of the movements of his constituency. This is his great study, his business, his trade—the very 'craft by which he has his gain.' " [5]

But Weld was more than a lobbyist; he was an evangelist as well, the genius of the abolition revival; and the power which had wrought miracles of inspiration in Tappan's Association of Gentlemen, among the students of Lane Seminary, in the rural communities of the West, in the Presbyterian General Assembly, among the Seventy—in every group which his magnetic presence had invaded—that power was still his own. With Weld, even the conversion of Congressmen may have been possible.

At this time he was at the very height of his capacities. His splendid vitality was completely restored; and while his voice would not permit regular public speaking, it no longer distressed him in private conversation.[6] He still preached the abolition revival. Though he lobbied for Whig Congressmen, he had no share in their faith "that Whiggery is the political salvation of the country"; his single purpose was the slave's deliverance. Surrounded as he was by the intense factionalism of the 'forties, "the desperate strugglings and vaultings of Ambition, the . . . fierce encounters of rivals for office and popular applause," [7] he perceived in Congress itself "mighty delivering providences, marshalled by God, [which] wait and are straining for the start, delaying only for the watchword of faith and prayer"; and this millennial vision sustained his labor. "But woe to abolitionists if they dream their work is well-nigh done," he cried. "What vigilance will be demanded for future crises! What high fortitude, daring, patience of hope, and labor of love! The infinite abolitionist must do the work, and He has begun it on a scale as broad as the world; and he will so accomplish the work that other mighty revolutions will follow in its wake, if not indeed ride upon its waves." [8]

However fruitful his proselyting may actually have been, Weld was much encouraged: "Quite a number of members of Congress who have never before taken an interest in the question of slavery are beginning to survey it pretty seriously." He labored with them, he thought, with some avail. "If spared and blessed," he decided, "I think

I can see plainly that it will be duty for me to be here a part of the next session." [9]

Next December, the insurgents called Weld back to Washington. At the Abolition House he found Slade, Gates, and Giddings, and many of the members who had boarded there before. There were several new members besides: ex-Governor Crafts of Vermont, who was vice-president of the Vermont Anti-Slavery Society; and two old abolition friends of his to swell the ranks of the insurgents, Clarke of western New York and Mixson of Ohio. The general welcome warmed Weld's heart. He called on Adams. "He greeted me with great cordiality, and talked in high force on twenty points of anti-slavery interest," Weld wrote the sisters. "Inquired after you both, and said he had just read in some of the papers that you had gone South on a tour for the purpose of lecturing against slavery. The slaveholders, he said, were so frightened at the inroads making at their 'peculiar institution' that they were quite at their wits ends." [10]

Weld planned his campaign. Insurgency had won its freedom: "I anticipate nothing like the contest of last winter. The truth is that the slaveholders got so smitten with consternation as the bolts of father Adams hurled through their ranks at the last session, that they have never been able to rally." On the various questions with an antislavery bearing, "not less than a dozen stand ready to advocate the right side. Among these are Mr. Adams, Andrews, Gates, Giddings, Calhoun, Slade, Winthrop, Barnard, and Henderson." It was a different situation from the desperate one which he had found the year before. Even the atmosphere had changed: "Abolitionism is talked not only at our table but all over Washington." The antislavery impulse had consolidated its victory.[11]

Among abolitionists, the Abolition House was growing famous. Several dropped in during the winter, some of the New York Committee, a British abolitionist, and—to Garrison's disgust—David Lee Child, who came to report the session for the *Anti-Slavery Standard*. He applied for a place at the Abolition House; "but," Weld wrote, "as Leavitt had already engaged the only room left here (at Mrs. Sprigg's) for me, he was obliged to go elsewhere. I am sorry for it; wish we could all be together." [12] Lewis Tappan also came: "He boards but a few rods from me with his brother, Senator Tappan of Ohio. Half a dozen slave holding members of Congress board there and treat L. T. with entire respect. Yesterday his brother took him into the Senate chamber and introduced Lewis to quite a number of slaveholding members, who all treated him with respect. A number of the senators talked with him about abolition." [13]

The Abolition House had become so prominent in the movement that even Giddings called it "the headquarters of abolitionism." Weld was so clearly the spokesman for the antislavery interest centering there that some of the abolitionists urged him to attempt a union of the antislavery factions throughout the North. But he refused to try. "All hopes of fusing into one the main divisions of the anti-slavery host seemed to me utterly vain," he told Lewis Tappan. "Deep, ir-reconcileable, personal animosities and repulsions, added to diverse other considerations made such a coöperation impossible. I see no other mode than for each 'to fight on his own hook' and deal blows when and where and as he best may—taking care only to keep the strokes falling thickly and on the most pregnable points." [14]

Weld was also urged to represent American abolitionists at the second World Anti-Slavery Convention in London. He would not consider for a moment going as a delegate of the American and Foreign Anti-Slavery Society. "The society well know that I will not be a member of their society, nor their representative anywhere, be-cause of their anti-woman feature. So individual members offer to pay my expenses and have me be the representative of no society." But Weld refused to go in this or any other capacity, even though the British abolitionists themselves urged him to come. "The earnest de-sire expressed by the committee of the British and F. A. S. S. and by so many leading abolitionists in this country to have me attend that convention, is quite unaccountable to me," he told his wife. "They all know that I have no taste for such gatherings and very little adapta-tion for them. . . . Very many abolitionists have for such scenes a strong taste, and let such attend them. They are doubtless of vast im-portance, but my calling is to other modes of promoting the great cause. Let each fill his niche." Weld still clung to his anonymity.[15]

The antislavery agitation for the session ran a quiet but fruitful course. Over certain issues—notably the claims for slaves killed or disabled in the service of the United States—there was "some pretty warm work." But on the whole the members from the Abolition House were permitted to speak their hearts on slavery, and never once was their freedom jeopardized. Weld labored ceaselessly, writing speeches, raising new issues for the agitation, planning strategic moves, yet finding time as a true lobbyist to "visit the members at their rooms, and talk with them and lead them into the subject." [16]

He stayed longer than he had intended, and when he went home the spirit of the antislavery lobby departed with him. "We miss you greatly since you left us," Giddings wrote him. "I now go down to Mr. Leavitt's room occasionally but my visits end there. He, Messrs. Gates, Slade and myself get together occasionally, but one is missing. . . . Oh my friend you left this quite too soon." [17] But gratitude for what Weld had done filled their hearts. "His labors and his counsels have been of the deepest importance," said Leavitt. "He has been doing foundation work, and we all feel that our future labors will be the more available for the services of a wise master-builder." [18]

At the next session of Congress the Abolition House took over the entire petition campaign. Gates was still to receive the memorials as before; but the appeal to the nation for petitions was signed, not by A. Tappan and J. Leavitt, but by the insurgents themselves, and John Quincy Adams' name headed the list. Formal leadership of the antislavery impulse was at last in Congress, where it had long belonged. [19]

The opening of the session found still more of the antislavery circle at the Abolition House, but Weld was not among them. The insurgents besought him to come. "I never wanted to see you more in my life," Giddings wrote him. "I never wanted to use you as much as at present. . . . We want help. 'Come over and help us.' " Lewis Tappan also urged him to go and offered to relieve his family of every care while he was away. But Weld was convinced that his foundation work was done. "I cannot feel that my *call* is to Washington this winter," he replied. "I know that much important work is to be done there and if it were impossible to get it done in any other way than by my going, I would go. But that, I know is not so." It was enough for him that the antislavery cause in Congress was now going forward; and neither the pride of leadership nor the subtler vanity which is fed by secret power moved him to share its triumphs. His own pioneering done, he quietly slipped out of the movement. [20]

But the impulse which Weld had quickened continued to enlarge. Antislavery insurgency increased in boldness and dexterity year by year. In each succeeding session new members were added to the antislavery ranks, some of them Weld's converts, others converts of the Seventy, like Thaddeus Stevens, whose eloquence and adroitness supplied those qualities for successful leadership which Giddings had lacked. A few of the Seventy themselves joined the insurgents, among them Owen Lovejoy, who had pledged his life to the cause years before beside his martyred brother's body. These new members brought no novel impulse to the insurgent bloc nor did they change its strategy. From first to last they followed the plan of Giddings and his early colleagues, to attack slavery upon every occasion which permitted its discussion.

The issues which they sponsored were various. Some were vital, others were trivial, and still others had small measure of reality. They all derived their importance from the fact that they provided an occasion for a fresh assault on slavery. Thus it mattered little to the insurgent Congressmen that an antislavery ordinance for the Western territories was needless, that it would, in Webster's phrase, merely "reaffirm an ordinance of Nature." To them the question of slavery in the territories, like many lesser issues, had a moral significance which transcended every economic aspect of the question. Indeed, the moral aspect of each issue touching slavery was the one for which the antislavery bloc contended from the beginning of the struggle to its inevitable end.

The insurgents were sustained by the antislavery host. Except for northern New England, the areas of their strength in marked degree were those where Weld and his disciples had preached the abolition revival, where the Seventy had later consolidated antislavery organization, and the petition volunteers had finally built up active majorities. Though these majorities embodied the antislavery impulse, they continued for many years to maintain their party affiliations, and in a corporate sense they acted as a unit only from time to time. When John Quincy Adams journeyed to Cincinnati in the summer of 1843, with reverent spontaneity they made his trip a triumphal progress such as few statesmen have experienced in our history. But at ordinary times only their antislavery convictions made a common bond between them. Still they formed a regimented group; and on each public issue concerned with slavery they found occasion to renew the struggle once again.

In the course of years, thousands of the antislavery host and thousands of their sons went west. Here in the new States and territories they advocated the creed which they had learned to reverence at home. Old members of the Seventy still served them as leaders: Codding in Illinois, Lee in Michigan, Wattles in Kansas, and many more. Though their proportion to the population of the West was smaller than it had been in the antislavery areas of the East, their efforts were enough to give to Western antislavery measures the character of "a religious cause—a moral cause" which the entire agitation had borne from its beginning.

Indeed from first to last, throughout the antislavery host the cause continued to be a moral issue and not an economic one. Neither in their propaganda nor in their sentiments was the economic issue dominant. Ministers, merchants, mechanics or farmers, their attitude toward slavery was determined by the chances of origin or personal influence and not by calculations of material advantage. Moreover, the areas of their antislavery strength coördinated with no single Northern interest. They were to be found near to the South and far away; tributary to Southern trade and independent of it; close to the territories in dispute between North and South and at the farthest confines of the nation. Except for northern New England and the new States of the West, their boundaries were largely coincident with the limits of the abolition revival, and with that circumstance alone.

Throughout the later agitation, from the 'forties to the 'sixties, the doctrine of the antislavery host thus continued in the moral tenets of the original antislavery creed. In this crusading spirit their support of men and measures was consistently maintained until 1860, when, county by county, the antislavery areas gave Abraham Lincoln the votes which made him President.

WORKS CONSULTED

This period of the antislavery movement is so familiar to scholars, and so much in the way of bibliography has already been published elsewhere, that I shall indicate here only the more important sources for this study.

My chief dependence has been upon the journals of the antislavery societies and the religious denominations.[1] The antislavery papers are not uniform in value. Before 1840, the *Emancipator* (New York and Boston, 1832–1844) was both the organ of the national society and a tract for national propaganda; it told only one side of the story and that in the most favorable light. After 1840, however, it became less the organ of a society and was therefore more revealing.

For the period before 1840, the State society papers are more valuable, especially Benjamin Lundy's *National Enquirer* (Philadelphia, 1836–1838), which was later replaced by Whittier's *Pennsylvania Freeman* (Philadelphia, 1838–1844); William Goodell's *Friend of Man* (Utica, N. Y., 1836–1842); Birney's *Philanthropist*—later edited by Dr. Gamaliel Bailey—(New Richmond and Cincinnati, 1836–1843); and Burleigh's *Christian Witness* (Pittsburgh, 1836–1840).[2] Lundy's paper was the most helpful of them all because it was the most outspoken. Almost as helpful was the *Friend of Man*. The *Philanthropist* records the progress of organization in the West, but in other respects it was not so useful for my purposes as other State journals. With Whittier in the chair, the *Pennsylvania Freeman* was edited with skill but with such discretion that it was of little use to me. However, after Whittier resigned, it too became more controversial. The *Liberator* (Boston, 1831–1856) is less valuable. It is the most carelessly edited, though incomparably the most brilliantly written, of them all; but it records only Garrison's view of the movement. The New Hampshire *Herald of Freedom* (Concord, 1835–1844) is but a pale reflection of the *Liberator,* and the *Massachusetts Abolitionist* (Boston, 1838–1841) is too factional to be objective. For events after 1840, the *National Anti-Slavery Standard* (New York, 1840–1850) has meaning only as long as the Childs edited it; thereafter it is mediocre. The organ of the American and Foreign Anti-Slavery Society, the *Anti-Slavery Reporter* (New York, 1840–1844), records the ups and downs of that organization after 1840.

Numerous lesser antislavery papers at certain times were helpful: the Methodist antislavery weekly, *Zion's Watchman* (New York, 1836–1841); *Freedom's Journal* (New York, 1827–1829); the *Abolitionist* (Boston,

[1] From all of the periodicals, I have listed only the volumes that are applicable to this study.

[2] I was unable to find a file of the *Witness* and have used only scattered numbers in private collections.

1833); and the *Genius of Universal Emancipation* (Baltimore and Philadelphia, 1827–1833). The pamphlet papers of the American Anti-Slavery Society—the *Slave's Friend* (New York, 1836–1838); the *Anti-Slavery Examiner* (New York, 1836–1840); *Human Rights* (New York, 1835–1838); the *Anti-Slavery Record* (New York, 1836–1837); and the *American Anti-Slavery Reporter* (New York, 1833)—are so much tracts for popular consumption that they proved almost worthless for my purposes. The colonizationists' *African Repository* (Washington, 1825–1844), and the British *Monthly Anti-Slavery Reporter* (London, 1825–1836) had some apposite items.

The denominational journals are second in importance only to the antislavery periodicals. For the early stages of the New York movement, the *New York Evangelist* (New York, 1830–1843) is indispensable. In New England, the Methodist *Zion's Herald* (Boston, 1829–1842) and the Baptist *Zion's Advocate* (Portland, Maine, 1833–1838) tell essential details of the agitation that escape the *Liberator*. The Congregational weeklies of New England are invaluable, especially the *Religious Intelligencer* (New Haven, 1834–1837) and the *Boston Recorder* (Boston, 1833–1838). I should have made more use of the latter. Two national religious weeklies, the *Presbyterian* (Philadelphia, 1831–1836) and the Methodist *Christian Advocate and Journal* (New York, 1829–1844), each contributed a few important notes. The regional religious weeklies are closer to the movement. I have already mentioned the New England papers. In the West, the Methodist *Pittsburg Conference Journal* (Pittsburg, 1833–1836) follows the Pennsylvania agitation in intermittent fashion. In northern Ohio, the Presbyterian *Ohio Observer* (Hudson and Cleveland, 1833–1838) and, in southern Ohio, the *Cincinnati Journal* (Cincinnati, 1832–1836) record the movement before 1836. The Methodist *Western Christian Advocate* (Cincinnati, 1834–1838) is a check on the first two. In the Far West is Lovejoy's Presbyterian *Alton Observer* (Alton, 1836–1837).

The denominational quarterlies contain unworked material both for the controversy between New- and Old-school theology and for the antislavery agitation. The most valuable is William Ellery Channing's *Christian Examiner* (Boston, 1824–1844). As the organ of the Unitarians, it took the rôle of impartial but interested spectator of the agitation. Next in value is Lyman Beecher's *Spirit of the Pilgrims* (Boston, 1828–1833). The *Biblical Repertory and Theological Review* (New York, new series, 1835–1844); the *Methodist Quarterly* (New York, 1825–1844); the *Christian Register* (Boston, 1828–1836); and numerous others of lesser importance, each contain studies of the antislavery agitation.

Finally there are certain reform journals, mostly queer little weeklies on the fringes of the benevolent empire: the *Genius of Temperance* (Providence and New York, 1828–1833); *MacDowall's Journal* (New York, 1832–1834); the *Journal of Humanity* (New York, 1831–1834); the *Non-Resistant* (Boston, 1839–1841); the *Protestant* (New York, 1830–1832); and the *Temperance Recorder* (Albany, N. Y., 1833–1835).

Contemporary and near-contemporary histories by participants in the antislavery movement are, of course, all written in accord with the traditional interpretation. William Goodell's *Slavery and Anti-Slavery* (New York, 1852), Oliver Johnson's *William Lloyd Garrison and his Times* (Boston, 1880), and the others are useful only as far as their statements can be verified. Similar histories of agitation in the denominations are more valuable, especially S. J. Baird's *History of the New School* (Philadelphia, 1868); L. C. Matlack's *American Slavery and Methodism* (New York, 1849); and *A History of the Late Division of the Presbyterian Church*, by a committee of the New York and New Jersey Synods (New York, 1852). I used numerous treatises on the Great Revival, two in particular: William B. Sprague, *Lectures on Revivals of Religion* (New York, 1833), and Charles G. Finney, *Lectures on Revivals* (New York, 1835, sixth edition).

I have quoted from only a few of the books of the period in criticism or in defense of immediatism: William Jay, *An Inquiry into the Character and Tendencies . . . of the American Anti-Slavery Society* (New York, 1835–1838, eight editions); Catherine Beecher, *An Essay on Slavery and Abolition* (Philadelphia, 1837); William Ellery Channing, *Slavery* (Boston, 1835); and J. T. Austin, *Remarks on Dr. Channing's Slavery* (Boston, 1835). Two bystanders' accounts are penetrating: Anonymous [Calvin Cotton], *A Voice from America to England* (London, 1839) and W. L. Stone, *Matthias and His Impostures* (New York, 1835).

The published collections of letters and diaries for the period are numerous. Three of the biographies come under this head. First, of course, is the monumental *William Lloyd Garrison* by his children (London, 1889, 4 vols.). I used the 1885 edition of the first two volumes. The second is Charles Beecher's *Autobiography and Correspondence of Lyman Beecher* (New York, 1865). The third is Catherine H. Birney's *The Grimké Sisters* (Boston, 1885). Then there is the classic diary of the period, *Memoirs of John Quincy Adams*. There are a few items in S. T. Pickard's *Life and Works of J. G. Whittier* (New York, 1894); the *Diary of Philip Hone* (New York, 1889, 2 vols.); and the Tappan papers in Abel and Klingberg, *A Side-Light on Anglo-American Relations, 1839–1858* (1927).

The biographies and autobiographies are of unequal value. The two autobiographies which I used most largely and also most cautiously— *Autobiography of Asa Mahan* (London, 1882) and *Memoirs of Charles G. Finney* (New York, 1896)—are in great part drawn from memory's storehouse. The biographies are mostly written by relatives and disciples, usually to elevate their subjects. This is less true of Lewis Tappan's *Life of Arthur Tappan* (New York, 1871), though even Lewis, by minimizing his own part, makes his brother's share in their joint labors for the cause far larger than it actually was.

As for the manuscripts, Weld's papers in the Library of Congress and the letters in the possession of his family gave to my story a reality which nothing else could have done. These manuscripts are to be published shortly by the American Historical Association on the Albert J. Beveridge foundation. I used a manuscript volume of transcripts of the letters of Elizur Wright Jr., made by his daughter, and also the papers of Lewis Tappan in the Library of Congress, a restricted collection to which the donor kindly gave me access. Several other collections were useful, especially the Giddings papers in the library of the Ohio Archæological and Historical Society. Mr. Dion. S. Birney of Washington permitted me to use the J. G. Birney papers in his possession (he has since donated them to the Library of Congress), and the Oberlin College Library generously sent me copies of several letters from the Finney papers. The tens of thousands of petitions in the House Files, Library of Congress, yielded data for the petition campaign and also contributed to the record of the enlarging antislavery areas in the North.

I found several volumes of manuscript minutes. The records of the old Anti-Slavery Society of Pennsylvania, 1829–1833, and the minutes book of the Philadelphia Women's Anti-Slavery Society, 1830–1831 (both at the Historical Society of Pennsylvania), throw light upon the beginnings of national organization. The American Anti-Slavery Society's Agency Committee Minutes, 1833–1840, and the second volume of the Minutes of the Executive Committee, which covers the years 1837–1840 (both at the Boston Public Library), are vital to an understanding of the society's inner history.

I have consulted most of the official documents of the various antislavery societies, the *Proceedings* and the *Reports,* as well as their antislavery tracts and pamphlets. A list of them would unduly extend this summary. For those from which I have quoted, I have given place and date of publication in the foot-note citations. I have referred in the same manner to contemporary pamphlets and books which were of minor importance to my story.

Secondary histories and monographs I approach with some embarrassment. If I have read the sources rightly, comment of mine upon other interpretations of the antislavery agitation would be unseemly. If I have read them wrongly, comment would only add to my errors.

NOTES *

CHAPTER I

THE GREAT REVIVAL

[1] Channing, *Memoirs,* III, 244.

[2] The quotations are from the *Sum of Saving Doctrine* of the Presbyterian Church (1832 ed.).

[3] A few of the New-School liberals in the Presbyterian Church considered conversion to be a natural phenomenon, the result merely of "excitement"; but the orthodox all maintained that conversion was a miracle wrought by the Holy Ghost and that to believe otherwise was heresy. For the orthodox position, see Sprague, *Lectures on Revivals of Religion,* pp. 229 ff. This is a symposium of the opinions of the greatest Presbyterian divines of the day regarding the nature of revivals.

[4] Long after 1830 the doctrine of infant damnation remained a part of Old-School Presbyterian orthodoxy, which maintained that, although infants "are not moral agents, yet they possess a nature not conformable to the law of God: they are depraved, 'children of wrath,' and guilty on account of their own personal depravity." (*Biblical Repertory and Princeton Review,* I, 499.) However, by 1830, most Congregational ministers refused either to subscribe to infant damnation or to denounce it. (See Griffin, *Park Street Lectures,* pp. 13–14, and *Spirit of the Pilgrims,* I, 160.)

[5] Even this timid concession to liberalism alienated Nettleton, the famous orthodox evangelist, who wrote as follows: "With all my love and respect [for Beecher] I must say that neither my judgment, nor conscience, nor heart can acquiesce, and I can go with you no farther. Whatever you may say about infants, for one, I do solemnly believe that God views and treats them in all respects, just as he would do if they were sinners." The letter is quoted in *Western Christian Advocate,* II, 190. The quotation from Beecher's position on infant damnation is in the *Spirit of the Pilgrims,* I, 88–89. His comment on original sin is in *Autobiography and Correspondence of Lyman Beecher,* II, 25. His discovery of the inadequacy of Calvinistic doctrine for revivals is recorded in *Christian Examiner,* first series, I, 78.

[6] An excellent summary of Beecher's abilities, with special reference to his weakness in philosophy, is in *Biblical Repertory and Princeton Review,* IX, 372.

[7] The quotations are from a letter from the Rev. Dr. John H. Church,

---

* The reference numbers in the text refer to items within the paragraph which precedes them, except where they occur within the paragraph itself.

one of the Andover interlocutors. It is printed in Baird, *History of the New School*, p. 200.

[8] *Christian Examiner*, third series, IX, 116.

[9] The letter from the indignant Calvinist, Rand, is printed in *ibid.*, p. 122. Beecher's prophecy of the millennium is in the *Spirit of the Pilgrims*, VI, 503.

[10] The two quotations describing the Great Revival are from the *Report to the Synod of Albany*, quoted in *Autobiography and Correspondence of Lyman Beecher*, II, 90, and the *Report of the Presbyterian General Assembly* for 1831, quoted in the *Spirit of the Pilgrims*, IV, 410.

[11] One especially obnoxious member of the Holy Band was a notable eccentric of western New York, an elderly Presbyterian minister called Father Nash, who would daily make up a list of sinners for whom he prayed in secret. Unfortunately "they could hear him pray half a mile off," and respectable people were scandalized. The quoted description of Finney in action is from *Bunker Hill Contest* (Utica, 1826), pp. 80–81. The comment of the President of Williams College is quoted in Wright, *Charles Grandison Finney*, p. 78.

[12] The Presbyterian summons to Beecher is in the *Biblical Repertory and Princeton Review*, new series, IV, 487. His comment on the parlous state of the church is in *Christian Examiner*, first series, IV, 265; and his invidious description of Finney as Satan is quoted from a letter to Nettleton, printed in *ibid.*, VI, 107.

[13] A full report of the conference is in *Christian Examiner*, IV, 359 ff. It is from this account that the resolutions are quoted. Finney's own comment on groaning in prayer is from his *Lectures on Revivals*, p. 95. Beecher's words to Finney, as recited by Beecher himself in after years, are in *Autobiography and Correspondence of Lyman Beecher*, II, 101.

[14] Finney's comments on his ministerial colleagues are quoted from his *Lectures on Revivals*, pp. 90, 194–195. The description of Finney is contained in Theodore Weld's narrative, in *Autobiography and Correspondence of Lyman Beecher*, II, 310 ff. The scene in Finney's revival is described by Finney himself in his *Lectures on Revivals*, p. 332.

[15] The last quotation is from the report of a committee to the Presbytery of Oneida, *A Narrative of the Revival of Religion in the County of Oneida . . . in the year 1826* (Utica, 1827), p. 36, regarding Finney's revivals. A similar report was made by the Oneida Presbytery to the synod, quoted in *Autobiography and Correspondence of Lyman Beecher*, II, 9; and the revival was described in similar terms in the *Narrative of the State of Religion in the Presbyterian Church* for 1827, a report to the Presbyterian General Assembly of that year. The description of Western Presbyterian revival methods is quoted from a letter written by Weld to Finney, Feb. 26, 1832 (Finney MSS.).

[16] The last quotation is from a sermon by Finney, *Sermons on Important Subjects*, Sermon 1; but Finney in turn quoted it almost word for word from a sermon by Jonathan Edwards. Finney's repudiation of "constitutional depravity" is contained in a sermon published in the *Pittsburg Conference Journal*, II, 76. The quotation regarding Finney's

connection with the theology of New Haven is from Baird, *History of the New School*, p. 217.

[17] Finney's "philosophical" interpretation of the Holy Ghost and revivals is in his *Lectures on Revivals*, p. 12; his analysis of the function of "excitement" in revivals is in the same work, pp. 10–11; and his description of the process by which the sinner secures a "new heart" is in his *Sermons on Important Subjects*, Sermon 2.

[18] Finney, *Lectures on Revivals*, pp. 374–375.

[19] Anonymous [Calvin Cotton], *A Voice from America to England*, p. 64. Not the least element in Finney's effectiveness was his entire unconsciousness of teaching novel doctrine. Quite the contrary; he invisaged his doctrine as the only true orthodoxy. He preached: "It is enough to make humanity weep to see the fog and darkness that have been thrown around the plain directions of the gospel, till many generations have been emptied into hell. . . . So much have you D. D.'s done to mystify and befool people's minds in the plainest matters." (Finney, *Lectures on Revivals*, pp. 347–348.) But among the Old-School Calvinists his doctrinal heresies were quickly detected. "The doctrines of . . . original sin, the entire dependence of the sinner on the special influence of the Holy Spirit in the work of . . . conversion . . . have almost invariably been either denied, or perverted," wrote Asahel Green, former President of Princeton. (Sprague, *Lectures on Revivals*, pp. 351–352.) But Finney was never tried for heresy. Men in whose churches he began his greatest revivals and who later were leaders in the New-School schism were tried or threatened with trial, but Finney was not touched. As the persecution of his colleagues became more severe, his scorn of orthodox ministers deepened; and in 1835 he declared: ". . . their contentions and janglings are so ridiculous, so wicked, so outrageous that no doubt there is a jubilee in hell every year about the time of the meeting of the General Assembly." (Finney, *Lectures on Revivals*, p. 269.)

[20] These early incidents in Weld's story I have pieced together from letters and newspapers. No connected account of his life exists. Unlike other abolitionists, Weld was not concerned with his place in history. His sister-in-law who lived with the Welds, wrote: "Theodore's history is, I suppose, a very remarkable one, but we shall probably never obtain it, as we only get it by scraps from his friends. He has an almost unconquerable aversion to speaking of himself, and therefore rarely mentions anything in which he is concerned." (Sarah M. Grimké to her mother, July 15, 1839, Weld MSS.) Beecher's apprehensions regarding the "host of ardent . . . young men" were expressed in a letter to Nettleton. (*Biblical Repertory and Princeton Review*, new series, IV, 477–478.) The quotation regarding Weld's success in revivals is from Finney's own words in his *Memoirs of C. G. Finney*, p. 188.

[21] The three quotations characterizing Weld are respectively from a letter from Stanton to Weld (no month), 1832; from the diary of Elizabeth Whittier, Sept., 1836 (transcribed by T. S. Pickard); and from a characterization of Weld written by H. B. Stanton in 1838, all in the Weld MSS. The quoted description of Weld's campaign for women's

right to speak in public is from a letter from Weld to Sarah and Angelina Grimké, Sept. 6, 1837 (Weld MSS.).

[22] Finney himself declared that he had had no part whatever in initiating the practice of women's speaking and praying in public. He had supposed when he first heard it that it was a local custom in Utica. (*Memoirs of C. G. Finney,* p. 178.)

[23] For Weld's association with Whittier, see Chapter XIII. Years later Whittier wrote Weld's daughter: "There is no one whom I more sincerely love and reverence than thy dear father—one of the ablest and one of the best men I ever knew." Whittier to Sarah Weld Hamilton, Dec. 19, 1889 (manuscript letter in the possession of Dr. Angelina G. Hamilton).

[24] Stuart wore "on all occasions and at all seasons a Scotch plaid frock, with a cape reaching nearly to his elbows." One of his former students in Utica Academy thus characterized him: "eminently pious, actively benevolent, unsurpassingly kind, rigidly austere, and wildly eccentric . . . with a most attractive smile and a thunderous frown . . . withal of the most humane and tender feelings; fond of children and youth, and of joining boyishly in their sports, but strict with them. . . . Of course he was the children's friend, for with the tenderness of a woman, he had the spirit of a child. How they would flock around him. How they would cling to him. They made him the willing partner of all their joys and sorrows, and of their sports as well." The description of Stuart as to "looks, dress, manners," etc., was by Weld's aunt, who nevertheless admired and loved Stuart. (See manuscript biography, "Charles Stuart," in the Weld MSS.)

[25] The four quotations above are from the following letters respectively: Weld to Angelina Grimké, Feb. 16, 1838; the same, March 7, 1837; the same, Feb. 16, 1838; and Stuart to Weld, July 9, 1829; all in the Weld MSS.

[26] The two quotations above are from a letter from Weld to Angelina Grimké, March 7, 1837, and Weld to the Grimké sisters, Dec. 28, 1837, both in the Weld MSS.

[27] For the record of this association see Stuart's letters to Weld, 1825–1830, a charming cycle. Weld's reference to his "indivisible existence" with Stuart is in a letter of his to the Grimké sisters, Dec. 28, 1837 (Weld MSS.).

[28] Upon occasion Weld's eloquence impelled liquor dealers to collective action. At Rochester, where he spoke on temperance at the close of 1830, eight or ten liquor dealers and manufacturers pledged themselves to abandon the business. "Indeed," remarked an editor, "we have been informed that a large number of wholesale grocers and others, have had a meeting with reference to abandoning the sale of ardent spirits, and we have no doubt they will generally do so. . . . We wish Mr. Weld could visit every town in this region with reference to the promotion of temperance. Should we say what we might anticipate from such a visit, we should be charged with enthusiasm." (*Western Recorder,* Jan. 7, 1831.) Weld's high place in the West as a temperance orator is estimated by John Keep, a leading

Presbyterian minister, in a letter to Weld, October 20, 1834 (Weld MSS.). For the details of Stuart's support of Weld at Oneida Institute, see Stuart to Weld, January 10, 1826; April 20 and July 9, 1829; and another of (no month) 1829. For Weld's work as a member of Finney's Holy Band, see Finney to Weld, March 27, 1828; March 20, 1829; and November 30, 1832 (Weld MSS.).

[29] Weld's refusals were probably due to Charles Stuart, who frequently admonished him to put first his training for the ministry. On July 5, 1828, for instance, he wrote: "Do not, on any account or for any consideration, overlook the main object of your residence at Whitesboro', your studious preparation for the gospel ministry . . . and whenever you find that local calls or duties interfere with these, cast them off without hesitation, pursuing steadily and in love your own more immediate calling." For invitations to Weld to come and hold revival, see Weld MSS., 1828–1831. One, John Keep, whose friendship with Weld was later significant to the antislavery cause, wrote as follows: "Our thoughts have been directed to you—but we are met by the apprehension that you cannot be induced to come. In the hope, however, that our fears are too strong, I now write to request you to visit. . . . My Son says do urge him, & take no denial— he must come—we cannot do without Mr. Weld or Mr. Finney." (John Keep to Weld, March 9, 1831.) Invitations from philanthropists during these years were numerous and pressing. For example, in 1831, several wealthy merchants of New York planned to establish a great Presbyterian revival church in New Orleans—"that wicked city, the Gomorrah of our nation"—on condition that Weld be its pastor. (T. Parmelee to Weld, May 12, 1831, and G. Winslow to Weld, June 30, 1831, Weld MSS.) This New Orleans pulpit was later established with Joel Parker as the minister. Lewis Tappan's summons to New York is quoted from a letter to Weld, October 25, 1831 (Weld MSS.). Lewis Tappan's two sons were students at Oneida Institute, and it was through them that he first met Weld.

[30] The quotation is from a letter from Finney to Weld, March 27, 1828 (Weld MSS.). Later, however, he wrote: "The scales have fallen from so many eyes that the rest are disturbed, and the charm seems to be breaking up, and the sorcery of hell in which they have been bewildered appears to be dissolving."

[31] Many observers at the time testified that the general conditions were favorable to revolutionary reforms which, in the early 'thirties, resulted from the Great Revival. An excellent summary is in Stone, *Matthias and His Impostures,* p. 321.

CHAPTER II

THE NEW YORK PHILANTHROPISTS

[1] The quotations descriptive of New York and the benevolent societies are from the following: *New York Evangelist,* I, 67; *Christian Examiner,*

first series, II, 247–248, and second series, VII, 105; and anonymous [Calvin Cotton], *A Voice from America to England,* p. 87.

[2] *Christian Examiner,* second series, VII, 105–106. The numbering of the Seamen's Friend Society among the "Great Eight" is accounted for by the fact that this was the day of the merchant marine's greatness, and saving the sailor was a major task quantitatively as well as qualitatively.

[3] The union of the temperance cause with revivals is explained in the *New York Evangelist,* IV, 6. The work of the New York Temperance Society is described in the same journal, IV, 191. The infant society movement was considerable. This work had a special agent, and a standard constitution for infant societies, in verse, and therefore "most wisely adapted to infant minds." It was as follows:

> "We, little boys and girls
>   Do not think
>   We'll ever drink
>   Whiskey or gin
>   Brandy or rum
>   Or anything
> That will make drunk come."

The instructions accompanying the constitution advised: "The promise contained in the line 'Do not think' is perhaps better calculated to inspire them with a sense of their dependence upon God for strength to keep their resolution . . . than a more positive pledge." (*Ibid.,* IV, 231.)

[4] The relation between the North and England was thus described by Senator Preston of South Carolina. (*Appendix to Congressional Globe,* first S., 24th Congress, p. 221.)

[5] Calvinists—Old-School Presbyterians—seldom appeared as officers in the benevolent societies. As a whole, Calvinists distrusted the societies; and when the Presbyterian Church divided in 1837, the Old-School General Assembly voted to exclude three of the greatest, the Home Missionary Society, the American Board of Commissioners for Foreign Missions, and the General Education Society, from their churches. The quoted indictment of Presbyterian control is from the *Christian Advocate and Journal,* June 14, 1833. In reply to this indictment, the editor of the *Evangelist* made unconvincing efforts, by naming Methodists on the boards of the societies, to prove that the charge was untrue. At least, he said, it was not true of the Seaman's Friend Society. "You can never make the sailors believe it. . . . You must 'tell that to the marines!'" (*New York Evangelist,* I, 58.)

[6] The quoted characterization of Lewis Tappan is from the *National Anti-Slavery Standard,* Dec. 30, 1841. A less flattering characterization by one of Lewis Tappan's merchant associates is in the *Diary of Philip Hone,* I, 167. The estimate of Arthur Tappan's work for the benevolent empire is from a letter by "an able writer," quoted in the *Life of Arthur Tappan,* p. 405.

[7] Founded in 1828, its introductory editorial announced, to provide the American public with a truly Christian newspaper, the current papers being "defiled with . . . laudatory dissertations upon half-naked ac-

tresses" and other "errors." The public did not want a truly Christian newspaper and after sinking the better part of a hundred thousand dollars, the Tappans had to sell it.

[8] The quotation is from a letter from Weld to Lewis Tappan some time in the 'fifties. (*Life of Arthur Tappan,* p. 370.)

[9] See *New York Evangelist* for 1831, vol. II, the first three numbers.

[10] *Ibid.,* IV, 71.

[11] The quotations are from a public letter from Arthur Tappan, *ibid.,* I, 30.

[12] This account follows a letter by Lewis Tappan to the Rev. Andrew Reed of London, printed in the *New York Evangelist,* VI, 29. To head the second Free Church, application was made without success to Weld. Joel Parker wrote him: "The whole church of New York laughed at our temerity in undertaking our church. They have felt the power of this blow and are shocked and stunned by it. Now while the old system of things is thus staggering and reeling, we want to strike it one dreadful blow and make it bellow and fall. This new church can do it. . . . What you say about want of qualifications is all very *pretty,* because a man must be modest. But . . . we all think you can sustain an establishment here with overwhelming interest. . . . There is a morning prayer meeting here on purpose to beg God to send you." (Parker to Weld, Nov. 8, 1831. See also Lewis Tappan to Weld, Oct. 25, 1831, Weld MSS. This is a peremptory summons for Weld to move to New York at once.)

[13] *New York Evangelist,* II, 275.

[14] *Ibid.,* II, 290.

[15] The propaganda for "pure wine" was carried on in the *Genius of Temperance, Journal of Humanity,* and *New York Evangelist,* for 1831. Hostility toward Arthur Tappan went so far that "some of the New York gentry appear to think that he ought to be drummed out of the city; if not honored with a coat of tar and feathers." (*New York Evangelist,* I, 71.) The quotation regarding Arthur's love of "unpopular causes" is from the *Life of Arthur Tappan,* p. 396.

[16] The actual connection of the Magdalen Society with England was more direct than the quotations indicate. The idea of the New York Magdalen was taken over bodily from the London Magdalen, which Tappan had visited on a trip to England. In the organization of a New York Magdalen Society, the London Magdalen Society was cited as a precedent so respectable that the opposition of prudish people to New York organization was ridiculous. The statistical basis for the estimated number of prostitutes in New York is discussed in *McDowall's Journal,* I, 35. McDowall found the statement quoted in the text, as to the ratio of prostitutes to the population of modern cities and as to the average life of prostitutes, in a French pamphlet; he applied the same ratios to New York. The remaining quotations are from the "Magdalen Report," which was first printed in the *New York Evangelist,* II, 263.

The Magdalen report made a great stir in the nation. The prudish 'thirties maintained a solemn silence on such subjects, so that, once opened, discussion flooded the news. Local Magdalen societies were formed by scores, college students being especially active. The Magdalen Society at Western Reserve College, for example, appointed a "Standing Committee on Lewdness," which ferreted out the marital scandals of rural communities around the village of Cleveland and proudly published them as "Society Reports" in the *Ohio Observer*, June 6, 1832.

[17] Arthur Tappan's letter to the public was published in the *New York Evangelist*, IV, 18. See also *ibid.*, V, 6.

[18] The organization was announced in the *Emancipator*, May 27, 1834. The speeches were printed in *ibid.*, Dec. 9, 1834. Application was made to Weld to be its general agent, at a thousand dollars a year, to conquer "this wonderful department of Satan's empire, where this arch deceiver works to brutify our nature and to damn the soul." (Committee on Moral Reform to Weld, March 29, 1834, Weld MSS.) Weld refused.

[19] Abraham Lincoln thus contrasted the temperance movement of the 'thirties with the saner "Washingtonian" movement of the 'forties: "Too much denunciation of dram-sellers and dram drinkers was indulged in. . . . This I think was both impolitic and unjust. . . . When the dram-seller and drinker were incessantly told . . . that they were the authors of all the vice and misery and crime in the land . . . it is not wonderful that they were slow, very slow, to acknowledge the truth of such denunciations, and to join the ranks of their denouncers in a hue and cry against themselves." (Speech before the Washingtonian Temperance Society of Springfield, Feb. 22, 1842.) The connection of temperance with revivals is described in *New York Evangelist*, V, 6; the "duty of rebuke" is quoted from *Right and Wrong in Boston*, No. 2, p. 53.

[20] See the *Life of Arthur Tappan*, Ch. IX, for the details of this project.

[21] *New York Evangelist*, II, 324. For Arthur Tappan's benefactions to Yale College during his residence at New Haven, which might well have been the reason for the coöperation of the Yale faculty in the Negro college project, see the *Life of Arthur Tappan*, pp. 77–78.

[22] The significance of this Convention of the People of Color to the course of Negro social history in America is remarked by Turner. (*The Negro in Pennsylvania*, p. 138.) Tappan's part in bringing Garrison to Philadelphia on this occasion is described in Garrison, *Garrison*, I, 259. Garrison's speech, urging his hearers to subscribe to the *Liberator* is summarized in the *Proceedings of the Annual Convention of the People of Color*, 1831. The importance to the *Liberator* of the subscriptions and the connection thus secured is explained more fully on pp. 50–51 of this book.

[23] *Poulson's Daily Advertiser*, Sept. 13, 1831.

[24] Lewis Tappan had opposed the society from its beginning. His brother Arthur had been a contributing member, but he had withdrawn from the society because its officers would not at his request prohibit the highly remunerative trade in ardent spirits which was carried on in Liberia. (*New York Evangelist*, IV, 103.) For the free Negroes' attitude to the Colonization Society, see *Freedom's Journal* for 1829. For the best summaries of the developing hostility toward the Colonization So-

ciety and its program, see *American Quarterly Review*, II, 237; *Christian Examiner*, first series, II, 463; IV, 210; new series, VIII, 200; *New England Magazine*, II, 13.

[25] Arthur Tappan's plea is printed in the *New York Evangelist*, I, 13. The antislavery program of the founders of the college is characterized on p. 28 of this book.

CHAPTER III

THE BRITISH EXAMPLE

[1] The quotation is from a letter from Stuart to Weld, July 9, 1829 (Weld MSS.). In another letter to Weld dated April 17, 1830, he is again in this country, having returned to the United States early in that year for a short visit. The letter of April 17 was written on the occasion of a second departure for England.

[2] The Southern editor was Robert J. Breckinridge, in the *African Repository*, IX, 330; the New York daily was the *New York American;* and the remark of Adams to Monroe is in *Memoirs of John Quincy Adams*, VIII, 269.

[3] *New York Evangelist*, IV, 139.

[4] New York *Whig*, Sept. 23, 1831.

[5] *Christian Register*, X, 138.

[6] The London Female Anti-Slavery Society was especially active in this correspondence. See the "Minutes of the Philadelphia Female Anti-Slavery Society," particularly for the year 1830, Historical Society of Pennsylvania. See the *Genius of Universal Emancipation*, 1829–1830, and the *Christian Examiner*, IV, 207, for notices of British antislavery pamphlets in America.

[7] The quotations are from letters of Stuart to Weld as follows: one dated March 20, 1830, and another, not dated, but probably written in January, 1830. In this letter Stuart asks: "How is the glorious Finney and the cause which makes him glorious?" Both letters are in the Weld MSS. Stuart's pamphlet campaign to convert Weld to abolitionism is recorded in the letters as follows: With an undated letter written sometime in 1830, he sent ten antislavery pamphlets, and in the letter of March twentieth, he mentioned a parcel he was sending, containing "several articles of information on the subject." He also asked Weld to send him "any late publications in the U. States on this subject." For Stuart's own tracts—all of which he sent Weld—see notes number 17 and 18 below. For an account of Weld's rôle as encyclopedist of the antislavery movement, see Chapter XIII of this book.

[8] The quotation regarding "Theodore's soul" is from a letter from Stuart to Weld, March 26, 1831 (Weld MSS.).

[9] The lag between the parliamentary debate and the antislavery meeting in New York is explained by the fact that in those days of slow sailing vessels, reports of the debate in parliament did not reach American newspapers until late in 1830. For the account of the antislavery meeting itself

I have followed in part the story Joshua Leavitt began, but never finished, thirteen years later in the *National Anti-Slavery Standard,* October 24, 1844. His story checks with current announcements in the *New York Evangelist* cited below and with the Weld MSS. He does not mention Bourne's participation, however. The Rev. George Bourne was the most notable pamphleteer of the old tradition. His pamphlet, *The Book and Slavery Irreconcilable* (Philadelphia, 1816), advocated the "immediate and total abolition of slavery." Garrison remarked that after the Bible itself, he owed most to this book for his views (Garrison, *Garrison,* I, 306). His later work, *A Picture of Slavery,* of which many editions were published, was a collection of gruesome and bloody tales of the slave régime. At this time (1831), Bourne was living in New York. He was editor of the *Protestant* (later the *Protestant Vindicator*), the first organ of the "anti-popery" movement in America. Among the sponsors for the paper were Leavitt, Finney, and a number of the Association of Gentlemen. (*The Protestant,* I, 2.)

[10] It should be remarked that this discussion group owed nothing of inspiration to the youthful Garrison. This point is important only because of the controversies regarding the origin of the antislavery agitation. The evidence of influence from other sources, especially from the British movement, is overwhelming; and contemporary evidence that Garrison or the *Liberator* had anything to do with their discussion is entirely lacking. Indeed the evidence that Garrison's influence was not a factor is conclusive. Leavitt so wrote in the account referred to above; and a year later, when Weld was becoming widely known as an antislavery orator, he replied to an invitation to speak in Boston: "It has been my misfortune never to have come in contact with the published views, arguments, etc." of Garrison (*Abolitionist,* I, 18). It should be remembered that Garrison's reputation for his work during these early years has been retroactive in character. At this time he was a humble, obscure young man in far-away Boston, just beginning the *Liberator,* which by the end of 1831 had only fifty white subscribers.

Finney's claim to have influenced the group to antislavery action (*Memoirs of C. G. Finney,* p. 324) is probably just as baseless. Indeed Weld later found it necessary to defend Finney against Tappan's charge that he had not given the subject of abolition "as much prominence in his preaching and at communion" as he should have: "I have no doubt but he ought to have given it more prominence in his public prayers and preaching. . . . This I told him in full. The truth is, Finney has always been in revivals of religion. It is his great business, aim and *absorbing passion.* . . . Finney feels about revivals of religion as you and I do about anti-slavery. . . . It is one of your besettings, my brother, to put upon others bad constructions, and to infer hastily wrong motives upon too light grounds. You recollect we talked this all over one night at your fireside." (Weld to Lewis Tappan, Nov. 17, 1835, Weld MSS.) While Finney's preaching had much to do with the reforming zeal of the New York philanthropists, it is not likely that his influence had any direct part in inspiring them to antislavery agitation.

The previous antislavery labors of the group had been as follows: Goodell had edited a paper, the *Investigator* (1827), devoted in part to the abolition of slavery. In his *National Philanthropist* in Boston, and his *Genius of Temperance* in New York he had continued to discuss slavery and its abolition, if not with great ability, at least with real devotion. Lewis Tappan had long been a member of the old New York Manumission Society. Jocelyn, a missionary to the Negroes, was an ardent abolitionist. Weld had worked with John Rankin, "the Martin Luther of the anti-slavery movement," whose *Letters on American Slavery,* written in 1824, were less important than his constant agitation of the subject in the presbyteries of southern Ohio and Kentucky. For Weld's relation to Rankin, see *Autobiography of Asa Mahan,* pp. 192–193.

[11] Elizabeth Whittier's description of Weld is quoted by Carrington (*Theodore Weld and a Famous Quartette,* p. 6). After another visit from Weld, on September second, 1836, Elizabeth Whittier wrote in her diary: "His smile . . . has been haunting me . . . ever since he left us. I did not see how Greenleaf could hear his affectionately sad farewell—his 'God bless you, dear brother,' with so much composure. I am sure I could have wept as bitterly as if I had said farewell to my own dear brother." (Transcribed by T. S. Pickard from Elizabeth Whittier's diary. Weld MSS.) Beecher's tribute to Weld's oratorical power is in James Monroe Jr., *Lectures and Essays,* p. 55, and Smith, *Liberty and Free Soil Parties,* p. 11.

[12] Weld's confession of the sin of pride is in a letter of his to Angelina Grimké, March 1, 1838. His attitude toward anniversaries he described in a letter to L. Tappan, April 5, 1836. Both letters are in the Weld MSS. His anonymous pamphlets are detailed in Chapter XIII of this book. His difficulties with those who wanted to publish his letters and his reproof of those who did are recounted in the following letters: Stanton to Weld, Nov. 7, 1832; E. Wright Jr. to Weld, May 26, 1835; and March 24, 1836 (Weld MSS.).

[13] *New York Evangelist,* II, 304.

[14] The mass meeting was reported in the New York *Whig,* Sept. 15, 1831. It was called the very day that the *New York Evangelist* published its prospectus for the new "American National Anti-Slavery Society."

[15] *New York Evangelist,* II, 324.

[16] *Religious Intelligencer,* Sept. 17, 1831.

[17] Official gratitude was expressed by the abolitionists for the services of "Captain Charles Stuart, E. I. C. E., who is already well known as a persevering, uncompromising friend of the cause" (*Report of the Agency Committee of the Anti-Slavery Society,* London, 1832, p. 2); and James Cropper, wealthy Quaker philanthropist and head of the Agency Committee, called him "one of the most devoted Christians I have known, and an unwearied advocate of the oppressed Africans." (Introductory letter to *Prejudice Vincible,* London, 1832.)

Stuart labored without compensation. He received a pension of eight hundred dollars a year for his military services, enough in those easy days to support him in his benevolent activities and to keep Theodore Weld in college. He wrote more than a score of pamphlets for the British propaganda. His Bible argument was entitled *Is Slavery Defensible from Scripture?* (Belfast, 1831). His tract, *The West Indian Question,* was printed as an article in the *British Quarterly Magazine and Review,* April, 1832, and then went through many editions on both sides of the Atlantic. The first American edition was printed in New Haven, at Arthur Tappan's expense, from a copy of the first British edition which Stuart had sent Weld as soon as it came off the press. Later, thousands of copies were printed by the American Anti-Slavery Society. In the "Special Instructions," issued annually to agents of the American Anti-Slavery Society, this tract was recommended as the standard defense of immediatism, at least until 1835.

[18] Stuart's anti-colonization pamphlets: *Remarks on the Colony of Liberia and the American Colonization Society* (London, 1832); *A Letter on the American Colonization Society* (Birmingham, 1832); *Prejudice Vincible* (London, 1832); *Liberia, or the American Colonization Scheme Examined and Exposed* (Glasgow, 1833); and *The American Colonization Scheme Further Unravelled* (Bath, no date). Stuart wrote in the last named tract: "It seems impossible that a people who exhibit, as the Americans of the United States are doing, their high susceptibility of moral motive in . . . Revivals, should continue much longer dead to the same sacred influence in relation to Slavery" (p. 19). For much of his material, especially as regards the opposition of free Negroes to the colonization scheme, Stuart was indebted to a colored agent from America, the Rev. Nathaniel Paul, who was touring England for funds to establish a Negro school. Paul had taken a prominent part in organizing protests in the Northern cities against the American Colonization Society. Stuart's pamphlet, *Remarks on the Colony of Liberia and the American Colonization Society,* was written in part to support Paul's agency.

For evidence of the success of Stuart's propaganda against the colonization cause, see the *Anti-Slavery Monthly Reporter,* V, 296 ff., and the *Abolitionist,* I, 88–89.

CHAPTER IV

Organization

[1] The spiritual state of Weld's disciples is the subject of most of their correspondence with Weld at this time. See particularly, S. E. Streeter to Weld, December 16, 1830; Theodore Clarke to Weld, December 24, 1830; J. L. Tracy to Weld, Nov. 24, 1831 (Weld MSS.).

[2] *Emancipator,* Oct. 22, 1840. In the biographies of Birney, this meeting is put at an earlier date; but I find that all contemporary references place it here.

[3] The story of this discussion at Western Reserve College I pieced together from the *Ohio Observer,* 1832–1833, and from four letters in the Weld MSS.: E. Wright Jr. to Weld, Dec. 7, 1832; Weld's reply, Jan. 10, 1833; E. Wright's rejoinder, Feb. 1, 1833; and a later letter from

E. Wright Jr. to Weld, Sept. 5, 1833. The quotations above and below are all from these letters. The conversion of Storrs was an achievement. He came of a family of able men. His brother Richard was editor of the *Boston Recorder,* and his nephew, Richard Salter Storrs, attained a reputation as one of the most eloquent pulpit orators in the United States. Storrs's conversion was the more notable in that he had served his church in South Carolina and Georgia, where he had seen slavery at first hand. His death, in 1833, was a serious loss to the antislavery movement.

A part of Weld's oration on temperance and most of his speech in defense of manual labor education, delivered at Cleveland and Hudson respectively, are printed in the *Ohio Observer,* Oct. 1, 1832. The Rev. John Keep was present at the Cleveland meeting; and since he was converted to abolition by Weld (Keep to Weld, Oct. 20, 1834), I assume that the conversion was at some time during this visit. For Weld's earlier acquaintance with Keep, see John Keep to Weld, March 9, 1831 (Weld MSS.).

[4] Asa A. Stone to Weld, Nov. 5, 1831 (Weld MSS.). Finney and N. S. S. Beman, a minister in whose church Finney had preached in the Great Revival, wanted the school still further east, at Troy—"a new school, low church, new measure, manual labour Theological Seminary," as Beman called it. "Dont now, I beseech you, by the love of Christ not to say nay," wrote Finney. "This is work that *must be done,* & be done by you. No one else *can do it."* (Beman and Finney to Weld, Nov. 30, 1832, Weld MSS.)

[5] J. L. Tracy to Weld, Nov. 24, 1831 (Weld MSS.). This letter evidently made an impression upon Weld. In his speech at Cleveland referred to above, he improved upon the letter as follows: "The Great Valley of the Mississippi is a cradle in which a giant in his swaddling clothes is sleeping. These swaddling clothes he will soon burst. And the time is not distant when he will sway the world! It lies with the present generation to decide whether he shall tread down the nations in blood or whether his march shall be the march of resurrection over the graves of ignorance and sin." (*Ohio Observer,* Oct. 1, 1832.)

[6] Most of the material facts in this account are from the *History of Lane Seminary* (Cincinnati, no date). The tribute to Vail's powers as a salesman is Beecher's (*Autobiography and Correspondence of Lyman Beecher,* II, 282). In his letter to Weld (*ibid.,* pp. 320–321), a part of which is quoted in the text, Vail added flattery: "We want now, my dear brother, first such a man as you are (I do not flatter you) to be the mainspring of the whole concern. We want the funds promised you exceedingly for buildings for 500 or 600 students, for more land, for workshops, tools, etc." Weld's report was approved and plans for Lane Seminary begun sometime before March, 1832. (H. B. Stanton to Weld, March 7, 1832, Weld MSS.)

[7] Speaking of the Lane students, Finney remarked: "They were most of them converts in those great revivals in which I had taken more or less part." (*Memoirs of C. G. Finney,* p. 332.) Some time before his removal to Lane, Beecher went out to Cincinnati to look over the ground. One of

Weld's fraternity talked with him on this occasion: "He [Beecher] told me in conversation on the subject that he had considered it a millennial enterprise—drew a glowing picture of our present generation of ministers—showed with biting sarcasm their criminal want of physical energy and consequent inefficiency, and then added with tears in his eyes, 'if there was anything which could make me want to live my life over it is to be instrumental in training up a corpse [corps] of *manual labor* young men and then leading them forth against the Infidelity and wickedness of a world!'" (Waterbury, in a "folio sheet" [Waterbury, Streeter, Stanton, etc.] to Weld, Aug. 3, 1832, Weld MSS.)

[8] Lundy told William Goodell the story of his interview with Beecher, and Goodell reported it in the *Friend of Man,* I, 55. Beecher's theological position is stated in the *New York Evangelist,* III, 29.

[9] Zachary Macaulay, editor of the *Anti-Slavery Reporter,* declared that he intended to quote regularly from Lundy's paper, the *Genius of Universal Emancipation,* which was the only American paper that would "serve to throw light on the whole institution" of American slavery. (*Anti-Slavery Monthly Reporter,* II, 8.) This was in June, 1827. Dr. Thomas Martin of the Library of Congress has found evidence that Lundy was in personal touch with the British abolitionists some years before that date.

[10] *Zion's Herald,* VIII, 29.

[11] Garrison's libellous statement in part was as follows: "FRANCIS TODD" and his like "should be SENTENCED TO SOLITARY CONFINEMENT FOR LIFE! They are the enemies of their own species—highway robbers and murderers; and their final doom will be, unless they speedily repent, to occupy the lowest depths of perdition." (*Genius of Universal Emancipation,* third series, I, 98–99.)

[12] Lundy described his differences with Garrison in the *National Enquirer,* III, 33. See also *Genius of Universal Emancipation,* new series, I, 130. The two quotations are from Garrison, *Thoughts on African Colonization,* p. 34, and Garrison, *Garrison,* I, 336.

[13] The first and second quotations are from Garrison's speech at an open meeting in Boston, which was reported almost entire in the *Christian Register,* IX, 170. The third quotation is from a later speech, which was reported in the *New York Evangelist,* Sept. 10, 1831.

[14] The story here is as told by one of the fifteen at the first meeting, Oliver Johnson, in *William Lloyd Garrison and His Times,* pp. 83–84.

[15] Garrison himself testified to his obligation to Charles Stuart's anti-colonization propaganda in England. (*Liberator,* I, 158.)

[16] The quotations are from Beecher's articles in the *Spirit of the Pilgrims,* VI, 399–402 and 542. Later events evidence Beecher's complete success in convincing the Congregational Associations of New England of the wisdom of united action. See pp. 61–62, and 92 of this book.

[17] *Autobiography and Correspondence of Lyman Beecher,* II, 314 (Weld's account).

[18] The article sent by Tappan was published in the *Spirit of the Pilgrims,* VI, 569 ff. The quotation is from Tappan's covering letter. The

article is anonymous, but its style suggests Joshua Leavitt. Beecher's reply to Tappan is printed in *Autobiography and Correspondence of Lyman Beecher*, II, 323.

[19] The Lane Seminary students are described in the *Emancipator*, July 15, 1834, and in the *New York Evangelist*, March 29, 1834. The student's letter from which the quotation is taken is in *ibid.*, IV, 139. Beecher's characterization of the Lane Seminary students is in a letter from him to Weld, a part of which was printed in the *Liberator*, V, 103.

[20] Wright's appointment as secretary to the New York Committee was probably at Weld's instance. Wright had already told Weld in a letter dated Dec. 7, 1832: "Should the storm that now seems to be gathering, or any other cause, drive me off [from Western Reserve College], I should rejoice to be deemed worthy to exert a more direct influence in favor of *immediate universal emancipation. . . .* What would benevolent men in N. York think of a convention on the subject?" Wright held his post as corresponding secretary of the American Anti-Slavery Society until 1839, and proved himself a prodigious worker, a loyal and enthusiastic abolitionist.

The request to form sectional societies is in a printed form on a letter from E. Wright Jr. to Weld, Sept. 5, 1833 (Weld MSS.). The agency to Ohio is described in the *Emancipator*, I, 6. The pamphlets which the New York Committee most widely distributed were Bourne's tracts and Charles Stuart's *The West India Question*, the former for "facts" regarding American slavery and the latter for arguments in support of immediatism. The first agents of the society were supplied with large numbers of these pamphlets. The questions to the secretary of the Colonization Society, and his replies, were printed in the *Emancipator*, Extra, June 25, 1833. The following reformers signed the letter to the secretary of the Colonization Society: Arthur and Lewis Tappan, Theodore Weld, Joshua Leavitt, George Bourne, Charles G. Finney, William Goodell, C. W. Dennison, and four merchant associates of the Tappans.

[21] The quotation from Tappan regarding the formation of an American Anti-Slavery Society is from a letter from Arthur Tappan to Jay, printed in Tuckerman, *William Jay and the Abolition of Slavery*, p. 45. The contents of the New York Committee's letters to the Pennsylvania Society for the Abolition of Slavery are inferred from the latter's reply to Arthur Tappan, a copy of which is preserved in the society's records. "We have been diligent," wrote their secretary, "in issuing the circulars of the New York Committee to various parts of the country, and in writing upon many of our citizens to obtain their coöperation." (Pennsylvania Society for the Abolition of Slavery, MSS. "Records," X, 205.)

[22] The suggestion of Philadelphia as the convention city is in *The Friend*, Oct. and Dec., 1832. The quoted editorial against the formation of a National Anti-Slavery Society is from the *Presbyterian* of June 5, 1833. I assume from the date of this editorial that Tappan's letter to the Pennsylvania Abolition Society asking them to prepare the way, must have been written some time before, possibly as early as March. The remaining quotations are from the reply of the Pennsylvania Society to Arthur Tappan's

letter, in the Pennsylvania Society for the Abolition of Slavery, MSS. "Records," X, 205.

[23] The quotations are from the *Address of the New York City Anti-Slavery Society* (New York, 1833), pp. 1–5.

[24] *Zion's Herald,* VI, 21.

[25] C. E. Beecher, *An Essay on Slavery and Abolition,* p. 43.

[26] The first quotation is from the *Pittsburg Conference Journal,* II, 195; the second quotation is from the *Biblical Repertory and Princeton Review,* VIII, 270–271. The last quotations are from a letter from Channing to Follen, July 26, 1834, printed in Channing, *Memoirs,* III, 160.

The adoption of immediate emancipation as the motto of the American Anti-Slavery Society effectively prevented union between Northern and Southern antislavery efforts. This was not significant as regards the Southern States east of the mountains; the antislavery movement in North Carolina and Virginia, which had been active a few years before, was losing ground there at this time. But the movement to the West, especially in Kentucky, was rapidly advancing. Its spokesmen were the Rev. John Breckinridge and President Young of Center College. The former was primarily a colonizationist; but the latter was a true gradual abolitionist, devoted and fearless. He preached an antislavery doctrine essentially like that of the New York Committee: "1. The system of slavery . . . is sinful. 2. It is not sinful in an individual to retain his legal authority over those of his servants whom he conscientiously believes to be unfit for freedom, while he is, by the application of proper and vigorous means, preparing them for . . . liberty. It is sinful . . . to delay the commencement of those benevolent and conscientious labors . . . thus retarding unnecessarily the day of complete emancipation." (*Cincinnati Journal,* Dec. 12, 1834.) Young also advocated this doctrine in application to political measures for gradual abolition. He secured the passage of resolutions embodying the doctrine in the Kentucky Synod, and he was instrumental in furthering the movement for gradual abolition in Kentucky, which a year later was lost in the legislature by a handful of votes. His controversy during 1834–1835 with the Rev. Samuel Crothers, an abolitionist of Ohio, in the *Cincinnati Journal,* was characterized by an almost perfect similarity of antislavery doctrine and a complete misunderstanding on Young's part as to the measures advocated by abolitionists. It is entirely possible that without the immediatist motto, Young's movement and much other antislavery agitation of the same character in the South could have been merged with the Northern agitation. For the interesting connection between this Kentucky agitation and Lyman Beecher's "American Union" movement, see note 19, Chapter IX.

[27] The reference to Arthur Tappan's odious reputation is from the *Philadelphian,* quoted in *New York Evangelist,* I, 71. "All the middle states are afraid of anything that Arthur Tappan favors. They must rub off the scent of Tappanism before it can be popular anywhere out of New England." (E. Wright Jr. to A. A. Phelps, Feb. 9, 1835, Wright MSS.)

[28] The record of subscribers to the *Liberator,* their history, where they were, and their division between blacks and whites, is told in the *Liberator,*

V, 3; in a circular, printed in 1837, entitled *Shall the Liberator Die?* and in the *Liberator*, March 7, 1835. The story of Garrison's appeal for subscriptions to the first Convention of the People of Color is told on p. 26 of this book.

²⁹ The quotation is from the circular, *Shall the Liberator Die?* Editorial courtesy restrained extended comment on the limited support of the *Liberator* among abolitionists. Now and then, however, it was discussed. See *Friend of Man*, Dec. 22, 1836, and Sept. 20, 1837; and *Philanthropist*, Oct. 30, 1838. The *Massachusetts Abolitionist*, of course, was more outspoken. Six months after its foundation, in 1838, its editor boasted that the *Abolitionist* then had more subscribers than the *Liberator* had secured at any time during its existence.

³⁰ Arthur Tappan's correspondent was the secretary of the Pennsylvania Society for Promoting the Abolition of Slavery. See MSS. "Records" of the society, X, 205.

³¹ When Southern demands for the suppression of Garrison poured into Boston, the mayor of that city, Harrison Gray Otis, was all the more embarrassed because he had never heard of either Garrison or the *Liberator* (Garrison, *Garrison*, I, 242–244). Even after Garrison and his *Liberator* had become news items in the North, the Northern papers continued to reflect the Southern news of his propaganda. Most of the early quotations from the *Liberator* in Northern papers referred to the Southern papers from which they were copied. Few were taken from the *Liberator* direct, even as late as 1834.

³² Channing, *Memoirs*, III, 178. "Nothing is really anti-abolition but apathy" (*Human Rights*, Sept., 1835).

³³ That this was Garrison's own conviction, I assume from the tone of his correspondence and from his course in England. "Garrison in England," one of his intimates wrote him, "will do the cause more good in three months than in twelve in America, by the reception he will there meet" (Arnold Buffum to Garrison, Oct. 11, 1832, Garrison, *Garrison*, I, 326).

³⁴ The story of Jocelyn's plan for a Negro school is told on pp. 26–28 of this book. Originally Garrison had in mind a first-rate Negro college like the one Jocelyn had planned; but his friend Buffum urged him to propose to the public an academy on the manual labor plan: "I am sure the idea of a farm school is much more acceptable to the public than that of a college. At the same time, when it is established we can make what we please of it" (A. Buffum to Garrison, Sept. 23, 1832. Garrison, *Garrison*, I, 327). Buffum then heard that the New York philanthropists would be more inclined to contribute to an institution of collegiate grade, such as Jocelyn had planned. So he changed his project to "an institution on the manual labor system for the education of colored youth. The location and arrangements to be determined at a general meeting of the contributors to the amount of ten dollars and upwards." (Buffum to Jocelyn, 11 Inst. [March?], 1832, *Journal of Negro History*, XVIII, 79.) This was the form in which the plan was published in the *Liberator*, II, 155.

The manner of Garrison's approach to the New York Committee for sanction and support is indicative of the relatively inconspicuous place in the agitation which was his before the trip to England. His partner, Isaac Knapp, wrote a letter to Joseph Cassey, a prominent Philadelphia Negro, asking him to lay Garrison's project before the New York Committee, but to keep his—Knapp's—name out of it. Cassey promised to do so, "without, however, intimating this suggestion as having originated with you" (Cassey's letter is in Garrison, *Garrison*, I, 327). Another approach to the New York Committee in Garrison's behalf was made by his intimate, Arnold Buffum, who wrote to Jocelyn as follows: "It is necessary to raise $500 to defray Garrison's expenses or to obtain for him a letter of credit in London for £100 sterling to be used in case of necessity. If Arthur Tappan will give him such a letter of credit we will at once furnish him with what may be necessary to carry him to London." (Buffum to Jocelyn, as above.)

For the list of those who did contribute to Garrison's mission, see *Liberator*, III, 86.

[35] *Ibid.*, III, 179. Garrison here told a British audience that most of the fund for his expenses had been contributed by Negroes. However, in the list of contributions referred to above, less than half the total amount was given by Negroes. It is possible that the contradiction arose from the circumstance that Garrison may have used a considerable fraction of the fund to provide for his own more pressing debts and for the relief of the *Liberator*, which was then in desperate plight; and that he chose to regard the balance of the fund, which paid his way to England, as the part contributed by Negroes. The total fund was much more than enough to pay all of Garrison's expenses throughout the trip; but since he had to borrow money to buy his return passage (see p. 53 of this book), I assume that part of the fund was used for other purposes.

[36] The story of Charles Stuart's campaign in Great Britain against the American Colonization Society is told on pp. 36–37 of this book. At Garrison's request, the board of the New England Anti-Slavery Society had recommended his British mission "for the purpose of . . . disseminating in that country . . . the truth in relation to . . . the American Colonization Society. . . . It is important that the Philanthropists of that country should be undeceived, and that the real principle and designs of the Colonization Society should be there made known." (*Liberator*, III, 39.) But as a matter of fact, this occasion for Garrison's mission had little more reality than the Negro school project, as Garrison himself must have known. For more than a year, every official organ of the British movement which reached his editorial desk had, at some time or other, condemned the colonization plan in unmeasured terms. This sentiment was the result of Charles Stuart's effective agitation, of which Garrison certainly had adequate knowledge, since Stuart's writings had had a part in inspiring his own *Thoughts on Colonization* (*Liberator*, I, 158). Moreover the leader of the antislavery cause in parliament, Thomas Folwell Buxton himself, had informed Garrison explicitly the year before, that his testimony against colonization was not needed in England. "It is wholly unnecessary," he wrote, "to set me, or any of the true Anti-Slavery Party in this Country,

on our guard against the delusive professions of the Colonization Society or its Agent" (*Abolitionist*, I, 88–89). Indeed, the greatest achievement of his mission in Garrison's own opinion—a "Protest against the American Colonization Society," which eleven of the leading British abolitionists prepared for Garrison to take back to the United States— was drawn up and signed without his knowledge. "In getting up this protest," Garrison told the New England Anti-Slavery Society on his return, "I had no agency whatever. It was altogether unexpected by me." It is not improbable that the "Protest" was prepared by Charles Stuart. Its language and arguments are those which Stuart employed in his anti-colonization pamphlets (see note 18, chapter III). Stuart was Garrison's companion during his stay in London and acted as his agent in England after his departure for America (see note 37 below).

[37] Garrison's benefactor, the Rev. Mr. Paul, whose school was later actually established in Canada, was the one whom Charles Stuart had assisted with his pen (see n. 18, Ch. III of this book). Of the loan, Garrison remarked: "It was exceedingly kind, and truly seasonable, in brother Paul to lend the money to me, so that I could return home without begging." The amount of the loan was $200. The quotations, the one in the text and the other in this note, are from two letters from Garrison to Lewis Tappan, Dec. 17, 1835, and Feb. 24, 1836 (L. Tappan Papers, Library of Congress).

Charles Stuart's assumption of Garrson's Negro school agency was not at Garrison's request. Stuart had planned to follow Garrison shortly to this country; but an "overruling sense of duty" compelled him to abandon this plan and remain in England to collect funds for the school. On October 26, 1833, he wrote: "About four hundred dollars has been already subscribed. . . . You may expect I think at least one thousand dollars through me for the above dear and sacred purpose." Evidently Stuart had been designated as Garrison's representative in England, for he added: "Many letters &c, &c. have come for you. I have opened them all and are [am] making use of them." Stuart closed his letter with this characteristic message: "If you meet with my Theodore Weld, tell him my heart is doubly his." (*Abolitionist*, I, 191.)

On the night of his arrival in America, Garrison joined the crowd that watched the mob storm Clinton Hall, but he did not make himself known, or participate in the formation of the New York City Anti-Slavery Society at Chatham Street Chapel. The next morning he departed for Boston.

[38] Elizur Wright Jr. to his father, Elizur Wright Sr., Nov. 2, 1833 (Wright MSS.).

[39] The story of Garrison's campaign for an early meeting is recounted in Elizur Wright Jr.'s letters to Amos A. Phelps, October and November, 1833 (Wright MSS.).

[40] Explaining his silence regarding his indebtedness, Garrison later wrote: "I landed in New York Oct. 2, 1833. In consequence of the uproar in the city, and my anxiety to reach home, I left for Boston immediately, without being able to say much about my mission to any of the friends in N. Y. My next visit to your city was in December." (Garrison to L. Tap-

pan, Feb. 29, 1836, L. Tappan Papers, Library of Congress.) During this interval, however, Garrison was in frequent correspondence with the Tappans, and in Philadelphia he had been with Lewis Tappan constantly for several days without once mentioning the matter of his indebtedness.

[41] A copy of the call is in the Weld MSS.

[42] Pennsylvania Society for the Abolition of Slavery, MSS. "Records," X, 205.

[43] Weld "on principle" at once resigned from the board. He had conscientious scruples against accepting any office of authority or honor. The new society also appointed him their agent for southern Ohio, Indiana, Illinois, western Virginia and Kentucky (Minutes of the Committee on Agencies, American Anti-Slavery Society, Dec. 16, 1833, and Jan. 14, 1834) ; but Weld refused the appointment.

The scanty attendance at the convention had been expected; but it reduced the organizing convention for the society to little more than a gesture. If the initial organization had been at the time of the anniversaries in New York the next May, there would have been more than three hundred delegates. (See *Proceedings of the First Anniversary of the American Anti-Slavery Society*, 1834.)

[44] Lewis Tappan's speech was reported in the *Abolitionist*, I, 181. Bacon's remark was quoted in the *New York Evangelist*, V, 122.

[45] "Let each member present feel solemnly bound to vindicate the character of Mr. Garrison" (Lewis Tappan's speech, *Abolitionist*, I, 181).

[46] This characteristic piece of Garrisonian financing, neither of the Tappans comprehended. Having told them how it was to be, Garrison departed content, leaving no written authorization with the treasurer for the payment of Arthur Tappan when—and if—the pamphlets should be sold, and—to do him justice—requiring no receipt for the transfer of the debt from himself to Tappan. It is not to be wondered at, therefore, that two years later neither Arthur nor Lewis Tappan had any memory of this arrangement. Poor Nathaniel Paul was the chief victim. Supposing that Garrison had paid his loan into Arthur Tappan's hands, Paul wrote a draft on Tappan for the amount of the loan, which he sold. On presentation of the draft, Tappan refused to pay it, and the purchaser of the draft brought suit against Paul for the amount. There is considerable correspondence in the Lewis Tappan papers regarding the matter ; though whether Paul ever got his two hundred dollars—or Lewis Tappan his two hundred and forty dollars—I do not know.

The quotations in the text are from a letter written by Garrison to Lewis Tappan, Feb. 29, 1836, in the Lewis Tappan Papers, Library of Congress.

[47] Weld to Sarah and Angelina Grimké, Oct. 10, 1837 (Weld MSS.).

CHAPTER V

Hostility

[1] The Tappan store employed twenty-five clerks, a large number for that day. In front of Lewis Tappan's home, for two days intermittent mobs

howled and rioted. "The unconverted part of my family were in much terror," Tappan wrote, "but the Christians remained firm." Tappan finally removed his family to the country, and that same night the mob wrecked his home. He refused to have the damage repaired: "It is my wish that my house may remain this summer as it is, a silent Anti-Slavery preacher to the crowds who will flock to see it" (L. Tappan to Weld, July 10, 1834, Weld MSS.).

² Bacon's summary appeared in the *Christian Spectator*, in 1834. It is reprinted in Bacon, *Slavery*, p. 73. Miss Beecher's summary is in C. E. Beecher, *An Essay on Slavery and Abolition*, p. 43.

³ The quotation regarding the popular "misconception" of immediate emancipation is from *Zion's Herald*, VI, 101. At antislavery conventions, resolutions of the following type were frequently adopted: "Resolved, That the opposition to the Anti-Slavery Societies arises in most cases from a misapprehension of their principles and measures, which, when rightfully understood, generally remove all objections and make proselytes of the objectors" (*Philanthropist*, March 12, 1839). The quotation regarding the "precipitate action" implied in immediate emancipation is from the *Pittsburg Conference Journal*, II, 195.

Channing, who was a man of outspoken antislavery conviction, pointed out that immediate emancipation had "contributed to spread far and wide the belief, that they [the abolitionists] wished immediately to free the slave. . . . They made explanations; but thousands heard the motto who never saw the explanation." (Channing, *Slavery*, p. 154.) The quotation regarding those "who cannot give up their grudge against Garrison," is from a letter from E. Wright Jr. to Weld, Sept. 5, 1833 (Weld MSS.). William Jay's difficulties were stated by him in the *New York Evangelist*, V, 103; and Gerrit Smith, before he joined, wrote a public letter to the *Emancipator*, asking for light: "Is not the *Liberator*, more than any other periodical, the favorite mouthpiece of the Anti-Slavery Society?" E. Wright Jr. replied: "It is . . . the 'mouthpiece' of its Editor," not of the society (*Emancipator*, April 21, 1835). Smith then joined the movement.

⁴ A typical expression of bewilderment is as follows: "How comes it that a despised band of pugnacious and awry speculators . . . are yet . . . enlarging alliances amid the very salt of the earth?" (*Quarterly Observer*, III, 44). Whittier, Lydia Maria Child, Gerrit Smith, and William Jay were the authors referred to in the text. Of all their tracts, William Jay's *Inquiry* was by far the most widely known; but even Jay's *Inquiry*, it was said, "acquired a celebrity from the character and standing of its author, to which the book itself, had it been left to its own merits, never would have attained." (*Christian Advocate and Journal*, IX, 150.)

⁵ Beecher's propaganda for unified antislavery action is described on pp. 44–46 of this book. The prominent abolitionists who were claimed for the movement are listed in *Zion's Herald*, VI, 10–11. Its platform and purposes are stated in *ibid.*, VI, 86; New York *Evening Post*, June 4, 1835; and *Liberator*, V, 49. Garrison's hostility to the new society is exemplified by the following announcement: "TO MY COLORED BRETHREN. The American

Union's object is TO PUT DOWN GARRISON AND HIS FRIENDS. Now, who are my friends if you are not? . . . Shall we suffer ourselves to be put down? No! Stand by me now, as you have hitherto done." (*Liberator*, V, 23.) Arthur Tappan's visit to Boston to secure Garrison's silence is described in Garrison, *Garrison*, I, 471.

⁶ Lewis Tappan's sympathetic letter to Garrison is in the *Liberator*, V, 19. The remarks regarding Garrison's subordinate place in the antislavery organization are in the *Emancipator*, Dec. 2, 1834.

⁷ The Union's survey of slavery: E. A. Andrews, *Slavery and the Domestic Slave-Trade in the United States* (Boston, 1836). Arthur Tappan's letter regarding Garrison's "severe and denunciatory language" was printed in the *Liberator*, V, 27.

⁸ *New York Evangelist*, Jan. 4, 1834.

⁹ From the first the executive committee had put the importance of agencies above that of journals and pamphlets. They were, wrote Elizur Wright Jr., "unanimous that the life of the Society depends upon efficient agencies" (E. Wright Jr. to A. A. Phelps, Dec. 31, 1833, Wright MSS.). The phrase characterizing the antislavery movement as "allied to revival" is from a letter of the Rev. H. G. Ludlow, one of the New York Free Church ministers, to Gerrit Smith, Jan. 12, 1837 (Weld MSS.).

Among the earliest agents, Whittier offered his "services in behalf of the cause during the ensuing six months, provided he can receive the sum of $150 to defray his traveling expenses and hire a substitute for the labors of his farm." His offer was accepted, but he was not a success. (Minutes of the Committee on Agencies, American Anti-Slavery Society, March 11, 1834.) Garrison's agency was his own idea. At his request, Williams of New York agreed to contribute a hundred dollars for expenses, and Garrison wrote that he expected to receive a like amount from Arthur Tappan. The American Anti-Slavery Society's Committee on Agencies assigned his territory (Minutes of the Committee on Agencies, American Anti-Slavery Society, Dec. 16, 1833), and he started out in the spring of 1834. He reported his adventures under his favorite *nom de plume*, "O. B." (Old Bachelor), to the *Emancipator*, June 17, 1834.

Beriah Green's style was characterized as quoted in a letter from E. Wright Jr. to Weld, no month, 1835 (Weld MSS.).

¹⁰ Charles Stuart, not suspecting that Garrison was not the representative of the abolition cause in America, as a matter of course paid over the thousand dollars he had collected for Garrison to the treasury of the American Anti-Slavery Society. Upon being told that all idea of a Negro school had been abandoned, he authorized the use of the money as the executive committee saw fit. But Garrison, when he heard of the transaction, was outraged. He demanded his thousand dollars at once. Unfortunately, Elizur Wright wrote him, the money had been spent. Then Garrison appealed to the board of the New England Anti-Slavery Society to support his claim. They had accredited his mission, he declared, and they therefore had title to Stuart's collections. The board, of course, took that view. See the correspondence of E. Wright Jr. to A. A. Phelps for May and June, 1834, especially the letter of June 20 (Wright MSS.).

Stuart defended himself from the charge that he was a "foreign emissary" in the *Emancipator,* Aug. 5, 1834. Evidently the charge militated against his success.

George Thompson's services were the material aid which Garrison had prescribed for the American cause on his visit to England the year before. Cropper, Sturge, and others advised strongly against sending Thompson, but it was supposed that Garrison was a competent judge of American conditions, and Thompson was sent. His agency was later admitted by all the British abolitionists—and no less by the Americans—to have been a serious mistake. Unfortunately for his agency, Thompson's past record had not been free from blemishes, as American newspapers were quick to discover. Serious charges were made against him, charges which Thompson could not deny. It is possible that some of the violence was due to this circumstance. See George Thompson to Theodore and Angelina Weld, June 15, 1839 (Weld MSS.), for Thompson's admission of these charges.

[11] The characterization of Phelps quoted in the text is Garrison's (*Liberator,* IV, 207). Elizur Wright Jr. thus described him: "Bro P[helps] is not after all a Demosthenes—he is logical, mathematical, convincing, but not passionate, moving, electrifying" (E. Wright Jr. to Weld, March 24, 1836, Weld MSS.). As the months of propaganda passed without effective achievement, the Agency Committee of the American Anti-Slavery Society grew desperate. Their agents had all failed. "Bro. Thompson if he has not sailed already, will soon, for England. Br. Phelps will be much occupied with his wife, who is sick. So it is hardly probable, that if you do not come we shall have a single agent in this immense state." (E. Wright Jr. to Weld, Nov. 18, 1835, Weld MSS.)

CHAPTER VI

THE LANE DEBATE

[1] The quotations are from the *Autobiography and Correspondence of Lyman Beecher,* II, 326, and 321. Weld later wrote his fiancée: "I should deplore it if you were to form your opinion of my natural traits of character from the representations of, for instance, my Lane Seminary fellow students. . . . They strangely and stupidly idolized me, and it used to distress me to see how blind they were to my great defects and how implicitly they yielded themselves to my sway . . . the whole mass of students who became Abolitionists." (Weld to Angelina Grimké, March 12, 1838, Weld MSS.)

[2] The quotations are from the *Autobiography and Correspondence of Lyman Beecher,* II, 319, 289, and 321.

[3] The quotations are from *ibid.,* pp. 315–316 (a letter from Weld), and from a letter from a student in the seminary, printed in the *New York Evangelist,* IV, 139.

[4] The opinion of the students as to abolition is quoted from a letter from Weld to Tappan, *Emancipator,* April 8, 1834. The students' opinion of

Garrison is quoted from a letter from Huntingdon Lyman to the *Emancipator,* March 25, 1834. The story of the conversion of William Allan is
told in the letter from Weld to Tappan. Several of the original members of
the ardent host, among them H. B. Stanton and Augustus Wattles, Weld
had converted to abolition some time before (Augustus Wattles to the
Emancipator, April 22, 1834).

⁵ Weld's words are quoted from the *Autobiography and Correspondence
of Lyman Beecher,* II, 322 (a letter from Weld), and from the letter from
Weld to Tappan, *Emancipator,* April 8, 1834.

⁶ Weld, Huntingdon Lyman of Louisiana, Augustus Wattles, and
H. B. Stanton wrote at length to the *Emancipator* and to the *New York
Evangelist.* Several unnamed students also wrote to friends, and their
letters were published in the *Emancipator.* It is from these that the story
of the debate is told. See particularly the *Emancipator,* March 25, April 22,
May 3, May 13, 1834, and the *New York Evangelist,* March 22, 1834.

⁷ Wattles to the *Emancipator,* April 22, 1834. These tales were usually
told as having occurred "down river," or "in the tidewater," or "out west,"
until after 1850, when various "tours of slave states" were widely sold.
In these the authors did not scruple to give names, dates, and places to the
ancient legends of cruelty, though internal evidence clearly indicates the
fraud.

⁸ One who refused to vote colonization down was J. F. C. Finley, son of
one of the founders of the colonization movement, and former agent of the
American Colonization Society. After the debate he persuaded the Ladies'
Auxiliary of the Cincinnati Colonization Society to raise funds for a visit
to Liberia. In a public letter from Liberia addressed to Stanton, he declared: "Almost everything I see raises Liberia so much in my estimation
that I feel as confident as I do of my existence that if my personal and
Christian friend [Stanton] who announced to a large audience in Chatham
Street Chapel, New York, in May last that the funeral knell of the Colonization Society had tolled, and who in the exuberance of his soul pronounced its eulogy . . . will come out and examine this country, this
infant republic, for himself, that in less than two months he will be as
ardent an advocate for the Colonization Society as any your country can
produce." (*Western Christian Advocate,* I, 147.)

⁹ The work of Wattles is outside the range of this study. For some
years he headed a school in Cincinnati, "as good as the best." He became,
in 1835, a regular agent of the American Anti-Slavery Society, but shortly
stopped lecturing (Aug. 5, 1836) in order to head a department of the
Anti-Slavery Society devoted to free Negroes, which was founded at
Weld's behest. (Weld to Lewis Tappan, Feb. 22, 1836, Weld MSS.) To
the society's program of education he added plans to settle Negroes in the
shop as mechanics and on the soil as farm owners. Having inherited some
property, he secured additional funds from certain men of wealth, and
used them all to purchase a large tract in Indiana where he established a
land office for Negroes. He founded trade schools. He published pamphlets
on farm methods for Negroes. He had a wide connection in Ohio and Indiana among Negro settlements, and he itinerated between them, encourag-

ing and aiding. His reports are evidences of extraordinary achievements, but year after year he and "Sister Susan," his indefatigable wife (one of the "Cincinnati sisters" referred to in note 11), labored without public recognition. His letters evidence his isolation; he is pathetically grateful to his friends for remembering him. He was one of the most admirable figures of the movement. His work among the Negroes of this country and the labors of two other Lane rebels—Hiram Wilson among the freedmen of Canada, and Ingraham among the emancipated slaves of the West Indies— were practical achievements of the highest order.

[10] The faculty later testified that the unprecedented level of scholarship which the class had attained the first term was maintained throughout their stay at Lane Seminary (*Emancipator*, Jan. 6, 1835).

[11] At least a foot-note in history is due these "paragons of womanhood," Phebe, Emeline, Lucy, and Susan—the "Cincinnati Sisters." Volunteering in response to a call in the *New York Evangelist* for missionaries to the blacks, they were sent at once to Cincinnati, where Weld, August Wattles, and Marius Robinson put them to work. They were all young, and three of them were charming; but the popular prejudice then prevailing toward the objects of their labors was so intense that they were outcast from the first. Despite the miracles of improvement that they wrought upon their "fighting, lying, stealing, swearing, wild and active" young charges, their unselfish labors did not win the regard even of the "good people" of the city; and not even their sex protected them from occasional mob violence from the baser sort. Inevitably—after years of service—they married Lane rebels. (See the series of joint letters from the "Sisters" to Weld, Weld MSS.)

[12] Thome's speech, and the closing quotation, are from the *Emancipator*, June 10, and June 17, 1834, respectively.

[13] Sometime during Birney's visit to Cincinnati, "Dr. Beecher tried hard to convert him over to his *neutrality* party [the American Union for the Relief and Improvement of the Colored Race]. But he found him little more *manageable* than Weld. We understand from Birney that the Dr. has concluded to defer the organization of his milk and water A. S. Society for a few months." (E. Wright Jr. to A. A. Phelps, Dec. 6, 1834, Wright MSS.) Beecher never did organize an Ohio auxiliary of his society, but the Kentucky auxiliary which he organized made history (see foot-note 19, Chap. IX). Huntingdon Lyman's description of Birney's talk with the Lane students is in *Oberlin Jubilee* (Oberlin, 1883), p. 65. Birney's description of Weld is quoted from Birney's diary, recorded a few days after meeting with Weld (William Birney, *James G. Birney and his Times*, pp. 149–151). Birney's letter of recantation was published in the *Emancipator*, Extra, Sept. 2, 1834. How completely isolated he conceived Weld's abolitionism to be is evidenced by the following passage from this letter: "Nor have I any acquaintance either personally or by literary correspondence, with any of the northern abolitionists." Birney was appointed agent of the American Anti-Slavery Society at fifteen hundred dollars a year and traveling expenses; but a covering letter told him: "In case he should think it best not to accept the commission . . . he will

obtain the proposed amount from individuals," retaining his freedom from official association with the Society. This arrangement was the one adopted (Minutes of the Agency Committee, American Anti-Slavery Society, April 18, 1834). It was continued until the summer of 1836 (Birney to Lewis Tappan, July 4, 1836, L. Tappan Papers, Library of Congress).

[14] Regarding the basis for the rumors of "social amalgamation," Charles Beecher, Lyman's son, remarks: "The young men, however, thought they saw the danger, and really tried to guard against it. Their opinion was, and probably still is, that no amount of prudence short of surrender of the enterprise altogether would have availed." (*Autobiography and Correspondence of Lyman Beecher*, II, 325.) But there had been unwise acts even according to the students' judgment. Wattles had boarded in a colored family, and the students testified: "Such intercourse is not . . . expedient even in respect to its influence on the colored people themselves" (*Liberator*, Jan. 17, 1835). A hostile editor, however, admitted that he was unable to find evidence for any of the stories (quoted in *Emancipator*, Oct. 28, 1834. See also *Cincinnati Journal*, Oct. 17, 1834, for a categorical denial of these stories by an editor by no means in agreement with the students). The students pointed with pride to the fact that out of their meager funds they had given three times as much to other causes as to the cause of the blacks. "And we add that though we have had repeated and urgent invitations to deliver public addresses upon the subject of slavery in various places throughout this region of the country, yet we have all uniformly declined these invitations without exception." (Statement of the Lane Seminary Students, *Emancipator*, Jan. 6, 1835.)

[15] Beecher's promise to Arthur Tappan to assure free discussion was made in the presence of John Morgan, a member of the Lane faculty (Morgan to Weld, Jan. 13, 1835, Weld MSS.). Not only was there little antislavery sentiment among college students before the Lane debate, there was much anti-abolition sentiment. At Wesleyan, Harvard, Princeton, and elsewhere, students had taken the lead in anti-abolition demonstrations.

The meeting of college representatives at New York, and their action, was reported by the president of the board of Lane Seminary to Asa Mahan, one of the trustees (*Autobiography of Asa Mahan*, p. 178), and by Beecher to the students (*Friend of Man*, Sept. 15, 1836). The policy of suppression was successfully executed at Amherst, Hamilton, Center, Union, Andover, Oxford (now Miami), Auburn, and Muskingum, and permissions to discuss and organize were generally denied at other institutions. Elsewhere, however, there were no "ardent hosts" for student bodies, and there were no more "Lane Debates," except at Center College, Kentucky, where Birney's son was a student and where one of Birney's converts, Dr. Buchanan, was on the faculty. The debate converted most of the students, but the school was nearly ruined thereby (*Western Christian Advocate*, II, 87). Buchanan was dismissed and went to Cincinnati to help Birney edit the first few numbers of the *Philanthropist*. Later he served on the Oberlin faculty.

[16] Weld evidently wrote Beecher to the same effect. Beecher replied: "I did not hasten home on the receipt of your letter because I could not do but

one work at a time,—and I did not answer it because being absent and un-acquainted with the necessary facts, I could say nothing without jumping in the dark, a thing which I do not like to do" (L. Beecher to Weld, Oct. 8, 1834, Weld MSS.). During the summer, while Beecher was away, a num-ber of the students remained on the ground, caring for the manual labor farm, studying, and teaching their classes of blacks in the city—Weld, Stanton, Lyman, Miter, etc. At first the young men were hopeful that all would be well. The rules promulgated by the executive committee would not be law until acted upon by the autumn meeting of the board of trustees, and it was believed that Beecher would not permit their passage. Professor Morgan was their whole-hearted champion (he had been re-employed for the next year at an increased salary), and Professor Stowe had assured them of his support. But as the summer advanced, their con-fidence waned. Morgan was summarily dismissed, with no cause assigned; resolutions were prepared in the executive committee for the immediate dismissal of Weld and Allan; finally the seminary dormitory was closed and the young men were turned out, despite the arrangement of continuous residence necessary to a manual labor school. Nevertheless they remained on the ground in the single hope that Beecher would fulfill his pledge of free discussion and free assembly. But Beecher did not return, and the board met. Weld had prepared to plead the students' case, and Mahan attempted to get a hearing for him; but the board proceeded at once to pass the obnoxious regulations entire. For the story of this summer, see H. B. Stanton to Thome, June, 1834; H. Lyman to Thome, August 17 and October 4, 1834 (Thome MSS. at Oberlin College).

[17] Beecher's movements during the summer were as follows: Upon re-ceipt of Mahan's letter, he abandoned the money-raising campaign which he had arranged in New England, and hurried west. But instead of turning south when he reached Columbus, Ohio, he remained there for several days. Then he turned north, visited for a time at Granville, and finally went east again to prosecute his financial campaign. Beecher's autobiography does not tally either with the students' statement or with any other con-temporary account. Whether the editor, Charles Beecher, glossed over his father's part in the affair, or whether Lyman Beecher conveniently forgot the facts, or both, the account in the autobiography cannot be reconciled even with the calendar. Beecher, apprised of events not only by Mahan but also by Weld (Weld MSS., as above), and by Judge Wright, president of the board (see *Autobiography and Correspondence of Lyman Beecher,* II, 327), stayed away from May to October. To the students Beecher de-clared when he returned that an unpopular teacher, Professor Biggs, had done it. "He has ousted you, and you have helped him. . . . He has led the trustees, who know nothing of such matters" (*ibid.,* p. 328). Charles Beecher puts the blame on the trustees: "The trustees declined to wait Dr. Beecher's return; the laws were formally promulgated" (*ibid.,* p. 329). But this can-not be so, because the resolutions when passed were not to be given the effect of rules until approved by the faculty, the trustees by their own statement being unwilling to take all the responsibility for the obnoxious regulations. Beecher remembered his tardy arrival thus: "When I got back I found all

in a flurry. If I had arrived a little sooner I should have saved them; but it was too late. . . . I went to the trustees and told them that the manner of reformation in my absence was untimely" (*ibid.*). All the direct evidence, as well as Beecher's own unhappy inconsistencies of action and statement, indicate that he permitted the trustees to do a distasteful job that he wanted done and had promised Tappan not to do, and then attempted to dodge the responsibility for it (see *Autobiography of Asa Mahan*, pp. 177–179; "Statement of the Lane Seminary Students," *New York Evangelist*, VI, 8; *Liberator*, Jan. 17, 1835; Rev. John Rankin's "Review of the Faculty Statement," *Emancipator*, April 28, 1835). This was the inference of Beecher's contemporaries: "I have no doubt that you are right in supposing that Dr. Beecher was privy to the concoction of the Lane Seminary laws. Nothing else can account for his acquiescence, his commentaries, his success at the East, &c." (E. Wright Jr. to A. A. Phelps, Dec. 16, 1834, Wright MSS.)

[18] From the "Statement of the Faculty of Lane Seminary." Beecher later persuaded the board to abolish the obnoxious resolutions, and vest the power of dismissal in the faculty itself. This was then presented in a public statement by the faculty as no more than the common law of all institutions of learning. But the students had then withdrawn, and the breach was too wide to be bridged. Moreover it was known that the trustees were determined that abolitionists and abolitionism should have no place in the seminary, under any consideration. (See *Cincinnati Journal*, July–Nov., 1834.)

[19] *Autobiography and Correspondence of Lyman Beecher*, II, 345. The enrollment in the seminary was as follows: of the forty in the theological department the year before, but two remained; of the sixty in the literary department, but five remained, and the literary department perforce was discontinued. Of sixteen new students for the theological department, eight left Cincinnati after they had talked with the Lane rebels. According to the "Students' Statement," letters from numerous prospective students had been received before the new rules were published. They had expected the enrollment to double the next year. In the end a class of only twenty theological students was secured.

[20] The quoted description of Finney is Beecher's own, from a letter to Nettleton, published in the *Biblical Repertory and Princeton Review*, new series, IV, 477. The final quotation is from a letter written by Lyman Beecher to William Beecher, July 15, 1835 (*Autobiography and Correspondence of Lyman Beecher*, II, 345).

[21] Catherine wrote a keen indictment of abolitionism, from which I have already quoted (p. 49 of this book). William, teaching in the East, wavered toward abolitionism, to his father's alarm (Beecher, as above). Edward, president of Illinois College, after a term of doubtful neutrality, went over to the abolitionists and helped Elijah Lovejoy organize the movement in Illinois. He was dismissed from his position for "his insidious attempts to instill the poison of Abolitionism into the tender minds under his charge" (*National Enquirer*, III, 71), but he was later reinstated. George early became an efficient and devoted agent for the American Anti-

Slavery Society in southern Ohio and in Rochester, New York (Minutes of the Agency Committee, American Anti-Slavery Society, Oct. 7, 1836, and *Friend of Man*, Oct. 6, 1836). In 1837, at an antislavery meeting in Putnam, Ohio, his burning words at last converted his brother, William, who was in the audience (*Zion's Herald*, VIII, 151). George died a young man. Charles also became an abolitionist.

Weld's *Slavery As It Is* was published in New York in 1839. Mrs. Stowe's defense, *Key to Uncle Tom's Cabin*, is composed largely of excerpts from Weld's pamphlet. Angelina Grimké Weld told her daughter, Sarah, that Mrs. Stowe had often described to her "how she kept that book [*Slavery As It Is*] in her work basket by day, and slept with it under her pillow by night, till its facts crystallized into Uncle Tom." (MSS. reminiscences in possession of Dr. Angelina G. Hamilton.)

CHAPTER VII

THE LANE REBELS

[1] The list of students who signed the "Statement" was not a full roll of the Lane rebels. Hedges of Virginia, an officer in their antislavery society, and many others, did not return for the fall term. Andrew Benton of Missouri left Lane with the rest, but he could not bring himself to sign the statement. He went to Oxford (now Miami) College. Augustus Wattles was too busy with his school to come out and sign, but he sent word that he approved. The Lane rebels were circularized by John Rankin of New York, a member of the Executive Committee of the American Anti-Slavery Society (not John Rankin of Ohio), in order to secure the entire body of students for Auburn Theological Seminary, of which he was trustee. He authorized "all the boys to draw on him for expenses to Auburn." Only two of them did, however (Stanton to Weld, "Folio Letter," Jan. 8, 1835, Weld MSS.). The story of the students' removal to their new home in Cumminsville is told by Mahan in the *Autobiography of Asa Mahan*, p. 189. The student teachers were assisted by John Morgan, the one member of the faculty who went with them, and by another Cincinnatian who had been stirred by the debate, a young physician named Dr. Gamaliel Bailey.

[2] Finney's refusal to go west is recorded in the *Memoirs of C. G. Finney*, p. 333. Tappan's plan for a new school is told in the *Emancipator*, Nov. 4, 1834.

[3] Leonard, *Oberlin—the Colony and the College*. Dr. Leonard naturally tells the story of the establishment of the college from the standpoint of the Oberlin colony; whereas the significant continuity is by way of Lane. This was recognized among Oberlin's founders. See, for instance, the statement of John Keep: "Oberlin—Oberlin—dear though persecuted—greatly blessed . . . owing its origin to the breaking off of the band of youth in Lane Seminary" (John Keep to Weld, Jan. 11, 1839). Before the Lane rebels arrived, the local support for Oberlin was negligible. When the 109 ministers of northern Ohio were circularized to ascertain their

wishes as to the future location of a theological seminary for northern Ohio, only six of the whole number designated Oberlin. (*Ohio Observer*, May 14, 1835.)

[4] The quotations in the two preceding paragraphs are from the *Ohio Observer*, July 17, and April 10, 1834.

[5] Shippherd met young Keep, the son of Weld's old colleague, John Keep, now the president of Oberlin's board of trustees. Keep was returning from Lane, one of the new students who had refused to matriculate after hearing the tale of the Lane rebels.

[6] Weld was pressed to accept the professorship at Oberlin by Mahan as well. Stanton wrote him: "You KNOW the aid such an announcement would bring to the institution from this State, New York &c., in the way of securing public reputation, students, funds, &c." (Stanton to Weld, Jan. 22, 1835, Weld MSS.) The trustees of Oberlin also urged him to come, but his reply was characteristic of the man: "I am totally unfit for the station which your partiality would assign me. . . . How I might regard it if I had enjoyed the advantages of a thorough education . . . as to qualify me for such high responsibilities, I cannot decide. . . . But as it is, the case is a plain one; and I cannot feel called upon to devote even a moment to the consideration of it before expressing my convictions both of propriety and duty." (MSS. Records, Oberlin College.)

[7] They did "not feel prepared till they have other and more definite information on the subject, to give a pledge respecting the course they will pursue in regard to the education of the people of color: wishing that this Institution should be on the same ground in Respect to the admission of Students with other similar institutions of our land" (Minutes of the Board of Trustees, Oberlin College, I, 26).

[8] For evidence of Keep's abolitionism, see his letter to Weld, Oct. 20, 1834 (Weld MSS.). For the attitude of the Lane students toward "the odious resolution," see the letter of John Morgan to Weld, Jan. 13, 1835 (Weld MSS.). The terms of the trustees' final resolution were equivocal. By it Oberlin was committed merely to an interest in Negro education, not to admit Negroes. It was probably understood, however, that this settled the issue of Negro students.

Oberlin's enlargement was a bitter disappointment to Western Reserve College. The authorities at the latter school pointed out that their doors had long been open to Negro students (p. 36), and that they had permitted the free discussion of abolitionism even by their faculty (see pp. 39–40 of this book). Their prior liberalism made them far more deserving of support by the New York philanthropists, they declared, than Oberlin's reluctant conformity. Strenuous efforts were made to obtain part of Oberlin's windfall for themselves. The faculty published a joint statement subscribing to the New York doctrine: "If the *whole work* be included under the head of emancipation, we must be gradual abolitionists. But if emancipation be considered as restricted to legal acknowledgment of the slave as a man, and legal protection and encouragement, we are immediate emancipationists." (*Ohio Observer*, April 30, 1835.) An inspired petition among the Presbyterian ministers of the Reserve, almost unanimously approved Western

Reserve College and deplored Oberlin (*ibid.*, May 14, 1835). The trustees of Western Reserve College elected Finney professor of theology and appointed a committee with instructions to convince the Oberlin trustees that it was their duty to transfer their gifts to Western Reserve (*Emancipator*, May 26, 1835). But their devices failed. Elizur Wright Jr. was convinced that the real temper of the Western Reserve trustees was hostile to antislavery agitation, and his conviction probably influenced Weld and the Lane rebels. (See Elizur Wright Jr. to Weld, Sept. 15, 1833, Weld MSS.; John Seward to Elizur Wright Jr., July 24, 1833; and Elizur Wright Jr. to A. A. Phelps [no month], 1834, Wright MSS.)

[9] Of the thirteen whom Weld summoned to Cleveland (H. Lyman in *Oberlin Jubilee*, p. 69), the *Third Annual Report of the American Anti-Slavery Society* lists only ten; but the others received commissions and reported their progress to the *Emancipator* (see Minutes of the Agency Committee, American Anti-Slavery Society, 1835–1836).

The story of Weld's invasion of Oberlin is told in a letter from Weld to the editor, *Oberlin Jubilee*, p. 350. Oberlin completed the abolitionizing of the Western Reserve. Reports to the *Philanthropist* from local societies of northern Ohio almost invariably indicated the leadership of some one from Oberlin. Much of the developing antislavery sentiment in northern Indiana and southern Michigan evidenced the same source of inspiration.

The best of the Lane rebel agents were Thome, Stanton, Whipple, Lyman, Gould, Wattles, Weed, Streeter, Allan, Alvord, and Robinson, a roll of heroes. Others of the Lane rebels just as competent labored in distant fields. Hiram Wilson and three more worked for the society among the free blacks of Canada. David Ingraham went as missionary to the freedmen of Jamaica, where he was later joined by Amos Dresser and four others of the Lane rebels. Ingraham's labors were so notable that they secured the commendation of the British colonial government. He paid for his achievements with his life. "His labors . . . were excessive, so much so that an iron constitution sank under them in less than four years." Dying of exhaustion, he sailed for this country, in 1841, and died at Weld's home the day after his landing. (Weld to L. Tappan, July 31, 1841, Weld MSS.)

[10] Thome to Weld, Feb. 9, 1835 (Weld MSS.).

[11] The first quotations are from a letter from Marius Robinson to the editor, *Friend of Man*, July 12, 1834. The letters to Weld from Thome, Allan, Streeter, Weed, Robinson, and Gould, 1835–1836 (Weld MSS.), tell of their fears and anxieties. There was one exception, James Alvord, a joyous warrior, who, said Thome, "has such a mob raising tendency that he needs some guardian." He was always a storm center: the following incident is typical of his adventures: After two days of discussion at Middlebury, Ohio, he reported to Weld: "Last evening Middlebury puked. Her stomach had evidently become overloaded by the amount of undiluted pokery she had taken at the two preceding discussions. The system would not endure it. Spasmodic heavings and retchings were manifest during the whole day. Toward night symptoms were alarming." That evening he found the Methodist Church where he was to speak locked up by its

timorous pastor. "Audience soon began to gather. . . . Abolition dander got a trifle started. Two of the trustees of the church with a growl put out. . . . One of them soon came back and invited us over. We found the door burst in. A goodly number soon gathered . . . when in came a broadside of eggs, glass . . . &c . . . A merchant of the place attempted to go out, when a volley was discharged at him and one of them hit him plump in the right eye. He came back groaning most piteously. I understand that he says this morning that he is an abolitionist. . . . I have been trying to clean off this morning but I can't get off the stink. . . . The mob today threatened dreadfully. Whether the citizens will cower before them or not I don't know. There are a few determined men here but the mob are set on by men of influence, most of them church members. . . . We must try to carry the day this time if possible. I forgot to tell you I am bound over to appear as witness at the trial of the Willoughby rioters," where several in Alvord's audience were hurt, and Alvord himself by a miracle was saved from serious injury. (Alvord to Weld, Feb. 9, 1835, Weld MSS.)

The Lane rebels maintained their first agency throughout the autumn and winter of 1835–1836. In the spring several of them returned to Oberlin. Birney, in charge of the Ohio antislavery office, wrote: "I greatly lament that our Oberlin agents have determined to quit their field of labor till autumn. They were doing well and advancing the cause with eminent success. We shall feel their loss during the approaching Summer. They seemed to have looked to a temporary return to Oberlin with so much certainty that I could not insist on their continuing their agency at this time." (J. G. Birney to Lewis Tappan, April 29, 1836, L. Tappan Papers, Library of Congress.) All but one of these young men returned to the field the following autumn (see n. 16, Ch. X of this book). However, many of the Lane rebels continued to labor for the cause throughout the summer.

CHAPTER VIII

Weld's Agency

[1] *Emancipator,* July 28, 1836. As early as the autumn of 1833, the New York Committee had assigned Weld the entire West as the area of his agency for antislavery effort and had urged him to begin (Minutes of the Agency Committee, American Anti-Slavery Society, Dec. 10, 1833). A year later their urgency was echoed in Ohio. John Keep wrote him from Cleveland (Oct. 20, 1834, Weld MSS.): "It is my heart's desire and prayer to God, that you may be persuaded to renounce for the present your connection with Lane Sy. & to devote yourself arm and soul to that cause which is so near your heart. . . . God in his mercy has prepared the way, at least in this region, by your previous labours in the Temperance Cause. . . . I hesitate not in saying that no man living could labor in this region upon this subject under as favorable circumstances and with so sure and certain expectation of success as yourself. How often do I hear this sentiment expressed."

[2] All of the quotations in the two paragraphs above are from the *Emancipator*, July 28, 1836.

[3] *Liberator*, V, 99. Garrison referred to Weld's method as "somewhat peculiar" (*ibid.*). This was written a few days before Stanton began to evangelize Rhode Island. His method of course was the same as Weld's: ". . . a course of five or six lectures in a place, sometimes more, until the people were made thoroughly acquainted with the subject" (*Emancipator*, April 1, 1836). All of the Lane rebels employed similar methods. The description of Weld's power as an orator is from J. H. Fairchild, *Oberlin, Its Origin, Progress, and Results*, p. 18. A despairing editor, after listening for sixteen nights to Weld's oratory, declared himself incapable of reporting any of it. He was too enthralled to make notes at the time, and when he attempted to recall the substance of the addresses, he failed. "You can't print thunder," he wrote.

[4] Non-Presbyterian Ohio's interpretation of immediatism is illustrated by a report on abolitionism adopted unanimously by the Ohio Conference of the Methodist Episcopal Church during Weld's agitation: Abolitionists proposed "the immediate, indiscriminate and unconditional manumission of all slaves, to remain among and commingle with the white population. . . . This doctrine of amalgamation is inseparable from the scheme of abolition." At this time the Ohio Conference of the Methodist Church included the entire State (*Western Christian Advocate*, II, 77). Weld stated his own doctrine of immediatism thus: "Slavery ought to cease at the first moment when it can be made to cease, consistently with the interests of those who are the subjects of emancipation."

[5] The first quotation is from a letter in the *Emancipator*, Sept. 5, 1835. The description by an indignant abolitionist of mob outrages was of events at Union Village, New York, where Weld spoke a few months later; but it is typical of what occurred in Ohio and Pennsylvania (*Friend of Man*, July 21, 1836).

[6] The stone-throwing incident is described in Weld's letter to E. Wright Jr., in the *Liberator*, April 4, 1835. *A propos* of the folded arms, Weld's daughter-in-law told me that he often said that his experience had been that a mob would seldom attack a man when his arms were folded. However in Ohio he was frequently attacked by mobs. Most of these assaults were more humiliating than deadly. To Weld the most painful memory of this year in Ohio was that "one entire suit and part of another was destroyed, or nearly so, by mobs." The loss was not a serious one, however. Weld's habitual garb was "a shag overcoat, linsey-woolsey coat and cowhide shoes. . . . However, I have always had to encounter the criticisms and chidings of all my acquaintances about my coarse dress. They will have it that I have always curtailed my influence and usefulness by such a John Baptist attire." In one respect only was he particular. Both as to his clothing and his person, Weld was scrupulously—even fanatically—clean. Every day, no matter what the weather or how great the inconvenience, he took a bath in cold water. All of these matters of personal habits and attire are described in a letter to a fellow abolitionist, Weld to Angelina Grimké, Dec. 28, 1837 (Weld MSS.).

⁷ *Friend of Man,* August 4, 1836. At Chardon, in Geauga County, the mob varied this technique: "The deputy sheriff had charge of the Court House and was inclined to abolition. At any rate we succeeded in getting permission to go into the court room and hold our meeting. I had only been on the judge's bench for a few minutes, when I heard a regular tramp, tramp coming up from the lower story. It kept coming nearer, and some four abreast, the mob came into the room and up to the platform, crowding me carefully right along until I came to some steps, when I was forced down the stairs. They then crowded in amongst the abolitionists, gathered and gradually crowded them out. Just as I came down the stairs, I met an earnest young man who said his school house was open, and if I went right over there I could fill it with my friends and the mob could not get in. We soon got together in this schoolhouse." (MSS. reminiscences by Weld, in the possession of his granddaughter, Dr. Angelina G. Hamilton.)

⁸ In Ohio Weld failed to conciliate the mob only once, at Granville. After a few nights of riot the town council met and resolved that Weld should go. He moved a few miles away and converted Granville citizens there. One Joseph Tuttle, a boy of sixteen at the time, later president of Wabash College, never forgot Weld's eloquence: "I was never more excited by a public speech than then, and never have I seen an audience more excited. . . . The speaker was a very manly, noble looking man. . . . He used no notes, but spoke with the utmost precision and fluency. . . . His imagination was brilliant, his humor, at times, overpowering, and his invective in all respects the most terrible I ever heard. His voice was wonderful in its compass and power. . . . There were times when his voice was as tender as a mother's to a dying child, and at others as fierce and loud as a winter storm. There was a quality of passion in his voice which magnetized his hearer to be what he himself felt. . . . He spoke with indescribable majesty and power. . . . Indeed, those two hours and a half that night in the brick Methodist Church in St. Albans, Licking County, Ohio, were the most soul-stirring of my life."

For Weld's success with Presbyterian ministers, see *Liberator,* V, 55. In contrast to the attitude of the Methodist Conference of Ohio noted above, the Presbyterian Synod of Ohio, in 1836, the year after Weld's agency, resolved to exclude all slaveholders from pulpit and communion—a striking testimony to Weld's effectiveness as an evangelist of abolitionism. This action was taken at the behest of the Cincinnati Presbytery, where it was proposed by George Beecher. It was Beecher who had the privilege of presenting the Ohio Synod's petition against slavery to the next meeting of the General Assembly.

⁹ The quotation is from a letter from Weld to F. A. Flower, author of *Edwin M. Stanton,* p. 31. See also Flower's letter to Weld, no date (Weld MSS.). Flower wrote that the story as Weld told it was numerously confirmed by old residents of Steubenville. Stanton was associated in Steubenville with Arthur Tappan's own brother Benjamin, but he got no abolition inspiration from that source. Benjamin Tappan was a convinced anti-abolitionist. He later went to the Senate, succeeding the one abolition

senator, Thomas Morris, and there spoke in bitter condemnation of the agitation.

¹⁰ Quoted from *Our Country* in the *Emancipator*, June 23, 1835. For Weld's success in converting slaveholders, see the *Emancipator*, Aug. 3, 1835, and *Liberator*, V, 55. A young Kentuckian, a student at Marietta college, where Weld spoke, wrote him: "I have received a letter from Kentucky, from a sister-in-law. She advised me not to come home, for it will go hard with me, she says. . . . I have had great change of circumstance since I became an Abolitionist. Before I had money as I wanted. My Father was a man of influence and as his son I was respected and loved both in Ky. and here. Now the people in Ky. would shun me as they would a rattle-snake. And the nobility of Marietta are as cool toward me as can be. And how do you think I feel? . . . Dear Brother, I think I never will prove recreant to that holy cause. . . . What I shall do I can't tell; but I don't think I shall stay in a slave state. If I never see you or write you again, be assured that I love you as I do my heart's blood." (James W. Davis to Weld, Feb. 22, 1836, Weld MSS.)

The only adverse mention of Weld that I have seen in the entire mass of anti-abolition newspapers, periodicals, and letters covering all the years of his antislavery service, is a newspaper skit which was probably published sometime during his Ohio agency: "Weldites—This is the name of a most deluded sect, the leader of which was a fanatic by the name of Theodore D. Weld, who under the *show* of great discernment, unequalled powers of mind, and more than apostolic self-denial, was at heart, a most proud, arrogant, self-conceited, disorganizing man. It was his glory to be at the head of a party, to lead about whithersoever he listed, his devoted satellites. In the year 1834, by the aid of a few men of some note in the religious world, he excited a great tumult on the subject of abolishing slavery at once, amalgamating blacks and whites, overturning the order and peace of the country, for the sake of giving liberty and equality to a set of men who were incapable of self-government. From one grade of folly or madness, he proceeded with rapid strides to another, until at length he was held to be a fit subject for a prison or a madhouse. All men of good sense recoiled from his projects, because of their treasonable and anti-christian character; while a few, who were heretofore held in some estimation by the better part of society, persisted in shouting the praises of their besotted leader." This is a clipping among the Weld MSS.

¹¹ At Jefferson, Weld reported proudly that after his last meeting the county clerk, the county auditor, and the county recorder all stood among the converts (see *Emancipator*, Oct. 20, 1835). During his twelve days at Jefferson, Weld was a guest at Giddings' home (Weld to L. Tappan, Dec. 14, 1841, Weld MSS.). The incident of Giddings' conversion is told in George W. Julian, *Life of Joshua R. Giddings*, p. 45. Weld's later association with Giddings is related in chapters XVIII and XIX.

¹² This dramatic story of the conversion of Zanesville (Weld to L. Tappan, March, 1836, Weld MSS.) was never published. Weld told it here simply to illustrate a point in connection with the treatment of people of color.

[13] See the *Proceedings of the Ohio State Anti-Slavery Convention, 1835*. Weld wrote the Declaration of Sentiments from which the quotations are made.

[14] Weld began his work at Ripley, on the Ohio River. Then he lectured in towns along the national road. During the summer he visited communities along the Ohio River, and in the autumn and winter he abolitionized the Western Reserve. The next year Ohio alone reported over a third of all the local societies in the nation. The society of four thousand was the Paint Valley Society, extending over several counties, the largest in the nation.

Garrison viewed Weld's success with covetous eyes. His British protegé, Geeorge Thompson, was finding the East increasingly difficult and dangerous, and Garrison wrote Weld that Thompson must come to work in Ohio. Weld replied that abolitionists in Ohio were seriously disturbed at the "mere prospect" of Thompson's coming. "As it is," he wrote, "I think it would be well to allay the apprehensions of our anti-slavery brethren, and tell dear brother Thompson to postpone his visit to Ohio." (*Liberator*, V, 45.) Shortly thereafter Thompson was sent back to England. "It is not fitting," an abolitionist remarked, "that the first martyr to the cause of freedom should be a foreigner."

[15] Theodore Clarke Smith reached the same conclusion regarding the importance of Weld's agency in the conversion of Ohio (*Liberty and Free Soil Parties*, p. 13). At the time, however, outside the little circle of anti-slavery leaders, the world knew nothing of the cause of this revolution in Ohio. Weld insisted that his letters and reports regarding it should not be published. Elizur Wright finally lost his temper. "Remember, we are asking the abolition public [for] *money*," he wrote Weld. "They say to us, what are you doing with the money? . . . Suppose, now, our agents write to us not a word but under the seal of secrecy; what shall we answer? Should not we judge of the 'egotism'? the 'vanity' &c? . . . Why should not your letters be published, when they will encourage all real friends and throw dismay into the ranks of the enemy?" (E. Wright Jr. to Weld, May 26, 1835, Weld MSS.) Weld, however, was obdurate. He would not permit his letters to be published.

[16] Weld's "irruptions into Vermont" are mentioned in the *Friend of Man*, I, 14. Weld spent only a few weeks in Vermont. Charles Stuart had been working there, however, for some months. Weld's conquest of Pittsburgh is described in the *Philanthropist*, Jan. 19, 1836. The ratio of abolitionists to the population before Weld's visit is mentioned in the *Philanthropist*, Feb. 12, 1836, and after his visit, in the *Cincinnati Journal and Western Luminary*, June 9, 1836. L. S. Gould of the Lane rebels was responsible for much of the antislavery sentiment in western Pennsylvania (See *Friend of Man*, July 21, 1836).

[17] Weld's dislike of anniversaries is quoted from a letter of his to L. Tappan, April 5, 1836 (Weld MSS.). The announcement by the committee that he was to speak, dated March 14, 1836, is also in the Weld MSS. The officers raged. Resolutions condemning his refusal (the New York City Young Men's Anti-Slavery Society to Weld, April 6, 1836, Weld

MSS.), and letters of protest, however, failed to change Weld's decision. The appointment to speak before the Rhode Island Legislative Committee is contained in a letter from E. Wright Jr. to Weld, April 21, 1836, and from the Rhode Island Anti-Slavery Society Executive Committee to Weld, May 29, 1836 (Weld MSS.). The appointment to speak before the Connecticut Legislative Committee is noted in a letter from S. Jocelyn to Weld, April 21, 1836 (Weld MSS.). In the Weld MSS. for 1836 there are scores of invitations to speak at cities large and small.

[18] The quotation is from a letter in reply to one of Weld's expressing indignation that Stanton had published one of his (Weld's) letters. Stanton, however, refused to apologize. Weld found that even Elizur Wright was not to be trusted. Wright was inclined to publish Weld's letters first— "with best intentions, and no small prudence, as I thought, and certainly with sage advisors"—and apologize afterward. (E. Wright Jr. to Weld, March 24, 1836, Weld MSS.)

[19] Some of the Lane rebels, notably Sereno Streeter, were laboring in the small towns and rural communities of the State.

[20] The first quotation is from a letter to the *Emancipator*, March 1, 1836; the second is from a letter in *Alvan Stewart on Slavery*, pp. 18–19.

[21] Weld's conquest of Rochester is described in the *Emancipator*, April 11, 1836. His experience at Lockport is told in the *Friend of Man*, Aug. 4, 1836.

[22] *Friend of Man*, July 14, 1836. A committee of the Troy Anti-Slavery Society published the story of the mob in a pamphlet, *The Mob at Troy*, Troy, 1836.

[23] Weld to Dr. Potter, *Friend of Man*, June 23, 1836.

[24] This account neglects perforce the effective work in New York of the Lane rebels—Huntingdon Lyman, Gould, Wattles, and Streeter (*New York Evangelist*, V, 81). Weld himself characterized Utica as the center of the abolition movement in the nation.

[25] *Emancipator*, July 28, 1836. Only two of the letters upon which this sketch of Weld's agency is largely based were published with his consent. At Elizur Wright's insistence, Weld reported twice to the Young Men's Anti-Slavery Society of New York, which had taken over the financial charges of his agency. Weld's modesty has buried a large part of his labors too deep for historical recovery.

CHAPTER IX

"GARRISONISM"

[1] The first quotation is from a letter from an Ohio clergyman in the *Liberator* March 20, 1835; and the second is from the *Spirit of the Pilgrims*, I, 341. For the perplexed historian, at a loss to account for the vitality of the legend that New England was the birthplace and home of the antislavery movement, it may be helpful to remember that nearly all the antislavery histories and biographies have been written by New Eng-

landers. For the number of New England abolitionists, see the report on membership made at the national meeting, May, 1837 (*National Enquirer*, III, 9). The entire enrollment in New England was then less than one-fourth greater than the membership in New York alone. A year later New York passed New England.

² *Right and Wrong in Boston*, No. 2, p. 53.

³ For a description of a meeting of the New England Anti-Slavery Society, see the *Pennsylvania Freeman*, April 12, 1838. The New England Anti-Slavery Society and the New Hampshire State Society did not embody community movements; but I hesitate thus to characterize the Vermont society. The State organization was strong, with, I suspect, a true local society system behind it; but aside from its political support of William Slade and the antislavery resolutions in its legislature, I know little about its activities. It is worth noting that Weld and three other Lane rebels worked there, and also Charles Stuart.

⁴ *Religious Intelligencer*, Nov. 12, 1836; March 18, 1837.

⁵ Stanton delivered one hundred and sixty stated addresses, as well as numerous informal talks, discussions, and debates. As a physical feat, his agency was surpassed only by Weld's in western New York, Pennsylvania, Ohio, and Vermont. Eastern abolitionists expressed astonishment at his methods: "His manner was to deliver a course of five or six lectures in a place, sometimes more . . . not so much directed to the organization of societies as in order that people may think for themselves and do their duty." His methods, like Weld's, were of course the "new measures" of the Great Revival.

Regarding the State convention, the *Sunday Morning News* of Providence said: "We believe that there is spunk enough in Providence to throw the fanatical wretches neck and heel out of the city if they presume to profane it with their unholy meeting." But no violence showed itself during the entire convention. "By delegation the whole state was there" (*Zion's Herald*, VII, 24).

⁶ In Connecticut, Stanton was assisted by Whipple, Allan, Dresser, and Streeter, all Lane rebels; and in Massachusetts he was aided by some of these, and by the Lane rebels, Gould and Alvord. His appearance before the committee on abolition of the Massachusetts State Legislature occurred during the following year. At the committee's public hearing several of the abolitionists testified, but Stanton was the bright, particular star. He spoke on three successive days, giving a summary of the Lane rebels' famous course of lectures. On the third day before a crowded audience—hundreds had been turned away—he spoke for an hour and a half, and then his voice failed him. "The committee were not satisfied; and one of them said, if there was any abolitionist who wished to follow Mr. Stanton they would gladly hear all he had to say, but all declined. . . . Such was the desire to hear more on this subject, that [Garrison] came directly to New York to get Weld to go and speak before them, but his throat is still so much affected that it will be impossible for him to do so." (Angelina Grimké to Jane Smith, no month, 1837. C. Birney, *The Grimké Sisters*, pp. 169–170.) The address of Stanton to the State legislative committee was the high

point in the Massachusetts agitation of that year. It is a revealing circumstance that when the committee asked for additional information, nobody among the Boston abolitionists was prepared to follow Stanton. Evidently none of them had the capacity for sustained exposition of antislavery doctrine. Only Weld and his disciples possessed it.

⁷ The quoted description of Scott is from the *Christian Advocate and Journal,* XII, 35. The story told here of Scott's conversion to the antislavery cause is the one which Whittier told Matlack a few years afterward (Matlack, *American Slavery and Methodism,* p. 101); but in an account dictated shortly before his death (Matlack, *The Life of Rev. Orange Scott,* New York, 1847), Scott described an earlier conversation with the Boston abolitionists, which he felt had influenced him to join the movement.

In the antislavery controversy in *Zion's Herald,* the editors attempted to maintain a neutral attitude. For example, when Scott summoned ministers through its columns to preach against slavery, the editor appended the following note: "Those who do not feel at liberty to preach on the subject of slavery would do well to give a sketch of Popery. We would recommend as a text: 'Mystery, Babylon the Great, the Mother of Harlots and abominations of the Earth.'" (*Zion's Herald,* VI, 41.)

⁸ The references and quotations as to Scott's doctrine are from *Zion's Herald,* IV, 30, and VI, 2. The Bible argument consisted in proving from the Bible either that slavery was a sin or that slavery was not a sin, as the case might be. Both positions could be conclusively established by the methods of handling Biblical "proof texts" then in vogue.

Merritt had been an editor of the national Methodist paper, *Christian Advocate and Journal,* at New York at the time of the Lane debate. Reading the documents of that discussion, he became a convinced abolitionist. Indeed, he ascribed the rise and growth of the antislavery movement to the efforts of the Lane rebels (*Zion's Herald,* VIII, 53). He continued as editor until his declared sympathy for the Methodist abolitionists in New England led to his removal (*Zion's Herald,* VIII, 49). He returned to his home in Lynn, Massachusetts, and devoted the remaining years of his life to the antislavery controversy. The statement of his position on immediatism is from *Zion's Herald,* VII, 206.

⁹ Before Scott began his labors, an abolitionist estimated that there were not five ministers or twenty-five laymen in the church who were abolitionists. This was an understatement. There was considerable old-line abolitionism in the church in the 'twenties, some of it radical in character. (See *Christian Advocate and Journal,* I, II, and III.)

The quotation as to the ecclesiastical status of the "national" societies is from the *Western Christian Advocate,* I, 15. The Methodists were inveterate schismatics, "highly censured by other denominations of Christians because they refused to unite in those societies called National or American," but persisting in their separate course of denominational Bible, Sunday School, educational, and tract activities, to the loss of the nation, Methodist church efficiency, and the national benevolent movement.

Originally two Wesleyan Conference societies in New England were organized. The movement quickly spread to the area of the Great Revival, and the Erie, Oneida, Genesee, and Troy conferences also formed Wesleyan Conference Societies.

¹⁰ The Baptist participation in New England abolitionism was neither as general nor, because of their loose ecclesiastical organization, as easily followed as the Methodist. Their work was more important in Vermont and Maine than in central New England. (See *Vermont Telegraph*, 1834–1837, and Willey, *Anti-Slavery in State and Nation.*)

The estimate of the number of abolitionists in the different denominations is that of the Rev. A. A. Phelps, himself a Congregationalist. It is based upon a questionnaire he sent out to New England abolitionists and is summarized in *A True History of the Late Division in the Anti-Slavery Societies* (Boston, 1840), pp. 33–34. The ratio of abolitionists which he found in the denominations probably prevailed even earlier. I analyzed the list of ministerial delegates at the New England Anti-Slavery Society's session of 1835 (*Liberator*, V, 86). Two thirds of the delegates were ministers, and two thirds of them were Methodists or Baptists. The Conference appointment lists in *Zion's Herald* and the Reports of Location list in *Baptist Zion's Advocate* served to identify the denominations of the ministerial delegates. This is not conclusive. Ministers might not have represented their congregations in antislavery affiliation. But it is probable that they did, ministers being what they were then, as now.

¹¹ That Boston was "the most important part of the field" was the opinion of an Ohio abolitionist (*Liberator*, March 20, 1835). It was not Weld's opinion: "What has been accomplished by all the expenditure in the shape of lectures in Boston? Something it is true, but if the labor of that sort which has been laid out there had been distributed in the country . . . depend upon it the Boston churches would have been open long ago." (Weld to L. Tappan, April 5, 1836, Weld MSS.) The epigram on Boston and New England's hold upon the nation is quoted from the New York *Evening Post*, Nov. 22, 1834.

¹² The quotation in the text is from the *Western Christian Advocate*, III, 111. In defense of Garrison it was urged by his friends that "Mr. Garrison's words cannot be taken in their literal meaning"—referring to his epithets, "thief and murderer," applied to a respectable New England clergyman. Leonard Bacon's comment was this: "Where the truth is covered with such rhetoric as this the mind naturally seeks relief in recollecting that a certain figure of speech . . . *hyperbole*, is sometimes known among men by a very different name, inasmuch as it is simply putting in the place of truth that which is not true." (*Christian Spectator*, IV, 319.)

¹³ *Religious Intelligencer*, Sept. 10, 1836.

¹⁴ This action was taken at the meeting of July, 1834. The Connecticut Association passed the same resolution. (*New York Evangelist*, V, 106.)

¹⁵ The situation in Congregational Churches with minority groups of abolitionists is described in the *Religious Intelligencer*, Nov. 12, 1836; and Garrison's warfare in behalf of these minorities is described in *ibid.*, March 18, 1837.

¹⁶ Lundy's characterization of Garrison's early theological views is in the *National Enquirer*, III, 33. Garrison's opposition to Sabbath observ-

ance alienated Lewis Tappan, secretary of the Sabbath Observance Society (*Liberator*, VI, 141). An indignant reader of the *Liberator* wrote that while he was "an abolitionist to the very back-bone, living or dying," Garrison's "opposition to the Sabbath—to the obligation to obey the fourth command, is no part of abolitionism. As a body I verily believe the abolitionists of the whole country would contemptuously reject the idea of acknowledging that man for their leader. *We brand him as the foe of his race!*" (*Ohio Observer*, X, 116.) Garrison's characterization of the Methodist Church is quoted from *Zion's Herald*, VIII, 123; and his descirption of the Presbyterian Church is in the *Liberator*, VII, 103.

[17] *National Enquirer*, III, 33.

[18] The quotations are from the *Religious Intelligencer*, Sept. 10, 1836. The Boston abolitionists arranged to finance a special paper, the *Non Resistant*, in the hope that thereby objectionable matter might be kept out of the columns of the *Liberator*. Garrison agreed to the arrangement, but he found it impossible to separate his enthusiasms.

[19] *Ohio Observer*, July 3, 1834. In 1834, however, Beecher and Calvin Stowe spoke to the Kentucky Colonization Society for the plan of union, with good effect. Gradual abolitionists organized the Kentucky Union for the Moral and Religious Improvement of the Colored Race. Its organization extended over the whole State, and it was instrumental the following year in bringing before the Kentucky legislature the famous bill for gradual emancipation, which barely failed of passage (Jones, *Religious Instruction of Negroes*, pp. 78–79). See the phillippic against slavery written by its secretary, President Young of Center College (*Zion's Herald*, VII, 77). This statement was also adopted by the Kentucky Synod of 1836, and was widely published to aid the gradualist agitation.

[20] Considering the important place which the Presbyterian Church held in the antislavery movement, the inconsiderable agitation on the subject in General Assemblies previous to the one which Weld attended, is worthy of remark. As late as the session of 1834, for example, the committee to which was referred an antislavery memorial from the Chillicothe presbytery refused to report it out of committee; and even when the matter was called to the attention of the assembly, no action was taken. (*Liberator*, V, 93. See also *Emancipator*, June 2, 1835.) One delegate reported that there were only two immediate abolitionists in the assembly of 1834, but that could not have been true. There was too much spontaneous immediatism in western New York and in Ohio for that. For a description of the 1834 assembly, see the *Emancipator*, June 16, 1835.

In order to attend this session of the assembly, Weld left his Ohio agency for the month of June, 1835. Though he organized the public meetings, he was too busy with his interviews with delegates to attend them until near the end of the session. Beman and Lansing, former colleagues of Finney, the leading New-School ministers, acted as chairmen. At one of the meetings a delegate, Dr. Nevin, a member of the faculty of Western Theological Seminary, was scheduled to speak; but he wrote Weld that the seminary authorities had forbidden him to appear. He proposed to resign his position, however, "for the sake of truth and a good conscience," as soon as a successor could be found. (*Liberator*, V, 97.) Another delegate, Dr. David Nelson, president of Marion College, Missouri, offered to plead the cause of the slave at home. At Weld's instance, the executive committee of the national society made the doctor agent for Missouri. His agency never got beyond its beginning. After a few abolition sermons from his pulpit in Palmyra, Dr. Nelson fled for his life to Illinois, and Marion College was closed. Dr. Nelson spoke powerfully for the cause in western Illinois, from 1836 to 1840. (See Minutes of the Agency Committee, American Anti-Slavery Society, 1835–1840, *passim.*) The quotations in the text are from Weld's report of his work at the General Assembly in the *Emancipator*, June 16, 1835.

[21] The quotation is from a letter, Samuel Galloway to Weld, Aug. 11, 1835 (Weld MSS.). Certain leaders of Presbyterianism suggested to Beecher that at the next assembly, in 1836, repressive measures should be taken to prevent the subject of slavery from coming up. Beecher replied that the subject must be considered; that it would not down; and that repressive measures would be sure to disrupt the church. (James G. Birney to Lewis Tappan, April 29, 1836, L. Tappan Papers, Library of Congress.)

[22] The quotation is from a letter from a delegate, *Western Christian Advocate*, II, 31. "The question is not between the new and the old school—is not in relation to doctrinal errors; but it is *slavery* and *anti-slavery*. It is not the standards which were to be protected but the *system of slavery.*" (Quoted from the *Cincinnati Journal*, in *Zion's Herald*, VIII, 106. See also *Alton Observer*, July 27, 1837, and *Philanthropist*, April 17, 1838, for similar observations.)

[23] *Ohio Observer*, X, 71.

[24] *Friend of Man*, July 14, 1836.

[25] Abolitionists' disdain of Beecher's plea for union was voiced by Gerrit Smith, who wrote Beecher an open letter of sharp reproof: "The opposition of the Anti-Slavery to the Colonization Society is as defensible and justified as its foundation doctrine of 'immediate repentance' is just; and never while one society continues to war upon that doctrine and the other cling to it, can there be an honest and thorough reconciliation between them." (*Ohio Observer*, X, 84.) The quoted description of Beecher's "enlarged . . . feeling" is from *Zion's Herald*, VI, 106. In evidence of Beecher's assimilative capacity for opposing doctrines: At this General Assembly he was to stand trial for anti-Calvinist heresy on appeal from presbytery and synod; but Dr. Wilson, his accuser, was persuaded to withdraw his charges. In the trial before the synod the previous year, Beecher had successfully defended his orthodoxy. Meanwhile he was recognized as a leading New-School theologian. The proceedings of his trial were reported in full in daily and weekly newspapers throughout the country.

[26] *Autobiography and Correspondence of Lyman Beecher*, II, 345.

[27] Since this Congregational Association met at Norfolk, Connecticut, the anti-abolition resolutions were known as the Norfolk resolutions. Beecher was now technicallly a Presbyterian, and his friend Leonard Bacon, therefore, proposed the resolutions; but Beecher said the necessary words. The quotations from his speech are from *Zion's Herald*, VII, 111.

28 The proceedings were reported in the *Ohio Observer*, X, 71. One poor minister, recently appointed antislavery agent, the Rev. E. R. Tyler, feared the consequences of this resolution upon the antislavery cause. Leonard Bacon unkindly paraphrased Garrison's famous doctrine of immediatism in his reply: "Abolitionists should never be troubled about the consequences." (*Religious Intelligencer*, March 18, 1837.)

29 *Ohio Observer*, X, 71.

30 This action of the Congregational churches marked the end of an ancient institution in New England. For generations the Congregational meeting house had been the community forum where any agitator, were he crank or prophet, could speak his heart. William Goodell discussed Beecher's part in the passage of these resolutions in the *Friend of Man*, I, 49. His words are quoted from the *Cincinnati Journal and Western Luminary*, Aug. 28, 1836.

31 In the antislavery journals, the action of the Connecticut General Association was variously accounted for; but when the Massachusetts association concurred, most of the editors ceased to explain it away. The only editor who went on talking about it in his columns was William Goodell, in the *Friend of Man*. Garrison was ill at the time, and the acting editor of the *Liberator* barely noticed it. Evidently he had no notion of its significance. Weld's and Stanton's mission to New Hampshire is noted in the *Friend of Man*, Oct. 13, 1836. The New Hampshire association's proceedings are recorded in the *Ohio Observer*, X, 105.

32 I follow here Whittier's interpretation of Garrison's animus. Whittier had been his loyal friend; but on this occasion he wrote Garrison: "Is this a time for contention among ourselves? For the avowal of petty personal dislike? . . . for SELF in all its vile and mean and despicable variety?" He rebuked Garrison for advocating his heresies in antislavery circles, "because they not only give offense, but, as recent circumstances show, 'cause my brother to offend.' I could never forgive myself . . . if I had ever sought to make use of abolitionism . . . for the purpose of covertly insinuating my own quiet and peculiar faith among my fellow laborers. . . . Let us then, consecrate ourselves anew to the work of humanity, and let pride and passion and prejudice and all unkindness be our first sacrifice." (*Friend of Man*, II, 70.) Garrison's threatening letter from which the quotations are taken is from Garrison to L. Tappan, Sept. 13, 1837 (L. Tappan Papers, Library of Congress). In reply to Garrison, Lewis Tappan declared that when Garrison denounced those who signed the "Appeal" for their opinions, he denounced at the same time "probably a majority of the members of the American anti-slavery societies in the United States." (Garrison, *Garrison*, II, 165.) See chapter III *passim*, for letters to Garrison in the same tenor from other national officers. Especially significant was the cruelly frank letter by Elizur Wright Jr. to Garrison. Commenting on Garrison's obsessions, he wrote: "It is not in the human mind (except in a peculiar and, as I think, diseased state) to believe them." (*Ibid.*, II, 168.)

33 Garrison's children—the authors of the *Life of Garrison*—derive Garrison's crisis of hostility to the churches from the documents published by the little group of authors of the various "clerical appeals." The action

of the Congregational associations is barely mentioned, despite its effect upon the agitation in New England. This is probably due to the fact that Garrison was ill during much of the year 1836, and the substitute in charge of the *Liberator* did not appreciate the importance of the action of the associations. Garrison's children built up their story from the files of the *Liberator*. (See Garrison, *Garrison*, II, chapters II–IV.) Garrison's own view of his place in the movement is illustrated by a passage in the *Liberator*, VII, 143: "You know something of the rise and progress of the anti-slavery cause through my humble instrumentality. I was a poor, self-educated mechanic—without important family connexions, without influence, without wealth, without station—patronized by nobody, laughed at by all, reprimanded by the prudent, contemned by the wise, and avoided for a time even by the benevolent. . . . You can realize nothing of the trials, discouragements and perils through which I had to pass. The pressure on me was like an avalanche, and nothing but the power of God sustained me. The clergy were against me—the rulers of the people were against me—the nation was against me. But . . . I commenced that warfare which is now going on with such glorious success. . . . I will not stop to trace the progress of this great enterprise. Suffice it to say, that its growth has been such as to astonish nations."

The first quotation in the text is from the *Liberator*, VII, 133; the second is from a letter from Garrison to Geo. W. Benson, Garrison, *Garrison*, I, 174.

[34] The list of delegates to the 1835 session of the New England Anti-Slavery Society is in the *Liberator*, V, 86. Even after the Norfolk Resolutions, the New England Anti-Slavery Society (now called the Massachusetts Anti-Slavery Society), found it impossible to prosper without the coöperation of the churches. The convention of 1838 memorialized all the New England ecclesiastical associations, praying for coöperation with the abolitionists. The Rhode Island Congregational Consociation rejected it unanimously (*Liberator*, VIII, 107). In the Congregational weeklies for 1838 I could not find a record even of its consideration in any other association. Thereafter the Boston agitation in the field assumed a curious complexion. Most of its agents, unable to attract audiences on their own account, went to the Sunday church services, where audiences were gathered, and spoke out from the congregations for abolition and against the clergy. They were regularly jailed for disturbing religious meetings. The *Liberator* only occasionally recorded this fantastic agitation, but N. P. Rogers in the *Herald of Freedom* (especially for 1839–1843) followed the agents' progress from jail to jail. Parker Pillsbury and Stephen Foster were the leading disturbers.

[35] Among the conservatives, many probably believed, like Dr. Farnsworth, that Garrison's "power for doing mischief" would be lessened "if we keep with him and surround him with our influence, which must restrain him to a very great degree." (Farnsworth to Phelps, Oct. 27, 1837, in *A True History of the Late Division in the Anti-Slavery Societies*, p. 11.) But among the majority, Garrison's fantastic views cost him dear. A. A. Phelps, with no sense of the true nature of Garrison's fixed idea re-

garding the churches, made a study of the New England movement to prove that he was wrong. It comprised the results of an elaborate questionnaire which showed that practically all abolitionists in the organization were members of churches, and that most of the leading abolitionists in the local societies were ministers. He secured the signatures of 124 ministers in his production. Garrison's comment was that if things were as bad as that, he despaired of the organization. The study was published in *A True History of the Late Division in the Anti-Slavery Societies,* referred to above. The quotation in the text is from a letter, Sarah Grimké to Weld, Sept. 20, 1837 (Weld MSS.).

[36] Among the resolutions framed by local societies here and there, in terms of the Garrison legend, I quote one example among many: The Delaware County Anti-Slavery Society of Pennsylvania could "discover no cause for this unmerited attack upon the noble pioneer in the field of liberty . . . who first marked out the path which all true abolitionists follow." (*National Enquirer,* III, 253.)

CHAPTER X

REVIVAL TRIUMPHANT

[1] The quotation is from the *National Enquirer,* III, 17. Elizur Wright Jr. wrote: "We . . . shall issue gratuitously from 20,000 to 50,000 of some publication or other every week. What seems now the greatest difficulty is to get the *names* of the right persons to whom we may send them. We want names of inquiring, candid, reading men who are *not* abolitionists." (Elizur Wright Jr. to Weld, June 10, 1835, Weld MSS.) The system for distributing bundles of petitions is described in the *Friend of Man,* Nov. 21, 1836. Nearly all the pamphlets in these bundles were brief appeals. Most of them were issues of newspapers: *Human Rights, The Anti-Slavery Record,* the *Emancipator,* and *The Slave's Friend.* (See *Emancipator,* Sept. 3, 1835.)

[2] The pamphlet campaign for the South is thus described in the New York Committee's own words: "We have sent no packages of our papers to any persons in those States [the South] for distribution, except to five respectable resident citizens at their own request. But we have sent by mail single papers addressed to public officers, editors of newspapers and clergymen." (Statement of the Executive Committee of the American Anti-Slavery Society to the Public, Sept., 1835.)

The Postmaster General wrote to the postmaster of Charleston: "We have an obligation to the laws, but a higher one to the communities in which we live, and if the former be perverted to destroy the latter, it is patriotism to disregard them" (*Philadelphian,* Aug. 20, 1835). The announcement that pamphlets would no longer be mailed to Southern addresses, together with the circumstances, is printed in the *Cincinnati Journal and Western Luminary,* IX, 90. By 1836, most Southern State legislatures had made the circulation of abolition pamphlets a felony.

[3] Still the collapse of the Southern campaign was a serious blow to the movement. As the South was closed to abolition propaganda, Wright in

desperation appealed to Weld for arguments to meet the situation, to be published in "The Annual Report, which is now in the stocks." He wanted "a plain common Sense view of the *how* emancipation and abolition are to be brought about by the correction of public sentiment at the North. . . . Can you not furnish me some *facts* pertinent to . . . the *effectiveness* of Northern abolition on the South? They will be thankfully recd." (E. Wright, Jr. to Weld, March 16, 1835, Weld MSS.)

⁴ Even experts in antislavery doctrine went wrong on the meaning of immediatism. For instance, Prof. Andrews, agent and author for the American Union (p. 62, of this book), objected to immediatism because the slave was not prepared for emancipation. He wrote, said a critic, "as if immediate emancipation meant setting the slave free," which of course it did not. "He imagines that the doctrine of immediate emancipation is altogether a different thing from what it is." (*Ohio Observer*, X, 74.)

⁵ The Society's *Particular Instructions to Agents,* a folder, first printed in 1833, for private circulation, gives the following warning: "Do not allow yourself to be drawn away from the main object, to exhibit a detailed PLAN of abolition. . . . Let the *principle* be decided on, of immediate abolition, and the plans will easily present themselves. What ought to be done can be done. If the *great* question were decided, and if half the ingenuity now employed to defend slavery were employed to abolish it, it would impeach the wisdom of American statesmen to say they could not, with the Divine Blessing, steer the ship through." These *Particular Instructions* were attached to agents' commissions at least until 1836. Several such commissions are in the Weld MSS. The first quotation in the text is from the *New York Evangelist*, I, 126. The second quotation, shifting responsibility to the Southern States, is from the *Emancipator*, June 3, 1834. The final quotation is from Austin, *Remarks on Dr. Channing's Slavery*, p. 6.

⁶ The first quotation is from the *Ohio Observer*, X, 74. For the beginning of the controversy regarding the meaning of immediatism according to the New York doctrine, see *Christian Spectator*, June, 1834, and the *Emancipator*, Oct. 21, 1834. The final quotation is from *Zion's Herald*, VI, 74.

⁷ The first quotation is from the *Christian Examiner*, third series, XXII, 13–14; the remaining quotations are from Jay, *Inquiry into the Character and Tendencies of . . . the American Anti-Slavery Society* (eighth ed.) p. 197. The statement first appeared in the third edition.

⁸ The description of an anniverary is from *Zion's Herald*, VIII, 90; the final quotation is from Jay, *Inquiry*, as above.

⁹ The first quotation is from the *Alton Observer*, Dec. 15, 1836. Benjamin Lundy's comment is from the *National Enquirer*, Aug. 24, 1836. Garrison's position was more theoretical than realistic: "Urge immediate abolition as earnestly as we may, it will, alas! be gradual abolition in the end. We have never said that slavery would be overthrown at a single blow; that it ought to be, we shall always contend." (*Liberator*, I, 129.)

¹⁰ The early propaganda was definitely religious. In 1834, for example, agents were directed to "insist principally on the SIN OF SLAVERY, because our main hope is in the consciences of men" (*Particular Instructions to Agents,* Weld MSS.). This propaganda never entirely ceased. The quoted

admission of the South is from the *Southern Quarterly Review,* Oct.,
1845, p. 334.

[11] Imminent disaster to the movement in 1835 is described in *Zion's
Herald,* VIII, 53. The controversy between the "slavery an evil" and
"slavery a sin" factions raged in the journals; but outside the debates in
the State societies, I have found no records of discussion among the anti-
slavery leaders particularizing this revolution in doctrine.

In a brief summary of the movement which Timothy Merritt, the
Methodist abolitionist, wrote for his people, he gave the Lane rebels credit
not only for solving the dilemma of immediatism, but also for originating
the doctrine that slavery was a sin. After indicating that, unless a way out
could be found, the abolition movement would have to go over to gradualism, he wrote: "Things were in this state when, three or four years since,
the students in Lane Seminary, Ohio, agreed among themselves to discuss
the question of slavery. They did so, and the discussions resulted in a conviction that slavery is a *sin.* For this, and for adhering to what they believed to be the cause of God and his truth, many were dismissed from the
Seminary, and God thrust them out, full of philanthropy and zeal, to awake
a slumbering nation." (*Zion's Herald,* VIII, 53.) But though there can be
no doubt that the influence of the Lane rebels favored the adoption of their
doctrine of the sin of slavery, it had long been a part of the antislavery tradition. See George Bourne's *The Book and Slavery Irreconcileable* (Philadelphia, 1816), for the most powerful early presentation of the Bible argument.

[12] Weld's pamphlet was entitled *The Bible and Slavery* (first ed., New
York, 1837). For years this pamphlet was the unquestioned authority to
abolitionists, both in England and America, for the Bible argument. It was
republished in England, and tens of thousands of copies were printed by the
national society. All ministers and theological students who applied for a
copy received one free.

[13] *Zion's Herald,* VIII, 53.

[14] The quotation is from the speech of Preston of South Carolina, in the
Senate. *Appendix to Congressional Globe,* 1st S., 24th Congress, p. 222.

[15] The best description I have found of this change in policy is in Lewis
Tappan's official announcement at the Pennsylvania State Anti-Slavery
Society Convention at Harrisburg, Feb. 1, 1837. Tappan said that already
seventy agents had been commissioned, and that the pamphlet printing had
been reduced to hardly more than one fourth of its former volume. This
reduction was probably close to a necessary minimum. The journals called
for a heavy part of it, and some funds were donated on condition that they
be used to print certain pamphlets. (*National Enquirer,* I, 90.)

[16] The appointment and labors of the Lane rebels are described in the
Friend of Man, Sept. 8, 1836; Feb. 1, 1837; Jan. 3, 1838; and Weld MSS.,
Aug.–Dec., 1836. Many of the Lane rebels had returned to Oberlin, to complete their preparation for the ministry; and when the commissions from
Weld arrived, the young men were sadly perplexed. Should they "lecture,
or . . . promote revivals of religion? Br. Finney has used his heart and
head and influence to convince us that it is our duty to preach. He groans

over the subject and speaks of himself as being agonized about it." Streeter
decided to preach, but Alvord, Thome, Allan, and the others could not agree
with Finney that their first duty was to revivals. News of the Cincinnati
mobs had just reached Oberlin, Allan wrote, and their fellow rebel, Weed,
who was already in the field, "has been hunted like a wild beast—life saved
by the ladies of his audience. Troubles are coming like a whirlwind. I have
helped to raise the storm. Shall I now avoid its fury by going into a less
dangerous field? God forbid! No, my brother, come life, come death, our
stand must be maintained." ("Folio letter," Allan, Streeter, Thome and
Alvord to Weld, Aug. 9, 1836, Weld MSS.) Allan continued: "Write
again, dear Brother, soon.—we not only want, but *need* your letters. To
feel and act together we must communicate often. Do keep us advised of
your movements. Sometimes we do not hear for months. It distresses us.
We can neither pray for you nor sympathize with you, unless we know your
circumstances."

In the search for agents, Stanton and Whittier canvassed the Pennsylvania colleges (Pickard, *Life and Letters of John Greenleaf Whittier,* I,
249–250). Stanton later joined Weld in western New York. Weld covered
Ohio, New York, and New England, and approved all the agents chosen by
Stanton and Whittier, as well as those suggested by the New York executives. (See Weld MSS. for 1836, and Minutes of the Agency Committee,
American Anti-Slavery Society, for 1836.) The first characterization
of the Seventy is from the New York *Evening Post,* quoted in *Zion's
Herald,* VIII, 25. The preponderance of ministers and theological students
among the Seventy is noted in *Friend of Man,* II, 98. When Amos Phelps
referred to the preponderance of clergymen among the Seventy to prove
that Garrison's anti-clerical statements were contrary to the facts, Garrison
replied that that very circumstance made him highly suspicious of the
abolitionism of the Seventy. (*Liberator,* Nov. 3, 1837.) The final quotation
is from the *Friend of Man,* as above.

¹⁷ At the Agents' Convention, Charles Stuart's speech was evidently a
panegyric upon Weld. In a letter to his fiancée, who had attended the
Agents' Convention, Weld expressed his regret that her opinion of him
should be based "upon the testimony and estimate of my too partial friends,
such as the almost passionate expressions of affection and respect for me
used by C. Stuart in our Agency Convention last winter. Charles has for
me more than a father's affection for his first born, and it strangely blinds
him to my faults. I have told him so a hundred times and tried to tear the
scales from his eyes, but he *will* hold them on." (Weld to Angelina Grimké,
Feb. 16, 1838, Weld MSS.) Regarding his own part in the convention,
Garrison wrote somewhat pathetically: "It was a happy circumstance . . .
that they had an opportunity to become personally acquainted with me: for
as I am a great stumbling block in the way of the people . . . it would be
somewhat disastrous to our cause if any of our Agents, through the influence of popular sentiment, should be led to cherish prejudices against me.
I was most kindly received by all . . . notwithstanding the wide difference
of opinion between us on some religious points, especially the Sabbath
question." (Garrison to his wife, Garrison, *Garrison,* II, 116–117.) The

description of Weld as the "central luminary" is from the same reference. This convention was the only one which Weld had ever attended. He could not escape the responsibility for its leadership. After he had promised to attend, Wright wrote him: "I do hope you will never regret *swallowing* your 'repugnancies,' modesty and all." (E. Wright Jr. to Weld, Nov. 4, 1836, Weld MSS.) The quotation regarding Weld's voice is from a letter from Sarah M. Grimké to Weld, Jan. 9, 1838 (Weld MSS.). Sarah Grimké, who was an agent at the convention, wrote: "He was the master spirit, the principal speaker in that assembly. His labors were intense. I have heard him speak eight or ten hours in a day at three sessions of the Convention. . . . Besides his speaking he would be up night after night till two or three o'clock. . . . Human nature could not endure it, she sunk." (S. M. Grimké to her mother, Mary S. Grimké, July 15, 1839, Weld MSS.) The quotations describing the work of the convention are from the *Friend of Man*, II, 98, and Garrison to his wife (Garrison, *Garrison*, II, 117.) The final quotation is from the *Friend of Man*, as above.

[18] The quotation as to Weld's "set purpose" is from a letter from Weld to Angelina Grimké, March 12, 1838 (Weld MSS.). Regarding what might have been achieved, if Weld had carried out his purpose, Theodore Clarke Smith remarks (*Liberty and Free Soil Parties*, p. 13) : "In view of the results attained in Ohio, where, until 1830, popular sentiment had been no further advanced than in its western neighbors, it seems possible that, had Weld, Stanton, Thome and the rest extended their work, those other States [Indiana and Illinois] might have developed an antislavery sentiment commensurate with that of Ohio." Without Weld to lead them, however, none of the Seventy were assigned to the far West. They were distributed among the antislavery areas already established. (See p. 105 of this book.)

Regarding his loss of voice, Weld wrote during his convalescence: "My general health is pretty good but I become very hoarse if I attempt to speak or even to discuss in conversation if at all excited. I don't understand it." (Weld to L. Tappan, June 8, 1837, Weld MSS.) He did not attempt to speak in public until after 1840, and even then his voice would leave him, if he attempted any "declamation." The final quotation is from a letter from Sarah Grimké to her mother, July 15, 1839. Weld himself declared: "I have never done half so much for Abolition as since I have stopped speaking" (Weld to the Grimké sisters, Nov. 21, 1837, Weld MSS.).

[19] See Weld MSS. from July to November, 1836, for references to this plan.

[20] *Zion's Herald*, VIII, 53.

[21] On the reorganized staff, Weld would take neither appointment nor salary: "I am not an agent of any A. S. society,—have no commission,—receive no salary—am under nobody's control or direction *in any sense,*—and yet am considered and called an agent of the Society. Why? Because I spend all my time in laboring in the anti-slavery cause—in doing here at the centre a hundred things which can't be named exactly nor defined, but enough to keep me busy as I ever was night and day." (Weld to the Grimké sisters, Oct. 1, 1837, Weld MSS.)

252 NOTES [Chapter X]

The last year, 1839, Birney, Weld, Stanton, and Leavitt were elected the sole executives of the society. Weld, of course. "on principle" immediately resigned.

²² The first quotation describing the "concussion" which the Seventy produced is from the words of Timothy Merrit in *Zion's Herald,* VIII, 53. Weld's words regarding the importance of work in the rural districts are from a letter written before the Agents' Convention had met, but it so exactly expresses Weld's policy that I have used its phrases here (Weld to Lewis Tappan, April 5, 1836, Weld MSS.). Elsewhere Weld recounted the experiences that taught him this propaganda strategy: "Sometimes in Ohio I found it utterly impossible to find rest for the sole of my foot in the capital of a county; but spend a few weeks in the towns round it among the yeomanry, and instead of being thrust out I would be invited and importuned to go to the county seat." As early as June, 1836, Elizur Wright Jr. wrote Weld that the Executive Committee had decided to follow his [Weld's] advice and "let the cities lie fallow." But they did not actually do so until Weld came to New York. Possibly demands for agents from the larger city societies were too strong to be denied. However, with Weld in the New York office, the Seventy were all assigned to the back country, and kept there.

²³ Five of the Seventy originally commissioned, by reason of illness, death, or changed circumstances, did not agitate abolition. The Seventy were really therefore sixty-five. Twenty of these were not reëmployed in June, 1837, for the next year's work. A few of them protested against their dismissals. The most persistent trouble-maker was H. C. Wright, who failed in Massachusetts, was shifted to Pennsylvania, and was finally dismissed. He was a "Garrison man," and he charged that his dismissal was on account of his loyalty to Garrison. The Boston abolitionists believed him, but the charge was untrue. He was a conceited, mischief-making incompetent, and his removal was demanded almost unanimously by abolitionists residing in his various fields of labor. (See Weld to the Grimké sisters, Oct. 16, 1837.) The quotation in the text is from this letter.

CHAPTER XI

THE RIGHT OF PETITION

¹ The first quotation is from Article II of the Constitution of the American Anti-Slavery Society. In the Declaration of Sentiments of the society, which Garrison wrote, there is a list of seven lines of activity for antislavery effort, but petitioning Congress is not one of them. Congress had exclusive jurisdiction over the District; slavery there was within the power of Congress; and petitions for its abolition were therefore in order. Regarding the work of the older abolition societies, the Pennsylvania Society for the Abolition of Slavery had operated a school for colored boys; but with that exception all the older groups made the presentation of petitions to Congress their main activity. The American Convention did little else.

Whittier's words are quoted from the *Salem Landmark,* June 20, 1835. This movement of 1828 was not formally organized, but through sympathetic editors it spread over the whole North, and even produced a large volume of petitions from the border slave States. Inhabitants of the District itself submitted a monster petition. Pennsylvania and New York were the leaders, and Ohio furnished a large number. In New England, Vermont was most active. This was due in part to the efforts of Garrison, who was then editing the *Journal of the Times,* at Bennington. Garrison sent out form petitions to postmasters in the State with directions to secure names to the petitions and return them. Since postmasters' mail went free, the expense of the campaign was nominal. Returns were secured from forty-one postmasters. This interesting campaign foreshadowed the systematic organization of the later movement. (See House Files, Library of Congress, Box 49.)

² *Appendix to Congressional Globe,* 1st S., 24th Congress, p. 221.

³ Letter attached to a petition (House Files, Box 90).

⁴ *Philanthropist,* Jan. 2, 1836. In the editorial of which this is a part, Birney foretold the gag, four months before its passage. Calhoun's attack on reception had occurred a few days before.

⁵ The first quotation is from Wythe [Weld], *The Power of Congress over the District of Columbia.* The position of the New York State Society is stated in the *Friend of Man,* II, 39. Stewart contended that since Patton had moved the previous question immediately upon proposing his gag— thereby cutting off debate—the Patton gag was a denial of the right of petition. For examples of dissenting county society opinions, that the Patton gag was only a "virtual" denial, see *Friend of Man,* March 14, 1838.

⁶ The orthodox abolition position on the standing gag is stated in the *Philanthropist,* Feb. 18, 1840. The resolutions of the antislavery mass meeting are in the *National Anti-Slavery Standard,* April 7, 1842.

⁷ Calhoun's argument was as follows: He quoted numerous standing rules of parliament—"Standing Orders"—by which petitions of certain classes on certain subjects were not to be received. He pointed out that in Congress petitions had been refused reception previously (see *Appendix to Congressional Globe,* 1st S., 24th Congress, pp. 224–225). He quoted Thomas Jefferson's *Manual of Parliamentary Practice* (1837 ed., p. 59), which had been adopted by both houses of Congress to govern their procedure. He quoted the Senate's own rule: ". . . that regularly a motion for receiving a petition must be made and seconded, and a question put whether it shall be received."

Franklin Pierce's statement is in *Congressional Globe,* 2d S., 25th Congress, p. 37; and James Buchanan's is in *ibid.,* p. 38.

⁸ *Congressional Globe,* 1st S., 26th Congress, p. 122.

⁹ The first two quotations are from the *Anti-Slavery Standard,* Jan. 4, 1844. Buchanan's statement is from *Congressional Globe,* 2d S., 25th Congress, p. 38. The final quotation is from the *Anti-Slavery Standard,* as above.

¹⁰ The inadequacy of the House Rules was notorious. In the first session of the twenty-sixth Congress, for instance, the Committee on Rules unan-

imously recommended that the desks in front of the members' benches be removed, "to make the seats of members as uncomfortable as possible," in the hope that "they would the sooner rid themselves of the tediousness of debate by vacating them. . . . It would expedite the public business more than any other rule that could be adopted." (*Congressional Globe,* 1st S., 26th Congress, p. 122.) The scene at the adoption of the Patton gag is described in the *New York American,* Dec. 23, 1837.

[11] *Congressional Globe,* 1st S., 26th Congress, p. 122.

[12] Such resolutions did not accompany the Patton gag.

[13] This was Atherton's description of the operation of the gag which bore his name. *Congressional Globe,* 3d S., 25th Congress, p. 23.

[14] *Ibid.,* p. 117.

[15] William Slade, a militant champion of petitions, did object to the "sweeping rule," pleading instead that petitions be disposed of "on *motion,* as they were presented"; but the basis of his plea was that action on petitions by a general rule was not according to "English rules of Parliamentary practice which we had adopted." This was not a valid objection, because parliament had frequently established standing rules not to receive petitions on designated subjects. Even Slade did not venture to argue that the gag violated the right of petition because it was a "prospective action." The final quotation is from *Appendix to Congressional Globe,* 1st S., 28th Congress, p. 242.

[16] *Appendix to Congressional Globe,* 1st S., 24th Congress, p. 402. Subjects acted upon could be brought up once by the motion to reconsider; but that motion once defeated, the measure could not be moved again.

[17] In the second session of the twenty-fifth Congress, Wise of Virginia made a determined effort to introduce the Senate's method of disposal. It worked smoothly enough for a time. Within a few days the routine was so well established that the Speaker regularly put the motion to lay the question on the table before Wise could speak. For several days William Slade suffered this procedure in silence. "I waited, in fact, till my spirit stirred within me, witnessing the contempt with which petitions of this description were treated by votes to lay them on the table with the avowed purpose of *nailing* them there. I waited till I could wait no longer." (*National Enquirer,* III, 66.) On December eighteenth he presented two of his petitions for abolition in the District, and after moving to refer them to a select committee, declared that "he could not but express his astonishment at the systematic arrangement which had been entered into" by Wise and the Speaker. "The mechanical arrangement for the disposal of these petitions was an insult to the people and unworthy of the House." Wise angrily denied any collusion between himself and the Speaker, and in the course of his explanation forgot to move to lay Slade's motion on the table. Under the forty-eighth rule, Slade was, therefore, entitled to claim the floor to discuss his motion, which he did on December twentieth (House Files, Box 103). For two hours he "shook the very hall into convulsions. Wise, Legaré, Rhett, Dawson, Robertson and the whole herd were in combustion. . . . The slavers were at their wits' end." (Adams, *Memoirs,* IX, 453.)

He was finally silenced and the House immediately adjourned. During the adjournment a caucus of all Southern members was called; it was attended by Southern senators as well. After a stormy session the caucus resolved upon another gag, which was presented by Patton the next day, December twenty-first. The Senate's procedure had broken down in the House and it was never systematically tried again.

In the session of 1835–1836, a select committee was appointed to receive abolition petitions. Immediately the number of petitions greatly increased. It was that unfortunate experience which turned the House against the plan urged by John Quincy Adams, which was to refer petitions to the standing committee on the District of Columbia, "the tomb of the Capulets," where, said Adams, they would die quietly. They would have continued to come, of course, as they did. The petition campaign even then was a major measure in the field among the abolition societies, and no device which the House could invent would stay the flood.

The fact that whatever device was adopted, petitions would continue, was a matter of common knowledge. Every week each member received a free copy of the *Emancipator,* which recorded the growing scope of the petition campaign, and more than once members quoted excerpts from the abolition papers on the floor of the House to show the need for action.

[18] During the years of experiment in parliament, for a time a special early morning session was instituted for the presentation of petitions, where twenty members were a quorum. By 1833, even this was insufficient (Cushing, *Law and Practice of Legislative Assemblies,* ninth ed., pp. 471–474). Such a device was not available in this country, for the Constitution states what shall constitute a quorum in Congress.

[19] The House of Commons in parliament had a rule refusing reception to any petition in which the prayer was either printed or lithographed; but Congress had no such rule. This made especially easy in this country a widespread petition campaign through the distribution of printed forms. For an impressive sample of the volume of these printed forms sent to Congress as petitions, see House Files, Boxes 70–136.

[20] Thomas Morris described himself in the words quoted in *Appendix to Congressional Globe,* 3d S., 25th Congress, p. 167. The quoted description of William Slade is from Adams's words on the floor of the House. In his diary he wrote that there were no more than five votes in the House for abolition in the District. (Adams, *Memoirs,* X, 63.) Franklin Pierce's characterization of the issue of the right of petition is in *Congressional Globe,* 1st S., 27th Congress, p. 27.

[21] *Appendix to Congressional Globe,* 1st S., 26th Congress, p. 251.

[22] The quoted description of the spirit of the Whig minority is in *Congressional Globe,* 1st S., 24th Congress, p. 513. There was no legal obligation upon members to present petitions sent them. Whigs chose to present them, and Democrats chose not to present them.

Botts, Stanley, Underwood, Arnold, Stuart, members from western Virginia and North Carolina, and eastern Kentucky and Tennessee, were intermittent defenders of the right of petition. An indignant member of the majority faction thus described Adams and Wise: "Ruling spirits of disorganization in this House . . . in this respect . . . a complete match." (*Congressional Globe*, 2nd S., 26th Congress, p. 183.)

²³ The phrase, "predetermined to reject" is in *Appendix to Congressional Globe*, 2d S., 24th Congress, p. 154. The proportion of petitions which Democrats in the House usually charged the Whigs with presenting was ten for every one presented by Democrats. The proportion was actually far greater, more than 'twenty to one. (See House Files, Boxes 52–136.) For the party alignment on the gags, see the roll calls on the votes for the gags in *Congressional Globe*, from the 1st S., 24th Congress, to the 1st S., 28th Congress. The gags were usually characterized as necessary·rules for House procedure by their Northern champions. They were "the best means of enabling the House to do the public business." (*Appendix to Congressional Globe*, 1st S., 28th Congress, p. 180.)

²⁴ Slade's admission as .o the right of reception is in *ibid.*, 1st S., 26th Congress, p. 889; and Adams' is in *ibid.*, p. 764. When the "general gag" described in the text came up in the twenty-seventh Congress, every Democrat voted against it, and every Whig save one voted for it. Adams alone, stubborn causist for the right of petition, cast his vote against it. By this gag, the only petitions to be received were those referring to subjects named in the president's message and to the bankruptcy act.

As evidence of the mixture of sectionalism and party politics involved in the standing rule, an illuminating incident occurred in 1842. During the early days of the first session, the Northern Whigs had a temporary majority, and they rescinded the standing gag, knowing that later arrivals would give the Southern Whigs and the Democrats a majority. Their declared purpose was to embarrass the Democrats by putting on them "the painful necessity of reënslaving the North." After more Democrats arrived, the rescinding vote was reconsidered and the gag was reëstablished. For the politics of this move, see *New York American*, Dec. 15, 1842.

²⁵ On the actual or "virtual" denial of the right of petition, the position of the various antislavery societies was as follows: The resolution by means of which the American Anti-Slavery Society presented their position was, as couched in Adams' ringing words: "a direct violation of the Constitution of the United States." The New England societies took the position of the national society, as did the State society in New York. The New York county societies, and the State and county societies of western Pennsylvania and Ohio, before 1840 pronounced the gags a "virtual denial" of their rights. Alvan Stewart's arguments moved the New York State Society. Possibly the position of John Quincy Adams influenced the New England societies.

The quotation referring to petitions unheard as "blank paper" is from the *National Anti-Slavery Standard*, Jan. 11, 1844. The demand to be "listened to" is in *Zion's Herald*, March 14, 1838. The quotation appraising the value of petitions as propaganda is from the *Emancipator*, Sept. 9, 1839. The final quotation is from *De Bow's Review*, XXIV, 425.

CHAPTER XII

PETITION STRATEGY

[1] *Appendix to Congressional Globe,* 1st S., 24th Congress, p. 221. Another irate Southern member remarked: "The language of the petitions is an insult to the South. . . . 'We thank God that we are not as other men, whoremongers and adulterers.' This was the language of the petitions, all of them." (*Congressional Globe,* 1st S., 24th Congress, p. 38.)

[2] *Appendix to Congressional Globe,* 2d S., 25th Congress, p. 59.

[3] For an example of Congressmen who were constrained to speak for their State, see Adams' *Memoirs,* XI, 256, giving Caleb Cushing's real opinion on the gag. The final quotation is from *Appendix to Congressional Globe,* 1st S., 26th Congress, p. 251.

[4] *Congressional Globe,* 2d S., 24th Congress, p. 119.

[5] This description is by the Washington correspondent of the *New York Express,* copied in the *Friend of Man,* II, 147.

[6] Adams' "wanton torture" of Southern feelings is described in *Appendix to Congressional Globe,* 1st S., 24th Congress, p. 333. The description of his stubbornness—"unmoveable as a pillar"—is quoted from the *New York American,* March 14, 1838. With reference to his spitefulness, Adams once apologized somewhat pathetically to the House: "I speak my mind sometimes perhaps too strongly, instigated it may be, by a momentary feeling of irritation which soon passes over, and which I am afterwards the first to regret." (*Congressional Globe,* 2d S., 27th Congress, p. 428.) The description of Adams' alternate "growling and sneering," and of his eloquence, is from the *Democratic Review,* I, 79. The correspondent added that at such times Adams "rises abruptly, his face reddens, and in a moment, throwing himself into the attitude of a veteran gladiator, he prepares for the attack; then he becomes full of gesticulation, his body sways to and fro—self-command seems lost—his head is bent forward in his earnestness till it sometimes nearly touches the desk; his voice frequently breaks." Adams was then seventy-two years old. Calhoun's description of him is in the Calhoun Papers, *Reports,* American Historical Association, 1899, II, 513. Andrew Johnson's description is in *Appendix to Congressional Globe,* 1st S., 28th Congress, p. 97.

[7] Adams wrote to his constituents (*New York American,* Sept. 18, 1838) that he "deprecated . . . discussion of slavery . . . in the House." His indignant defense of the right of petitions to a hearing is in *Appendix to Congressional Globe,* 1st S., 26th Congress, p. 763. His defense of the presentation of petitions one by one is in *ibid.,* 2d S., 25th Congress, p. 263. The final quotation is from *Congressional Globe,* 2d S., 27th Congress, p. 181.

[8] Adams' real doctrine as to the right of petition was stated most clearly during his long filibuster covering fifteen morning hours in June and July, 1838: "The right of petition is suspended if the motion to lay on the table a petition of a class not approved by the majority is regularly applied, either by a general rule or by habitual procedure." (See *National Intelligencer,* April 23, 1839, for an excellent discussion of this view.) To

defend his position, Adams argued that it was incumbent upon the House to take definite action on all petitions. Laying them on the table was neither rejection, which was in the power of the House, nor consideration, which was the right of the petitioner; it was simply an avoidance of the question. With admirable consistency, he claimed that all petitions so disposed of— for a National bank, for the relief of the Cherokee Indians, for restricting immigration—were as truly gagged as abolition petitions. (*Speech of John Quincy Adams . . . June 16–July 7, 1838.*) In fact, he wrote in a public letter that "the right of petition for any object not agreeable to the ruling majority of the House must be considered as suspended" (*National Intelligencer,* April 23, 1839). This stand was logical, but it involved as a major premise the impropriety of making the tabling motion a means of avoiding action upon any subject embarrassing to the majority—a premise which few in the House would grant.

In 1840, Adams moderated his position on the right of petitions to reception, contending, however, that if a petition was not received, it must be because "special objection exists against it"; but in 1842 he was once more arguing the unqualified right of petitions to reception. At times in the House, and usually in his public letters, Adams argued the right of petition on the popular ground, that the gags were a denial in advance of the rights of the petitioners. This was the only argument that the general public could understand, and Adams was a practical politician.

Adams' definition of a proper "general rule" is in *Congressional Globe,* 2d S., 24th Congress, p. 79. His speech in defense of such a "general rule" is in *Appendix to Congressional Globe,* 1st S., 26th Congress, p. 764. Several antislavery Whigs informed Adams that they considered this measure a gag, and they refused to support it (Adams, *Memoirs,* X, 199 ff.). It was strongly condemned by abolitionists (*Emancipator,* Feb. 13, 1840). The record of the passage of the "Adams gag" is in *Congressional Globe,* 2d S., 27th Congress, p. 267. In this session Adams was the leading Whig. Of course his hostility to the Twenty-first Rule, the standing gag, was as bitter and as violently expressed as ever.

[9] *Ibid.,* p. 79.

[10] The quotations as to Adams' real sentiments at the time of the first debate on the gag are from a letter from Adams to S. Lincoln, April 4, 1836 (Massachusetts Historical Society, *Proceedings,* second series, XV, 439). Adams' definition of slavery as a "deadly disease" is from a public letter to his constituents, *New York American,* Nov. 13, 1838. The final quotation is from Adams, *Memoirs,* IX, 418.

[11] The description of Adams as "the glory of three ages" is from the *New York American,* Feb. 22, 1843. The "moral grandeur" of Adams' accepting a seat in the lower House was remarked by the New York *Whig,* Dec. 27, 1831.

[12] Adams, *Memoirs,* VIII, 707.

[13] *Ibid.,* X, 79.

[14] Giddings' diary, in Buell, *Joshua R. Giddings,* p. 79. After the manner of proud and sensitive natures, Adams was inclined to refer his loneliness to others. He wrote in his diary: "To be forsaken by all mankind seems to

be the destiny that awaits my last days. In such cases a man can be sustained only by an over-ruling consciousness of rectitude." (Adams, *Memoirs*, IX, 58.)

[15] The characterization of Adams—"none other . . . to take his place" —is from the *Anti-Slavery Standard*, Nov. 10, 1842. The words were spoken to his constituents by Marshall of Kentucky. The description "enfeebled, but yet . . . never tired" is in the *Democratic Review*, I, 79. The final quotation is from *Congressional Globe*, 2nd S., 27th Congress, p. 175. These were the words of Adams' chief antagonist, Henry Wise of Virginia.

[16] Adams, *Memoirs*, IX, 302. The position that his battle was for the right of petition only, Adams took in most of his public letters before 1840. See, for example, his letters in Massachusetts Historical Society, *Proceedings*, second series, XV, 459, 473.

[17] The two quotations are from Adams, *Memoirs*, IX, 418 and 348. For examples of attacks in Democratic papers on Adams, see an article from the *New Era* in the *Emancipator*, Dec. 19, 1839; and the *Extra Globe*, IV, 343–344.

[18] Adams, *Memoirs*, IX, 365. For the course of his interesting and significant friendship with Lundy, see Adams, *Memoirs*, VIII, 316; IX, 302, 365; Lundy's *National Enquirer*, Dec. 17 and 31, 1836; Jan. 4, and March 15, 1837; *Pennsylvania Freeman*, March 15, May 10, and June 6, 1838.

[19] Adams' boast that he could bring up the slavery issue "tomorrow" is in the *Appendix to Congressional Globe*, 1st S., 26th Congress, p. 761. His promise to devote the remainder of his life to the overthrow of slavery is in the *Anti-Slavery Standard*, June 22, 1843. The final quotation is from *Appendix to Congressional Globe*, 28th Congress, p. 97. It was quoted in the House from a letter written by Adams to the secretary of the Pennsylvania Anti-Slavery Society, Western Branch, and published in a Pittsburgh paper.

[20] The following is an example of "pure farce." On a petition day in 1837, Adams asked the Speaker whether a petition he held, "purporting to come from slaves," came under the gag. Immediately Southern members took fire, and a resolution was offered censuring Adams for presenting an abolition petition from slaves. After much had been said, it appeared that Adams had not actually presented the petition, and the resolution of censure was modified accordingly. Heated debate ensued. Finally Adams let the House know that the prayer of the petition was for his expulsion from the House; and on examination, the petition itself proved to be a hoax, got up to insult Adams. After one more attempt to censure him for "giving color to the idea" that he intended to present a petition from slaves, the disgusted House laid the whole question on the table.

CHAPTER XIII

THE PETITION FLOOD

[1] Daniel Webster's phrase, *Appendix to Congressional Globe*, 2d S., 24th Congress, p. 155.

² Whittier's efforts in the Essex County Society are described in the *Emancipator*, June 24, 1834. His example was not followed in New England. Among the scores of constitutions of local societies printed in the *Liberator* during 1834 and the first three months of 1835, only three pledged their members to petition Congress. None of those fathered by A. A. Phelps at this time did so. Throughout 1833, however, the *Emancipator* had urged abolitionists to petition, and each year a large petition originating in Boston and another in New York were presented in Congress. (See House Files, Box 52.)

The resolution of the New England Anti-Slavery Society to get petitions is printed in the *Liberator*, V, 86. The final quotation is from the *Boston Recorder*, copied in the *Emancipator*, June 24, 1835. See also *Emancipator*, Jan. 6, 1835, for notice of a like hostility to petitions in New York.

³ The Western case for petitions is stated in the *Observer and Telegraph*, May 2, 1833. The Cincinnati petition is noted in the *Emancipator*, April 14, 1835.

⁴ *Ohio Observer*, Nov. 9, 1833, and *Observer and Telegraph* as above.

⁵ The first national plan for petitions is outlined in the *Emancipator*, Dec. 16, 1834. See *ibid.*, July 20, 1833, for directions as to petitions. The calculation as to the number of names to be secured is in *ibid.*, Nov. 18, 1834. The final quotation is from a broadside sent out by the New York office. A number of these broadsides are in House Files, Box 69.

⁶ A summary of current newspaper opinion is in *Proceedings of the New England Anti-Slavery Society*, 1836, p. 8.

⁷ See the numerous forms presented during the session of 1836–1837, in House Files, Boxes 71–81. Massachusetts and New York had official forms, but in the back counties hundreds of local forms were circulated. Pennsylvania and Ohio had no official forms. The most widely used form was the famous "Fathers and Rulers" petition for females, written in 1834 by Weld. That these petitions were started too late was Stanton's judgment, and the petitions themselves bear him out. (See *Friend of Man*, Aug. 2, 1837.)

⁸ The diverse methods of getting names on petitions in 1834–1836 show clearly the difference between the community movements of the West and the locals of New England. Societies in New England usually adopted some such resolution as this: "That an energetic man be employed . . . as an agent to go through the county to procure signatures to a petition." An agent of the national society who had been laboring in the East, on a visit to Trumbull County, Ohio, in October of 1836, noted with surprise a method of circulating petitions he had never seen before. Instead of hiring a special agent, the county society laid out the work of circulating petitions by a system of regional volunteers. (*Friend of Man*, Feb. 1, 1837.) The two final quotations regarding "false representation" and "emesaries" are from petitions in House Files, Box 87 and 79 respectively. See Boxes 79–84 for more literate protests.

⁹ The first quotation is from a form petition, numerous copies of which are in House Files, Boxes 79–84. Caleb Cushing's letters to Whittier, from which the two final quotations are taken, are in *Whittier Correspondence* (Oak Knoll Collection), pp. 43–44, and 40.

The charge as to forged petitions is in *Congressional Globe,* 1st S., 24th Congress, p. 258. A large proportion of the names on the petitions of that year were evidently not *bona fide* signatures. It does not follow that they were all copied with the intention of deceiving Congress. Frequent notes on the petitions themselves, to the effect that the original petitions were so badly "used up" in their circulation that they were not fit to send, explain some copying. But thousands of names were obviously forged, especially on "female petitions" near the latter end of the lists, when the fair volunteers grew weary. (See House Files, Boxes 78–87.) The difference between British and American parliamentary attitudes toward forgeries on petitions indicates clearly the different status of petitions in the two representative bodies. The forging of names on petitions to parliament was a felony, and forgers were vigorously prosecuted. In this country such forgeries were not actionable and little was made of them. These different attitudes grew out of the dissimilar principles of representation in parliament and Congress. Before the Reform Bill, only a part of parliament were directly responsible to the people of their constituencies; whereas every member of the House of Representatives was directly responsible to the people of his district. In Great Britain, petitions were thus the only means open to a large part of the population for informing parliament as to their legislative will. Petitions were therefore guarded from fraud by law. For the same reason, the right of petition for general objects had an importance to the people of Great Britain which it did not possess in this country. It was often pointed out in Congress that petitions for antislavery legislation were superogatory. If a majority for such legislation could be secured in the members' constituencies, the members would vote for it without petitions. So long as no such majority existed, the members could not be expected to heed the petitions of a minority. Petitions for general objects, it was therefore contended, had no practical importance in American legislative procedure.

[10] The quotation regarding "the feelings of his own constituents" is from the printed "Directions for Petitions" on the backs of early form petitions of the American Anti-Slavery Society, in House Files, Box 69. Daniel Webster spoke for the Senate: Though they "had received many abolition petitions," he asked, "had they presented them from day to day, and annoyed the Senate?" (*Appendix to Congressional Globe,* 2d S. 24th Congress, p. 155). Nearly all the petitions of 1834–1836, and many of 1837, were sent in duplicate to both the Senate and the House; but the petitions presented during that time in the Senate were very few as compared with the multitude presented in the House. Caleb Cushing's plaint is from a letter to Whittier in *Whittier Correspondence* (Oak Knoll Collection), pp. 38–40. As to Whigs, Adams frequently noted in his diary the names of Whig members who told him that they would not present petitions that they had received (*Memoirs,* VIII, IX). The final quotation is from a letter attached to a petition sent to Thomas Corwin of Ohio. The writer told of a number of petitions sent to Webster of Ohio. "I heard no more of them, though he sent me some documents in return." (House Files, Box, 93.)

[11] Weld to Lewis Tappan, June 8, 1837 (Weld MSS.). Birney was not

a powerful speaker or a brilliant writer. In the councils of the movement his influence was negligible. He was fearless, honorable and devoted—an admirable but not a great man.

[12] Weld to Angelina Grimké, April 15, 1838 (Weld MSS.). His refusal to take an appointment or a salary is noted in another letter to the Grimké sisters, Oct. 1, 1837 (Weld MSS.).

[13] This analysis of the national movement is based partly upon the annual report of the American Anti-Slavery Society for 1837. It brings the organization up to April, 1837, though it is incomplete even for that date, especially for the New York State Society. Only 173 societies with a total of 17,664 members were reported from New York in time for the 1837 report. The *Friend of Man* had neglected to gather statistics soon enough to get them in. Delayed reports brought the total to 217 societies, with more than 20,000 members.

[14] The first quotation describing the lack of names is from a form letter sent out by the committee, May, 1837. Directions in detail as to the appointment of county leaders are in the *Alton Observer*, June 29, 1837, and the *Friend of Man*, May 31, 1837. Wherever it was possible the committee worked through the State societies. In Illinois, Indiana, and elsewhere, the committee managed the campaign from the New York office. Wherever an individual named for township and county supervision was not known as an antislavery man, the leaders were asked to name "a responsible person to vouch for him, to guard against imposture." In corresponding with county and township leaders, Stanton alone wrote over a thousand personal letters this year. How many were written by Weld and Whittier I do not know. A copy of the committee's circular, containing minute directions as to obtaining signatures is in the *National Enquirer*, II, 62. The way the petitions were to be handled in the central offices is described in *ibid.*, II, 57.

[15] Because of their brevity, the millions of official form petitions contained only what was required to be read to Congress as titles when they were presented. It is an ironical circumstance that those petitions were, therefore, really read on the floor of Congress. They were not gagged.

[16] The readiness with which the Texas memorials were signed is noted in the *National Enquirer*, III, 1. Hundreds of Texas petitions which did not originate with abolitionists are in House Files, Boxes 86–93.

[17] The two quotations identifying the signers of petitions with abolitionists are from *Appendix to Congressional Globe*, 24th Congress, 1st S., p. 17, and *ibid.*, 25th Congress, 2d S., p. 25, respectively.

The convention of the "Friends of the Integrity of the Union" (at Harrisburg, May 1 and 2, 1837) was called by a Kentuckian, the Rev. T. W. Haynes, then of Allegheny. Every county in the State was requested to send delegates. In Gettysburg, at a mass meeting called to select a county delegate, Thaddeus Stevens, just converted to abolitionism by J. Blanchard, one of the Seventy, spoke eloquently against the purpose of the convention, and he was elected as a delegate. The proceedings of the convention began by resolving that "no individual holding the abominable, wild and fanatical doctrine of the Abolitionists could, consistently with the honor of a gentleman, hold a seat in the convention"; but Stevens refused to be a gentleman. He remained in his seat and proceeded to break up the convention. When an anti-abolition resolution was introduced, Stevens would move an amendment taken from the Pennsylvania bill of rights, and then call for the yeas and nays, that "those who had become wiser than their fathers might be handed down to posterity." His adroitness and eloquence were such that the delegates insisted upon his being allowed to speak. On the second day he spoke for over two hours on the principles of abolitionism. The convention then broke up in disorder, "entirely used up, root and branch, routed horse, foot and dragoons." (See *Alton Observer*, June 4, 1837, and *National Enquirer*, May 6, 1837.) Two months before this convention the society had voted Stevens an antislavery agency (Minutes of the Agency Committee, American Anti-Slavery Society, March 15, 1837), which he did not accept.

The plaint of the discouraged volunteer at the end of the paragraph is from L. M. Child, *Letters from New York*, first series, p. 31.

[18] Wythe [Weld], *Power of Congress over the District of Columbia*, pp. 5–6, and 13.

[19] The first quotation is from a letter from S. W. Streeter to Weld, July 10, 1836 (Weld MSS.). When Thome and Kimball were ready to start, the Agency Committee resolved "That the agents to the West Indies be advised to sail in the first vessel to St. Thomas provided she does not sail on the Sabbath. Otherwise . . . that they go by Havanna." (Minutes of the Agency Committee, American Anti-Slavery Society, Nov. 17, 1836.) Thome's original manuscript would have filled a thousand pages. Ultimately Weld wrote it down to 128 pages. It bears little trace of Thome's diffuse style. For a time Thome was grieved, but he recovered. See Weld's letters to the Grimké sisters from October, 1837, to January, 1838, and Thome's letters to him covering the same period (Weld MSS.).

The final quotation is from the *Philanthropist*, April 24, 1838. The revolution in doctrine was among orthodox abolitionists only. The newspaper public had never supposed that immediatism was anything but immediatism. *Emancipation in the West Indies* simply made the official doctrine what the general public had always supposed it to be.

[20] Weld told this story of his researches for "the manufacture of *Slavery As It Is*" years later in a letter to Catherine H. Birney, who published it in *The Grimké Sisters*, pp. 258–259. Weld continued: "After the work was finished we were curious to know how many newspapers had been examined. So we went up to our attic and took an inventory of bundles, as they were packed heap upon heap. When our count had reached *twenty thousand* newspapers, we said, 'There, let that suffice.' Though the book had in it many thousand facts thus authenticated by the slave-holders themselves, yet it contained but a tiny fraction of the nameless atrocities gathered from the papers examined." Several copies of Weld's form letter requesting facts for this tract are in Weld MSS. The quotations in the text are from one of these.

Slavery As It Is was published at a time when the various antislavery leaders were at feud; and secondary accounts of the movement, concerned at this period with personal controversies rather than with the antislavery agitation, have none of them rated this tract at its true worth. Provision for its circulation was unprecedented (*Proceedings of the Sixth Anniversary of the American Anti-Slavery Society,* pp. 21–22, 48), and the number of copies printed far exceeded any other antislavery publication until *Uncle Tom's Cabin* appeared. For the latter work it was an inspiration (H. B. Stowe, *Key to Uncle Tom's Cabin*). In England it produced an extraordinary impression. It was favorably reviewed by numerous quarterlies, religious and literary, and, in Great Britain, it had much the widest circulation of any of our antislavery literature. The British and Foreign Anti-Slavery Society put it in the hands of the principal officers of the government, deposited it in libraries, in colleges, etc. (A letter from England to the *National Anti-Slavery Standard,* July 13, 1843.) It was not published until 1839, but like Weld's other tracts it was a standard volume in the "anti-slavery libraries," so I have included it here.

[21] The resolution directing Weld and Whittier to prepare the libraries is in Minutes of the Executive Committee, American Anti-Slavery Society, 1837–1840, pp. 30–31, and p. 76..Typical resolutions by antislavery organizations, urging the antislavery libraries upon their auxiliaries, are to be found in the *Friend of Man,* March 15, 1838, and the *Philanthropist,* Feb. 15, 1838. The quoted resolution in the text is from the latter reference. For a more extended survey of antislavery library distribution, see the *Friend of Man,* April 25, 1838, and the *Emancipator,* Sept. 19, 1839. The large number of such libraries explains the wide distribution of the later pamphlets of the American Anti-Slavery Society. They were distributed from stores in Albany, Utica, Cleveland, etc., to the nearby counties. For the vast increase of printing by the national society, see the *Annual Reports* of the American Anti-Slavery Society for 1838 and 1839.

[22] The two quoted admonitions to women to circulate petitions are from the *Emancipator,* Jan. 21, 1834, and a circular of the American Anti-Slavery Society printed in the *Liberator,* V, 198. But the women needed no such admonitions. As early as 1830, Philadelphia women had petitioned Congress for abolition in the District. This was probably done at the instance of their British correspondents of the London Female Anti-Slavery Society, who urged petitions as the most effective measure that women could take for the slave. (Minutes of the Philadelphia Female Anti-Slavery Society, MSS. "Records" for 1830.) Lucretia Mott, a minister of the Hicksite sect of Quakers, took the lead in this petition, which was signed by more than two thousand women. In a note attached to the petition, Mrs. Mott somewhat apologetically expressed the hope that women's applications to Congress would not "be considered intrusive. But we approach you unarmed. Our only banner is Peace . . . Nothing less than a deep conviction of the necessity of the measure could have induced" the petitioners "to appear in this public manner." It was sent to the Speaker of the House and was presented by him. (House Files, Box 52.)

[23] *New York Evangelist,* Nov. 30, 1833.

[24] Mrs. A. J. Graves, *Women in America,* Introduction, p. xiv.

[25] *North American Review,* April, 1836.

²⁶ The reproach that woman should "unsex herself" is in *Zion's Herald*, VII, 38. The member of Congress who was "pained to see" women's names on petitions recorded his words in *Congressional Globe*, 24th Congress, 1st S., p. 337. Benjamin Tappan's speech is printed in the *Emancipator*, Feb. 20, 1840. At the close of this speech, Senator Preston of South Carolina thanked Senator Tappan in the name of the South. The epithets "devils" and "old maids" were those applied to women petitioners by Wise and Garland respectively.

²⁷ Quoted from the *Religious Magazine and Family Miscellany*, in *Right and Wrong in Boston, No. 3*, pp. 57-58. Toward the ladies who declined to give their names on the ground that "it is such an odd, *unladylike* thing to do," one of the "female brethren" expressed herself thus: "We have never heard this objection, but from that sort of woman who is dead while she lives. . . . Her infancy was passed in serving as a convenience for the display of elegant baby linen. Her youth in training for a more public display. . . . This is the woman who tells us it is *unladylike* to ask for the abolition of slavery in the District of Columbia. . . . The case of such a woman is the case that makes us feel the powerlessness of mere human effort for the conversion of the sinner. Nothing but the spirit of God can elevate that debased mind or give true life and joy to that ossified heart." (*Right and Wrong in Boston*, no. 2, p. 27.) The bitterness of this outbreak probably measures the difficulties of the women's campaign.

²⁸ The coincidence of the simultaneous call for national organization from the three cities was noted in the *National Enquirer*, I, 89. The quotation in the text is from the same reference. A copy of the call is in the *National Enquirer*, I, 105. The best account of the convention—better even than the official *Proceedings of the Anti-Slavery Convention of American Women* of 1837—is in the *National Enquirer*, II, 42, 49, 54, 66.

²⁹ In the larger States there were eastern and western, or northern and southern, offices of control for both men and women volunteers.

³⁰ The circular appeal also declared that "the Hon. Mr. Peyton, Member of Congress from slave-holding Tennessee, assured one of our friends that he dreaded the influence of women on this subject more than any other influence." In the circular appeal of 1839 to the women of the North is this statement: "John Quincy Adams is known to have expressed the opinion that if slavery was ever peacefully abolished in our country, women must do it." The latter appeal is attached to a petition in House Files, Box 133.

³¹ "—qualified, however, as it must be, with the regret" that by opposing abolition in the District of Columbia, "he did not sustain the cause of Freedom and of GOD."

³² The quotation describing petitions as women's "only mode of access . . . to Congress" is from the *Philanthropist*, June 6, 1838. The quotation ascribing to petitions for women the inauguration of "a new era" is from an appeal "TO THE WOMEN OF THE UNITED STATES" pasted above a petition form (House Files, Box 133). The final quotation is from an "Address to Women" on a petition form, House Files, Box 84.

³³ Petitions that Susan B. Anthony circulated are in House Files, Boxes 126, 128.

[34] In House Files, Boxes 52–146, among the thousands of petitions, women's petitions predominate. The first quotations are from a widely used petition form for women, the only one that was comparable in numbers to the short sentence forms of the national society. (See Boxes 81–126, House Files.) The final quotation is from *Congressional Globe,* 1st S., 24th Congress, p. 337.

[35] The most important central offices for petitions were in New York, Utica, Boston, Philadelphia, Pittsburgh, Cleveland, and Cincinnati. There were smaller central offices at Concord, N. H.; Middlebury, Vt.; Portland, Me.; and Farmington, Mich. At Green Plains, Ohio, petitions from the huge Paint Valley Society were checked and transmitted to Congress. A large number, possibly one fourth of the total, was sent to Congess directly from the towns in which they were circulated. (See House Files, Boxes 87–102.) Of the central offices, the New York office alone sent out one hundred thousand blank petitions (*National Enquirer,* III, 103).

Whittier's letter to his sister is in the *Whittier Correspondence* (Oak Knoll Collection), p. 53. The final quotation is from the *New York American,* copied in the *Friend of Man,* Jan. 24, 1838. By April the mass of abolition petitions presented at that session filled a room 20x30x14 feet, close-packed to the ceiling. Adams moved that these petitions be printed, together with their names. The correspondent of the *New York American* talked with the clerk in charge of the petition file. At the very thought of printing them, he said, "the poor clerk was nearly frightened out of his wits." Quoted in the *Friend of Man,* April 11, 1838.

[36] *Pennsylvania Freeman,* March 22, 1838.

[37] *National Enquirer,* III, 17.

[38] *Friend of Man,* Sept. 27, 1837.

[39] The exhortation to the petition volunteers is from a circular to all the volunteers, copied in the *National Enquirer,* II, 62. The increase in the number of signatures on the thousands of petitions in the House Files is as follows: the number of signatures on petitions presented in 1836–1837 averaged 32; on petitions in 1837–1838, 59; on petitions in 1838–1839, 91; and on petitions in 1839–1840, 107. (See House Files, Boxes 62–147.) The admonition to volunteers to "answer all the questions" of prospective signers is in the *Emancipator,* Sept. 19, 1839. The final quotation is from a letter with a petition in House Files, Box 133.

[40] The bulk of these and later antislavery petitions are no longer in existence. The House Files are fairly representative of the number and character of antislavery petitions—though not by any means complete—for all the sessions to 1838–1839. Thereafter antislavery petitions were not received by the House, and only a chance few thousand were filed. Twenty years ago there were several truck-loads of abolition petitions stored here and there about the Capitol. The late Dr. C. H. Van Tyne used to tell his classes at the University of Michigan how, when he was making his *Guide to the Archives,* he found a caretaker in the Capitol keeping his stove hot with bundles of antislavery petitions. There were so many of them, the caretaker said, that those he used would never be missed.

CHAPTER XIV

DECENTRALIZATION

[1] The transfer of the petition campaign in lower New England to the local societies is noted in the *Pennsylvania Freeman,* July 18, 1838. Township and ward agents were to be appointed in every county. The transfer in Pennsylvania to the county societies is noted in *ibid.,* Sept. 5, 1838. The transfer to county auxiliaries in New York is noted in the *Friend of Man,* Feb. 21, 1838. Some of the State society offices continued to send such petitions as they received to the national headquarters until the end of 1839, when the Executive Committee of the American Anti-Slavery Society requested them thereafter to forward their petitions directly to Congress. (Minutes of the Executive Committee, American Anti-Slavery Society, Dec. 5, 1839.)

[2] For the locally printed forms after 1837, see House Files, Boxes 89–106. For directions as to the mailing of petitions under the new régime, see the *Friend of Man,* as above.

[3] The first quotation is from a letter of Abel Manning to the Hon. Levi Lincoln, Feb. 10, 1837 (letter attached to a petition). The second quotation is from the *National Enquirer,* Nov. 26, 1836.

[4] A resolution in the Pennsylvania State Society Convention, advocating uniform "political action" throughout the State, was later withdrawn (*National Enquirer,* Feb. 18, 1837). The New York State Anti-Slavery Society advised abolitionists to question candidates: "In our judgment it is proper and important" but not a duty (*ibid.,* III, 17). The Anti-Slavery Convention for Northern Ohio resolved that even county societies should dispense with the questioning of candidates for office. Political action should never be accomplished through associated action, but by abolitionists "as independent freemen and electors." (*Emancipator,* Oct. 3, 1839.)

[5] *Christian Examiner,* third series, XXIV, 243.

[6] For the activities of the New York Committee in furthering the petition campaign, see the following: furnishing blank petitions, the *National Enquirer,* III, 103; distributing new petition forms, Minutes of the Executive Committee, American Anti-Slavery Society, 1837–1840, pp. 21, 180; timely documents mailed to local petition supervisors, *National Enquirer,* as above; correspondence with Congressmen in Washington, Minutes of the Executive Committee, American Anti-Slavery Society, 1837–1840, pp. 35, 108. See also the letterbook of Lewis Tappan, 1839–1840 (L. Tappan Papers, Library of Congress), for numerous letters to Congressmen.

[7] The quotation as to the removal of the struggle "from its proper ground" is from the *Philanthropist,* Feb. 18, 1840. The resolution of the conference of conservatives is in the *Friend of Man,* Jan. 31, 1838. This was at the Rochester Convention, Jan. 10–12, 1838. The quotation regarding "human government" is from the DECLARATION OF SENTIMENTS of Garrison's Non-Resistance Society. The quotation condemning "praying to men" is from the *National Anti-Slavery Standard,* May 26, 1842. The final

quotation is from an editorial of N. P. Rogers in the *Herald of Freedom*.

⁸ *Massachusetts Abolitionist*, II, 1.

⁹ Societies formed for the single purpose of petitions, according to their constitutions, were most numerous in New York, Pennsylvania, and Ohio. See *Friend of Man, Pennsylvania Freeman, Philanthropist*, and *Christian Witness*, for 1838–1839. For petitions signed by non-members of abolition societies, see House Files, Boxes 92–106.

¹⁰ In Ohio decentralization took a different form. Several county societies refused to pledge any money to the State society unless they were promised its equivalent in a series of lectures by State agents (*Philanthropist*, June 9, 1838). For decentralization in New York, see the *Friend of Man*, Oct. 25, 1837.

¹¹ The difficulties of the Pennsylvania Society, Eastern Branch, are described in the *Pennsylvania Freeman*, May 31, 1838. Whittier was now its editor. For a complete account of their financial troubles, see the *Freeman* for April 5, 1838. The difficulties of the Ohio society are described in the *Philanthropist*, Oct. 30, 1838. The regional conventions in New York were held at Rochester in January, at Lockport in June, and at Ballston in September, 1838. See *Friend of Man*, Jan. 31, 1839, and *Pennsylvania Freeman*, Sept. 20, 1838. When the break occurred, eighteen counties formed the Western New York Anti-Slavery Society in October, 1839 (*Emancipator*, VI, 103). Later an Eastern New York Anti-Slavery Society was also organized. Wade's speech for union in the Ohio society is printed in the *Philanthropist*, Oct. 30, 1838; but a year later "The Anti-Slavery Convention for Northern Ohio" was in existence. (*Emancipator*, Oct. 3, 1839.) The story of the organization of the Pennsylvania State Anti-Slavery Society is told in the *National Enquirer*, I, 90. Later the eastern branch split apart and the Anti-Slavery Convention of Northern Pennsylvania was formed. (*Pennsylvania Freeman*, Feb. 13, 1840.)

¹² The competition between State and national organs for subscribers is discussed in the *National Enquirer*, II, 57. When the *Friend of Man* was proposed, the executive committee attempted to save *Emancipator* subscriptions by offering to print any given number of the latter paper at half the expense of the *Friend of Man*. "The funds of this cause are *needed, greatly needed*, to support more agents" (E. Wright Jr. to Weld, Jan. 22, 1836, Weld MSS.). By 1839 there were ten State organs, and special newspapers for the Methodist abolitionists and the antislavery Negroes.

The resolution of 1834 for joint State and national action in financial agencies is printed in the *Emancipator*, Jan. 6, 1835. The 1837 resolution on the same subject is printed in the *Friend of Man*, May 31, 1837. The workings of this plan, to the satisfaction of the national officers, but to the disadvantage of the State societies, is described in the *Emancipator*, Dec. 19, 1839. The rebellion of the State societies is chronicled in the *National Enquirer*, II, 91, 103. The resolution of 1838, closing the State society territories to the financial operations of national society agents, is printed in the *Friend of Man*, II, 186.

¹³ *Anti-Slavery Reporter*, June, 1840. In the report of the Eastern District of the Pennsylvania Anti-Slavery Society for 1837, it was suggested

that "in the future a sufficient amount should first be raised for carrying
on Anti-Slavery operations in the State, and that the surplus should be
appropriated to general purposes under the direction of the Executive
Committee of the American Society" (*National Enquirer*, III, 91). The
next year the society made its pledge to the national society on condition
that the entire amount be expended within Pennsylvania.

On June 13, 1838, Alvan Stewart, eccentric champion of the rights of
the State societies, informed the national executive committee that the demands of the New York State Society's program were so heavy that the society could pledge nothing to the national treasury, "excepting what this [the
national] committee may gather in the counties south of Albany," territory
over which the State society had no claim at all. (Minutes of the Executive
Committee, American Anti-Slavery Society, 1837–1840, p. 73.) Later,
however (July 19, 1838), the New York society pledged $10,000 (*ibid.*,
p. 86).

¹⁴ In 1835, Preston of South Carolina remarked in the Senate that
Tappan's Association of Gentlemen "with a spirit worthy of a better cause
have bound themselves to contribute forty thousand dollars a year to the
propagation of abolition doctrines through the press. Five of these pay
twenty thousand dollars a year, and one, one thousand dollars a month"
(*Appendix to Congressional Globe*, 24th Congress, 1st S., p. 222). Whether
this was so or not, I have been unable to determine. The financial records
of the society do not show such large contributions as these; but in Weld's
correspondence for 1835–1839 there is occasional mention of gifts for
pamphlet issues, agents' necessities, and the like, that were not to be made
public. These, of course, never got into the financial records. Much of the
financial distress during 1838–1840 in the society's affairs was probably
due to the cessation of these unmentioned contributions by the New York
Committee.

¹⁵ Arthur's spirit had begun to fail as early as November, 1836. Wright
wrote Weld: "The Wall Street fever is terrible, and has seized some of
our committee. A. Tappan especially was afraid to go ahead any more till
he could see where the funds were to come from. . . . A. T. should be
disabused of the idea that if he & G[errit] Smith & one or two others
should fail to pay their notes at three o'clock some day, the cause of God's
oppressed would fall through. Our Committee once in a while falls
into a fit of 'practical expedience,' and puts *prudence* against *faith*."
(E. Wright Jr. to Weld, Nov. 4, 1836, Weld MSS.) However, Joseph
Sturge, the British abolitionist, on a visit to the United States in 1840–
1841, still found that "in the just estimate of the pro-slavery party, ARTHUR
TAPPAN is ABOLITION personified" (Sturge, *A Visit to the United States,*
p. 3).

¹⁶ *History of Broadway Tabernacle,* pp. 36–38, and *New York Evangelist,* 1838–1840. Finney had resigned; and the pastor, Joel Parker, quite
changed in his antislavery sentiments by a residence in New Orleans, told
Lewis Tappan that he considered his influence in the church a bad one,
and he proposed to do all he could to limit it. He denounced the Church
Anti-Slavery Society, and opposed the use of "pure wine" at communion.

In his usual "somewhat peremptory manner," Lewis expressed his mind to Joel Parker. Certain of his fellow members thereupon charged him before the church with slander. At his trial, he demanded a reporter, and was condemned for contumacy. He appealed unsuccessfully to the presbytery and then to the General Assembly of the Presbyterian Church. The assembly reversed the decision of the presbytery, but his church refused to reinstate Tappan. All of the antislavery members thereupon withdrew, and their departure wrecked the church. It was sold at chancery sale, July 2, 1840.

CHAPTER XV

The Woman Question

[1] From the "Pastoral Letter" of the Congregational Association of Massachusetts for 1837.

[2] See D. L. Child to Angelina Grimké, Feb. 12, 1838 (Weld MSS.), and the *Massachusetts Abolitionist*, II, 24. Maria W. Chapman, the most ardent champion of women's right to speak before mixed assemblies, did not venture to do so herself until the meeting in Pennsylvania Hall in May, 1838.

[3] The father of the sisters, John F. Grimké, had been chief justice of the South Carolina supreme court, and the Grimké family were related to many of the prominent families of the South. The brother, T. S. Grimké, helped to organize the American Temperance Society and the American Peace Society. He also pioneered a change in college curricula, the substitution of the Hebrew and Greek of the Bible for the Latin and Greek of the classics. By a curious coincidence, Oneida Institute was the first school to adopt this reform. The General Education Board thereupon dropped Oneida Institute from its list of accredited schools. See Grimké's Phi Beta Kappa Address at Yale, 1832, for details of his reform. Characteristically, he refused to accept an LL.D. from Yale on the occasion of this address. His promise to examine the question of slavery is recorded in a letter from Sarah Grimké to Weld, Jan. 21, 1837 (Weld MSS.). During 1833, however, another sister had begun a lively correspondence with her brother upon the subject. He replied: "With regard to the principal topic of your letter, slavery, I should have no difficulty on the score of interest, in parting with all I own. I keep them because I have them. I do not free them, because the law will not let me, and I am not disposed to do indirectly, and by secret trusts and concealment, what I cannot do openly." (T. S. Grimké to Mrs. Anna Frost, Feb. 9, 1833, Weld MSS.) Another brother, Judge Frederick Grimké of the Ohio State supreme court, in his book, *The Nature and Tendency of Free Institutions*, wrote one of the most penetrating criticisms of abolition doctrine that I have found in contemporary literature.

The final quotation in the text is from a letter written by Angelina to Sarah Grimké, Jan. 6, 1832 (Weld MSS.).

[4] Sarah Grimké told her experiences in the Society of Friends in a letter to Weld, an undated note written sometime in 1837, in the Weld MSS. The

final quotation is from a letter from Angelina to Sarah Grimké, July 3, 1836 (Weld MSS.).

⁵ Angelina recounted her conversion to immediatism, as told in the text, in a letter written Oct. 2, 1837 (*National Enquirer*, III, 25). Years later she was inclined to put her conversion to immediatism back to Charleston days. The first quotation of Angelina's words is from a letter written by her to Sarah Grimké, July 4, 1836; the second quotation is from a letter to the same, Aug. 5, 1836, both in Weld MSS. At first Sarah was opposed to Angelina's antislavery stand. Angelina converted her.

⁶ Minutes of the Agency Committee, American Anti-Slavery Society, July 13, 1836. A Miss Wheelwright was appointed at the same time.

⁷ The quotation is from a letter signed by Sarah and Angelina Grimké, and written to Sarah Douglass, Feb. 22, 1837 (Weld MSS.). "I will just mention that our friends in N. Y. think the less said at present about what we are doing the better; let us move quietly on for a while and the two 'fanatical women,' as the Richmond papers call us, may thro' divine help do a little good." In a letter from Weld to Sarah Grimké, March 29, 1838, in the Weld MSS., Weld pointed out to Sarah her faults as a speaker, and advised her, in the interest of the cause, not to speak again. "A loving and faithful letter," Sarah wrote upon it.

⁸ The first quotation is from a letter from Sarah Grimké to Gerrit Smith, June 28, 1837 (Weld MSS.). Sarah, devoted, humble, and self-sacrificing, added that Angelina was the one to speak. "I only pick up chips for her." The final quotation is from a letter from J. Sumner Lincoln to Weld, no date (Weld MSS.).

⁹ Weld to the Grimké sisters, July 22, 1837 (Weld MSS.).

¹⁰ In those dark days Garrison would not even grant the propriety of women's petitions to Congress (*Genius of Universal Emancipation*, Dec. 25, 1829).

¹¹ Stanton's suggestion that Angelina should speak to the legislative committee was not his first suggestion that she should appear before a "promiscuous assembly." Like Weld, he had championed the sisters' right to speak before men from the first. During their New England tour, in order to silence opposition, he proposed to them a joint meeting, where he and the sisters would speak alternately; but they shrank from such public association with a man. They did consent, however, to his arranging a debate with two Southern gentlemen on slavery, which was held at Amesbury, Massachusetts, August 19, 1837 (C. Birney, *The Grimké Sisters*, pp. 193–194). All the quotations in this paragraph are from a letter from Angelina Grimké to Weld, Feb. 11, 1838 (Weld MSS.). The tardy approval by the Boston abolitionists of Angelina's appearance before the legislative committee is noted in a letter from Sarah Grimké to Gerrit Smith, Feb. 16, 1838 (Weld MSS.).

¹² At her first hearing she was very nervous. "It was not one of my happiest efforts," she wrote Weld (Feb. 21, 1838). But after her second lecture she wrote (Feb. 25, 1838): "I am sorely tempted to believe I have had a *triumph* this afternoon, but I pray to be delivered from such sinful, presumptuous thoughts." After the third lecture, however, she informed

Weld (Feb. 26, 1838) that she was "spared that distressing feeling of ex-altation with which I was so sorely tempted after the last meeting. I feel that I am a poor, miserable sinner, *a worm of the dust.*" Weld's news of the results of Angelina's lectures is quoted from a letter from Weld to Sarah Grimké, March 29, 1838 (Weld MSS.). Wendell Phillips agreed. "Those two sisters doubled our hold on New England in 1837 and 1838," he de-clared. (C. Birney, *The Grimké Sisters,* p. 189.)

[13] The words of the clergyman regarding "Female Orator" are quoted in *Right and Wrong in Boston,* no. 3, p. 48. The resolutions of the Massa-chusetts Congregational Association were embodied in a "Pastoral Letter," from which the quotation is taken. This is the "Pastoral Letter" which provoked Whittier's indignant poem of the same title.

[14] The first quotation is from a letter from Angelina Grimké to Weld, no month, 1837 (Weld MSS.). Angelina's argument for speaking for the rights of women was as follows: *"We must establish this right,* for if we do not, it will be impossible for *us* to go on *with the work of Emancipa-tion. . . .* If we surrender the right to *speak* to the public this year, we must surrender the right to petition next year & the right to *write* the year after & so on."* (Angelina Grimké to Weld and Whittier, Aug. 20, 1837, Weld MSS.) Sarah Grimké's letters to the *Spectator* were published in 1838 under the title, *Letters on the Condition of Women and the Equal-ity of the Sexes.*

[15] The quotations are from two letters from Weld to the Grimké sisters, Sept. 6, 1837, and Aug. 15, 1837 (Weld MSS.).

[16] Whittier's letter to the sisters is printed in full in C. Birney, *The Grimké Sisters,* pp. 203–205. The discussion between Whittier and Weld and the sisters was complicated by the sort of publicity which the Boston radicals gave to the Grimkés. There appeared in the *Liberator* (VII, 118), a skit entitled "A Domestic Scene," written by H. C. Wright. The char-acters were Wright and the Grimké sisters. The three argued the sisters' par-ticipation in the woman's rights controversy, and "the conclusion was unanimous." Then they argued the "no human government" question, but without a "unanimous" conclusion. This "unseemly display" of the Grimké sisters before the *Liberator's* public incensed both Weld and Whittier. H. C. Wright also published a weekly bulletin in the *Liberator,* recording the Grimkés' agency, which he entitled "The Labors of the Miss Grimké's." Birney asked: "Can he not be stopped from writing the Misses Grimkés' bulletin? What a blunder and that of a most ridiculous kind he has fallen into—the 'LABORS'! of the Miss Grimkés!!" (Birney to Lewis Tappan, Aug. 23, 1837, L. Tappan Papers, Library of Congress.)

Weld characterized the sisters' habits of reasoning, as quoted in the text, in a letter to the Grimké sisters, October 10, 1837 (Weld MSS.). Nevertheless both of the sisters for the moment were completely under Garrison's influence. Sarah wrote: "I believe there is to be a deadly war waged between Righteousness and Sin, between the theoretical and phari-saical and time-serving clergy, and practical christianity. I believe they are the Man of Sin sitting in the temple of God and showing himself that he is God. Brother Garrison is sustained by the Lord. We hope that he will be less trammelled next year than he has been this, and that the *Liberator* will be open to the discussion of the great subjects of Peace, Perfection, Government, the Clergy, Woman &c. &c." (Sarah Grimké to Jane Smith, Nov. 8, 1837, Weld MSS.).

[17] The first quotation is from a letter from Angelina Grimké to Weld, February 11, 1838. This was the letter in which she accepted Weld's proposal. The quotation regarding woman's rights "or any other extraneous doctrine" is what the Welds and Sarah Grimké told Joseph Sturge (*A Visit to the United States*). Sturge added: "I could not but wish that those of whatever party, who are accustomed to judge hastily of all who cannot pronounce their 'shibboleth' might be instructed by the candid, charitable and peace loving deportment of Theodore Weld." Garrison's realization that Angelina had freed herself from his influence came upon the eve of her marriage. He asked Angelina whether she intended to join Theodore in family worship after their marriage. "She answered in the affirmative. If so I fear she will be prepared to go further. For I did hope that she had been led to see that . . . all stated observances are so many self-imposed and unnecessary yokes." (Garrison to his wife, May 12, 1838, Garrison, *Garrison*, II, 211–212.) The final quotation is from a letter from Sarah Grimké to Augustus Wattles, May 11, 1854 (Weld MSS.).

[18] *Anti-Slavery Reporter*, June, 1840.

[19] Birney, Leavitt, Stanton, and Weld were elected to the executive offices. Weld of course, "on principle," immediately resigned. Weld's name was probably put forward in order to carry the others into office. He was the only man in the New York office who was universally loved and respected. The New York leaders must have known that he would never accept the position.

[20] The Anti-Slavery Convention of American Women had drifted away from its first purpose, the oversight of the petition campaign. The convention of 1838, at Philadelphia, was nearly three times as large as the convention of 1837, but over three fourths of the delegates were from Pennsylvania, and two thirds were from Philadelphia and its vicinity. Juliana Tappan headed the conservatives. She wanted a program of "five for every one petition rejected by the National legislature the preceding year." But instead of planning a campaign to carry out this program, the members of the convention spent most of the session debating their duty to withdraw "from churches receiving slaveholders to pulpits or communion tables." Most of the leading figures of the petition campaign opposed this measure, but by a small majority the Philadelphia vote carried a resolution that abolitionists should come out of such churches. The 1839 convention, also at Philadelphia, clearly showed the effects of decentralization. It was less than half as large as the previous one (most of the Massachusetts women were at New York attending the national society's anniversary), and only one fifth of the delegates came from a distance. Almost none of those who had organized the convention in 1837 to supervise the petition campaign were present. In its "Address," the convention paid lip-service to the circulation of petitions; but all of its time was taken up with debates on such subjects as the duty of antislavery women to

identify themselves with free Negroes "by worship, by appearing with them in our streets, by giving them our countenance in steam-boats and stages, by visiting them at their homes, and encouraging them to visit us." The convention resolved to meet next year at Boston, but they never did. Instead they raided the 1840 anniversary of the American Anti-Slavery Society. (See Anti-Slavery Convention of American Women, *Proceedings,* for 1838 and 1839.)

[21] From the Constitution of the Massachusetts Abolition Society, the anti-Garrison organization.

[22] The conviction that Garrison was the champion of women's rights and that his opponents were its enemies prevailed even among the Boston abolitionists. Sometime in the 70's, at a reunion of abolitionists in Boston, a speaker remarked that among the New York executives only Whittier had championed the rights of women. Weld, who was present, broke a life-long resolve to engage in no controversy between abolitionists and spoke from the floor in indignant repudiation of the views ascribed to himself and his old colleagues. (Reminiscences of Weld's daughter, Sarah G. Hamilton, in possession of Dr. Angelina G. Hamilton.) The quotation in the text is from a letter written by Angelina Grimké to Weld, Feb. 11, 1838 (Weld MSS.).

The story of Weld's attempt to secure Lydia Maria Child for the Seventy, and the Boston abolitionists' opposition thereto, has been told on p. 153 of this book. In 1837, Maria W. Chapman proposed founding a paper to further the agitation of woman's rights. Angelina Grimké urged her to begin instead the practice of woman's rights by lecturing like herself for the cause of the slave. Mrs. Chapman was intrigued by the suggestion, and Angelina wrote to a friend: "We greatly hope that dear Maria Chapman will soon commence lecturing." But Garrison and the Boston abolitionists opposed the suggestion, and it was abandoned. Weld later persuaded a New England woman, Abby Kelly, to enter the lecture field (Abby Kelly to Weld, Jan. 14, 1839, Weld MSS.). The story of the Boston abolitionists' unwillingness to sponsor Angelina Grimké's appearance before the committee of the Massachusetts State Legislature has been told on p. 156.

The practical championship of woman's rights by Weld, Whittier, and Stanton has been related in the text, pp. 154–155, 157–158, and in note 11. It was Wright who persuaded Angelina Grimké to speak for the slave (p. 154); and Leavitt had favored the woman's cause from the first. In the convention of 1839, as delegate from New Jersey, he voted for the right of women to sit and speak in the national society, even though he knew that Garrison's faction might thereby gain control of the society (*Sixth Annual Report of the Executive Committee of the American Anti-Slavery,* p. 29). Later Whittier, Leavitt, and Stanton served the American and Foreign Anti-Slavery Society with the understanding that they did not favor its "anti-woman" feature. Wright later served the Massachusetts Abolition Society on the same terms. Weld, however, declined to be associated with the former society because of its refusal to admit women on the same basis as men (p. 176).

[23] The original action of the Executive Committee with reference to the

Grimké sisters has been described (p. 154). Its later course, however, was not above reproach. Taking advantage of the circumstance that
when the question of appointing Angelina Grimké came up in 1836, they
had passed the question of her employment back to the agency committee
with power, in 1837 the Executive Committee took the position that they
had never appointed the sisters as agents. Members so informed Weld. "I
confess I had supposed till I inspected the records," Weld wrote the sisters,
"that the Exec. Com. had by vote made some sort of recognition of you"
(Weld to the Grimké sisters, Oct. 1, 1837, Weld MSS.). However Weld's
supposition had been correct. Though the sisters paid their own charges
and determined their own itinerary, and though in a sense, therefore,
Angelina was not a regular agent, nevertheless she had been regularly
appointed. Lewis Tappan had first opposed, then favored the appointment
of female agents (Weld to the Grimké sisters, Sept. 6, 1837, Weld MSS.);
but when the question of female agents became involved in the Garrison
controversy, he changed his position again.

CHAPTER XVI

COLLAPSE

[1] *Report on the Condition of the Church,* Presbyterian General Assembly
(New-School), 1839.

[2] The first quotation is from the *Philanthropist,* Feb. 18, 1840. That
slavery had become one of the leading public questions of the time was
the universal testimony. A comprehensive summary of the state of public
opinion in the churches on the subject is in the Address of the Bishops of
the Methodist Episcopal Church for 1840 (*General Conference Journal
and Debates,* 1840–1844, p. 136). The quotation regarding "the sin of slaveholding" is from *Zion's Herald,* VI, 140.

[3] The first quotation is from a speech by Calhoun in the Senate (*Appendix to Congressional Globe,* 25th Congress, 2d S., pp. 61–62). The second
quotation is from a sermon by the Rev. J. B. Postell of South Carolina.

[4] The quotations are from a letter from Finney to Weld, July 2, 1836
(Weld MSS.). Finney went on to illustrate his thesis: "We made temperance an appendage of the revival in Rochester. . . . I was almost alone in
the field as an Evangelist. Then 100,000 were converted in one year, everyone of which was a temperance man. The same wd. be the case in Abolition.
We can now with you and my Theological class [at Oberlin] bring enough
laborers into the field to under God move the land in 2 years. If you will
all turn in I will get dismissed from my charge in N. York if need be, and
lay out what strength I have in promoting the work. . . . Our leading Abolitionists are good men, but few of them are wise men. Some . . . are so
denunciatory as to kill all prayer about it. . . . Unless we can come to a
better understanding among ourselves . . . I fear that all the evils and
horrors of civil war will be the consequence."

The final quotation concerning "the bewildered Southern brethren in the
Lord" is from *Zion's Herald,* VI, 140. Not all abolitionists by any means

abandoned the evangelical objective. Gerrit Smith spoke for many: "The grand object of the anti-slavery enterprise is to abolitionize the public mind —to break the strong, slave-holding heart of this nation. . . . If every pro-slavery law in the land shall be repealed and yet the nation not be brought to repentance for the sin of slavery . . . the grand object will still remain undone." (From a letter to Leavitt, dated Dec. 24, 1839, *Pennsylvania Freeman*, Jan. 23, 1840.)

[5] Early in 1839, less than four months after the publication of *Slavery As It Is,* more than twenty-two thousand copies had been sold, five thousand over the counter in the New York antislavery book store. Before the end of the year, nearly a hundred thousand had been sold (*Pennsylvania Freeman*, Sept. 26, 1839). All of Weld's tracts had unprecedented sales during these last days. He wrote that the New York office alone had cleared more than ten thousand dollars on his pamphlets during 1839–1840 (Weld to Angelina Weld, Feb. 27, 1842). The quotation in the text is from a letter from Beriah Green to Weld, April 14, 1839 (Weld Papers, Library of Congress). Weld had refused the office of corresponding secretary, to which he was elected in May, 1839. He continued to refuse an appointment to the Executive Committee (Minutes of the Executive Committee, American Anti-Slavery Society, 1837–1840, p. 180). During the previous year, Weld had been so successful in getting his editorials and articles published, especially in the New York *Sun*, that the Executive Committee resolved that he should put all his time on this work. Weld refused (Minutes of the Executive Committee, American Anti-Slavery Society, Sept. 20, 1838.)

[6] To further his project for showing the support of slavery by the North, Weld sent out a form letter to the nation for information regarding the connection of the North with slavery. Several copies are in the Weld MSS. The resolution of the Executive Committee—"That Mr. Weld be authorized to employ an agent for three months in each of the cities of New York, Philadelphia, and Boston, to procure the information he is in search of, respecting the Connections of the North with Slavery"—is in Minutes of the Executive Committee, American Anti-Slavery Society, 1837–1840, p. 182. On November 21 Weld secured additional funds to hire two more agents for the "copying of facts in records." One of these five agents was James A. Thome (appointed Oct. 17, *ibid.,* p. 187), who was now an instructor in Oberlin. On a visit to his father's plantation in Kentucky, Thome, at some peril to himself, had assisted an ill-treated slave on a nearby plantation to freedom. An Oberlin student indiscreetly told the story—an exciting one—to the editor of a newspaper. The story reached Kentucky, and Thome's relatives informed him that the sheriff was securing papers for his arrest. Thome fled to New York, and Weld put him to work (see the letters of Thome to Weld for September and October, 1839, Weld MSS). Later Thome helped Weld in preparation of "an elaborate statistical document on American Slavery." This was undertaken at the request of the British and Foreign Anti-Slavery Society. "The unexampled interest excited by the disclosures of *American Slavery As It Is* and the anxiety created thereby to receive at the same hand an exhibition of the causes and fruits of pro-slavery at the North" was its occasion (*Emanci-*

pator, May 15, 1840). This report was published and widely distributed in England by the British and Foreign Anti-Slavery Society under the title: *Slavery and the Internal Slave Trade in the United States* (London, 1841).

⁷ The promised donation is noted in the *Anti-Slavery Reporter*, June, 1840. To select the twenty agents, Weld was appointed, but he refused. Whittier was then appointed for the same object, but he also refused. The committee finally secured the agents by correspondence. The most successful of the Seventy refused to serve again. (See Minutes of the Executive Committee, American Anti-Slavery Society, pp. 170, 173–180, and Weld to Angelina Weld, June 21, 1839, Weld MSS.)

The promised donation probably never was paid. Up to November eighth, the year's receipts from donations and pledges were only $6,500 (*Emancipator,* Nov. 14, 1839). The dismissal of the agents is recorded in the Minutes of the Agency Committee, American Anti-Slavery Society, Nov. 7, 1839. On the same date Weld was told to dismiss his five fact-finding agents (Minutes of the Executive Committee, American Anti-Slavery Society, 1837–1840, p. 204).

⁸ The protest of State societies against the financial circular is recorded in *ibid.,* p. 192. A copy of the financial circular is in the Weld MSS. The Cleveland conference is described in the *Anti-Slavery Reporter*, June, 1840. Toward the end, even the executives went unpaid. For two years Stanton had not received his salary (Weld to L. Tappan, April 10, 1840, Weld MSS.). Birney and Weld (who had received a salary only since his marriage) both proposed that their salaries be reduced. Weld asked that his be reduced from $1,000 to $700 a year, and Birney asked for a reduction of $250 (Minutes of the Executive Committee, American Anti-Slavery Society, 1837–1840, pp. 148, 202), but even then the society could not pay them what was due.

⁹ The committee's reproof of Leavitt is in the Minutes of the Agency Committee, American Anti-Slavery Society, Feb. 15, and March 1, 1838; and it is noted in the *Emancipator*, March 12, 1840. Lewis Tappan's reproof was printed in *ibid.,* Nov. 14, 1839.

¹⁰ Birney's suggestion of a new party to be led by Channing is in a letter from Birney to S. P. Chase, June 5, 1837 (Chase Papers, Library of Congress). Channing's interview with Adams is described in Adams, *Memoirs*, X, 38. Channing's plan for a new society is printed in the *Christian Examiner*, third series, XXVI, pp. 301–318.

¹¹ The quotations are from Adams, *Memoirs*, IX, 451. This was in December, 1837.

¹² When Adams made his address upon abolition, William Slade of Vermont was much disturbed. He talked the speech over with Giddings. "He seemed to be very apprehensive that the speech would have a bad influence on the subject of abolition," wrote Giddings in his diary. He discussed the advisability of having it out with Adams, but Giddings, with a greater faith in the aged statesman than his more experienced colleague, advised against it. (Buell, *Joshua R. Giddings*, pp. 88–89.)

Adams' three amendments proposed that gradual abolition should begin in the States after a three-year period, that immediate abolition should occur in the District after seven years, and that except for Florida no new State should be admitted with slavery (*Congressional Globe*, 25th Congress, 3d S., p. 205).

Adams' public letter, from which the quotation is made, was published in the *National Intelligencer*, May 27, 1839. Adams' public letters to his constituents had enjoyed each year a wider fame. His letters of 1837 and 1838—especially his letter dated Aug. 13, 1838—I have found in almost every daily and weekly that I have consulted. But his letters of 1839 to the petition volunteers not only had a national circulation; they created a national sensation. They were two in number, printed in the *National Intelligencer* for April 23 and May 27, 1839. Bound, they made a pamphlet of book size and length. The story in Adams' diary of how he dragooned Seaton of the *Intelligencer* into making room for his letters is a tale in itself. The first letter is an account of the gags and an argument for the right of petition. The second is a history of the Southern "aggressive defense" policy (from Adams' partisan viewpoint) and an analysis of the various organizations concerned with antislavery measures,

[13] The doggerel is printed in the *Emancipator*, Sept. 26, 1839. This alluded to Adams' defense of Andrew Jackson's French policy in 1836. See also the *National Anti-Slavery Standard*, Aug. 18, 1842, and March 3, 1843. Garrison made his attack upon Adams in the "Decennial Meeting," Dec. 5, 1843 (*National Anti-Slavery Standard*, Dec. 14, 1843).

[14] The first quotation is from the Minutes of the Executive Committee, American Anti-Slavery Society, 1837–1840, p. 207. At the convention seventy-one were present. Only one delegate came from Pennsylvania and only one from Ohio. Vermont was holding a State convention and did not send a delegate. The turn-out was "a great disappointment" (*Emancipator*, Jan. 23, 1840). The result, "practically a decision of bankruptcy," is thus characterized in the *Anti-Slavery Reporter*, June, 1840. On Lewis Tappan's proposal only thirteen voted affirmatively. Most of the delegates refused to vote, their refusal being of course the equivalent of a negative.

[15] *Pennsylvania Freeman*, Jan. 16, 1840.

[16] *Philanthropist*, Feb. 18, 1840.

[17] *Massachusetts Abolitionist*, II, 30.

[18] Lewis Tappan to Weld, May 4, 1840 (L. Tappan Papers, Library of Congress).

[19] *Emancipator*, April 23, 1840.

[20] The permission of the Massachusetts Abolition Society to let Stanton solicit in their State, and the refusal of Garrison's society to pay its pledge, are both recorded in the Minutes of the Executive Committee, American Anti-Slavery Society, 1837–1840, Feb. 20, 1840. All of the State auxiliaries except the Massachusetts Anti-Slavery Society finally paid their quotas. Total receipts and total expenditures for the fiscal year were thus nearly $50,000. The Garrisonians made the charge that this amount was illegitimate: "The society had by formal vote expressed its will that expenditures be limited to $30,000." This was not the case. The annual meeting of 1839 had voted pledges from the State societies to the national society amounting to the total sum of $32,000. Nobody dreamed that the

Executive Committee should refuse private donations, orders for books, etc., in addition to this amount. The Garrisonians also charged that over $18,000 had been dissipated by Birney, Leavitt, Stanton, "and one other" (Weld: they did not have the temerity to charge him by name with financial misconduct), for high salaries and needless expenses. This too was a misrepresentation. Weld, for instance, disbursed funds assigned to him for his researches under the head of expenses, and the others followed similar methods. In view of the pecuniary sacrifices that all four men made during the last year, the charge that they devoted improper sums to their own uses is ridiculous (see *National Anti-Slavery Standard*, Oct. 12 and 20, 1843, for the charges made by Garrison's adherents). As a matter of fact, even the reduced salaries due the executives had not been paid. Stanton, the only bachelor on the staff, had received no salary at all during this last year or during the previous year; and during the final year Sarah Grimké had loaned Birney a thousand dollars to provide for his necessities. (See the letters from Weld to Lewis Tappan, 1840–1842, Weld MSS.)

The resolution transferring the society's property to Lewis Tappan and another is recorded in the Minutes of the Executive Committee, American Anti-Slavery Society, 1837–1840, April 16, 1840. The reason for this transaction, the committee recorded in the minutes as follows: "1st. To secure Mr. Rankin's endorsement. 2nd. To secure themselves for their personal liability on behalf of the Society. 3rd. To provide for the remaining debts and liabilities of the Society." The real reason was the fear that, if Garrison's raid should be successful, the new régime would not pay off the old obligations. There was an appended note to the above reasons: "Such property to be retransferred to the Ex. Com'te or their successors on security being furnished for the payments of said debts and liabilities." The fear was well grounded. The new régime refused to pay any of the obligations of the old. (See *Anti-Slavery Reporter,* Oct., 1840.)

[21] This was Lewis Tappan's description of the delegation from Massachusetts.

[22] The quotations are from a letter from Garrison to his wife, May 15, 1840 (Garrison, *Garrison,* II, 355). The executive committee had restricted its activities to general appeals "to come to New York to the annual meeting to secure a majority." A description of their campaign to attract delegates is in *Herald of Freedom,* Dec. 8, 1840.

CHAPTER XVII

RESIDUES

[1] The suggestion for a World Anti-Slavery Convention first appeared in the *Emancipator,* March 21, 1838. The correspondence between the New York and London abolitionists on the subject is summarized in the *Proceedings of the General Anti-Slavery Convention,* London, 1840, p. 20.

[2] The first quotation is from *ibid.,* p. 29. The "self-constituted Committee" was the Executive Committee of the British and Foreign Anti-Slavery Society, which had called the convention. There had been two letters of

invitation. The first invited simply "the friends of the Slave of every nation and of every clime." But, as the secretary of the British and Foreign Anti-Slavery Society explained to the convention, after the first letter had been sent, "we did become aware . . . that there was a disposition on the part of some of our American brethren . . . to construe the document in question . . . that it might include females." Accordingly a second letter was sent specifying the delegates as "gentlemen." (See *ibid.*, pp. 25, 31.)

The State society of Pennsylvania, eastern branch, also appointed women, Lucretia Mott among them; but unlike the Massachusetts delegates, the Pennsylvanians did not officially protest the exclusion of their women associates.

Upon receipt of Weld's refusal to attend the World Convention, the New York Committee appointed Gerrit Smith and then William Jay; but neither of them accepted the appointment. Smith finally went as delegate for the New York State Society, but Jay refused to go in any capacity. (Minutes of the Executive Committee, American Anti-Slavery Society, 1837–1840, p. 204.)

[3] The quotations are from the *Proceedings of the General Anti-Slavery Convention,* pp. 44, 45.

[4] Elizabeth Cady Stanton to Sarah Grimké and Angelina Weld, June 25, 1840 (Weld MSS.).

[5] A public statement of the British society upon the subject of Garrison and his course is printed in the *Emancipator,* Feb. 25, 1841.

[6] It was the divided counsels of the delegates from America that moved Joseph Sturge, the leading member of the British and Foreign Anti-Slavery Society, to visit this country shortly after the convention, on a mission to bring together the hostile factions. Whittier accompanied him. His mission was a failure. (J. Sturge, *A Visit to the United States,* 1841.)

[7] Minutes of the Executive Committee, American Anti-Slavery Society, 1837–1840, May 15, 1840. The Garrisonians proudly recorded their own proceedings in the old book of minutes.

[8] For the distribution of affiliations of State and local societies, see footnote 15, below. The strength of the Garrisonians was in the Massachusetts Anti-Slavery Society, which now was largely composed of radicals in Boston and Lynn, and in the remnants of the Pennsylvania Anti-Slavery Society, Eastern Branch, which was dominated by the Philadelphia women under Lucretia Mott. The Pennsylvania northeastern counties had separated from the eastern branch, and had formed a society of their own, which later affiliated with the secessionists.

The financial difficulties of the Garrisonians are recounted in the Minutes of the Executive Committee, American Anti-Slavery Society, 1837–1840; Sept. 25, and Dec. 3, 1840; and Jan. 20, 1841. Except for the record of the first meeting, the minutes were written some time after the meetings they recorded. There is much window-dressing, but the desperate straits of the *Standard* was the central theme. One of the greatest difficulties of the new Executive Committee was that there was often not a quorum in New York City. It proved a hard task to manage its affairs from Massachusetts. The mission to England is noted in *ibid.,* Sept. 25, 1840.

⁹ *Emancipator,* Feb. 25, 1841. The agent had asked for a "grant of £2,000," or, if that was impossible, "an expression of their cordial desire for the success" of his agency. The executive committee of the British and Foreign Anti-Slavery Society refused both requests.

¹⁰ The degree of interest which British reformers, especially among the evangelical denominations, showed in the progress of the antislavery cause in America is astonishing. There were at least two periodicals whose primary purpose was to keep their readers informed upon the subject. The one which was published by the Baptists, for example, *Slavery in America* (London, 1836–1839), "was undertaken principally with a view to awaken attention to the fact, that in the republican States of America, and among the Christian Churches in that land, SLAVERY . . . was not only permitted to exist, but even palliated. . . . Upon the passing of the Abolition Act in this country, having, as we supposed, washed our hands of all participation in the foul crime . . . it was equally the dictate of principle and benevolence, to look abroad, and exert our energies for its destruction wherever in other countries it had struck its pestilential roots." (*Slavery in America,* II, 289.) The annual letters from denominations in England to corresponding sects in the United States, containing admonitions regarding slavery, exhibited a thorough knowledge of the leading personalities and the progress of the antislavery cause.

Charles Stuart had been in England some time before Collins arrived. He had been active since 1838 in a survey of the West Indies, "at his own charges," in order to ascertain the result of the apprenticeship system upon the freedmen. (See Weld to Gerrit Smith, Nov. 28, 1838, Weld MSS., and numerous letters from Stuart to the *Emancipator,* 1839. See also Stuart's letters to Weld during 1839–1840, Weld MSS.) He had returned to England in 1839, and had attended the World Anti-Slavery Convention. When Collins appeared in England, Stuart began at once to write and speak against his mission. (One of Stuart's pamphlets attacking Collins and the Garrisonians is in the Weld MSS.) The British abolitionists had shown their appreciation of Stuart's labors in a substantial manner. His friends in parliament had secured his promotion from the rank of retired captain to that of retired major, with attendant increase in pay. He was also made "honorary life member" of the British and Foreign Anti-Slavery Society.

Stuart's opposition to Collins did not prevent a considerable degree of success for the latter's mission. Collins' first draft, for nearly a thousand dollars, reached New York just in time to save the *Standard* (Minutes of the Executive Committee, American Anti-Slavery Society, Feb. 3, 1841). Later, "British gold" sustained the Garrisonians as well as the New York paper. Reports of the Massachusetts Anti-Slavery Society after 1846 show an increasing proportion of British support.

¹¹ The account here is a summary of the story that David Lee Child, himself, told of his own and his wife's editorial difficulties with Garrison (*Anti-Slavery Standard,* May 23, 1844). The new editor was Oliver Johnson. He had been assistant editor of the *Liberator* and, during Garrison's illness, had served as acting editor.

¹² Under the Garrisonians, the American Anti-Slavery Society published no reports until 1853, and then they were largely summaries of public events with an antislavery bearing which had occurred during the year. The quotation glorying in the absence of a plan for emancipation is from the *Anti-Slavery Standard*, Aug. 29, 1844. The small number of accredited delegates at the anniversaries of the society was surprising. At the May anniversary of 1844, for example, there were 449 names on the roll of the meeting, but only 78 were eligible to vote on resolutions (*Anti-Slavery Standard*, May 23, 1844). The number of members in the society recorded in the text is from the membership roll of 1843. Their opponents contended that the membership was even smaller, but I have taken the Garrisonians' own figures. Many even of these six hundred belonged to societies which were moribund. (*Ibid.*, April 27, 1843.)

¹³ *Massachusetts Abolitionist*, II, 23.

¹⁴ The quotations are from the following letters: Weld to Lewis Tappan, Jan. 23, 1843 (Weld MSS.), and Gerrit Smith to Weld, July 11, 1840 (Weld Papers, Library of Congress). Smith's letter continued: "I have come to the conclusion that the benefits our anti-slavery organization yields are not adequate recompense for the danger it does our cause . . . and that it is therefore better that it should be abandoned." The final quotation is from a letter from Whittier to Courtland, July 2, 1840 (Pickard, *Life of Whittier*, I, 259). Though Whittier would not join at this time, he later edited the society's organ, the *Anti-Slavery Reporter*.

¹⁵ The Connecticut State Society, the Massachusetts Abolition Society, one of the new State societies in New York, the New Jersey State Society, and numbers of the county societies in New England and the middle States which no longer recognized the authority of their State organizations, affiliated with the American and Foreign Anti-Slavery Society. (See *Anti-Slavery Reporter*, July, 1840, and the *Emancipator*, June–Nov., 1840.) The Ohio State Society, the old New York State Society at Utica, the western branch of the Pennsylvania State Society, and others, though they withdrew from the American Anti-Slavery Society, would not affiliate with the new organization.

Notices of the withdrawal of auxiliaries from the American and Foreign Anti-Slavery Society after May, 1841, are in the *Emancipator*, August to November, 1841. The resignations of Birney and Stanton, and Leavitt's admission of failure are in *ibid.*, Nov. 25, 1841.

References to Lewis Tappan's labors are as follows: Abel and Klingberg, *A Side-Light on Anglo-American Relations*, for his correspondence with British abolitionists; the *National Anti-Slavery Standard*, April 27, 1843, for his most famous achievement as treasurer for the antislavery impulse. It was Lewis Tappan who took over the care of the Amistad Captives, a cargo of slaves who had captured their vessel and landed on American shores. He collected the funds for their maintenance, for their defense, and for their return to Africa. Their battle for freedom in the Supeme Court, with Adams speaking in their defense, was a thrilling chapter in the public propaganda of the 'forties. For Tappan's embassy to England for the slaves, see note 13, Chapter XIX.

¹⁶ *Emancipator*, Nov. 12, 1840.

CHAPTER XVIII

THE TURNING POINT

¹ The Washington lobby was discussed in the *Friend of Man*, May 31, 1837. Weld's official notice of appointment to Washington is in the Weld Papers, Library of Congress. His refusal to go is recorded in the Minutes of the Executive Committee, American Anti-Slavery Society, 1837–1840, p. 75. He refused on account of his health; at that time he had not entirely recovered from his breakdown. Senator Morris' letter suggesting a lobby first appeared in the *Philanthropist* and was summarized in the *Emancipator*, Nov. 12, 1840. An editorial unfriendly to the project is in *ibid.*, Dec. 17, 1840. The *Philanthropist* concurred in pronouncing the project inexpedient.

² Giddings' letter to Leavitt was in part as follows: "Why should you deem it necessary to diminish the influence of the few individuals who are now placed between you and the common enemy; or why should you strike from their hands the weapons raised in defense of Northern rights?" (Giddings to Leavitt, no date.) Giddings added that Borden of Massachusetts concurred in his censure of Leavitt. The letters from Slade and Giddings were printed in the *Emancipator*, July 15, 1841, some months after they had been written. Meanwhile more friendly letters from the congressmen had been published. See especially the letter from Giddings to Leavitt, in the *Emancipator*, May 6, 1841. Various others from the antislavery members were published in the *Emancipator* during the next three months.

³ All the quotations in the text are from a letter from Leavitt to Giddings, Oct. 29, 1841 (Giddings Papers).

⁴ *Ibid.*

⁵ The quotations characterizing Leavitt are from a letter written by Seth M. Gates to Giddings, Dec. 6, 1843 (Giddings Papers). Leavitt's second mission to Washington was financed by the Massachusetts State Liberty Party Convention. The convention adopted a resolution expressing characteristic New England thrift: "Brother Leavitt's presence and able pen at Washington as a reporter, will do more to advance the cause of humanity than any one else we can employ at that price." The price was two hundred dollars (*Emancipator*, Oct. 28, 1841). The final quotation describing the changed program of the Congressmen is from a letter from Weld to L. Tappan, summarizing a letter of Leavitt's to Weld, Dec. 14, 1841 (Weld MSS.).

⁶ The first quotation is from the New York Committee's directions to petitioners for 1841, printed in the *Emancipator*, Sept. 16, 1841. Wise's speech is in the *Congressional Globe*, 27th Congress, 2d S., p. 172.

⁷ Weld to L. Tappan, Dec. 14, 1841 (Weld MSS.).

⁸ *Ibid.* The "select committee" also planned to force debate on the constitutional rights of free colored citizens in the South, and on the recognition of Hayti.

⁹ For preliminary discussions regarding this project, see the letters of Lewis Tappan to Giddings, Gates, and Slade during the late summer of

1841 (Letter Book of Lewis Tappan, 1840–1841, L. Tappan Papers, Library of Congress). The appeal for funds, from which the quotation in the text is taken, was printed in the *Emancipator*, Sept. 16, 1841.

[10] I have summarized the account of the plan for the Congressmen's lobby which Leavitt wrote Weld and which Weld in turn wrote to Lewis Tappan, Dec. 14, 1841 (Weld MSS.).

[11] *Ibid.* All of Weld's mail was to be sent to Giddings, who told Leavitt that he would frank Weld's outgoing letters. Several of Weld's letters from Washington bear Giddings' frank, but many are franked by Gates, Slade, and Andrews. (See Weld MSS. for 1842–1843.)

[12] "I was never qualified nor prepared for the station in which by a train of circumstances I have found myself," Giddings wrote Weld. "My education is not equal to it, my habits have in some respects unfitted me for it and I long to leave it." (Giddings to Weld, Feb. 21, 1843, Weld Papers, Library of Congress.) As evidence of Adams' regard for Giddings: two years after the lobby began its work, he wrote a poem "To Joshua R. Giddings." Two of the stanzas are as follows:

> "And here, from regions wide apart
> We came a purpose to pursue,
> Each with a warm and honest heart
> Each with a spirit firm and true.

> "And here, with scrutinizing eye,
> A kindred soul with mine to see,
> And longing bosom to descry
> I sought, and found at last—in thee."

It is printed in Buell, *J. R. Giddings, A Sketch.*

[13] During the previous Congress, when Bynum of North Carolina had challenged Gates to confess his faith, he had risen and declared to the House that he was an abolitionist. Bynum expressed sardonic admiration: "That man is the first who has had the candor to own his being an abolitionist . . . and although I detest his principles, I cannot but admire his courage as a man." The quotations in the text are from a letter from Weld to his wife, Jan. 1, 1842 (Weld MSS.).

[14] *Ibid.*

[15] The first two quotations describing the "select committee" are from a letter from Giddings to his wife, Feb. 18, 1842 (Giddings Papers). The facts regarding the religious affiliations of the antislavery members and the final quotations are from a letter from Weld to his wife, Jan. 18, 1842 (Weld MSS.).

[16] The first quotation is from the same, Jan. 1, 1842 (Weld MSS.), and the last is from the same, Dec. 27, 1842 (Weld MSS.). Mrs. Sprigg was too late to save some of the slaves, however. One they called "Poor Robert" left on a Monday evening, "and the next he was heard from he was 'way up there in York State,' full tilt for Canada." (Giddings to his son, Addison Giddings, Aug. 15, 1842, Giddings Papers.) Six years later Gates enter-

tained another of the former servants of the Abolition House at his home
in Warsaw, N. Y.—John Douglass, who had escaped soon after Poor
Robert. After eighteen months in Canada he had returned to this country,
and was living prosperously in Rochester. Poor Robert, Douglass said,
had moved from Canada to Buffalo, where he had a family. He was cook
on a lake steamer, had steady work, and was doing well. The underground
railway agent in Washington for these and numerous other fugitives was
one Smallwood of the Navy Yard. Smallwood would collect slaves one by
one, and hide them in a garret. It usually took three weeks or more to collect a gang of eighteen, enough to make a trip north worth while. When
the gang was collected, it was rushed north at night and picked up somewhere near Philadelphia by an agent of the railroad. Such at least were the
details of the underground railroad from Washington to Canada, as told
to Gates by John Douglass. (S. M. Gates to Giddings, Dec. 5, 1848, Giddings Papers.)

[17] Weld to his wife, Jan. 25, 1842 (Weld MSS.).

[18] The same, Jan. 2, 1842 (Weld MSS.).

[19] The same, Jan. 9, 1842 (Weld MSS.).

[20] From Giddings' *Creole* Resolutions, *Congressional Globe,* 27th Congress, 2d S., p. 342.

[21] Giddings told the story of the origin of the *Creole* resolutions in a
public letter to his constituents (*Anti-Slavery Standard,* April 28, 1842).
For Weld's development of the municipal theory of slavery in his tract, see
pp. 137–138 of this book.

[22] The quotations from Adams' speech are taken from a letter from
Weld to his wife, January (no date), 1842 (Weld MSS.). The quotation
describing the dinner at Adams' house is from another letter to the same,
January 9, 1842 (Weld MSS.). Giddings told of Adams' uniting with the
"select committee" in a letter to his wife, Feb. 18, 1842 (Giddings Papers).
In this letter Giddings records Adams' identification with the "select committee" more than a month after the dinner with Adams; but the letter
makes it clear that Adams' association with the insurgents was not of
recent origin. This circumstance, together with Adams' actual opening of
the warfare shortly after the dinner, leads me to ascribe the occasion of
Adams' identification with the "select committee" to the dinner meeting at
Adams' house.

[23] This caucus was referred to by Adams during his trial and its existence was admitted by Marshall of Kentucky (*Congressional Globe,*
27th Congress, 2d S., p. 211).

[24] The two quotations are from a speech by a Democrat, Black of
Georgia, who thus characterized the attempt to censure Adams (*Appendix
to Congressional Globe,* 28th Congress, 1st S., p. 205).

[25] Weld to his wife, Jan. 30, 1842 (Weld MSS.). In the course of the
trial, their association became more personal in character. Adams shortly
discovered that Weld was the son of his old Harvard classmate and distant
relative, Ludovicus Weld. Moreover, Adams told Weld, his grandfather,
the Rev. Ezra Weld, Congregational minister at Braintree, Massachusetts,
had baptized him "in the half-way covenant." At times during this associa-

tion they would suspend the business of the trial, and Adams would tell
Weld stories of his father at Harvard, of his grandfather at Braintree, and
reminiscences of his own boyhood, charming tales which Weld later told
his children. (See the MSS. reminiscences of Sarah Weld Hamilton, in the
possession of her daughter, Dr. Angelina G. Hamilton.) It is unfortunate
that Adams was not keeping up his diary during these crucial days. At
later dates, however, he mentions Weld with reference to their coöperation.

[26] Weld to his wife, Jan. 25, 1842 (Weld MSS.).

[27] The same, Jan. 30, 1842 (Weld MSS.).

[28] *Ibid.*

[29] *Congressional Globe,* 27th Congress, 2d S., p. 208.

[30] Weld to his wife, no date (sometime in early February), 1842 (Weld
MSS.).

[31] The same, no date (about Feb. 28), 1842 (Weld MSS.). Giddings'
motion to refer another petition for the dissolution of the Union to a committee is in *Congressional Globe,* 27th Congress, 2d S., p. 268. The factional
character of the move to censure Adams for presenting a petition to dissolve the Union is indicated by the refusal of the House on three separate
occasions after Adams's trial to consider resolutions condemning the
presentation of such petitions. (See *Congressional Globe,* as above, and
ibid., p. 342.)

[32] The rumor of Adams' compromise with Whig leaders was widely
repeated: "Mr. Adams has abandoned the principle of the right of petition
in refusing to present petitions for the dissolution of the Union, ever since
the compromise by which the resolutions of censure upon him were abandoned, and he became a leader of the slave-holding Whig party" (*Anti-
Slavery Standard,* March 16, 1843).

[33] The antislavery members expected the case of the *Creole* to be brought
up in the House by Southern members. It had already been brought up in
the Senate by Calhoun; and Holmes of South Carolina, Giddings' seat mate
in the House, "had in his desk a string of resolutions on the subject of the
Creole for 2 weeks, and Giddings has been pushing him to present them, but
H. refuses on the ground that the Abolitionists will make capital by it. So
Giddings will present nine resolutions on Monday." (Weld to his wife,
no date, 1842, Weld MSS.) Elsewhere Weld reported Giddings' and
Holmes's conversation: Giddings asked Holmes why he did not present his
Creole resolutions. " 'Because,' said Holmes, 'you abolitionists will pounce
upon us with your discussions of slavery.' 'Yes,' said Giddings, 'that we
will. Now you had better make the best of it—for you have *got* to bear it.' "
(Weld to his wife, Jan. 9, 1842, Weld MSS.).

The correspondent of the New York *Evening Post* thus summarized the
politics of Giddings's censure: "It was somewhat singular . . . that the
most urgent desire to drive the matter to its extremity was discovered on
the part of certain strong Whigs. It was General Ward of New York who
first moved the previous question on the passage of the resolutions, thus
to force a vote upon questions which are vital almost to the prosperity of

our government without an instant's deliberation; it was Botts who prepared the censure, even while the resolutions were reading, and immediately moved the previous question on adopting it; it was Weller of Ohio
who next took it up and pressed it forward." (New York *Evening Post,*
March 24, 1842.)

For the discussion in the House as to the parliamentary details of Giddings' censure, see *Congressional Globe,* 27th Congress, 2d S., pp. 324–
346, 348–349, 353, 356. The previous question was moved upon the resolutions of censure, and the Speaker interpreted this as cutting off all debate,
even Giddings' defense. The House sustained the Speaker's decision. At
the very last, however, just before the final vote, a demand was made that
Giddings be allowed to speak. The Speaker had already ruled that Giddings
would be out of order, and the House had sustained the Speaker; so that
his defense now could be heard only by unanimous consent of the House.
Giddings rose to read a protest but was immediately called to order by
Cooper of Georgia. Cooper was persuaded by his more astute colleagues to
withdraw his objection, and Giddings was again asked to speak. His colleague Goode went over to his seat and, as he later admitted, implored him
not to do so, since if he spoke at all at such a time, it would be only by
favor of the unanimous consent of the House, subject at any moment to
the objection of any member, and not regularly, as a right, without interruption. But Goode's persuasions were not needed. One of the insurgents,
W. B. Calhoun of Massachusetts, realizing that what the Whig leaders
were trying to secure was the appearance of an opportunity for Giddings
to speak in his own defense, immediately renewed Cooper's objection, as-
signing as his reason that "as Mr. GIDDINGS had been denied the privilege of defending himself as a *right,* I would not consent that he should
exercise it as an act of grace, *courtesy* or *favor."* This objection by Calhoun
should have made it impossible for the Whigs to claim as they did, that
Giddings had been given an opportunity to speak in his own defense and
had refused it. But unfortunately Calhoun's objection, with his remarks,
were not recorded in the official account in the *Globe.* They were recorded,
however, by several of the other papers. The original account of the proceedings in the *National Intelligencer* was largely correct; but a later more
detailed account (*National Intelligencer,* March 31, 1842) told the story
according to the official Whig position. Calhoun's letter describing his objection and remarks in detail, is in *ibid.* for April 2, 1842. The account in
the *Globe,* which was used by Whig spokesmen to prove that Giddings had
been given a chance to speak in his own defense but had refused to do so, is
quite clearly incorrect, although it was made up from official sources.

[34] S. M. Gates to Giddings, April 4, 1842 (Giddings Papers). The quotation regarding the Northern Whigs is from a letter from Giddings to his
wife, March 22, 1842 (Giddings Papers). The story of Gates's attempt to
call a caucus of the Whigs in Giddings' support is in a letter from
S. M. Gates to Giddings, March 25, 1842 (Giddings Papers).

[35] This is the comment of "R. M. T. H." (Dr. D. F. Bacon), correspondent of the *New York American,* May 7, 1842.

[36] See the letters from Gates to Giddings referred to above, and also the *New York American,* March 28, 1842, for the course of this under-cover campaign.

[37] See Giddings to his son Addison Giddings, May 8, 1842 (Giddings Papers), recounting the anxiety of his colleague.. Adams' emotion at their parting is noted in a letter from Giddings to his wife, March 22 (dated March 12 by error), 1842 (Giddings Papers). The anxious correspondents were Dr. Bacon ("R. M. T. H.") of the *New York American,* and Brower of the Boston *Courier.*

[38] The quotation regarding Giddings' majority is from the *New York American,* May 7, 1842. In point of *f*act, however, Giddings's majority at his reëlection was not as large as his majority at his previous regular election. The perplexity of Whig leaders over Giddings' reëlection is related in the Baltimore *Sun,* May 6, 1842. Wise's compliment to Giddings was quoted in a letter from Giddings to his son Addison, May 19, 1842 (Giddings Papers).

[39] Giddings told his son Addison of the attempt that would be made to censure him again in *ibid.* The words of the Congressman who warned the die-hards that Giddings could not be stopped are quoted from the *Congressional Globe,* 27th Congress, 2d S., p. 576. The quotation regarding the majority ready to censure Giddings "for anything and everything" is from a speech by Black of Georgia (*Appendix to Congressional Globe,* 28th Congress, 1st S., p. 205).

CHAPTER XIX

The Broadening Impulse

[1] "Theodore D. Weld," MS. by H. B. Stanton, written sometime in 1838 (Weld MSS.).

[2] See Weld to Angelina Weld and Sarah Grimké, Feb. 17, 1842 (Weld MSS.). Weld's letters record numerous occasions on which Adams sent for him to talk over some new point in the campaign.

[3] For this reason Weld would not seek out Angelina's first cousin, R. Barnwell Rhett of South Carolina: "I am unwilling to be introduced to him without taking up the subject of slavery, and I can serve the cause here far more effectually than by talking on the subject of slavery with inveterate slave-holders of the McDuffie school." (Weld to his wife, Jan. 30, 1842, Weld MSS.)

[4] The same, Feb. 20, 1842 (Weld MSS.).

[5] "R. M. T. H." in the *New York American,* Dec. 29, 1842.

[6] Regarding his recovered vitality, Weld wrote: "I walk, run and jump about an hour every morning before breakfast. Am admirably situated for this, the Capitol square park being directly in front of our house. . . . A better place for exercise could not be had." (Weld to his wife, Jan. 20, 1842, Weld MSS.) For the sake of his mission, Weld gave up his "John Baptist attire." "All my clothes are in very good state," he wrote his wife. "I shave every other morning, and Leavitt testifys that I keep in very re-

spectable plight." (Weld to his wife, Jan. 30, 1842, dated 1841 by error, Weld MSS.) Regarding the recovery of his voice, he wrote: "You speak of my preaching, beloved. I have ceased to lay plans. That I should have sufficient strength of voice to take upon me a permanent responsibility of public speaking I have not much expectation; but that I shall be able still to speak considerably I have no doubt, if spared. What God would have me do specifically, I have as yet no strong indication; but that he will call me to some one particular mode of doing good, I have no doubt. May HE direct who never errs. And to whatever He leads, let us watch and pray without ceasing, for faith to follow." Weld to his wife, Jan. (no date), 1842 (Weld MSS.).

[7] The same, Jan. 26, 1843 (Weld MSS.).

[8] The same, Feb. 17, 1842 (Weld MSS.). The quality of Weld's anti-slavery inspiration—its profoundly religious content—sets him apart from most of the other abolitionists. His language, like his spirit, was after the model of the Hebrew prophets. From the midst of Adams's trial, for example, he wrote regarding Adams's opponents: "Oh that they knew in their day the things that belong to their peace! The slave-holders of the present generation, if cloven down by God's judgments, cannot plead that they were unwarned. Warnings, reproofs, and the foreshadows of coming retribution have for years freighted the very air; and should sudden destruction come upon them now at last, well may the God of the oppressed cry out against them: 'Because I have called and ye have refused; I have stretched out my hand and no man hath regarded; but ye set at naught my counsel and would none of my reproof. Therefore will I laugh at your calamity and mock when your fear cometh like a whirlwind. Then shall ye call but I will not come; ye shall seek me early but ye shall not find me. Therefore shall ye eat of the fruit of your own ways and be filled with your own devices.'" Weld to his wife, Feb. (no date), 1842 (Weld MSS.).

[9] The same, Feb. 20, 1842. Weld left Washington earlier than he had planned: "Until two days since I expected to stay here two weeks longer at least; but upon looking at the whole matter, I feel as though I had better go home now, and if any great emergency should arise before the close of this session that will make any labors [?] of mine here very important, the brothers here will at once let me know, and (D. V.) I must return. However, I shall leave behind me a mass of materials on the subjects that will come up, besides having conferred at length with those who will debate them, so that I feel quite at liberty to leave, and quite confident no emergency will arise requiring me to return." Weld to his wife, March 2, 1842 (Weld MSS.).

[10] Weld to Sarah Grimké and Angelina Grimké Weld, Dec. 27, 1842 (Weld MSS.).

[11] The first two quotations are from a letter from Weld to his wife, Jan. 1, 1843 (Weld MSS.). The final quotation is from another letter, the same, Jan. 4, 1843 (Weld MSS.).

[12] The same, Dec. 27, 1842. Child told with pride an adventure which he had with a "slaveite": "Shippard of North Carolina came up to a corner in the Capitol where Giddings, Gates and myself were in conversation."

Shippard made some invidious comment, and Child retorted. "He turned away, muttering something about 'hangers-on,' which I supposed was intended especially for my benefit." (*Anti-Slavery Standard,* March 2, 1843.)

[13] Lewis Tappan's private embassy to England in the spring of 1843 was one of the most extraordinary antislavery events of that year. He had a talk with Adams, in the course of which Adams told him that he believed British abolitionists, if properly informed, could persuade their government to refuse recognition to the Republic of Texas unless slavery were abolished. "I deem it the duty of Great Britain as a Christian nation," said Adams, "to tell the Texans that slavery must be abolished—that it shall not be planted there, after all the efforts and sacrifices that have been made to abolish it all over the world. . . . If slavery is abolished in Texas, it must speedily fall throughout America; and when it falls in America, it will expire throughout Christendom" (From Lewis Tappan's speech to the World Convention of 1843. *Proceedings of the General Anti-Slavery Convention,* London, 1843, p. 305.) Tappan immediately sailed for London, where he was introduced to the great men of the empire, and communicated his message from Adams. According to Duff Green, unofficial representative for Southern interests in London, he did more. A reciprocity treaty between the United States and Great Britain was in negotiation, and Lewis Tappan testified against it. "So," said Green, "the reciprocity treaty is destroyed in inception." He bitterly condemned the British authorities and "their allies, John Quincy Adams & Co." The story of Lewis Tappan's mission is told in the *Anti-Slavery Standard,* Oct. 19, 1843.

[14] Weld to Lewis Tappan, Feb. 3, 1843 (Weld MSS.). The characterization of the Abolition House as abolition's headquarters is in a letter from Giddings to his wife, May 15, 1843 (Giddings Papers).

[15] The first quotation is from a letter from Weld to his wife, Jan. 25, 1843 (Weld MSS.). The British invitation from John Scoble (Secretary of the British and Foreign Anti-Slavery Society) to Weld, Dec. 30, 1842, is in the Weld MSS. The final quotation is from a letter from Weld to his wife, Feb. 1, 1843 (Weld MSS.). With pardonable gratification he added: "By the way, I have from three different quarters the offer of having my expenses paid if I go."

[16] Giddings to Weld, Jan. 28, 1844 (Weld MSS.). Weld wrote regarding his labors: "The anti-slavery questions are liable, some of them, to come up hourly, yet none of them may be up for two weeks. But whether they come up or not little affects my employments. Come up they will at *some* time, and preparation for them all is business enough." (Weld to his wife, Jan. 9, 1843, Weld MSS.) On the report from the Committee on Commerce regarding the status of colored seamen in Southern ports, for example, Weld furnished such material. "Mr. Winthrop . . . is to report on it. . . . After presentation the first thing will be to secure the printing of it. That passed, some anti-slavery member—probably Mr. Adams or Andrews of Ohio—will move the printing of an extra number of copies, and on that motion, enter on the debate. (Inter nos) I have prepared an argument on the subject in detail, which is in the hands of two of the members who designed to speak upon it." (Weld to his wife, Jan. 4, 1843, Weld

MSS.) For other questions upon which he prepared briefs, see Weld to his wife, Jan. 12, and Jan. 19; and to Lewis Tappan, Feb. 3, 1843 (Weld MSS.).

[17] Giddings to Weld, Feb. 21, 1843 (Weld Papers, Library of Congress).

[18] J. Leavitt to Angelina Weld, Feb. 7, 1843 (Weld MSS.).

[19] The appeal had been framed and signed by the antislavery insurgents during the previous session, either while Weld was still in Washington or shortly after his departure. They had planned to publish it to the nation after Congress had adjourned, in time to get petitions started for the next session. But by some mischance a copy of the appeal got into the hands of the editors of the *National Intelligencer,* and they promptly published it, with objurgations. See Gates's letter dated March 3, 1843, to the *Emancipator,* copied in the *Anti-Slavery Standard,* June 1, 1843.

[20] Giddings' appeal to Weld to "come over and help us" is in a letter from Giddings to Weld, Jan. 28, 1844 (Weld MSS.). In the same letter, Giddings remarked: "Here I am not exactly alone, for abolitionists are not as rare as they used to be even in this *abolition* boarding house." Weld's refusal to return to Washington is quoted from a letter from Weld to L. Tappan, Jan. 11, 1844 (Weld MSS.). It appears from other passages in this letter that Lewis Tappan had written several times previously, urging Weld to go, and that Weld had steadfastly refused. This letter evidently contained his final refusal.

Lewis Tappan, however, continued to labor for the cause. He refused to give Weld up: "Perhaps he will burst out one of these days and surprise us all, like the sun after a partial eclipse" (L. Tappan to J. A. Thome, Jan. 20, 1844, L. Tappan's Letterbook, 1842–1844, L. Tappan Papers, Library of Congress). Meanwhile he not only maintained Leavitt at Washington to be "the *watchman* at headquarters," but he also maintained a secretary for the lobby in order that Leavitt might have "some liesure to see and converse with members of Congress, etc." (L. Tappan to Leavitt, Jan. 9, 1844, reference as above). He proposed an antislavery library for the use of members of Congress and applied to friends of the cause to fill its shelves. He maintained a correspondence with abolition leaders throughout the North, which was, he wrote, "more than would be sufficient to occupy all my time" (L. Tappan to A. A. Phelps, reference as above, p. 556). He urged upon his correspondents the need for an antislavery newspaper at Washington; and finally he succeeded in establishing one, the *National Era,* which soon became the organ for the antislavery host. He selected for its editor the man who years ago had taught the Lane rebels at Cincinnati, Dr. Gamaliel Bailey (see foot-note no. 1, Chapter VII); and in its columns the world first read the tract of another who had heard the Lane debate, Harriet Beecher Stowe's *Uncle Tom's Cabin.* (See p. 73, and the accompanying foot-note.)

INDEX

Abolition House, 182, 193, 194, 195
Abolition of slavery, *see* Emancipation, plan of
Adams, John Quincy, 29, 109, 113, 118, 119, 145, 178, 188, 191, 193, 195, 196; protests against Pinckney gag, 110; method of conducting petition agitation, 122-124; doctrine of right of petition, 124-125; antislavery convictions, 125; qualifications for leading petition agitation, 126-127; relations with abolitionists, 127-128; defends women's petitions, 141, 143; leader of antislavery cause, 165; condemns American Anti-Slavery Society, 165-166; meets Weld at Washington, 183; joins insurgent congressmen, 184; opens their campaign against slavery, 184-185; trial on resolution of censure, 185-187; assisted by Weld, 185-186
African Repository, 67, 69
Allan, William T., 39, 46, 65, 66, 71
Alton riots, 162
American and Foreign Anti-Slavery Society, 175-176, 178, 194
American Anti-Slavery Society: proposed, 35, 47; founded, 55-56; first pamphlet agitation, 59-61; agitation by agents, 104-106; reorganization, 106-107; dominance of Great Revival influence, 107; organizes national petition campaign, 133-136; survey of the organization, 134; second pamphlet agitation, 139; relinquishes petition campaign to local societies, 146; friction with State societies, 151; financial difficulties, 152; report repudiated by State societies, 158; admits women delegates, 159; involved in woman's rights controversy, 159-160; financial collapse, 164, 167; liquidation, 168; captured by Garrison's faction, 169; withdrawal of auxiliaries, 170; under control of Garrison, 173-174
American Colonization Society, 27-28, 36-37, 39, 42, 44-45, 46, 47, 53, 67
American Union for the Relief and Im-

provement of the Colored Race, 61-62, 92, 94-95
Andrews, Sherlock J., 122, 181, 182, 193
Anthony, Susan B., 143
Antislavery congressmen, 122; urged by Leavitt to attack slavery in the House, 178-179; organize as "select committee on slavery," 180; finance antislavery lobby to bring Weld to Washington, 180; belief in their mission, 182; enlist Adams, 184, who opens their campaign against slavery, 184-185; attempts of Whig leaders to discipline them, by censuring Adams, 185-187, by censuring Giddings, 188, and by preventing Giddings' reëlection, 188-189; significance to antislavery agitation of Whig leader's failure, 189-190; later course and policy of insurgent congressmen, 195-196
Anti-Slavery Convention of American Women, 142-143, 159, 169
Antislavery libraries, 139-140
Antislavery lobby in Washington: projected by American Anti-Slavery Society, 177; by Thomas Morris, 177; by Joshua Leavitt, 178-179; by American and Foreign Anti-Slavery Society, 180; organized by antislavery congressmen, 180; headed by Weld, 181; headquarters at Abolition House, 182; operations, 191-195
Antislavery petitions in Congress, *see* Petitions for antislavery objects
Antislavery petitions in parliament and rules as to their disposal, 116-117
Antislavery tracts, *see* Pamphlet program of agitation
Association of Gentlemen, 151, 192; organized by the Tappans, 20; plans national antislavery movement, 33-34, 36
Atherton gag, 111, 119

Bacon, Rev. Leonard, 56, 59
Baptist abolitionists in New England, 91, 93, 175
Barnard, Daniel D., 193

293

INDEX